Tyranny and Revolution

The Philosophy of Freedom from Rousseau to Heidegger launched a great protest against modern liberal individualism, inspired by the virtuous political community of the ancient Greeks. Hegel argued that the progress of history was gradually bringing about greater freedom and restoring our lost sense of community. But his successors Marx, Nietzsche and Heidegger rejected Hegel's version of the end of history with its legitimization of the bourgeois nation-state. They sought to replace it with ever more utopian, apocalyptic and illiberal visions of the future: Marx's Socialism, Nietzsche's Overman and Heidegger's commitment to Nazism. This book combines an exceptionally clear and rich study of these thinkers with a deep dive into the extent to which their views fed the political catastrophes of revolution, tyranny and genocide, including the Jacobins, Bolsheviks, Nazis, Khmer Rouge, ISIS and populist nationalism, but argues that the Philosophy of Freedom remains indispensable for understanding today's world.

WALLER R. NEWELL is Professor of Political Science, Philosophy and Humanities at Carleton University.

Tyranny and Revolution

Rousseau to Heidegger

WALLER R. NEWELL
Carleton University

CAMBRIDGE
UNIVERSITY PRESS

CAMBRIDGE
UNIVERSITY PRESS

University Printing House, Cambridge CB2 8BS, United Kingdom

One Liberty Plaza, 20th Floor, New York, NY 10006, USA

477 Williamstown Road, Port Melbourne, VIC 3207, Australia

314–321, 3rd Floor, Plot 3, Splendor Forum, Jasola District Centre, New Delhi – 110025, India

103 Penang Road, #05–06/07, Visioncrest Commercial, Singapore 238467

Cambridge University Press is part of the University of Cambridge.

It furthers the University's mission by disseminating knowledge in the pursuit of
education, learning, and research at the highest international levels of excellence.

www.cambridge.org
Information on this title: www.cambridge.org/9781108424301
DOI: 10.1017/9781108333856

First published 2022

Printed in the United Kingdom by TJ Books Limited, Padstow Cornwall

A catalogue record for this publication is available from the British Library.

Library of Congress Cataloging-in-Publication Data
NAMES: Newell, Waller R. (Waller Randy), 1952- author.
TITLE: Tyranny and revolution : Rousseau to Heidegger / Waller R. Newell, Carleton University,
Ottawa.
DESCRIPTION: Cambridge ; New York, NY : Cambridge University Press, 2022. | Includes
bibliographical references and index.
IDENTIFIERS: LCCN 2021050110 (print) | LCCN 2021050111 (ebook) | ISBN 9781108424301
(hardback) | ISBN 9781108440042 (paperback) | ISBN 9781108333856 (epub)
SUBJECTS: LCSH: Despotism–History. | Political science–Philosophy–History. | Rousseau,
Jean-Jacques, 1712-1778–Political and social views. | Heidegger, Martin, 1889-1976–Political and
social views. | BISAC: POLITICAL SCIENCE / History & Theory
CLASSIFICATION: LCC JC381 .N434 2022 (print) | LCC JC381 (ebook) | DDC 321.9–dc23/eng/
20211213
LC record available at https://lccn.loc.gov/2021050110
LC ebook record available at https://lccn.loc.gov/2021050111

ISBN 978-1-108-42430-1 Hardback

Contents

Contents

Preface

What is the purpose of political life? Is it meant to protect our rights as individuals, leaving us free to work hard and prosper, protected from illegal infringements on our liberty, free to do as we please in our private lives so long as others are not harmed, including the freedom to ignore politics and public life altogether? That is the recipe for the classical liberalism of Locke, Montesquieu and their heirs including the American Founders for good government: Secure the maximum net material gain for every member of the social contract to enable them to live in comfort and otherwise get out of the way – for, as Jefferson put it, that government is best which governs least. Government is not about teaching people how to be virtuous – that is a matter for individual choice. Politics is about means, not ends. As Madison wrote, the sources of factional strife are sewn into human nature. Their causes cannot be removed, but their harmful effects can be controlled by the social contract.

But what if political life is about much, much more than this? What if it is meant to give us a sense of belonging to and participating in a community of our fellow citizens, to promote virtue over vice in our public and educational institutions, to ensure a spirit of individual self-sacrifice on behalf of the common good, to shape us to be public beings first and private individuals only second, if at all? What if, in short, the purpose of political life is not merely utility but *nobility*?

The thinkers we examine in this book believed that political life should not merely protect our freedom as individuals but involve us in a communal experience that would bring us true happiness, a happiness that classical liberalism could do no more than leave to whatever private avocations and amusements we chose to pursue as a reward for our pursuit of economic self-interest. And in looking for this higher set of expectations from political life, these thinkers, unable to find what they wanted from the modern social contract thinkers like Locke and Montesquieu, searched for it in its original and unforgettable pure source – the civilization of the ancient world, especially the ancient Greek polis, where citizen life meant a full-time involvement in public affairs promoted by an education in virtue. How could it be brought back? That is what preoccupied European political philosophy from Rousseau to Heidegger.

And yet – strangest paradox – precisely this longing to make politics noble again, beautiful again, and more entirely just than before, culminated in projects for revolutionary violence and extremism that surpassed anything in previous human experience for the scale and depravity of their cruelty and slaughter – beginning with the Jacobin Terror of 1793, continuing through the Bolshevik and National Socialist revolutions, third world socialist revolutions such as Maoism and the Khmer Rouge, and contemporary Jihadist terrorism. For every one of the thinkers we examine in this book had a connection, genuine or least alleged, to one or more of these extremist revolutionary movements. How could the attempt to raise the level of modern political life beyond mere material self-interest simultaneously launch such dangerous extremist longings? How could the desire to ennoble modern life lead to the political catastrophes of totalitarianism and utopian genocide? Exploring that paradox is the aim of this book. At its core lies not only a radically new way of looking at human experience but, more fundamentally, a radically new way of understanding the character and structure of the entire world, of all reality. The longing for political wholeness launched by the Philosophy of Freedom as the balm for the spiritual impoverishment and utilitarian crassness of bourgeois modernity, and the dangerous consequences that longing entailed, including their totalitarian implications, hinged on a massive *metaphysical* shift in the meaning of existence, the transition from nature to history, which emerged from the difficulties of reconciling the eros for human happiness with the modern materialistic conception of nature.

This book is the promised sequel to *Tyranny: A New Interpretation*, but it stands in a somewhat asymmetrical relationship to it. The first book discussed the history of tyranny as a theme in political thought from ancients to early moderns. Although the notion that an entire nation could be a tyrant was touched upon (as when, for example, Pericles tells the Athenian people they are viewed by their allies as a "tyrant city") along with an exploration of the ancient and modern understanding of imperialism and its relationship to republican self-government, that book's main focus was the assumption common to both periods that tyranny was mainly about the lawless rule of an individual. I ended the book by edging up to what I termed millenarian populism, first emerging with Rousseau, which differs from either the classical or early modern account of tyranny by treating it as a collective force, the revolutionary will of "the people." Whether observed in actuality or not, this was its principle of legitimacy. Its leaders like Robespierre, Stalin and Hitler, were not autocrats supposedly ruling for their subjects' good like Julius Caesar or the Tudors, but vehicles of that popular will and of history itself. *Tyranny and Revolution* is the elaboration of this peculiarly modern category of tyranny, focusing on Rousseau, Hegel, Marx, Nietzsche and Heidegger. It can also be read in conjunction with the intervening book, *Tyrants: Power, Injustice, and Terror*, a brief history of tyranny from ancient times to the present intended for a general readership, accordingly fairly low on pure theory and high on biography, psychology and historical narrative. My aim here is, hopefully, to provide the philosophical depth to the subject matter of Part III of *Tyrants* – millenarian tyranny since the Jacobin Terror of 1793 – that I aimed to provide in *Tyranny: A New Interpretation* for ancient and early modern tyranny, including the intrinsic connection between the philosophies of the thinkers examined and the real or conjectural implications of their thought for extremist political movements in practice. In the case of all three books, I have endeavored not to limit myself to the theme of tyranny narrowly or exclusively speaking, but to demonstrate how this cardinal theme can be a window to the entire range of ancient and modern political and moral philosophy including its psychological, aesthetic, political and cosmological dimensions. So the three volumes comprise something of a trilogy.

Acknowledgments

I gratefully acknowledge the encouragement and stimulus I received for my interest in the Philosophy of Freedom going back to my student days, from classmates, teachers, colleagues and former students of mine now embarked on their own careers.

They include Samuel Abraham, Gerald Owen and Katherine Anderson, Edward Andrew, Ronald Beiner, Jeffrey Bernstein, Allan Bloom, Leah Bradshaw, Timothy Brownlee, Timothy Burns, Gary R. Clewley, Mark Cordover, Tom Darby, Norman Doidge, Alex Duff, Jonathan Eayrs, Peter Emberley, Emil Fackenheim, Charles Fairbanks, Arthur Fish, Bryon-Paul Frost, Michael Gillespie, Kenneth Hart Green, Marc Hanvelt, Karsten Harries, Henry Higuera, Martin Jaffe, James H. Nicholls, Greg MacIsaac, Sophie Marcotte-Chenard, Kenneth Minogue, Douglas Moggach, Clifford Orwin, Thomas L. Pangle, Matthew Post, Farhang Rajaee, Nalin Ranasinghe, Stanley Rosen, Abraham Rothstein, Kenneth Schmitz, Robert Sibley, Steven B. Smith, Erik Stephenson, Robin Varma, Bernard Yack, Catherine and Michael Zuckert.

Thanks again to my editor, Robert Dreesen, without whose advice this book (and its two predecessors) would not have been possible.

As with all my books, my wife and colleague, Jacqueline Newell, provided a superb edit and multiple suggestions for improvement.

Acknowledgments

Introduction

The Recollection of Freedom

This book is about an extraordinary transformation in the history of modern political thought that begins with Rousseau and unfolds through Hegel, Marx, Nietzsche and Heidegger in their pursuit of the path to human wholeness.

Hitherto in the Western tradition, it was believed that human happiness, justice and satisfaction came from aspiring to transcend the world of time and changing circumstance and orient oneself by what is immortally lasting and eternal. That transcendental aim had been identified with metaphysical concepts such as Plato's Idea of the Good and with the Christian belief in immortal salvation through faith in God. Sometimes those aims were treated as a single path, sometimes as alternative paths to the same goal.

Beginning with Rousseau, and elaborated by the great historicist thinkers we variously identify with the Philosophy of Freedom or German Idealism, a complete reversal takes place. Happiness is now sought, not in a transcendental realm of pure unity and rest beyond the earthly realm of multiplicity and becoming but, on the contrary, in the realm of becoming itself. No longer are human happiness, justice and satisfaction to be sought through escaping the world of historical action, but through immersing oneself in its vital energies.

Why was this path taken? A hallmark of virtually all the political theories we consider in this book is their profound admiration for ancient Greek civilization, the world of the polis. All of them use their particular evocation of the ancient Greeks as a foil for exposing the shallowness, vulgarity, selfish individualism and materialism of the modern age. The Greeks' devotion to community and virtue, their striving for nobility and beauty, their disdain for the merely useful, shone forth as a stunning refutation of the utilitarian political reasoning of Hobbes, Locke and the Enlightenment. As Schiller saw it, every meaningful experience in life was given to the Greeks as a direct gift of nature in all its shining freshness. In order to rescue ourselves from the dreary commercial materialism of the modern age, we must try to recollect and re-energize those latent traces of the ancients in ourselves.

But one apparently insurmountable obstacle stood in the way of this attempt to recapture the nobility and harmony of the ancient polis – the seemingly irrefutable triumph of the modern physics of matter in motion over the metaphysical cosmologies of the ancients. For the physics of Bacon and Newton appeared to have shattered forever the classical belief that the cosmos was primarily characterized by rest over motion, by unity over multiplicity, and by permanence over becoming. That cosmological belief of the ancients had been indivisibly connected to their prescriptions for human happiness. Because the world at large was characterized by the preeminence of the immortal truth over chance becoming, mirrored in the movement of the heavenly bodies or the eternal structures of geometry, it made sense to argue that we as human beings could achieve in our own souls a degree of that cosmic stability through cultivating the virtues of wisdom, justice and moderation. The ancients' prescription for happiness, in other words, was not merely anthropological. When Plato argues that the study of the Idea of the Good is the source of all human prudence and virtue, that is not simply the Idea of the *human* Good, but the transcendental unity that informs the entire world. Nature is primarily characterized by stability, balance, harmony and proportion, and because human nature is a part of nature, that, too, is the best way of life for man. Hence, to return to Schiller, we cannot directly experience, as could the ancients, the "naive" openness to the revelation of nature that enfolds us in its sweep because, for us, nature is an external object, the nonhuman world of physics. He sums up the paradox this way: The ancients "felt naturally, while we feel the natural."

All the thinkers considered in this book took it for granted that there was no way back behind the triumph of modern natural science to those ancient cosmologies. Nature, we now know, is random happenstance, a realm of sheer accident, chance and becoming. The human mind, far from being, as the ancients thought, the crown of nature and the mirror of its orderliness, has no intrinsic connection with nature as matter in motion at all. Instead, the mind is an external instrument that can, through an exercise of will, master nature so as to make it yield the material security and well-being that human beings need for bodily survival and physical comfort. Any talk of a higher realm of virtue and the longing for immortality was merely, as Hobbes scathingly put it, "absurd" and "insignificant" speech with no counterpart in measurable physical reality.

Ancient thinkers like Plato had believed that the eternal order of the cosmos provided a unifying third term between subject and object, self and other, and citizen and community. In the famous Image of the Sun in the *Republic*, the Idea of the Good makes it possible for things to come into being and for us to understand what they are. Modern natural science removes that third term, launching an irresolvable debate as to whether the mind imposes all structure on purposeless matter or whether the mind is passively determined by those same empirical processes. Locke frankly confesses that he cannot explain why things have the coherence they do. When the mind has analyzed the attributes and properties of any phenomenon, there remains an elusive underlying unity, neither solely in the mind nor solely in the thing, that can only be described as "something I know not what."

Beginning with Hegel, drawing upon the path-breaking speculations of Rousseau, the Philosophy of Freedom discovers a new third term, a new source of unity – the time-bound realm of historical change itself. The unity of life will no longer be seen as transcendental and timeless, but as a sheer matrix of origination, the fecund source of all existence, both natural and human, what Hegel terms a "self-originating wealth of shapes." Even more remarkably, Hegel argues that it is precisely in this realm of flux and contingency, supposed by the ancients to be the enemy of all virtue, that human virtue, including civic virtue, along with the sources of political community and artistic and intellectual merit, are to be found. Through the understanding that human existence is historical through and through, that everything is time-bound and mutable, that there is no such thing as a permanent human nature because human beings are self-makers – through that new understanding, paradoxically, we will be able to reclaim the precious Greek heritage that the victory of modern natural science and its political equivalent, the Enlightenment, had seemingly forever closed to us. Plato had famously likened human life to a cave of shadows, a mixture of light and darkness. Only the philosopher could find the path up and out of the Cave, to stand in the sunlight of the eternal. We now must understand, according to Hegel, that there is nothing *but* the Cave, nothing but historical existence. Whatever truth we can uncover will be intertwined with that mixture of shadow and light that is the condition of man's time-bound existence.

The Philosophy of Freedom, as I argue in this book, was the attempt to return to a classical conception of human existence rooted in our communal connectedness with one another, a synthesis of the ancient Greek polis with the individual liberty of the modern age. This historicist philosophy tried to restore a full sense of cultural, aesthetic and civic satisfaction as against what was widely viewed as the vulgarity, narrowness and philistinism of Enlightenment individualism and the concept of the state as nothing more than a heartless utilitarian contract among producers and consumers of commodities. Plato and the classical conception of the good life provided both a precedent and a foil for German Idealism, especially Hegel, whose *Phenomenology of Spirit* is, I will argue, a conscious reenactment of the Platonic ascent of the soul to wisdom and happiness on historicist grounds. Rousseau, severe critic of bourgeois materialism, had been the first modern thinker to attempt to recover the classical vision of the polis on the basis of modern natural right. His struggle to reconcile freedom with happiness provided German Idealism, as we will see, with its central enigma. Kant and Schiller each take up one of the two poles inherited from Rousseau's thought – the mastery of the inclinations through the freedom of will and the Romantic longing for oneness with nature, respectively – setting the stage for Hegel's grand synthesis of freedom and community, the "Absolute Science of Spirit," designed to promote both individual liberty and the common good while avoiding revolutionary violence. After exploring the Hegelian Absolute, I will examine a series of ongoing assaults on it from the Left (Marx) and (in the European sense of the term) the Right (Nietzsche and Heidegger). Of special importance will be the internal debate among these thinkers as to whether history is rational and progressive (Hegel and Marx) or a cycle of existential experiences deeper than any rational account can penetrate, and with no teleological direction (Nietzsche and Heidegger). With Heidegger, I will argue, we reach the fragmentation of the Philosophy of Freedom into the twentieth-century schools of critical theory, neo-Marxism and postmodernism, and a growing despair over the benevolent progress of history as the twentieth century is faced with the juggernaut of world war and global technology.

Throughout this whole debate, each thinker's reinterpretation of the historical process is mirrored in his reinterpretation of the ancient Greeks, and those differing visions of the ancient Greek polis provide roots for the practical and political implications of their political philosophies. In general, the increasingly illiberal tone of historicist philosophy after Hegel is mirrored in his successors' marked preference for an older, archaic epoch of ancient Greece in contrast with the classical age of the fifth century BC. In other words, because Hegel defends a moderately progressive liberalism, with an emphasis on the teleological and rational progress of history, his Greeks are those of Periclean and democratic Athens, with its shining achievements in art, music, literature and philosophy, a balanced civilization in which the life of the mind and a reasoned civic-spiritedness flourished. While Hegel appreciated the older Homeric and chthonic Greek religious traditions with their emphasis on heroism, tragic fate, the limits of human reason and freedom and a distrust of individualism, he believed that history was definitely on the side of the ethical universalism that was introduced by Plato and which mirrored the best in Greek culture, outlining a world to come in which the tribal societies of the polis would give way to the first world states of Alexander the Great and Rome.

By contrast, both Nietzsche and Heidegger, because they renounced the Hegelian faith in the teleological unfolding of history and its culmination in what they saw as the bourgeois, materialistic and egalitarian world of the present, and regarded this outcome as in truth a calamitous debasement of human greatness and rank, they also rejected the rational, cultural and political equipoise of the "aesthetic democracy" (to use Hegel's phrase) of the Periclean Age in favor of returning back behind it into the primordial tribal depths of Homeric heroism and what Nietzsche called "the tragic age of the Greeks" in its greatness, before these vital energies and sense of human greatness and mastery began to be leveled by the rationalism of Socrates. Whereas Hegel had viewed the gradual displacement of the older chthonic religion of reverence for blood and soil as an unqualified step forward for mankind, Nietzsche famously deplored how the symbiotic interaction of the Dionysian and the Apollonian – the chthonic and the rational – reaching a supreme flowering in Homer and Sophocles, was destroyed by Socrates, who allowed the hyper-rationality and formalism of the Apollonian to overwhelm and desiccate the vital Dionysian forces of passion, rank and strife in which its sublime beauty had originally been rooted. Nietzsche's early enthusiasm for Wagner stemmed from his belief that Wagner's operas were restoring the mythical and heroic to the modern age. As the detestation of modernity among Hegel's successors grew ever more intense, and as their wish to tap into the primordial energies of the pre-Socratic Heracleitean view of existence as "war" intensified, Hegel's moderate progressive liberalism gave way to Nietzsche's vision of a coming planetary battle for rule by a master race, and Heidegger's commitment to the National Socialist "community of destiny."

MY INTERPRETIVE APPROACH

There is a rich pedigree of commentary on the purely political teaching of Hegel's works. To varying degrees, they underemphasize the ontological premises of Hegel's historicism and try to extract from it pragmatic prescriptions about justice, virtue and civil society that can be stated in their own terms, similar to the approach one might take to the political theories of Burke, Tocqueville or J. S. Mill. There is another body of commentary that stresses, on the contrary, the formidable technical dimensions of Hegel's philosophical concepts and mostly, and again to varying degrees, underemphasizes their implications for ethics and a legitimate civil order. The same might be said of Marx, Nietzsche and Heidegger – some approaches to their works are more straightforwardly about political theory, while some pay more attention to their underlying ontological presuppositions, although it is not a consistent relationship. For reasons we will explore, Marx and Nietzsche deliberately avoid the sort of technical metaphysical speculations associated with Hegel, while in Heidegger, they come back strongly to the fore. My approach is to try to show how these two dimensions are inseparable, why it is ultimately not possible to extract an ethical discourse or pragmatic political prescription from the Philosophy of Freedom that is not necessarily grounded in, and intertwined with, its historicist philosophical principles at every turn.

The wish to extract the political theory from the historicist philosophy is, to be sure, understandable in view of the current extreme skepticism toward any such comprehensive "Absolute Science of Spirit" of the kind Hegel believed he had elaborated, not only on the grounds that no such monistic account of reality has withstood scrutiny but also on the grounds that the belief in it has had some unfortunate practical political consequences perhaps best expressed in the Marxist-Leninist formula "the unity of theory and practice." My point, however, is that if we wish to attempt to understand these thinkers as they understood themselves, then we have to think their philosophies through as a synthesis of real-world prescriptions and a historicist account of the whole. Critiques can proceed from there, and there are certainly critiques to make.

My approach is a synoptic one, tracing a common pedigree of themes from Rousseau to Heidegger. Although I am in good company here, it is valid to ask whether linking these figures together as parts of one unfolding dynamic might undermine the claim each makes to originality and the need to study each author's works strictly in their own right. This might especially seem to be the case for Nietzsche, who deliberately tries to shed the clanking baggage of German academic philosophy and speak more in the voice of a poet, artist or man of letters, re-evoking from the world around him a freshness buried under Hegel's convoluted grey concept nets. My answer will be, first of all, that there is a very high degree of intertextual continuity among these thinkers in which they address each other explicitly. Schiller and Kant both engaged with Rousseau, and Hegel attempts to synthesize all three. Marx discusses Rousseau and Kant, and his terminology is heavily derivative from, while at the same time highly critical of Hegelianism. Nietzsche takes on Rousseau, Schiller, Hegel, and if not Marx by name, certainly socialism. Heidegger, who died in 1976, addresses all of his predecessors stretching back to the Hegelian original, forming a dialogue spanning a century and a half. Moreover, precisely because each of these thinkers believes that life is historical through and through, that no Platonic ascent from the Cave into the sunlight of the permanent truth is possible, they are unavoidably involved in criticizing what they see as their predecessors' flawed understandings of the meaning of history – understandings that contributed to the actual flawed unfolding of history itself – and using those flaws as the point of departure for what they believe to be their own healthier understanding of mankind's past and future. I will also argue that Hegel's original concept of existence as a "self-originating wealth of shapes" remains the underlying core assumption of his successors, modified as species-being (Marx), Will to Power (Nietzsche) and the ontology of Being (Heidegger). Even Nietzsche, it will emerge from this perspective, is rather more of a "technical" thinker, less of an artist, than meets the eye. I have also tried to compensate for any exaggerated uniformity that my synoptic approach might impose on such a richly varied continuum of thinkers by presenting their work in a series of highly exegetical, textually focused studies, attempting to show how their more general principles emerge from a thorough immersion in selective works. Finally, given the enormous range of scholarly interpretations of the theories and issues examined in this book, I have included a brief bibliographical essay for each chapter that attempts to give readers the lay of the land and direct them toward further reading, should they be interested.

Escape to Lake Bienne

How Rousseau Turned the World Upside Down

During September and October 1775, Jean-Jacques Rousseau lived on the small, forested island of St. Peter's on Lake Bienne in Switzerland. There, as described in the Fifth Promenade of *The Reveries of the Solitary Walker*, he experienced a revelation of unsurpassable pleasure about nature that made him want to stay there for the rest of his life, for, as he wrote, no other place had made him "so truly happy." This revelation supplies, in my view, the elusive link that Rousseau always maintained united his hugely disparate, on occasion flatly contradictory, writings around a single theme. It also unleashed a powerful tidal wave of forces that in the coming century and a half would sweep away much of the civilization of the Enlightenment and usher in some of the noblest achievements of modern thought and art along with the worst political catastrophes in human history.

Rousseau rocketed to fame with his attack on the Enlightenment and was a famous and controversial figure for his entire life. The first philosophical celebrity, he was known simply as "Jean-Jacques," rather like our one-name celebrities today (Oprah, Bono). Dressed in a flamboyant lilac-colored fur-edged caftan, he was the star of his own life. Responding to his call to live naturally, the French upper orders took walks and suckled their children for the first time. Since it was still a crime in France to dispute the biblical origin of man, he was frequently in hot water for his own views. More seriously, he has been called the intellectual godfather of the French Revolution – a revolution that aimed for the absolute equality of the human condition and not merely the Lockean rights to representation and the acquisition of private property. He has also been called the founder of Romanticism, an inspiration for Shelley, Heine and Holderlin, and the notion that the life of the artistic outsider is superior to citizen life and philosophy. His influence on Goethe's *Werther* is widely acknowledged. Goethe described how Rousseau had "touched the sympathies" of his generation of young men – "scattered far and wide over this country was a community of silent admirers who revered his name," set free by him from the "fetters" of "the conventional world." Finally, although their styles of thought could not have been more diametrically opposed, Rousseau was a major inspiration for Kant, who dubbed him nothing less than "the Newton of the moral universe."

The extraordinary range of Rousseau's influence reflects the difficulty and diversity of his thinking, although he maintained that the contradictions among his works were merely apparent, not real. Each of them expresses its particular viewpoint with powerful rhetorical force, making their interrelatedness even harder to uncover. I suggest that the different political, moral and aesthetic alternatives he explores flow from three major themes: the critique of modern times, the state of nature and how the state of nature might be recovered in the present. After discussing them, I will return to the Fifth Promenade, where I believe the fundamental experience uniting them all can be discovered.

THE CRITIQUE OF BOURGEOIS LIFE

Rousseau burst into prominence when he won an essay prize competition set by the Academy of Dijon in 1750. The academy's question was, "Has the restoration of the sciences and arts tended to purify morals?" Rousseau's answer was a shocking No, the sole such response, and therefore the most attention-grabbing. It became his first major work, *A Discourse on the Sciences and Arts* (hereafter referred to as the *First Discourse*). It was also the beginning of Rousseau's ability to send a frisson of contrarian excitement through the ranks of the very *philosophes* whose drawing-room refinement he made a career out of attacking. To understand the shock value, we have to consider the background of the Enlightenment.

By the time Rousseau wrote, England and France had undergone remarkable transformations since a century or so earlier. The old feudal order was giving way to powerful monarchies that actively promoted the spread of commerce and the advancement of knowledge for the benefit of ordinary people. Bacon had urged the use of science "for the relief of man's estate," a science that transforms the world and does not merely contemplate it, derived from Machiavelli's summons to the conquest of Fortuna. Hobbes and Locke had argued that the social contract exists for the protection and security of the individual; that governments should encourage the rise of commercial private enterprise and that people should otherwise be left free to live as they wished – the state should not legislate personal morality. The American Constitution established the first formal separation of Church and State, the way of the future.

The classical view had been that man's natural perfection came through performing the duties of a citizen toward the community. Man could not be fully human except in this way. Strictly speaking, there was no such thing as individualism by nature. This tradition had been built upon by medieval Christian, especially Thomistic, theology so that man is seen as fulfilling his duty to God in part by fulfilling his duties as a subject. The modern view, by contrast, was that human nature is fundamentally individualistic. That is, man is complete in his nature prior to and apart from his formation by civil society. What makes man an individual is that he is naturally concerned above all with his own self-preservation. Duties are not an intrinsic part of man's natural fulfillment, so that common duties are replaced by individual rights. According to Hobbes, the adjuration to duty was a deception by which people were oppressed by corrupt civil and religious authorities. At the same time, that adjuration invited the "vainglorious" to disrupt functioning governments in the belief that they possessed superior virtue. The solution was to understand that civil society exists expressly to facilitate the individual's pursuit of self-preservation and even comfortable self-preservation. Any society that achieves this is legitimate because it protects us from one another and redirects contumacious political ambition into the competition for economic advancement.

These processes took a long time to take root and did so at an uneven rate. Their most momentous beacons to date were the two great modernizing liberal revolutions in England and America. By Rousseau's time, the French monarchy had found its own power increased by promoting these measures for economic advancement, while the *philosophes* mounted attacks on remnants of the old premodern public morality – against censorship, religious intolerance and retrograde habits such as dueling. Rousseau attempted to put a brake on the progress of modernization, and he knew many would perceive him to be a philistine for doing so ("Here I am a barbarian because no one understands me" was the quote from Ovid with which he begins the *First Discourse*).

The core of Rousseau's great counterattack is best summed up in a later work, *Emile*. Modern man, he writes, is a "bourgeois," a word that originally simply meant a townsman (like the German *Burger*) and therefore a person likely to engage in commerce, but which Rousseau was the first to invest with the negative, even detestable qualities it was to assume for subsequent critics of modernity including Marx. Although the number of actual *bourgeoises* in the France of his day was likely no more than 8 percent of the population, Rousseau sees in this emerging human type a loathsome vision of everyone's future, not unlike Nietzsche's later vision of the spread of the Last Man.

According to Rousseau, the bourgeois is strung between two authentic alternatives. Natural man lives entirely for himself, but he is entirely self-sufficient. At the opposite extreme, the citizen is devoted entirely to the common good and the laws, a way of life that is completely alienating and unnatural but dignified in its austerity. In his evocation of the citizen, Rousseau departs from the Enlightenment preference for the Athens of the classical age in its view of the ancient world – Periclean Athens, cultured, affluent, tolerant and democratic, appeared to provide an ancient antecedent and inspiration for the improvements being spread by modernity. For Rousseau, by contrast, the grimly collectivist republics of Sparta and early Rome were the high-water marks of the manliness, honor and patriotism of true citizenship.

It has been suggested that Jacques-Louis David's famous painting *The Oath of the Horatii* symbolizes the dichotomy in Rousseau's thought between these two authentic and opposite alternatives – on the left-hand side of the painting, stern Roman men with swords pledging a fight to the death against Rome's enemy Alba Longa; on the right-hand side, a family group tenderly comforting each other over the impending loss of their loved ones. A large space in the middle of the canvas separates these alternatives of patriotic duty and familial affection. One way of viewing the French Revolution in its most radical Jacobin phase is as the attempt to use the harshness of citizen virtue from the left-hand side of the painting to bring about a world that releases the sweet natural ties on the right-hand side. We will return to this later when we discuss the possibility that Rousseau's writings were responsible for the Terror.

The bourgeois, Rousseau argues, is a bastardized half-way house between the two authentic ways of life of natural man and citizen. Like natural man, the bourgeois lives for himself. But unlike natural man, he needs others to take advantage of, and is dependent on them for this very reason. In Rousseau's estimation, this has encouraged secret avarice and fraud under a mask of hypocritical politeness and civility. There is little real virtue in modern times, so more artificial civility is needed to paper over the fierce struggle to get ahead. The Enlightenment thinkers encouraged people to get along with others, to be "sociable," because it was best for their own individual interests. Virtue toward your fellow man is not practiced for its own sake but as a means for your own selfish ends.

The modern view of human nature as universally individualistic, along with the materialistic modern science that underpins it, Rousseau argues, broadcasts its cosmopolitanism and thereby reduces all societies, traditions and beliefs to these universalistic explanations of human behavior, making it difficult for people to believe unreservedly in their own particular peoples, traditions or faith – a corrosion of morality that further encourages an absorption in self-interest. The spread of prosperity and new productive techniques pampers the body, makes one weak and hungry for ever-new luxuries, and therefore more selfish and unable to rise above one's own good. For Rousseau, therefore, scientific and economic progress go hand in hand with despotism, because people abdicate more and more of their responsibilities as citizens to a central authority so as to devote themselves completely to their own self-advancement and pursuit of riches.

Finally, the progress of the arts and sciences, Rousseau argues, increases inequality because it rewards mental talent and makes all other human qualities seem worthless by comparison. As he mordantly remarks, one might think France suffered from having too many farmers and too few professors. The Enlightenment considered as one of its proudest achievements the spread of the idea that individuals should be able to rise in life through their own ability and hard work, a meritocracy rather than a caste system based on inherited privilege. This was one reason why, early on, the spread of modern ideas found its strongest supporters among the commercial classes, who were not bound to the land by feudal hierarchy. Rousseau is the first major thinker to argue that liberal meritocracy was in fact leading to the *most* inegalitarian society in history, spawning ever wider divides between the economic winners and losers. Even more important, meritocracy was psychologically tormenting in a way that the old regime of inherited privilege had never been. A person born into the lower orders of feudal society had no expectation of rising in life, and therefore did not need to blame himself for failing to do so. For the bourgeois, by contrast, the failure to rise in life through our own merits proves that we are inferior beings who have only ourselves to blame for being bested in the contest. This theme is later developed by Tocqueville in his diagnosis of American society, and can be seen all around us today in the obsession with getting one's children into "a good school," even beginning with daycare centers said to "track to the Ivy League." Because mental ability has more prestige today than any other walk of life, Rousseau adds, it invites charlatans to promote themselves as thinkers and artists out of vanity. Rousseau's attack on philosophy in this context is partly rhetorical because, while he believes that modern learning has been corrupted by the pursuit of academic and scientific honors, he also believes that there *are* real philosophers (he alludes to Bacon here and in the *Discourse on the Origins of Inequality* praises "the wise Locke") who know what they are from early on and who do not pursue knowledge for the sake of public renown. Nevertheless, in the end, I think Rousseau does abandon philosophy in its traditional meaning for a new form of insight. This abandonment can be seen in the *First Discourse* in his portrayal of Socrates, whom he detaches from Plato and any concern with metaphysical speculations about the cosmos, transforming him into an "honest man" in his plainspokenness, populism and simple common sense. Ultimately, Rousseau will replace the philosopher in the traditional sense as one who seeks knowledge of the eternal truth with the poetic artist and visionary.

THE NATURAL CONDITION OF MAN

Rousseau's critique of the modern age might appear to be a grumpy jeremiad, akin to Swift, if he had no alternative. But the alternative is natural man. What animates Rousseau's writings is that he wants people to recover their natural characteristics from the vain distinctions and soulless competitiveness of civilized society – to the degree possible. For reasons we will explore, Rousseau does not believe our natural condition can be fully recovered. His works therefore spring from the attempt to find various approximations of the natural life *in* the civilized world. His *Discourse on the Origins of Inequality* (henceforth the *Second Discourse*) is his most sustained effort to evoke our original natural condition and how we lost it.

By nature, according to Rousseau, man is an individual, concerned above all with self-preservation. In other words, despite his loathing of the new modern type, the bourgeois, Rousseau accepts the fundamental premise of modern political philosophy since Hobbes and, by implication, the new Baconian science of matter in motion in which it is grounded. However severe his criticisms of the modern age might be, however much he may long for the virtuous republics of ancient times, for Rousseau there is evidently no way back behind the demonstrable truth of modern physics, which has permanently refuted the Platonic and Aristotelian concepts of an ordered and eternal cosmos in which excellence of soul was to be achieved by cultivating those same qualities of balance and harmonious proportionality in the city and in oneself. Whereas the ancient thinkers held that rest was superordinate over motion in the cosmos, unity over difference, being over becoming – and that through education we can instantiate that balance in our souls – we now know nature to be systems of matter in motion, that rest is a temporary pause in a more fundamental perpetual motion, and that man is one such system, impelled to preserve his own motion by satisfying his desires.

But – and here is where Rousseau begins his great countermovement – by nature man does not have any desires he cannot satisfy on his own, by (so to speak) gathering the nuts and berries and hunting. Self-preservation is easy because we do not need much, and therefore, contrary to Hobbes and Locke, we do not need to fight with others or lay up huge stores. Moreover, contrary to Hobbes' depiction of the state of nature, we experience no fear of death and therefore no anxiety about constant threats to our survival. We live from day to day, never wanting more than what is available. Natural man, according to Rousseau, is even capable of pity, though only in the limited sense of being able to identify with a fellow creature being torn apart by tigers nearby before running away. Later, however, Rousseau will build upon this slender natural tendril of pity to encourage compassion as a desirable trait for citizens within the social contract.

So far, in Rousseau's state of nature, we have an animal untroubled by thoughts of mortality and easily able to survive. But why is this a condition anyone should long for? Because, Rousseau adds, life in the state of nature is also *sweet*. This unselfconscious, instinctual, sensuous enjoyment of simply being alive is totally absent from Hobbes and Locke. For them, we are compelled to pursue self-preservation because we fear death and deprivation. At best, success in attaining power and property also allows us to enjoy material pleasures and status beyond the level of bare survival, but there is nothing intrinsically happy about it – enjoying a big meal is not a blissful experience like falling in love. According to Hobbes, man's natural condition is anxiety throughout one's entire life prompted by the fear of violent death. That anxiety is alleviated by the safety provided by the social contract but it never entirely vanishes. Moreover, for both Hobbes and Locke the natural condition of man is untenable, inevitably leading to danger for everyone and the self-evident need for government. According to Hobbes, even those who in the state of nature would be content with enough to survive and to leave others alone are compelled to fight because of a minority of men who naturally delight in mastery for its own sake. They will steal what you have and kill you for the hell of it, so you have to be ready to strike preemptively if anyone approaches you with uncertain intent. According to Locke, while people are capable of establishing their ownership of property in the state of nature even absent a government (in this he departs from Hobbes), eventually the losers in the competition, the "quarrelsome and contentious," awakening one day from their slumber under a tree to find that the land and stores are mostly in others' hands, will set upon the "industrious and rational" and invade their possessions. In other words, for Hobbes and Locke, living in the state of nature contradicts the aim of one's nature, which is survival and safety. Our natural desire to preserve ourselves is contradicted by the practice of this desire, which maximizes everyone's fear of violent death. In Rousseau's view, however, Hobbes and Locke are reading back into the state of nature passions and aggressions that were acquired only after the state of nature was left behind by civilization and the progress of the arts. They are completely unwarranted, in Rousseau's judgement, in assuming that this was our original condition. Originally, we were happy.

It would be difficult to overestimate the profundity of this new synthesis. Like the early modern thinkers, Rousseau also identifies nature with motion and chance becoming. Like them, therefore, he also rejects the classical view that reason, order and virtue are entailed by nature – that is, by a teleological conception of the cosmos. Unlike the early modern thinkers, however, Rousseau regards nature as beneficent and as the source of human happiness and repose. He thus restores the classical concern with happiness on the basis of the modern account of nature as origination and of human nature as individualistic. For the classics, happiness was an ascent from the moral virtues to the intellectual virtues, so that the aspirations of the mind for its fullest satisfaction entailed along the way our duties as family members and citizens. The higher we climb on this ascent, the more people drop off on the lower rungs. A few progress far enough upward in the development of the contemplative virtues that their minds are drawn close to, and in some manner harmonize with, the orderly cycles of the cosmos. It was, as is made clear by Plato's Image of the Cave in the *Republic*, Diotima's Ladder in the *Symposium* and the Seventh Letter, an arduous ascent requiring our utmost striving before we are finally borne aloft by the light of immortal being. For Rousseau, by contrast, happiness is the immediate and immanent gift of nature to all human beings. No effort on our part is required. Not only is it not necessary for us to ascend through the hierarchy of moral and intellectual virtues, but these products of civilization actually alienate us from the sweet sentiment of existence that is given to every human being. The ascent takes us further away from human happiness.

In this connection, we should note the parallels between the account of man's evolution out of the state of nature in the *Second Discourse* and

Lucretius' *On the Nature of Things.* Lucretius was an exponent of philosophical hedonism, which held that happiness came from the avoidance of pain, and
that in order to avoid pain, we had to avoid excessive pleasures, which required
us to toil for money, prestige and power over others. It was a variation of an
argument made by Socrates, but with the crucial difference that, for Lucretius, a
happy man was best off living in total privacy, in the garden of his villa,
avoiding the dangers and distractions of political life and ignoring the claims
of civic virtue. In this way, Lucretius departed from the mainstream tradition of
classical natural right, which stressed that philosophy must be civic-spirited. He
also took a materialistic view of the whole as having evolved out of the atoms, a
view of life as bodily that reinforced the identification of happiness with the
avoidance of pain. One way of looking at Rousseau is that he takes this
doctrine of philosophical hedonism – which Lucretius, typical in this respect
of all classical philosophy, believed could only be practiced by those with the
education to reflect on it and the financial means to live independently – and
transposes it to the unselfconscious instinct of every individual in the human
race in the primitive state of nature. Lucretian hedonism, which was antipolitical and aristocratic, in Rousseau's hands becomes pre-political and egalitarian. Rousseau's adaptation of Lucretius bolsters the dimension in his thinking
that also identifies political life as one of toil and sacrifice, with the consequence
that the practice of citizen virtue of the most authentic ancient Spartan kind
must be at the expense of *any* vestige of natural happiness, a life of constant
law-bred self-sacrifice.

Rousseau transposes to the origins of man the erotic wholeness and pleasure
that for the mainstream classical tradition could only be aimed at through a
teleological ascent solicited and guided by the final end. This puts him at odds
with both ancients and moderns. For the early moderns, nature is bad –
dangerous and hostile; what Machiavelli calls "the malignity of Fortuna."
Reason is the anthropocentric tool for nature's repression and reshaping (both
our own natures and the external world at large). For Rousseau, by contrast,
nature is good, the source of our happiness. Because modern rationality –
including the rationality of the social contract – represses nature, it can therefore never be deemed beneficial without qualification. Even granting that it
yields the utilitarian benefits of security and economic well-being, these must
pale in comparison to the repression of our natural happiness. Rousseau
thereby begins to drive a wedge between happiness and reason, which would
have been inconceivable to the ancient philosophers (for whom the life of the
mind was the happiest life), and which portends ominously for the future
unfolding of modernity.

Further, Rousseau is not arguing that man in the state of nature is virtuous.
He is good, but only because he has no reason to be bad and exploit others,
since he is not possessed of desires that he cannot fulfill on his own or any
proclivity toward aggressiveness or a love of victory. In this way, to the wedge
Rousseau drives between reason and happiness we can add a further wedge

between goodness and virtue – equally inconceivable from a classical perspective. For the classics, man perfected his goodness through cultivating the virtues required to live in a political community. For Rousseau, by contrast, there is no need for virtue or vice in the state of nature, and virtue arises only out of a need to restrain vice in an already corrupted and unnatural society. Therefore, as we observed in reference to the *Emile* and the dichotomy between the natural man and the citizen, virtue can have a certain dignity but it is not a good or happy life, as Plato and Aristotle argued.

So to summarize Rousseau's new synthesis, he agrees with Plato and Aristotle that human nature is good when it is fully developed. But he also agrees with Hobbes and Locke that human nature is fully developed before society ever arises, that it is by nature individual and not – as the classics had argued – communal. At the same time, he rejects Hobbes' and Locke's contention that, in the absence of government, the human condition is naturally wretched. This leads to the fundamental break with Hobbes, Locke and the early modern social contract theorists. For Rousseau, because the state of nature is not bad but is on the contrary our only experience of happiness, there is no need to escape from it. For Hobbes and Locke, as we have observed, the competition to survive eventually makes the state of nature unbearable. Only the social contract can protect us by restricting us universally from acting on our natures – by invading and tyrannizing over others – thereby increasing the maximum net gain in security and prosperity that we derive as individuals living under its sovereignty. But for Rousseau, the state of nature will *always* be preferable to civil society, even to a virtuous civil society, because it will always make us happier. He is on the verge of opening a Pandora's box that arguably makes it impossible to legitimize any form of political authority.

However, the wedges that Rousseau has driven between nature and civil society, between happiness and virtue, and between happiness and reason expose a serious problem with his own argument: If the state of nature made us happy without effort, why would human beings ever have left it? How did human nature even develop the capacity for social and political life, since it is not innate? For Hobbes and Locke, it is always in our natural self-interest to join the social contract if we are guided by reason. For Rousseau, it is never in our natural self-interest to do so, at least not fully or strictly speaking. For Rousseau, there is an enormous gaping chasm between nature and society or nature and convention. Modern society is so perverted, so artificial, that there hardly seems to be anything natural surviving in it. For Hobbes and Locke, by contrast, nature is very close – we are not all that different in society, just more restrained. For Rousseau, nature is immensely far away, a "distant shore," as he puts it in the *First Discourse*, to which we look back with longing as our distance from it widens. (Did he remember this image later when he was leaving Lake Bienne?) We have to strip away many eons of acquired, artificial traits in order to uncover it. This is why the turn to an account of historical progress is unavoidable. From the beginning, that historical genealogy is riven by the contradiction that it is a kind of technological and economic advancement chronicling an ever greater loss of our natural happiness that leaves us progressively more miserable.

And now we reach a passage that forms one of the foundation stones of German Idealism, bequeathing a set of paradoxes with which all of Rousseau's successors including Hegel wrestled, and which explains how Kant, arguably the most systematic of "technical" philosophers, could have found in Rousseau, arguably the least (if indeed he even conceived of himself as being a philosopher), the "Newton of the moral universe." It is worth quoting at some length:

> In any animal, I see only an ingenious machine to which nature has given senses to restore itself and to protect it, up to a point, from everything which tends to destroy it. I see precisely the same things in the human machine, with this difference, that nature alone causes all the operations in any animal, whereas man helps to bring his about, in his capacity as a free agent. One chooses or refuses by instinct and the other by an act of liberty. This means that the animal cannot deviate from the rule which is prescribed for it, even when it would be advantageous to do so, and that man can deviate from the rule often to his own prejudice.

Rousseau concludes by limiting the validity of physics to explaining the lowest sphere of human existence, below that of the "soul":

> Nature commands every animal, and the beast obeys. Man experiences the same sensation, but he recognizes that he is free to obey or to resist, and it is above all in the consciousness of this freedom that the spirituality of his soul reveals itself. For physics explains in some manner the mechanical working of the senses and the formation of ideas, but in the power to will ... and in the feeling of this power one finds only purely spiritual acts, about which nothing is explained by the laws of mechanics.

Nature prescribes an animal's instincts and it cannot depart from them. Nature also prescribes that man's desires need not exceed his needs, but a man is free to choose or not choose to act on an inclination to upset that equilibrium by becoming, for example, a glutton. Therefore, our freedom of will must be rehabilitated and placed solely at the service of preserving our natural self-sufficiency and lack of superfluous passions. Modern natural science ("physics" and "the laws of mechanics") explains human beings only insofar as we are "machines" constructed to preserve our lives. Its sphere is limited to sense data. Our "power" to choose, even to oppose nature and our own natural inclinations, is not bodily but "spiritual," and therefore beyond the sphere of physics. It is also "spiritual" because it has no specific natural content – no innate potentiality for virtue, no innate passion or appetite; it is entirely plastic and contentless.

In this way, Rousseau locates in the realm of freedom all those higher human capacities for which the modern physics of matter in motion cannot account. It explains how Rousseau is able to escape the reduction of human nature to the bourgeois self-interest with which he identifies modern social contract theories like those of Hobbes and Locke while conceding the validity, within their limits, of the materialistic and empirical natural science upon which those political prescriptions were based, witnessed by his references to Bacon as a true philosopher and, in the *Second Discourse*, "*le Sage Locke*" (to whose epistemology there is probably an allusion in Rousseau's concession that modern physics can in some measure explain the formation of ideas).

In Rousseau's new synthesis, the highest sphere of human experience, of the "spirituality of [man's] soul," is now identified with freedom as the pure will to resist nature, a radical departure from Plato and Aristotle, for whom the highest development of the soul would constitute the *fulfillment* of (and subordination to) nature. This is the portal from Rousseau to Kant. For Kant, like Rousseau, "physics" or natural science is limited to explaining what is empirically verifiable in nature, including human nature, and so would be limited to man understood solely in terms of appetitive self-interest. "Pure reason" for Kant means the kind of reasoning that guides modern natural science, for which the universality and necessity that structures causal rationality must in every instance have an empirical correlate in the realm of sense-experience, so as to organize all of nature in thought. The "critique" of pure reason is that it cannot enter the realm of man's freedom to resist the natural inclinations, because freedom is the only "fact" that possesses the structure of reason itself – universality and necessity – while possessing no empirical content or correlate. Man's exercise of freedom is observable, but it is not empirically verifiable or measurable. Therefore, empirical knowledge must recognize the limits of its own validity and "make room" for "freedom, God and immortality." More on this later, along with the contribution of Spinoza.

It remains to be seen how, on the one hand, Rousseau can identify free will as one of our faculties (along with "perfectibility") in the purest, original state of nature, characterize it as our capacity to resist our own natural inclinations, and yet identify this cluster of seemingly contradictory qualities, equal measures of instinct and the ability to rise above instinct, as in some overall sense our unified "nature." This conundrum, as we will see, is wrestled with by his successors beginning with Schiller and Kant. For now, we can observe that in Rousseau's moral philosophy, the exercise of our free will over our inclinations applies principally to our ability to repress natural inclinations already corrupted by the progress of civilization after that capacity for free will has been rehabilitated by being disentangled from the service of those corrupt passions. This is another reason why the historical genealogy is inevitable, and we turn to it now.

Along with this fundamental distinction between nature and freedom in our earliest, most pristine natures, Rousseau endows natural man with the additional faculty of "perfectibility." The history of man's fall from the state of nature through the ever greater progress of the arts, economic growth and finally the emergence of civil society results from man's capacity to abuse his freedom of will by devising new means toward ever more superfluous and bloated pleasures, losing his original self-sufficiency. The misuse of free will to serve increasingly bloated passions is closely linked to the psychological emergence of *amour propre* or vanity. While natural man's love of self or *amour de soi* is limited to what he naturally needs, leaving him self-sufficient and in no need of others, *amour propre* emerges as our capacity to extend ourselves into what we imagine others think of us, so that our pursuit of greater wealth and pleasure goes hand in hand with our craving for prestige in the eyes of others – to be admired, loved or feared by them, which requires ever more power, status and adornment. Rousseau's other writings explore how our proper use of the natural faculty of freedom might be disentangled from its corruption through the unfolding of history fueled by *amour propre* and restored to its "spiritual" purity as the power to resist our natural passions – the basis, for instance, in the *Social Contract* of the true citizen's sacrifice of self-interest to the common good in order to safeguard public liberty.

To remain with Rousseau's central distinction between freedom and nature, I find the most difficult thing to explain to students is how, for the classical thinkers, the life of the mind and, ranked just below it, the exercise of civic virtue comprise the most "natural" way of life – as in Diotima's Ladder – so thoroughly have they been exposed to Rousseau's identification of living naturally with spontaneous instinct and feeling, and his identification of freedom with our ability to throw off all of nature's restrictions. This is a testament to the brilliance of his new synthesis. Ever since he unfolded it, we now almost unthinkingly regard moral and intellectual cultivation as artificial and created, even if we admire it, something added on top of our natural, spontaneous emotions. Moreover, it is hard not to include one's autonomy, one's freedom from natural limitations, among the supreme benefits of free societies. But on another level it is one more stick of dynamite that Rousseau bricks into the foundation of his revised version of modernity. For what if the feeling of our sheer "power" in exercising freedom outweighs any ethical limitations or civic responsibilities? Rousseau's deep interest in education, both personal and civic, flows from his awareness of this problem, and it is one that will only intensify among his successors.

The open-endedness of freedom and the potential dangers it might pose was not a problem in principle for the early moderns. For Hobbes, the purpose of free will was to secure the material means for self-preservation. Every act of free will in this sense is limited to an appetitive gratification, the maintaining of one's motion. If you live under a sovereign authority that restrains us all so as to prevent the war of all against all by providing a neutral umpire to enforce the laws of contract whereby we may strive to prosper through the peaceful arts of commerce, then you are free in any meaningful sense of that term, and the yearning for some higher, allegedly noble, or open-ended autonomy would for Hobbes constitute an example of "absurd" and "insignificant speech" lacking a correlate in the concrete means toward self-preservation, as well as the kind of "vainglory" that induces ambitious young men to suppose that their superior virtues entitle them to usurp established authority and claim it for themselves, plunging us back into the rapacious chaos of our natural condition. But after Rousseau, these dragons menacing the bourgeois social contract will not be put to rest. For if freedom is plastic and has no innate content, how can our wills be in any way impeded?

The state of nature, in Rousseau's genealogy, is irrevocably lost when civil society is formed. Just as for Locke, the purpose of civil society is to protect the right of individuals to acquire unequal amounts of property. But whereas for Locke this authority is self-evidently legitimate, for Rousseau it is a fraud, since human beings do not by nature need or seek private property. As he puts it, the haves "seduced" the have-nots with "specious reasons" into giving up their natural liberty, and "for the profit of a few ambitious men henceforth the whole human race" was subjected to "work, servitude and misery." It was an unsurpassed human tragedy in which "all ran to meet their chains thinking they had secured their freedom." In other words, according to Rousseau, the very point at which for Hobbes and Locke we are secure from the terrors of the state of nature is the point at which our happiness is lost forever. This is the strongest indictment of private property rights and their protection by the social contract to be found in Rousseau's writings, obviously incendiary in a proto-Jacobin way, though sharply qualified or even retracted elsewhere.

I will not dwell on the details of this perplexing and controversial genealogy of loss through progress, but a sketch is necessary. Since man in his original natural condition was solitary and had no innate leaning to form communities, their existence could only be explained as the consequence of some natural cataclysm – a tidal wave or volcanic eruption – that forced people to bind together for mutual safety. In other words, human society originated through chance. Those short associations gradually led to the building of settlements, the growth of permanent families and family sentiments, and the first seeds of vanity through comparing our hut with the hut next door.

Interestingly, there is a midway point between these earliest associations and the full-blown alienation from nature to come, where the experience of communal living remains comparatively inured from the most corrosive inequalities of wealth and status and people can enjoy the simple satisfactions of working, eating and raising children together – a temporary condition Rousseau terms a "golden age" between the solitariness of the pure state of nature and the burdensome oppression of civilization. Many have noted the ambivalence of praising a phase in human evolution that, however comparatively innocent compared with what was to come, still represented a profound and irreversible departure from the solitary self-sufficiency that Rousseau otherwise maintains was our only true experience of happiness. Is it because he is building a platform upon which some notion of a reformed civil society, relatively close to nature, might be built, one that would require some natural inclination toward a collective association, if only natural in the sense that it was bred in us over time, a sort of second nature? This is only one instance of the ways in which Rousseau uses the term "natural" on a sliding scale from the earliest, purest and solitary version to the fleshpots of Paris, a continuum along which he ranges numerous admixtures of the natural with the unnatural as history unfolds. Our original, purest nature is mixed by successive degrees with corruption.

At any rate, the chains truly tighten as agriculture leads to the division of labor – the first instance of inequality based on talent and effort – and finally to private property and institutionalized inequality. As in Hobbes' and Locke's versions of the state of nature, at this for Rousseau very late stage of our loss of our original natural condition strife erupts between the haves and have-nots, and in Rousseau's depiction the social contract is created as a plot by the haves to make their superior status permanent. Even so, Rousseau begins to build a case for how even this most wretched eventuality in our fall from the state of nature might be partially rehabilitated based upon his understanding of our original nature. Freedom, we recall, is one of our original natural "faculties" from the earliest origins, and therefore, Rousseau argues, it is one that we cannot "alienate" or yield to the social contract if it is to have any basis in nature at all. The desire for the acquisition of property, on the other hand, was not one of our original natural faculties, is therefore entirely conventional and the product of our history of progressive alienation from nature, and therefore in principle can be alienated for the sake of minimizing the degree to which the social contract further cuts us off from our natural happiness. Freedom, in short, is inalienable, whereas – in direct opposition to Locke – property rights are not. Together with his observation that democracy is the form of government "least removed" from nature because it recognizes that we are all equal by nature, we can see that Rousseau is already reaching for a conception of government that is at least relatively close to nature and therefore legitimate.

How literally is this history to be taken? Some have said that it is purely hypothetical, a kind of thought experiment. I think this is true to the extent that the events surrounding our departure from the purest, earliest state of nature need not be taken literally as having happened at some verifiably specific time and place. But in order to explain how we became what we are now, Rousseau is implying, we have to infer that *some* such rupture occurred as a natural catastrophe, a tsunami or volcanic eruption, that forced the original solitaries to band together for survival, out of which the habit of living together gradually emerged. The rupture could have been something else, somewhere else and at some other time. But I would not go so far as to say that Rousseau's genealogy is purely hypothetical, for Rousseau believes that a green shoot of our original connection to nature dwells within us even now, however weakened, and in order to explain how such vastly different beings as we are today still preserve that green shoot from the origins, a real historical account is required. According to Hobbes and Locke, our natures dwell just beneath the surface of the social contract that restrains aberrant extremes of power-seeking, such that were the force of law to be removed we would immediately relapse into our full natural savagery, ready to kill rather than be killed; for Rousseau, by contrast, civilized man is almost a completely different being than natural man, separated by an enormous chasm that only an account of historical evolution can explain.

The same argument can be made about Rousseau's use of anthropological evidence gleaned from travelogues and early accounts of the Caribbean and Africa. For him, they do not constitute a strict historical and empirical proof of how man emerged into civilization from nature, especially since much of the evidence then and since repudiates his view that human beings ever lived solitarily, or lacked property, hierarchy, adornment and economic interdependence. All Rousseau need do is cherry-pick among these bits of evidence to furnish illustrations of what is already his certainty – that this is indeed how natural man originally lived, which at bottom rests on the bedrock assumption that there is a primordial individual wholeness that each of us once possessed that has been almost irrevocably lost but which can still be stirred within us and nurtured. This is a premise behind which no antecedent premise resides in Rousseau's thought. Moreover, whenever Rousseau is confronted with evidence that as far back as we know people lived in communities with private dwellings and property, he can always respond that we have not reached far enough back into the *pure* state of nature, only to an already contaminated level. The state of nature is a vanishing point where our animality hangs together with a sack of "faculties" that are pure formless potential.

Many readers have wondered how Rousseau can possibly add onto the innocent, robust animal that is natural man the mysterious faculties of freedom and perfectibility, which do not seem derivable from a being whose natural condition is in all other respects akin to that of an orangutan. Moreover, Rousseau's understanding of human nature at its most pristine as entirely individualistic, fully formed for happiness and self-sufficient in its natural condition prior to the emergence of society would appear to bar him from endowing natural man with any innate potentialities, such as Aristotle does when he defines man as by nature an animal that lives in a city through whose civic deliberations he exercises his capacity for reasoning. A cynical reader might even suggest that it is all too convenient for Rousseau to simply lard these formless, contentless faculties into an animalized understanding of human nature with which they are utterly incompatible, so as to have a basis upon which to explain natural man's evolution into the great civilizations of today with all their power, riches and vices. While I share these reservations about the soundness of his argument, I think Rousseau's response would be akin to the one I just sketched about how literally the historical account is to be taken: At bottom, he might say, I cannot explain precisely how or when natural man could have possessed these latent faculties, but I do know that the natural life and the way we live now is separated by eons of development (to our cost), and since I cannot depart from my fundamental conviction that originally we *were* happy and solitary, I must *infer* that some such plastic powers of transformation had to be sewn into human nature at the very outset – otherwise, our loss of our natural happiness through our own actions could never be explained.

As we have seen, Rousseau's location of man's prospects for happiness in his pre-political natural condition generates a number of characteristic dualisms that do not exist in principle for either classical or early modern political thought but with which his successors must grapple – nature versus freedom, nature versus reason, the Is versus the Ought, natural man versus the citizen, happiness versus virtue. Is there a unifying third term that might reconcile these dualisms? The rest of Rousseau's thought explores a number of compromises between nature and political society meant to narrow the gap between nature and convention so as to make life in civil society as natural as possible. I will discuss what I see as the three main alternatives.

THE SOCIAL CONTRACT AND THE GENERAL WILL

The first of these alternatives is a social contract that minimizes inequality by making everyone equally subject to laws of which they approve, set in a relatively austere economy that discourages extremes of wealth and luxury. The aim of Rousseau's work *On The Social Contract* is to preserve as much of our remaining natural equality and freedom as possible by setting up institutions that prevent any citizen from ruling despotically over any other citizen and forestalls to the degree possible the misery of the competition for wealth and social status characteristic of the bourgeois age. Hence, the social contract will provide a kind of institutional simulacrum of our original natural condition. The prescription has something of a classical aura but it is informed more by a nostalgia, and limited at that, for early ancient historical practice – the virtuous republics of Sparta and Rome – than by classical political philosophy.

Whether the regime is democratic, monarchical or aristocratic, it must recognize the equality of all citizens in principle and with respect to their rights, because, as we learned in the *Second Discourse*, a regime based on equality is the one "least removed" from nature. For the legitimacy of the social contract is *connected* to nature, but is not directly *from* nature. In contrast with ancient thinkers such as Aristotle, for whom each regime type embodies a different substantive conception of virtue and justice, for Rousseau, equality is the only principle of legitimacy, and all regime types are merely different modalities for institutionalizing it. The classical prescription for the best regime is aristocratic in principle, since human beings in their view are not equal by nature or by circumstance – for example, Aristotle does not believe manual laborers should be citizens in the best kind of regime because they lack the leisure to deliberate on public affairs. For the classics, the aim of political life is to enable the best people to cultivate their moral and intellectual virtues as fully as possible through their participation in public affairs. For Rousseau, by contrast, a legitimate social contract will conserve what remains of man's natural equality by establishing institutions that discourage the growth of any entrenched, inherited superiority of status. It will be governed by what we might term a "leadership elite" rather than an aristocracy.

Rousseau's prescription also differs from that of the classics because of its emphasis on the citizens' freedom rather than their virtue – for, as we recall from the *Second Discourse*, freedom is natural to man, whereas virtue is not. Man's nature has been corrupted by the progress of history, so that in the bourgeois age, the individual ordinarily uses his freedom to advance himself at the expense of others, whether economically, through political power-seeking, or by the pursuit of status. Rousseau's aim is to rehabilitate man's natural faculty of freedom as the vehicle for his commitment to a society that will curtail this competitive strife. The means to this end is the General Will. According to the General Will, we choose only those laws which not only we but everyone else in society would be willing to obey. This means that I as a citizen cannot will a law that would be exclusively in my own self-interest, or that of my family, class or faction. The exercise of my freedom as a citizen comes through voluntarily choosing the laws that we all will obey. The General Will is a rule of generalizability: It prevents any law that would enable others to take advantage of me or me to take advantage of others. Thus, the exercise of our innate natural freedom within the structure of the social contract guarantees the protection of our individual interests by limiting everyone's pursuit of their individual interests.

Much as with Kant's Categorical Imperative later, to will only a law that could not be exclusively in one's own self-interest virtually guarantees a moral outcome. In this respect, the exercise of the General Will requires no substantive content such as a regime principle that promotes virtue – the classical understanding of aristocracy – or any specific virtues of character such as those in the *Nicomachean Ethics*. It is purely procedural. Nevertheless, an education is needed to inculcate in citizens the proper, that is to say disinterested and generalizable, application of the General Will – hence Rousseau's return to the classical concern with education, including a possible need for the censorship of art and literature conducive to vice. For the ancients, freedom is at the service of virtue – we are free to acquire through education the proper ordering of the soul, the harmony of mind and affects, which will make us free from base passion, from risk of disgrace. For Rousseau, by contrast, virtue is at the service of freedom. The core of citizenship is the exercise of freedom – if there is no freedom, there can be no civic morality. In order to exercise our freedom, we require a sound character not mired in the craving for wealth, luxury and status. Morality arises primarily from the exercise of free will, not from virtue or education. To put it another way: For Plato, the education of eros to ascend toward virtue and wisdom enables us to be free because it fulfills our nature. For Rousseau, freedom is an ideal to be sought beyond the boundaries of a human nature already corrupted by the progress of civilization. Rousseau sees education as a means to shaping a character that can exercise freedom responsibly. The deistic "civil religion" of the *Social Contract* aims to form a civic psychology capable of the selfless exercise of freedom and the promotion of "sociability" (a somewhat opaque mixture of patriotism with the state-promoted belief in a Supreme Being who is not the God of revealed religion and obligatory tolerance toward all creeds while banning atheism).

In the social contract, according to Rousseau, a common power and a common will must outweigh private interests and individual freedom. Otherwise, we would revert to the late, corrupted state of nature where strife, greed and oppression would reign unchecked. One's alienation of one's individual liberty to the social contract must be "total" as long everyone does so equally, so no one can be the judge of his own private interest – giving myself to all avoids giving myself to one or a few. The General Will does not, we should stress, obliterate self-interest but on the contrary secures it. The pursuit of self-interest does, however, require limitation if it is not to exceed what is best for society as a whole – this is the sense in which we must be "forced to be free." The General Will is meant to prevent one's dependence on any arbitrary power through our total dependence on the public power. We exchange our unlimited natural freedom for civil freedom and property, both of which receive a more favorable account in the *Social Contract* than they do in the *Second Discourse*. Our natural freedom is now supplanted by civic and moral freedom so as to conserve what remains of the former. Political equality remedies the natural equality lost during the late stages of the state of nature. The General Will, by requiring that each citizen wills no act that would enable him to exploit others or be exploited by others, establishes the right of the individual to live securely but also imposes on him the spiritual test of exercising his freedom of will to rise above the passions. In this way, to use Isaiah Berlin's famous pairing, it combines the negative freedom of Locke's social contract with the positive freedom to live autonomously in cooperation with others, each citizen improving his own character through this joint endeavor.

Rousseau's overall prescription is therefore more social democratic than proto-Jacobin or communist, protecting both negative and positive freedom. Despite the fiery formulations, in Rousseau's expectations it will not require a huge degree of coercion by the state to "force" us "to be free," because our interests are protected as well, although not without limitation. Moreover, because, in contrast with Locke, for Rousseau compassion and freedom of will are natural, pre-political faculties, their incorporation in the social contract will in his view raise modern society's moral tone. Compassion is not merely to be tolerated or permissible as an aim of politics. Its active promotion by the state is arguably required, since along with freedom it is an important green shoot within an artificial compact of our original natural happiness, and can be strengthened through education and institutions in the social contract, whereas in the original state of nature it was limited to fleeting intervals of pity for another solitary.

Rousseau's view of precisely how much inequality of wealth is permissible before it interferes with our basic equality and our equal participation in the General Will is unclear since, like other social contract theories, his is mainly procedural, the rules of state umpirage. But because Rousseau, unlike Locke, thinks property rights are not natural, it follows that title is only created by the social contract, so that, upon its formation, the state takes away our possessions and returns them to us legitimized as property. Contrary to Locke, in other words, property rights cannot precede the state, which strictly speaking owns everything. The state is the only basis for all such rights, because natural man is so little in need of rights that they are inconceivable apart from the installation of political convention. In principle, the state may act in the public interest to curtail severe inequalities of wealth that might lead to factional strife or bribing the poor to buy their votes.

Civic freedom is a simulacrum of our freedom in the state of nature, but whereas our natural freedom was spontaneous and unselfconscious, our civic freedom is willed and self-conscious – a second, specifically moral, freedom gained by membership in the social contract. This, as I have already implied, helps to explain the ambiguous status of the Golden Age in the *Second Discourse* – it provides a quasi-natural social basis for the General Will to build upon, making no attempt to return to the purest state of nature where we were solitary. In the *Social Contract*, the history of the state of nature is truncated in comparison with its lengthy exposition in the *Second Discourse*, minimizing the huge distance between nature and civilization that we encountered in that earlier work, and is mostly confined to its later, most strife-ridden stages, so as to underscore how much we are in need of government – a revealing example of how Rousseau tailors his rhetoric for different contexts. Any hint of a possibility of returning to or recapturing the solitary condition of the pure state of nature is excluded here. Nevertheless, much as Rousseau underplays his account of our original human nature in the *Social Contract*, he still cannot argue that it is ever in our natural self-interest strictly speaking to unite in a society without completely ignoring what he argues elsewhere.

This explains why the despotic role of the founder of society, the Legislator, looms in a way that it does not for Hobbes and Locke. Exactly as in Hobbes' account of the state of nature, for Rousseau, in contrast with the ancients, there is no such thing as a superior ruler or statesman by nature. However, the Legislator, while not superior by nature, will have to employ despotic powers to put the "machine" of the social contract in motion in the transition from the state of nature. For the early modern social contract theorists, once you live under a stable and lawful government, in Hobbes' case even that of an absolute despot, you will retroactively assent because only now are your rights secure. For Rousseau, however, you do not need that protection in the pure state of nature and therefore, absent any innate leaning toward society or innate predisposition to recognizing the rationality of the need for government, we can only be dragged kicking and screaming by a "god-like" ruler who will breed in us, forcibly if need be, sociable habits. He must then step aside and never "enter into" the regime he has created, like Cincinnatus returning to his plough after resigning his dictatorship. The Legislator possesses unlimited power in order to create the republic, but its future leaders will exercise only those powers voluntarily designated to them by the people. The aim of the social contract is to prevent anyone like the Legislator from ever emerging again, though it could not have been created except by him. Call it the withering away of the despot.

In this way, just as Rousseau revived the classical concern with education (albeit as shaping the character able to repress his inclinations so as to exercise the General Will, as opposed to cultivating our moral and intellectual virtues in the ascent toward the contemplative life), here he revives the ancients' concern with the possible need for a just regime being founded by a tyrant, as in Book 4 of Plato's *Laws*, with the difference that the regime to be founded will recognize only human equality as its principle of justice, as opposed to the classical preference for aristocracy. But the tyrannical potential of Rousseau's Legislator, in my view, exceeds that of either the ancients' exploration of the foundation of the city through coercion or of the Hobbesian Sovereign. For the ancients, human beings already have a natural leaning to political community even before it is founded. For Hobbes and the early moderns, the destructive consequences of acting upon our individual freedom make the need for its curtailment by the Sovereign self-evident according to reason. But for Rousseau, the distance between the state of nature and civil society is so enormous, with no innate natural leaning toward community or capacity to rationally assent to our own constraint, that the Legislator must literally "change human nature," "destroy" our natural independence so that each becomes "nothing." Moreover, given Rousseau's conception of human nature, people will not be able understand the benefits of the social contract until after it has been constructed, meaning that they cannot consent in advance to something – citizenship – they cannot experience until it is established. Perhaps echoing Machiavelli, Rousseau says that, at the earliest inception of the transition from the state of nature to "the founding of a people," the Legislator will need to employ some form of religious belief in order to overawe natural man's innate incapacity for living in society with divine sanction and threat of retribution. Not surprisingly, the charisma of Rousseau's Legislator and his power to attempt to change human nature makes some commentators envision a Robespierre or Lenin. We can already anticipate the dynamic of millenarian collectivism where a "transition phase" of dictatorship is supposed to create a society in which arbitrary political power will henceforth be impossible and unneeded.

The totalitarian potential in Rousseau's theory of government is in my view more evident in the Legislator than in the doctrine of the General Will, where commentators frequently locate it. Take, for instance, the notorious maxim: "The General Will Can Never Err," in which some have detected a presage of

Stalinism or Orwell's *1984*. All it amounts to is the tautology that, as long as the General Will is operating properly, it cannot make a mistake. But, according to Rousseau, it does not necessarily always operate properly, and the people can be fooled by a fraudulent use of it. Precisely because the social contract is not grounded in an innate human propensity but must be compelled to some degree by force, its legitimacy through recognizing equality and protecting individual rights is crucial to justifying that power. The individual's natural liberty can never be completely absorbed by the social contract. We alienate to it only that degree of liberty that will prove useful to us, though that alienation of liberty must be done equally by all. The generalizability of the General Will makes "each" the same as "each." The General Will therefore cannot make decisions about particular individuals. As long as no one is singled out for exceptional treatment – good or bad – our natural liberty is preserved. Accordingly, Rousseau does not favor majoritarian or populist democracy like that of ancient Athens. The General Will is not "the will of all," which is only the sum of private wills. Instead, the General Will achieves an equilibrium of interests across the board. Even if 99.9 percent of the citizens favored discriminatory treatment toward the remaining few, that would not be the General Will, merely a single majoritarian faction. Hence Rousseau's dislike of political factions – they encroach upon the common good, where "each" should be the same as "each." If factions cannot be avoided, better to have many than few, so as to diffuse their ability to coalesce into "the will of all," as opposed to the General Will. There is another contrast here with Aristotle, whose conception of popular authority is one where the middle class rules, leading in the best instance to the promotion of an aristocratic element through rewarding the virtuous and educated with public office. For Rousseau, Aristotle's "polity" would merely be rule by a faction.

According to Hobbes and Locke, our legitimate self-interest is "represented" by the state at a distance. For Hobbes, at its most effective, it is an autocracy. For Locke, it requires the consent of the Commonwealth, but that consent does not necessitate ongoing political participation. For Rousseau, by contrast, our direct participation in political life is necessary if we are to exercise our moral and civil freedom to assent to how we are ruled. In this way, Rousseau revives yet another classical rubric set aside by the early moderns – the view that a just civil society needs to be limited in size so that the citizenry can participate directly in its deliberations. Again, however, he revives a classical rubric for opposite reasons: Whereas for Aristotle, a political community should be small enough for citizens with sufficient economic wherewithal to cultivate their moral and intellectual virtues through a full-time devotion to "politics and philosophy," and is hence an aristocracy, for Rousseau, small size is optimal because it enables an equal citizenry to exercise its freedom. The central such exercise is the right of the citizenry to affirm or revoke the powers exercised by the state to promote the General Will.

In Rousseau's social contract, we still have property and other self-interested rights, just as in that of Locke. Despite some inflammatory language, his social contract theory does not advocate the obliteration of the individual by the collective or the complete equality of condition. It is not an attempt to return to the pure citizen virtue of the ancient republics but an accommodation with modern bourgeois self-interest. Moreover, even though Rousseau says that all human beings are equal in principle, in practice he hints that the political predominance of the propertied classes arguably provides an element of stability because those with more have a greater stake in preserving the state – quite like Locke. Discussing the Roman Comitia in Book 4 of the *Social Contract*, Rousseau appears to approve of the way in which the oligarchs of republican Rome rigged the voting by centuries so as to ensure the election of candidates friendly to the propertied orders.

For Rousseau, in contrast with Hobbes, the government itself is not synonymous with the social contract, only a "commission" from the sovereign people. The different regimes of democracy, aristocracy and monarchy are not, as they are for Aristotle, distinct substantive claims based on a "part" of justice and virtue intermixed with self-interest, and their intermediate forms are limitless. Political right (after the Legislator has forged the Sovereign People out of human nature) cannot be derived from force – an implicit disagreement with Hobbes, for whom a legitimate Sovereign can be established through war or conquest as much as by voluntary assent as long as his authority is used to protect us from relapsing into the state of nature. In reality, for Hobbes, a people's voluntary assent to the Sovereign's rule would probably be impossible were they still living in the war of all against all, meaning that their assent is in effect retroactive once they have been brought by force to see its necessity for their own survival and prosperity. That is why the preferable form of sovereignty for Hobbes is absolute monarchy, and its powers must be limitless. For Rousseau, by contrast, one cannot alienate all of one's freedoms to a monarch, and even such rights as are transferred to him cannot be for more than one generation without the people being asked to ratify his authority or revoke it. Were the people to give up its freedom entirely to one man, that would not constitute the security of the social contract but, on the contrary, its dissolution through tyranny.

Because Rousseau does not believe in the possibility of citizens, monarchs or statesmen deserving political authority because of their superior natural virtue, as in the classical account of government, the procedural mechanisms for legitimizing rule are of supreme importance – the sovereign is a "machine." Rousseau's ranking of all regimes follows from their structural capacity to conserve the General Will and human equality. Even though in the *Second Discourse* he pronounced democracy in its historical origins to be "least removed" from the state of nature because it recognized and mirrored our natural equality, viewed from the perspective of promoting the civil freedom added by the social contract to our original (and now largely lost) natural freedom, he now criticizes democracy for weakening the General Will because it encourages the wills of private individuals: There is not enough of a separation between the people and the state to guarantee the degree of coercion needed to "force" people to be free. He believes an elective aristocracy is the best regime because it preserves a middle ground between the excessive equality of democracy and the excessive inequality, accompanied by the danger of despotism, of monarchy, with the proviso that, in contrast with Aristotle's view that an aristocracy based on virtue and education is itself the best kind of regime, Rousseau envisions a kind of egalitarian-minded leadership elite that would govern on behalf of the General Will of citizens equal through their exercise of freedom, not on the basis of the elite's own innate superior merit.

Rousseau believes there is an inverse relationship between the size of a state and the successful exercise of civic freedom – smaller is better. But he also recognizes that, in the modern age, societies small enough to facilitate direct political participation are increasingly rare. The larger the country, he argues, the more frequently there should be assemblies of the people, because more power is concentrated in the hands of the state, but the larger the country, the harder it is to convene them. Nevertheless, it is crucial to the legitimacy of the regime that the people be asked on a regular basis to affirm the "commission" they have given it to exercise power on their behalf. Even if the people cannot participate more widely or thoroughly in public affairs, this minimum standard for the exercise of their free will must be met, or the state will be by definition a despotism, benign or otherwise. This standard does not exist in the social contract theories of Hobbes and Locke, because they do not recognize the "spiritual" importance, to use Rousseau's term from the *Second Discourse*, of the citizens' exercise of freedom to overcome their natural inclinations and to voluntarily submit to a collective authority of their own choosing. For Hobbes and Locke, so long as every individual's "life, liberty and ... pursuit of property" is secured by their representatives governing the social contract, any meaningful definition of freedom is thereby met.

Rousseau propounds a version of federalism that would ameliorate the difficulties of large states having their commission regularly ratified by the people by providing for leagues of towns, each of which would convene such assemblies, or by assemblies that would rotate throughout the country. Among Rousseau's more benign political influences was the promotion of this understanding of federalism by Tocqueville in his exploration of American democracy, with its emphasis on the importance of townships and states as local incubators of liberty to mediate between the individual and an already large and expanding national republic. Interestingly, few if any modern democratic nation-states would live up even to Rousseau's most relaxed standard for minimal legitimacy, since, for example, in the United States, the constitution can – with very great difficulty – be changed, but no law requires that it be periodically returned to the people for its ratification.

Unlike Kant's Categorical Imperative later, which applies to mankind as such, Rousseau appears to assume the primacy of "peoples" rooted in their traditional territories – an important antecedent for Hegel, as we will see. Even though the *Social Contract* is presented as a universally applicable and valid teaching about legitimate government, its content is so underdetermined due to its proceduralistic character that the distinct history of each "people" begins to fill it up with its unique and particular worldview, its *moeurs*. Viewed in this light, one might say that the doctrine of the General Will is a conceptual membrane within which the particular experience of a given people is immanentized, or that Rousseau's understanding of distinct peoples walks up to the line of being entirely historical with no mooring in nature but does not cross over it (that move must await Hegel). Whereas nothing in principle prevents Hobbes' and Locke's theories of the social contract from virtually limitless expansion, swallowing up hitherto distinct peoples, Rousseau believes in patriotism and does not regard its heart as dead even in today's bourgeois. As we observed, the General Will does not equal the majoritarian will of all; in principle, to oppress even one citizen would violate it. But what would prevent a distinct "people" from decreeing that its boundaries and traditional identity excluded certain members of the population from its sovereign body? Could they then be oppressed as, in effect, internal enemies? In other words, while it might be the case that, as conceived by Rousseau, the General Will could not oppress its own members, might it not conceivably tyrannize over those whom it deems to be noncitizens? This quandary will continue to haunt the Philosophy of Freedom.

LOVE AND FAMILY

Rousseau's teaching about the social contract reveals the extent to which he keeps one foot planted in the early modern outlook on political legitimacy, despite being highly critical of it. But with the second alternative way of bridging the chasm between nature and convention a very different Rousseau emerges: one of the founders of Romanticism. That alternative, most fully realized in the *Emile*, prescribes a life in the provinces devoted to the family, far from the most alienating influences of society, closer to what remains of the state of nature because it is in a rustic rural setting. Rousseau regarded the family as the least alienating and artificial of human dependencies, based on simple and touching sentiments of affection. We recall from the *Second Discourse* that families appeared very early in the state of nature, after its purest stage of solitude had been left behind, but well before the wholly baleful development of private property and the social contract – another instance of Rousseau's ingeniousness in building into the unfolding of the state of nature a minimal kind of sociality that, like the faculty of freedom and the instinct for compassion, provides a link for prescribing a comparatively less alienating form of civil society that at least mirrors our original freedom and equality.

Emile is a boy who, being raised in the country and thereby insulated from the full panoply of modern vices, is educated by stages so as to conserve his innate natural goodness and innocence as he is gradually exposed to the world of simple manual labor – suitable for someone whose material needs will never go beyond the most basic – and, eventually, an education in the wider world led off by *Robinson Crusoe* (to reinforce Emile's natural self-reliance) followed by historical classics such as Herodotus and Thucydides. It is an education emphasizing facts, including real-life models of virtue, rather than abstract speculation: "With its help he will read the hearts of men without any lessons in philosophy." The capstone of Emile's education is the identification of the unity and harmony of nature with a Supreme Being accessible through our sentiments – Rousseau's variant of Deism, a creed for which the *Emile* was publicly burned by the authorities on the grounds that it rejected Christian revelation.

When Emile hits adolescence, his *amour propre* also emerges because, being erotically attracted to girls, he is able to wonder in his imagination whether or not they find him attractive in return. "Jean-Jacques" (Rousseau, oddly enough, appears as a character in his own pedagogical drama) rehabilitates Emile's ability to live through the expectations of others, ordinarily a source of vanity and craven dependence on those whom one wants to win over, by focusing it entirely on his perfect future partner, Sophie (who has in the meantime fallen in love with the ancient Greek hero Telemachus from Fenelon's tale and is looking to find him in real life). By educating himself under Jean-Jacques' guidance to be attractive to her – morally upright, self-reliant and trustworthy – Emile projects Sophie as his ideal for his own improvement, for he attributes to her all virtue and goodness; in his complete absorption in her, Emile's passions are further sluiced away from their ordinary modern outlets in vice, luxury, libertinage and the craving for prestige. Emile, the modern Telemachus, loves Sophie, his ideal of wisdom (*sophia*). The projection is not necessarily a reflection of the truth about Sophie, but a dream of love in which he can totally lose himself. As Rousseau puts it in a classic *apercu* of Romanticism:

There is no true love without enthusiasm, and no enthusiasm without an object of perfection, real or chimerical, but always existing in the imagination ... In love everything is only illusion. I admit it. But what is real are the sentiments for the truly beautiful with which love animates us and which it makes us love. This beauty is not in the object one loves; it is the work of our errors.

As the final stage in his preparation for marriage and family life, Rousseau introduces Emile to the concept of civil society, a new version of his argument in the *Social Contract*. Rousseau now argues that family life weds us more firmly to civil society than our freedom as citizens alone. If we have only ourselves to worry about, we might not be willing to limit our own selfishness even in exchange for everyone else limiting theirs. But if we have a family to worry about, according to Rousseau, we have a greater motive for preferring a safe and peaceful civil society to the dangers of factional strife and revolution caused by selfish interests. The General Will, it appears, may have been too austere as originally formulated, relying too much on the satisfaction each of us gains from the exercise of our free will. Modern bourgeois man needs a greater private motive for loyalty to the common good, and for Rousseau, the family is a private interest which is at the same time relatively unselfish, since it involves not merely our own individual security and comfort but caring for the people dearest to us. Whereas the General Will is an institutional procedure whereby otherwise corrupted modern individuals might, by imposing their will to repress their inclinations, achieve a simulacrum of the freedom and equality of the state of nature – a kind of top-down solution to the conflict between nature and freedom – the *Emile* suggests how someone living today might be shaped in such a way that his nature will be conserved and channeled into blossoming through his education and love of another – a kind of bottom-up solution, or an aesthetic blend of the natural and conventional. As we will consider in detail in Chapter 2, the top-down solution to the tension between nature and freedom anticipates the moral idealism of Kant, while the bottom-up solution anticipates Schiller's idea of aesthetic culture. Neither response embodies the purity of either of Rousseau's two original authentic alternatives, Natural Man versus the Citizen. But they do try to bridge the chasm between them.

In the *Emile*, Rousseau concedes again that we cannot aim for the true citizen virtue of the ancient republics, the obliteration of the distinction between the individual and the common good. Modern bourgeois man must have a self-interested stake in an orderly society, and the family, which includes our own property and wealth, is the healthiest such stake because it gives him a personal motive for behaving justly. In sum, the social contract will accommodate man's transformed nature in a bourgeois epoch and raise it to a comparatively higher moral pitch. To return to the David painting, Rousseau begins but does not end with the dichotomy between severe Roman virtue and the natural sentimental-ity of family life, but attempts to bring them together in the modern social contract while diluting both extremes. Of course not everyone was content with this compromise – they wanted to use the painting's left-hand side of stern Roman virtue to bring about the right-hand side of natural happiness.

THE SOLITARY DREAMER

The *Emile* may contain Rousseau's most successful search for a way of recon-ciling the powerful dualisms he has diagnosed in the bourgeois age, the unifying third term to be provided by education and an aesthetic flowering of human nature into a civilized man. But what about Rousseau himself? What about the individual who does not find primary satisfaction in citizen life, or in the provinces with his family (to say the least), but spends all of his time thinking about how to recover the natural life? There is a powerful, perhaps insuperable dilemma here, because Rousseau cannot claim that the philosophic life is superior to the life of an individual seeking the authentic experience of nature. It might even be better to have been a citizen of Sparta mindlessly conforming to the laws of a virtuous republic than a philosopher, whose way of life according to Rousseau has a huge potential for vanity and for carrying us away from the natural life, and our compassion for others, into a realm of fanciful abstraction. For Plato and Aristotle, the philosophic way of life is the closest that human nature can come to perfection, an ascent that can only take place by way of the moral and civic virtues, and whose pinnacle only a very few will reach. By contrast, for Rousseau, if he is to be considered a philosopher at all, or if he considered himself to be one, the best kind of philosophy can only point the way to a natural happiness which is not philosophy itself, and which all people were capable of experiencing in the state of nature prior to any hier-archical moral and intellectual ascent.

This leads to the third solution for narrowing the chasm between happiness and freedom: Rousseau replaces the philosopher conceived of as someone who seeks knowledge of the eternal causes of the whole with a kind of dreamer or poet, an authentic individualist who uses his intellectual powers to free himself *from* the intellect, in order to commune with his natural sentiments. Replicating natural man's original solitariness, this individualist is a solitary who stands outside of civil society, not because he is wiser in the traditional sense of philosophical contemplation but because he is more natural and authentic. He takes an artistic view of life in order to evoke and express the sentiments that are most natural in himself. Poetry and literature, not treatises, are his medium. His experience of nature is aesthetic rather than contemplative – not the search for the eternal truth, but summoning up and releasing into himself nature's underlying potency and sublimating those energies through their expression as art. Rousseau's autobiographical writings, especially the *Reveries*, his novel and his music reveal his attempt to be this kind of dreamer. It helped begin the Romantic tradition in art and literature and the elevation of the artist over the rational thinker as the true voice of being, a cardinal theme, as we will see, of German historicism. For Rousseau, the daydreams of the solitary walker are the best chance of opening a portal to the inner truth of what remains in us of our original natural condition, and he could not give up those dreams for a devotion to either citizen or family life.

And that carries us back at last to the shores of Lake Bienne, the scene with which this chapter began, where Rousseau experienced the happiness that in my view provides the unifying thread among his many diverse, often seemingly contradictory, works. Let us look at it in detail. As evening approached, Rousseau tells us, he went down from the summit to the lake shore. We know that Rousseau read Plato's *Republic*, which he thought to be "the most beauti-ful educational treatise ever written." The *Reveries* may accurately describe events in Rousseau's life, but they are also works of autobiographical art and are in a manner meant to instruct and educate. I am going to assume, therefore, that there is an allusion here to Plato's Image of the Cave. In diametric opposition to that image, in which one ascends from the shadowy, time-bound twilight toward the summit and the sunlight of the eternal truth – also the opposite of Diotima's Ladder in which eros draws us "on up" toward the unchanging Idea of the Good – Rousseau goes *down* for insight into nature, down from the fading sunlight into the approaching night and the flux of the temporal, down to what Plato presents as the lowest level of the Divided Line, the level of light playing on water, hazy images and sensations prior to illumination by reason. (Rousseau describes them as "smiling images," prompting one to remember that for Plato the lowest level of the Divided Line was the level of "images" and the faculty of "imaging" [*eikasia*].)

In short, Rousseau's reverie presents us with the complete and total reversal of classical ontology, the world turned upside down. Whatever stability is to be found in life is no longer traced to the eternal ends that structure the cosmos but to the stable current of ceaseless becoming, the stability of floating along a stream of motion and chance. It is nature as origination. Moving down into it is to reverse the evolution of the self-conscious self out of the unselfconscious pre-self; not the transcendence of time that the classics identified with the love of wisdom but, on the contrary, a descent, a recessional movement from selfhood back into the moment where self and becoming intersect and the self dissolves. As Rousseau evokes the recollection, as he lay on the shore the sound of the waves and water "plunged" his soul "into a delicious reverie." The ebb and flow of the waves interacted with the "internal movements" of his reverie, merging the inside with the outside, so that he felt his "existence with pleasure without taking the trouble to think" – a phrase which, again, turns the entire meaning of philosophy on its head, since for the classics, and in an attenuated way even for the moderns with their reductive account of human satisfaction, living in a satisfactory way was inseparable from thinking, as much so for understanding the rationality of the modern social contract that insulates us from nature's irrationality as for understanding the contemplative life in the classical meaning of the term as the fulfillment of our nature. For Rousseau, happiness comes *from* nature's disorder; thinking is an impediment to this happiness.

Here, then, is his own personal solution to the dichotomization of virtue and natural happiness symbolized in the David painting – the third term underlying all of these dualisms is an originary unity, a unity of motion, what Schelling was to term "the infinitely finite." The underlying flow of movement and disorder becomes a place for the soul to "repose" upon, where it can "gather together all its being" without needing to recall the past or think about the future, where "time counts for nothing," where "the present lasts forever without marking its duration," where there is no sentiment of enjoyment, pleasure, pain, desire or fear other than the solitude of one's existence, which this feeling can "fill entirely." For as long as this state lasts, one is happy – not merely a relative happiness, as in the fleeting pleasures of life, but "perfect and full," leaving no "void" in the soul, drifting "at the will of the water" on the "agitated lake." In other words, everything about existence that for the classics prevented us from being happy – chance, accident, disorder, motion – and that we aim to transcend through the ascent of the mind, for Rousseau is the very locus of happiness, "without taking the trouble to think." As he sums up this revelation: "What is the nature of one's enjoyment in such a situation? Nothing external to oneself, nothing except oneself and one's own existence; so long as this state lasts, one suffices to oneself, like God."

This language takes a familiar formulation from classical and Scholastic philosophy and completely reverses its meaning. The traditional view had been that our soul can achieve self-sufficiency, true independence, to the extent that we can minimize our desires, which depend for their satisfaction on perishable external objects and the acquisition of wealth, honor and power, distracting us from the life of the mind and the contemplation of the eternal verities. Thus, for Plato and Aristotle, although a life devoted to civic virtue and statesmanship was admirable, it was not the highest or fullest kind of happiness available. Only philosophical contemplation could provide that, if only at intervals. For Plato, the eros for knowledge of the whole was so overpowering that it sluiced off erotic energies for any lower, less perfect kinds of happiness such as the pleasures that could be attained through pursuing wealth and power, and whose objects, being perishable, chained one to a slavish round of procuring them again and again, since they could not last, and also involved one constantly in vying with others for wealth and status.

Rousseau reverses all of this by arguing that precisely by descending *behind* reason and virtue to the point where even our awareness that we are human selves is blissfully obliterated, descending into the matrix of sheer happenstance, flux, movement and origination, do we cease to depend on external goods for the gratification of our passions and thereby achieve true self-sufficiency – not by transcending such desires, but by descending behind their distinct identities and respective objects in the world down into sheer inchoate feeling. And whereas, for the classics, the pursuit of happiness can only be conducted in a political community – because one needs friends with whom one can pursue wisdom through conversation, and because, while the moral and civic virtues are but way stations to the higher happiness of contemplation, they are necessary for forming in potential philosophers the traits of moderation and prudence that are necessary for philosophy itself – for Rousseau, these moments of true happiness *cannot* be achieved with others: "It is necessary to admit that this was done better and more favorably in a fertile and solitary island, naturally circumscribed and separated from the rest of the world, where nothing offered itself to me but smiling images."

The meaning of nature as origination provides, in my view, the underlying unity among Rousseau's works, but it also helps to explain their extraordinary diversity and at times considerable tension with one another. As usual, a contrast with Plato is apt. All Platonic dialogues lead us toward the One, the

Idea of the Good, that brings our soul into conformity with the eternal reason-
ableness of the cosmos. The paths toward the One vary with the dialogic
situation and the psychological make-up of the interlocutors – Glaucon
requires a different kind of shaping than Theaetetus. But the goal does not
vary – hence, as so many Platonic images of philosophizing limn, it is a vertical
ascent toward a unifying height. Rousseau's works, by contrast, are
related to each other horizontally, not hierarchically. For whether he is discussing political life, family life or strictly personal life, all of these experiences
are offshoots from the underlying flux of nature, offshoots that embody whatever still resides in us of nature to varying degrees and through different,
sometimes contradictory modalities, summed up in the dichotomy between
natural man and citizen. Only in his *Reveries*, as I think the foregoing discussion makes clear, is Rousseau able to experience nature in a pure, uncompromising and unmediated way, if only at intervals, and this solitary interlude of
happiness – a solitude that is his portal to the natural condition of man in
its purest, most pristine solitary form – provides him with the bedrock conviction that nature *is* still able to speak to us, summon us back, and
therefore also provides him with a standard in accordance with which he can
criticize the politics and personal life of the modern bourgeois age and
show how its vices might be ameliorated through varying blends of nature
and convention.

There have been other plausible interpretations of the unifying thread in
Rousseau's writings. According to one, his explorations of nature throughout
his lifelong ramblings was a response to his abandonment by his father and the
need to leave his birthplace, Geneva, symbolically an expulsion from Eden and
his wandering exile in a fallen world as he sought readmission. Seen in this
light, the *Emile* might be viewed as the attempt by "Jean-Jacques" to raise and
educate a new version of himself, a boy who will be shielded from the searing
injustice with which he was treated, and the immersion in vice (chronicled in the
Confessions) which followed upon his expulsion – a Rousseau made whole.
While plausible as explanations of the course his life took, these other interpretations of the unifying thread among his writings are to my mind secondary
to his revelation on Lake Bienne, because however worthy citizen life, education and family life may be, however comparatively close they may come to
conserving or approximating something of the state of nature, only in his
Reveries is Rousseau the solitary able to merge with nature completely: the
font of all his other arguments and insights.

UNRESOLVED PARADOXES: ROUSSEAU'S BEQUEST

Even if I am right in suggesting that the revelation of nature in the *Reveries* is
the underlying source for Rousseau's diverse explorations of political, family
and aesthetic life, however, it does not point to a clear and unambiguous
endorsement of any one of these alternatives as preferable to the others or

provide a direct basis for them. Nature is still too far away to invoke in a binding manner. While the solitary poet's meditations upon nature and attempts to evoke it through his imagination may come closest to the pristine experience of the natural life itself, a dedication to that quest forecloses any lasting involvement with society at large, including the family and especially civil society.

As we have observed, for Rousseau, citizenship at its best is achieved by the obliteration of the self and its complete submergence in a law-bound collective, a high-water mark achieved by the ancient republics such as Sparta and Rome – in other words, by one's total alienation from one's natural condition. The modern social contract Rousseau eventually prescribes retreats from that draconian Spartan standard, relaxing the duties required of citizens by civil society so as to ensure a degree of individual material self-interest is protected. But while this prescription for the social contract arguably avoids the worst excesses of bourgeois materialism and selfishness, it remains no more than a half-way house between unalloyed nature and the highest standard for citizenship, a mélange of artificial institutional mechanisms and natural desires that are universally restrained but have still been inherently corrupted by the progress of history; a social contract whose institutions promote no more than an artificial simulacrum of the equality and freedom we spontaneously experienced in the state of nature. Emile's life as a husband incentivized by family ties to assume his responsibilities as a citizen, along with the insulation from bloated passions provided by his boyhood education to keep his desires on a level with the simplest needs of natural self-preservation, arguably introduces a further layer of natural sentiment into the exercise of the General Will. But it still does not make civil society a natural way of life, strictly speaking; and, after all, even the family, while it emerged comparatively early in the evolution of the state of nature and the Golden Age of simple communality, is not strictly speaking natural in the fullest, purest, earliest and most pristine sense as the original solitary.

At the end of the day, it remains mystifying to me that Rousseau insists that man at his most natural is solitary. If the state of nature *began* with the primitive sociality of the later stage of the Golden Age, it would have been a much simpler matter for Rousseau to propose it as a healthy substratum beneath the corruption that set in with civilization, a natural communality still salvageable to some degree in the present. But Rousseau, as it were, throws a monkey wrench into his very effort to strike that equipoise between a legitimate social contract and an underlying residue of natural communality by stressing a *more* natural and original solitary condition that must fatally undermine it. Perhaps that insistence is another sign of the influence of Lucretius, whose philosophical hedonism was confined to enlightened individuals who avoided the realm of political strife and ambition. Or did it mirror a tension in Rousseau's own psyche between his desire to belong and his love of being apart?

In sum, the side-by-side, centripetal and horizontal character of Rousseau's various and conflicting attempts to bridge the chasm between nature and convention remains. Whereas the classics' account of the natural life as the ascent from family life to civic virtue and, at the highest level, contemplation thereby provided a way of ranking different ways of life as well as the comparative justice and injustice, virtue and vice, rationality and irrationality of different regimes grounded objectively in the permanent truth about the whole, Rousseau's account of the natural life as a matrix of origination underlying all human, social and political phenomena flows equally into all of these different channels, with no objective ranking according to reason possible.

Hence, as we will consider in Chapter 2, at the end of the day Rousseau bequeathed to his German successors Kant and Schiller a series of only partially resolved tensions between nature and convention to which they responded by extracting one dimension or another of his thought, assigning it priority, and thereby attempting to make it the basis for the others. In the ensuing decades, meanwhile, Rousseau's influence over French intellectual, cultural and political life would assume an importance that one of Robespierre's biographers compares to that of the King James Bible for Protestant England, and especially for the leader of the Jacobins. Robespierre believed that, in launching the Terror of 1792 – whose death toll would reach a quarter-million across France – he was literally implementing "Jean-Jacques'" teaching about the General Will. By exterminating those classes in French society most thoroughly corrupted by bourgeois vices, along with the other vices accompanying aristocratic and religious hierarchy, the Jacobins believed that they were returning the rest of France to the pristine condition of the Golden Age of the state of nature, incoherently blended with a collectivist republic, with no inequality of condition, a community of the virtuous and pure in which the individual would be totally submerged. It was the return to "the Year One."

This was the beginning of what I have elsewhere termed utopian genocide – to be repeated with a mounting scope of savagery and intensity by the Bolsheviks, Nazis, Maoists and Khmer Rouge, down to today's Jihadist revolutionaries such as ISIS. The common motif is that, if society can be ridded of its corrupt classes in a single massive blood-letting, then everyone will be released from the psychological torment of having to compete for property and status, the corrupt forces that, in Rousseau's view, had alienated us from the state of nature and our original happiness. We will live together in collective bliss and, the enemies of peace, justice and freedom – the offending classes or races standing in the way of that collective bliss – having been wiped from the face of the earth, war, violence, political exploitation and competitive strife will never arise again, because no one would want the pain of such struggles once they had fully felt the sweet balm of release from them. Unless, of course, the first round of terror had not been *completely* effective and the corruption of self-interest began to creep back into the human character, which would require a new round of liquidation to uproot, and as many rounds as necessary after that.

As we will see in Hegel's diagnosis of the French Revolution, where he argues that this dynamic of permanent revolution first arose, the Jacobins sincerely believed they were implementing Rousseau's General Will, and, whether Rousseau intended to have this practical effect or not – and on any fair reading of the *Social Contract* he did not – for Hegel, his intention is of no more than secondary importance compared to the fact that this is how Robespierre and his comrades interpreted his teaching. So in this sense if in no other, to return to my opening observation, Rousseau's walk along Lake Bienne did indeed turn the world upside down, ushering in cultural Romanticism – the great movement in art, music and literature to displace what was taken to be the effete, polished and arid rationalism of the Enlightenment with the exploration of the inner self in all its emotional turmoil and richness – but also, through the inflammatory rhetoric with which he denounced bourgeois alienation in comparison with the lost wholeness and sweetness of the natural condition of man, summoning the dark forces that would attempt to construct heaven on earth with the guillotine.

2

Redeeming Modernity

The Erotic Ascent of Hegel's Phenomenology

Hegel's solution to the dualisms of Rousseau's thought is as simple as it is brilliant: He transposes the Golden Age of human happiness from the origins of history to its completion. In this way, he can plausibly claim to have resolved the central paradox of Rousseau's account of mankind's evolution – that it is at one and the same time a morally neutral kind of "perfectibility" in the sense of the progressive development of economic, political, technological and military power through our freedom to transform nature and a steadily increasing decline from the happiness we originally enjoyed.

Rousseau transposed the erotic satisfaction that the ancients believed could only be achieved through the arduous ascent of the soul through civic virtue toward the immortal truth to the instinctive and effortless sweetness of life in its pre-civilizational origins. Hegel transposes this erotic satisfaction back to the final fulfillment of our teleological development through an arduous ascent by way of civilization toward wisdom. But he locates its aim not as the philosopher's contemplative union with the immortal truth but with mankind's collective advancement through the unfolding of history itself. The Platonic philosopher's recurrent ascent toward intervals of transcendence is replaced by mankind's progression a single time to the final outcome, the actualization of wisdom at end of history. Everything that Rousseau lamented must carry us away from our original happiness – war, conquest, exploitation, sophistication, refinement, affluence, abstract thought – was for Hegel the necessary guarantor of its attainment.

Our portal to this grand reversal of Rousseau is Hegel's first mature master-piece, the *Phenomenology of Spirit*. The young Hegel was an avid reader of both Plato and Rousseau, especially the *Emile*. In this chapter, I will try to show how the *Phenomenology* was an attempt to synthesize the educational philosophies of the West's two leading titans of pedagogy. In a remark on the *Emile*, Hegel argued that, instead of attempting to educate an individual according to nature by keeping him isolated from civilized life, education should treat human beings from the outset in the shared context of their lives as social and political beings, enabling human nature to rise to the level of the "ethical" (*Das Sittliche*), in effect a "second nature" aiming to make each of us (Hegel alludes to a Pythagorean saying about the purpose of education) "a citizen of a state with good laws."

Put more broadly, the implication of Hegel's respectful criticism is that the *Emile* should not only have been the history of one isolated individual, but of the human race as a whole. It is not difficult to surmise that, in writing the *Phenomenology*, one of Hegel's purposes was to do just that – to historicize, as it were, an ascent from childhood and simple sense experience to an understanding of morals, gradually emerging into the world of love, imagination and the sentiments, and the transition to a responsible role in civil society. In the *Phenomenology*, the human race enacts an analogous ascent progressively over the eons. But if it is plausible to view the *Phenomenology* as Hegel's way of delivering on his criticism of the *Emile*, I think the reverse is equally true: Just as the *Phenomenology* is the history of mankind, it is at the same time the history of a fully evolved and fully integrated individual personality in the modern present.

In this sense, the *Phenomenology* does not merely universalize a version of the education of a single individual in the *Emile*, but combines the history of mankind with the history of the individual, which makes it both a work of philosophy and an educational classic. The book is not limited to presenting the outward chronology of mankind's teleological advance over time, but is also meant as a therapeutic aid to the individual's crystallization of his moral and intellectual virtues in the present, drawing upon the accumulated intellectual, cultural and practical energies of the past. Moreover, since for Hegel, the individual is always already "intersubjectively" involved with others in communities and nation-states with their range of private and public associations, these moral and intellectual virtues are ways both by which individuals can relate to one another and peoples can relate to other peoples.

Rousseau had explicitly linked the *Emile* to Plato's *Republic*, which for him was primarily a work about education rather than a political teaching. Hegel, too, I am arguing, attempts through the *Phenomenology* to assimilate the Platonic ascent of the soul to the teleological unfolding of history, in effect arguing that mankind as a whole has ascended from sense experience through moral and civic virtue into what Hegel terms (in an obvious echo of the Image of the Cave from the *Republic*) "the spiritual daylight of the present." The key to this ascent is what Hegel terms "recollection" (*Erinnerung*), a hermeneutical engagement with the whole panoply of ethical, aesthetic and philosophical "shapes of consciousness" accumulated within the all-embracing ambit of Spirit (*Geist*), a trove of latent in-dwelling experiences from which individuals and nations can draw in the present for guidance and inspiration. In a way that anticipates Gadamer's concept of the fusion of horizons, for Hegel, recollection, as the key to educational culture and development (*Bildung*), is not merely the passive ingestion of fixed facts and data, but a dynamic interaction between the learner and what is given in learning, a reciprocal rejoinder with the accumulated shapes of consciousness in which the content of education is transformed as it transforms the learner, so that the possibilities of the past emerge in new and unanticipated ways as they are shaped by the concerns we bring to them in the present. In this way, Hegel attempts to restore the famous Platonic doctrine of education as "recollection" in the *Meno* on the basis of an ontology of time-bound historicity, and in a manner that serves both the noblest aspects of the modern longing for freedom and the need to temper individualism within the context of heritage, community and experience.

In this way, then, some central tenets of both the *Republic* and the *Emile* are historicized by the *Phenomenology* and offered as the actual, concrete embodiment of wisdom in the present epoch. At the same time, however, the *Phenomenology* is much more than the positive account of mankind's progressive triumph over the past. As Hegel remarks in the lectures published as the *Philosophy of History*, "nothing in the past is lost" for Spirit. Because the *Phenomenology* issues both in the collective progress of mankind and in the evolution of a fully integrated modern personality in the present, it is never a matter of simply negating the past and looking down on it as irrelevant. Instead, history, or to use Hegel's term for the cosmos, Spirit, should be seen as a constant present. History is not a straight-arrow, linear progression in which one era is superseded by the next. Instead, it is a moving whole within which ever richer, ever more complex patterns of moral, intellectual, cultural and aesthetic alternatives evolve, all flowering in the modern personality and providing it with an organic heritage of resources for the challenges of the present and future. In this way, Spirit is analogous to the classical conception of an ordered whole, except that its elements have emerged progressively over time as that historicized whole has continually developed itself, culminating in (as he puts it in the *Philosophy of History*) the "self-actualization" of God in history. By showing how, in effect, a Platonically ordered, metaphysically transparent whole emerges teleologically out of an ontology based on impermanence and flux, Hegel can claim to have reconciled the Heracleitean cosmology of motion with the Platonic metaphysics of eidetic permanence.

I hope this approach to Hegel will shed some light on a number of perplexities that often beset his readers. One is the notorious vagueness of Hegel's historical references in the *Phenomenology*. A few opaque references to the Crusades and to bells and incense must suffice to connect the Unhappy Consciousness with medieval Christianity, while the discussion of the natural law and the human law within the ethical realm of *Sittlichkeit* in the ancient Greek polis is situated historically with a few broad and nameless allusions to Aeschylus and Sophocles. In my view, Hegel's manner of writing is no mere oversight, the product of haste or of a deliberate intention to be obscure – he is eminently capable of exhaustive historical precision when he needs to be – but follows the pedagogical premise I sketched above. For, when Hegel is discussing Stoicism, Skepticism, the tragic consciousness or any of the other "shapes of consciousness" in the progress of history, he is not merely referring to the specific historical epochs of the past. He is simultaneously maintaining that these "shapes" dwell with us in the *present* – that all of us can crystallize, through "recollection," these cultural, psychological and theoretical stand-points and draw upon them for our lives today. They are archetypes whose successful recollection has a therapeutic value for the modern reader, who might raise them to consciousness through reflection on the completed odyssey of Spirit, and not as mere historical information, however fascinating, instruct-ive or diverting. In other words, all of us are still, to some extent, Stoics and Skeptics, just as we are, in different spheres of life, masters and slaves. We have all experienced the exuberant optimism of modern liberty, humble veneration before cherished traditions, and tragic resignation in face of our mortality and how necessity and blind chance limit whatever happiness we can achieve. Each of these "shapes" is simultaneously the evocation of a specific epoch of the past and a map of man's mind and character in the present, at once the outward progress of the human race and the inward development of the modern personality. Spirit's achievement of wholeness through its own self-development, Spirit's success in having developed this whole panoply of moral, intellectual, religious and artistic riches in its longing for completion, entails and grounds the capacity of modern peoples, and the autonomous individual personalities who make them up, to complete this journey for themselves. Because the Spirit of the whole world fulfills itself by developing through its human agents, we are able to lay claim to its evolutionary heritage and enjoy its fruits in ourselves. The "absolute science" of Spirit, as Hegel sums up his system, is both the actual, lived history of the world from the earliest origins to the present day and a cognitive map of the mind's patterns. Spirit is simul-taneously the structure of reason, the history of the world, and the psycho-logical profile of every living individual as he or she lays claim to the organic *Bildung* of moral energies evolved over the centuries. Every section of the *Phenomenology* should be read on these multiple levels.

Before exploring the movement of the *Phenomenology* in detail, however, we must pause to consider how, in order to effect this synthesis between historical progress and happiness, resolving the contradictions in Rousseau's thought between nature and freedom, Hegel had first to reconcile two pro-foundly different interpretations of Rousseau's legacy, each of which attempted its own way of resolving those contradictions. As I first suggested in Chapter 1, Kant and Schiller undertake, respectively, what we can term a top-down and a bottom-up solution to the antinomies of Rousseau – Kant develops Rousseau's prescription in the *Social Contract* for our freedom of will to repress our natural inclinations, whereas Schiller develops Rousseau's exploration in the *Emile* and the *Reveries* of how the nature of an individual might, properly conserved and educated, blossom into psychological wholeness, happiness and

virtue in the modern present. We should look more closely at these
two responses.

THE PARADOXES OF ROUSSEAU AND THE RESPONSES FROM
KANT AND SCHILLER

The question inherited from Rousseau by German Idealism is this: How can
reason be reconciled with nature when nature is understood as an originary,
pre-rational source of human happiness and wholeness, whereas modern
reason is identified with utility and bourgeois alienation, and both alternatives
block any return to the classical account of nature as an orderly cosmos that
entails both reason and happiness? A corollary of that question is: How can
freedom be reconciled with nature when freedom is identified as man's most
spiritual quality precisely because of its freedom to *resist* nature?

One answer to these questions is broached by Rousseau himself and is given
full expression by Kant. Very much as in Rousseau's discussion of the state of
nature that we examined in Chapter 1, Kant begins the *Groundwork of the
Metaphysics of Morals* by arguing that if our desires are not inflamed by
bloated pleasures and luxuries, they operate according to a natural equilibrium
that, by not aiming for more than what we need to live, makes us happy.
However, our capacity for free will and thinking can introduce into that
equilibrium new desires that exceed what we need for self-preservation and
plunge us into competitive turmoil, sometimes leading us to hate reason itself
for alienating us from our simple, natural happiness. Ordinarily, reason and the
will are used to stimulate the desires beyond their simple, natural equilibrium
and devise the selfish means to gratify these inflamed, sophisticated passions.
Kant's aim is to extricate the will from its service of these bloated passions and
to rehabilitate it as what Rousseau termed our "spiritual" faculty – the pure
will to restrain all such inclinations.

For Kant, human beings are necessarily divided inwardly between their
capacity for natural happiness and a self-conscious, rational and willing half
that alienates them from the effortless equilibrium of the inclinations. By
formalizing the will, by willing only what can be willed for mankind in general,
our alienated, unnatural half can turn back against the natural desires now
corrupted by civilization and paradoxically restore a simulacrum of the equality, austerity and repose that nature originally gave us as an unselfconscious
gift for which no such spiritual striving is necessary. This generalized will
has willing itself as its object to the degree humanly possible, and therefore
does not have as its object the satisfaction of any natural inclination with its
empirical correlate in the world governed by scientific reasoning and necessity.
The generalized will, or will to will, cannot *heal* the division in the self
and return it to the spontaneous innocence of nature. But it can achieve a
certain dignity, employing the purified will as a bulwark against the corruption

of whatever remains in us of nature's beneficent residue. This is Kant's Categorical Imperative, whose first formulation runs: "I should never act in such a way that I could not also will that my maxim should be a universal law."

The Categorical Imperative is a very revealing example of how German Idealism strove to recover the high moral standards of classical philosophy but could only do so by repudiating its fundamental premises. Plato had argued that passions such as spiritedness or eros could lead to tyrannical, belligerent and corrupt behavior. However, properly sublimated and educated, those same passions could energize the cultivation of civic virtue and, in the highest instance, the longing for wisdom about the eternal causes of the whole. To the extent that these passions were directed toward just aims as opposed to base ones, it was perfectly permissible for a citizen to enjoy the honor conferred on him by his fellow citizens and for the philosopher to admire himself for his single-minded pursuit of wisdom.

Kant, by contrast, accepts the apparent truth of the modern account of nature as matter in motion. As a consequence, he also implicitly accepts the Hobbesian reduction of human passion to nothing but self-interest, even when disguised by claims to want to serve the common good – usually a mere camouflage for a bid for tyrannical power. Because the cosmos as a whole is bereft of purpose, nobility and moderation, it is pointless for human beings to claim they are attempting to internalize these qualities in their own souls. Every professedly noble motive for morality is just another form of selfish desire, or a way of flattering one's own vanity for being superior to others. Whatever residue may dwell in us of our innocent natural equilibrium is helpless before this modern dynamic of power-seeking.

Accordingly, for Kant, the only way to overcome the downward drag of the appetites is through an ethic of pure intentionality. We know we are behaving morally when we have no self-interested motive – not only in the obvious sense of crass desires for wealth or physical pleasure, but even in the more subtle sense of wishing to be admired or to admire ourselves for being good. From this perspective, one might say, Mother Teresa was nothing but a publicity hound in her care for the dying. Every incentive to virtuous behavior that the ancients would have recognized as valid – a longing for public honor, gratitude from our beneficiaries, love, friendship, patriotism, philanthropy – is rejected by Kant as tainting the purity of our motivations. He dismisses this "pathological" approach to moral philosophy as a "disgusting jumble of patched-up observations and half-reasoned principles" and criticizes the Stoics' pursuit of inner "perfection" for suggesting that virtue deserves the reward of self-esteem and a soul that is happy because it is inwardly well-ordered and just. Kant concedes that happiness as a practical matter generally accompanies what he regards as an ethical intention, but claims that they have no intrinsic motivational connection to one another. The classical notion that virtue understood as moral duty makes us happy is, as he put it in the *Critique of Practical Reason*, "an optical illusion of self-consciousness." Treating others justly is a better way of life than treating them unjustly. But a wish to benefit from treating them justly or to be esteemed for doing so should never be our incentive for exercising the Categorical Imperative, even though those good consequences for us will tend to accompany our attempted exercise of it.

In an analogous manner, Kant by implication dismisses as scandalous the Aristotelian view that certain virtues cannot be practiced without a degree of economic wherewithal. For Aristotle, only a well-to-do person can exercise the virtue of magnificence by funding, for example, a temple or a library. Those who lack such means may be able to practice other virtues, but not this one. For Kant, by contrast, all that matters is the purity of our intention to benefit everyone. Accordingly, a poor man who gives a few dollars to a beggar is more ethical than a wealthy man who gives millions to a charity or a university, because the poor man is sacrificing a far greater proportion of his means than the wealthy man, who can easily afford his good works. Similarly, Kant argues, someone who is misanthropic and does not like people in general is more to be admired when he is the benefactor of others than someone who is by nature affable and empathetic. Kant does not deny that the standard he sets for properly autonomous moral conduct demands such a pure disinterestedness that it is possible that no such act has yet occurred in human history. But that does not excuse us from the obligation to continue aspiring to this level of selflessness.

Another important way in which Kant attempts to restore the high moral level of the ancients by departing from their basic premises is this: For Kant, although we aspire toward actions that are generalizable and meant to benefit the rest of mankind, the seat of moral striving – the freedom of will – is located in each individual. It is not a shared or communal experience, and not the outcome of a shared civic pedagogy. Kant shares with the early modern political theorists the assumption of the ontological and epistemological priority of the separate individual. That is why, among the thinkers we are considering in this book, Kant is perhaps the least sympathetic toward, and evinces the least nostalgia for, the vanished ancient polis and its subordination of the individual to the community. He shares this comparative disregard for the heritage of the ancients with Marx, although, as we will see, for very different reasons.

Kant's adaptation of Rousseau's theory of morality differs from it in two significant ways. Whereas for Rousseau the morality of disinterestedness enacted by the General Will was housed in the distinct territorial and historical existence of various "peoples," Kant in effect extends this morality to mankind as a whole. As a universal prescription for mankind's moral aspirations, the Categorical Imperative is detached from considerations of specific constitutions and regimes. Indeed, Kant in general is disdainful toward questions of ordinary political reasoning, which he identifies with the realm of low "cleverness" or "cunning" (*Klugheit*) in the calculation of self-interest.

The second major difference from Rousseau is that for Kant there is no prospect for the wholesale or even partial recovery of the natural equilibrium of our desires, only a perpetual struggle by the will to master the inclinations. In this respect, he banishes Rousseau's ceaseless waffling between, on the one hand, pronouncing that natural wholeness to be lost forever and, on the other, searching for some way of re-evoking it in the present, whether in civic life or in the poetic experience of the solitary wanderer. All that is left for us is the struggle to rise above desire. This amplifies our observation that, in contrast with most of the other German inheritors of Rousseau, Kant displays virtually no longing for the communal virtue that Rousseau attributed to the ancient republics: For Kant, not only is there no going back, but we should not want to, because ancient morality was flawed in its core principles.

Kant's identification in the *Groundwork* of the will as "the only good thing" in the world "that is good without limitation" makes striving to achieve freedom of will something akin to the automatic guarantor of moral autonomy. There is a distinction between philosophical and moral knowledge, but the philosophical knowledge of moral freedom already presupposes our moral obligation. Philosophy, in other words, demonstrates the truth of moral freedom, but freedom is *not* the philosophic life, and the philosophic life is *not* the zenith of the good life – another diametrical opposition to Plato. For Kant, freedom is transcendental, meaning that it has the formal structure of reason (universality and necessity). But it is not "theoretical" in Kant's sense because it has no empirical correlate. Following Rousseau, Kant wishes to limit reason's claims to give an account for our higher faculties because modern utilitarian rationality tends to debunk them, as we observed in Chapter 1 in connection with Hobbes. Kant therefore identifies "pure reason" with the empirical study of nature and preserves the realm of freedom as an independent and higher sphere. But because freedom possesses the structure of reason, although it has no empirical correlate, freedom is still a "fact of reason" – the only such fact. Our attempt to exercise freedom of will is observable but not empirically measurable. This opens the door to Kant's argument that, by exercising the Categorical Imperative, we strive to inject moral freedom into the very structure of nature otherwise studied by empirical science. This raises it from a mere human rule for conduct to a force for improving all of reality. Hence, whereas the first formulation of the Categorical Imperative stressed that one should never act in such a way that one's will could not also be a universal law – in other words, a rule guiding merely human conduct – the second formulation has a far broader sweep: "Act as though the maxim of your action were by your will to become a *universal law of nature*" (my emphasis). Is there a project for the open-ended historical transformation of reality hiding between the lines of what is usually taken to be Kant's attempt to maintain an equipoise between the realm of nature and the realm of freedom? We will return to this question in due course.

The other answer to Rousseau's question of how nature might be reconciled with freedom (also broached by Rousseau himself) comes from Schiller, who argues that the perpetually divided Kantian self of the *Groundwork of the Metaphysics of Morals* is both unbearable and unnecessary. According to Schiller, the divided Kantian self can achieve unity and wholeness only through aesthetic fulfillment. Nature as a void of origination expresses itself, achieves a certain flowering, as the work of art – as Schiller puts it, aesthetic education is a path to freedom "through beauty." We do not so much will art as the product of an isolated ego as let it come forth through us, an upsurge from the origins that finds clarity, form and sublimity through its interaction with human creative faculties.

Schiller's main riposte to Kant comes in a book much admired by Hegel, and one of the best points of departure for understanding the centrality of education to Hegel's enterprise. Schiller's *Letters on the Aesthetic Education of Man* is an especially important work for understanding the attempt made by German thinkers in the wake of Rousseau to explore the possibility of an education in culture as a way of healing the alienation caused by modern rationalism – an alienation not only between man and nature, but within human beings between their rational and passionate selves, crystallized in Kant's categorical imperative. In the Preface to his *Philosophy of Fine Art*, Hegel paid tribute to Schiller's originality: "It is Schiller to whom we must give credit for the greatest service of having broken through the Kantian subjectivity and abstractness of thought, daring to transcend them by intellectually apprehending the principles of unity and reconciliation as the truth, and realizing them in art." The very title of the work recalls the subtitle of Rousseau' *Emile*, "On Education," and thereby connects it with a holistic conception of *paideia* stretching back behind the Enlightenment to the ancients. In Schiller's concern with human wholeness, echoed by Hegel's prescription for an educational "recollection" of the classical heritage, we encounter one of the wellsprings of contemporary liberal studies.

Kant, the foil for Schiller's argument, might well be seen as a philosophical hero of modern moral education. He uses the characteristically modern tension between reason and nature to defeat the basest consequences of Hobbesian power-seeking and materialism. If we follow the Categorical Imperative, we do not try to become sovereigns of others and masters of nature, but masters of our own natures and sovereigns of ourselves. But as Schiller and Hegel complain, Kant achieves this suppression of the worst excesses of modern appetitive individualism at the cost of a permanent rift between, on the one hand, moral reason seen as an imperative to repress nature and, on the other, natural feelings that, bereft of rational purpose, are reduced to indiscriminate impulses. The task of modern education must be to heal this rift between arid rationality and irresponsible impulse; to find what Schiller calls a "third character" through education and culture. Before going forward, we should note that Schiller's critique of Kantian morality is primarily aimed at the version of it Kant presented in the *Groundwork of the Metaphysics of Morals*. Kant's

Critique of Judgement develops his own understanding of aesthetics as mediating the opposition between natural inclination and moral will, implying that in his considered view, not all natural inclinations are reducible to self-interested drives requiring repression, but can be ranked insofar as these sentiments give rise to an appreciation for beauty, as Schiller himself argued.

According to Schiller, whereas a life spent in fulfilling low appetites in the Hobbesian manner is "savage," Kantian morality creates a more complicated problem for the education of character. Having learned that reason requires us to rise above natural inclinations in the pursuit of our duty, we run the risk of utterly impoverishing the world of feeling, treating its sublime and coarse expressions alike as equally deserving of suppression by the moral will. In other words, Kantianism runs the risk of producing a prude who regards a passion for Raphael and a passion for gin as defects equally deserving of curtailment. Schiller therefore tries to demonstrate that there is a route to Kantian morality – whose content he does not dispute – *through* an aesthetic education; that a beautiful life can entail a morally well-ordered one.

This blend of nature and morality is aesthetic culture. In attempting to beautify Kantianism, Schiller tries to restore the erotic dimension of virtue explored in Plato's *Symposium* on modern subjectivistic grounds, in this important way anticipating the *Phenomenology of Spirit*. He accepts the modern definition of human nature as an individual subject. But for Schiller the pursuit of moral freedom requires not only the repression of the passions, but their sublimation and re-expression in the work of art, which reflects nature back to man as transformed, beautiful and made harmonious as the home of his achieved freedom. Aesthetic culture, then, has a different ontological basis than Platonic eros. It is not, as in Diotima's teaching in the *Symposium*, the summons of erotic longing toward the immortal nobility of civic virtue and, at the highest level, the imperishable Idea of the Good. Instead, aesthetic culture is man's self-conscious transformation of nature to create an organic unity between his subjective will and the sensuous embodiment of his ideal in the work of art. Hence, as Schiller tells us, modern aesthetic education will have an undertone of self-doubt, moodiness and anxiety – a quality of "sentimentality" – that the ancients did not experience in their "naive" conviction of an immediate openness to the permanent truth about the world, a contrast that is further explored by Hegel. Whereas for the Platonist, the world is a rationally ordered and benevolent whole, the Romantic is prone to be tormented by the mystery of whether nature is receptive or indifferent to the beauty he both projects upon and discovers in the world outside of man. For, as Rousseau had put it in the *Emile*, "That beauty is not to be found in the object of our affections, but in the creation of our illusions."

In this way, then, Schiller tries to infuse Rousseau the solitary dreamer back into Rousseau the egalitarian moralist as taken up by Kant. Their positions embody a division between beauty and duty, between the poetic inwardness of the *Reveries* and the stern moral voluntarism of the General Will, a division that Hegel sets himself the task of overcoming in a synthesis that fully encompasses both. According to Schiller, modernity is characterized by two powerful and contradictory forces. One is the realm of "necessity." As a devotee of Kant's moral idealism even as he attempts to aestheticize it, Schiller understands the realm of nature as the realm of necessity – of material drives for self-preservation. The political and economic counterpart of the modern scientific understanding of nature as matter in motion is the contractual bourgeois liberalism of Hobbes, Locke and the Enlightenment. As Schiller sums up that now regnant culture, "Utility is the great idol of the age, to which all other powers must do service and all talents swear allegiance." The other great modern force is the realm of freedom, a superior realm which transcends the realm of nature, which is synonymous with material necessity and a utilitarian credo. Echoing both Kant and Rousseau, Schiller claims that our true dignity and nobility reside in our spiritual capacity to "abandon actuality and soar with becoming boldness above necessity." Specifically like Rousseau in the *Emile*, and emphatically seconded by Hegel, Schiller does not believe that the aesthetic experience can be a purely private concern or a mere diversion. Its purpose is to contribute to the character and tastes appropriate to free men and women: "Art is a daughter of Freedom, and receives her commission from the needs of spirits, not from the exigency of matter." Again we see how, in the wake of Rousseau, the German Idealists and Romantics try to restore the comprehensiveness of classical civic education on the basis of modern individual rights and freedom and the modern Baconian account of nature in which they are grounded.

For Schiller, the aesthetic is the crucial middle realm of experience between the sometimes degrading downward pull of natural necessity and the sometimes too austere dictates of moral freedom. Art cannot serve the commercial interests of contractual liberalism without losing its soul. Art must contribute to mankind's progress toward the Ideal by showing that "it is through Beauty that we arrive at Freedom." For Schiller, however, the problem is that the Understanding – the human intellect with its powers of empirical observation and analysis – is both the ally and the enemy of aesthetic culture. It is the Understanding that, by discovering the Categorical Imperative, establishes the supremacy of freedom and human dignity over the degradation of the natural inclinations and "the noisy mart" of liberal-contractarian politics. But the Understanding also appears to destroy the aesthetic experience. Kantian morality tends to banish the aesthetic to the realm of the other inclinations, treating it as merely another selfish indulgence. Modern rationality threatens to destroy the validity of sentiment, even though the imperative to moral striving that reason demonstrates in a rigorous manner is first experienced *as* a sentiment in the heart of the ordinary man. As Schiller observes:

You have only to free [these moral sentiments] from their technical [Kantian] formulation, and they will emerge as the time-honored utterances of common reason, and as data of that moral instinct which Nature in her wisdom appointed as Man's guardian until clear insight should bring him to maturity.

The problem, however, is that the "clear insight" of reason may undermine that "moral instinct" itself:

But it is just this technical formulation, which reveals the truth to our understanding, that conceals it once again from our feeling. For unfortunately the Understanding must first destroy the objects of the inner sense before it can appropriate them. Like the chemist, the philosopher finds combination only through dissolution, and the work of spontaneous nature only through the torture of Art. In order to seize the fleeting appearance he must bind it in the fetters of rule, dissect its fair body into abstract notions, and preserve its living spirit in a sorry skeleton of words.

Schiller formulates with exceptional precision a problem that, as we saw in Chapter 1, bedeviled Rousseau throughout his writings – how to promote the highest and noblest kinds of human experience given the validity of the modern account of nature as matter in motion. Whereas for Plato and the ancients, a noble life was the culmination of our natural fulfillment, for the moderns, such aspirations have no basis in nature, which is reduced to appetitive self-interest. Like Rousseau and Kant, Schiller identifies the faculty of Understanding with modern science and analytical rationality. His likening of reason to a "chemist" who dissolves nature into its elements and who "tortures" our inner sentiments by dissolving them into empty, abstract concepts clearly is meant to remind us of Bacon, who acknowledged Machiavelli's project for the mastery of nature as his own inspiration and compared scientific analysis to the "torture" of nature.

Kant, following Rousseau, had believed that the basic precepts of morality comprised what Rousseau termed a "sublime science of simple souls" likelier to be found in ordinary folk relatively unspoiled by civilization than in those who were intellectually more sophisticated and therefore had more bloated and superfluous desires and vain pretensions of brilliance. As he wrote in the *Groundwork*:

The most remarkable thing about ordinary reason in its practical concerns is that it may have as much hope as any philosopher of hitting the mark. In fact, it is almost more certain to do so than the philosopher, because he has no principle which the common understanding lacks, while his judgement is easily confused by a mass of irrelevant considerations, so that it easily turns aside from the correct way. Would it not, therefore, be wiser in moral matters to acquiesce in the common rational judgement ... than to steer the common understanding from its happy simplicity in practical matters...?

Kant believed it was the duty of philosophy to use its technical capacity of rational demonstration (what Schiller here terms Understanding) to raise the common folk's instinctive grasp of morality to full intellectual clarity and consciousness, thereby rehabilitating reason by severing it from its usual role of stimulating new and excessive passions or sources of vanity and using it instead to purge the inclinations to a healthy minimum. Schiller, however, reminds us of the Rousseauan paradox that Kant tends to gloss over: Since reason itself – which is to say modern scientific and analytical rationality – alienates us from nature and the sublime sentiments aroused by the beautification of nature through art, how can reason aid us in living closer to nature? How can reason help us achieve what Schiller calls the "third character" between selfless morality and indiscriminate sensuality without destroying it?

LOVE AND UNDERSTANDING: THE EMERGENCE
OF HEGELIAN HISTORICISM

In his early writings, Hegel moved within these same trammels, unable, like Kant or Schiller, to fully reconcile the realms of Beauty and Understanding. Love, he wrote, "excludes all oppositions" and is "infinite life," whereas reason is confined to the finite realm which it breaks down into its elements – a "killing" relationship based on "conceptual abstraction." Whereas reason remains "one-sided" and brings existence under its corrosive "determining power," love is "all-living and all-powerful," is God. "Philosophy must therefore stop short of religion ... and place the true infinite outside its confines." Whereas for Plato, eros properly educated by philosophy guides our longing for the imperishable Good, for Hegel at this stage of his thinking, the love of God must *exclude* philosophy.

But by the time he writes the *Phenomenology of Spirit*, Hegel has arrived at an answer to Schiller's question (earlier his own) of how the will to moral freedom and the spontaneity of nature might be reconciled through educational culture. The answer is the teleological progress of history. We now enter the realm of "historicism" proper – *historismus*, a term coined by Schlegel and fully elaborated by Hegel – for the first time. Rousseau, who, as I earlier observed, still had one foot in the Enlightenment, identified happiness with an underlying substratum of human nature that had never entirely been extinguished by the history of alienation and corruption since mankind evolved. Kant and Schiller both accepted the existence of this natural substratum as well – their adaptation of different elements of Rousseau's thought was an attempt to show how its residue might best be conserved. By transposing the Golden Age from its origins in Rousseau's state of nature to the final outcome of the progress of history, Hegel, in contrast with his predecessors, recasts man as a historical being through and through. His way of synthesizing Kant's and Schiller's attempts to resolve the contradiction between nature and freedom inherited from Rousseau was through the complete jettisoning of the concept of human nature.

All of the dualisms of early modern thought going back to Hobbes and Locke and including Rousseau and Kant are now subsumed within the organic historical life-world Hegel terms Spirit. Those dualisms can still be abstracted from the totality of Spirit by the Understanding for analytical clarification, so long as it is understood that they do not exist as truly independent entities, and so must always be returned to the dialectical process from which they have emerged. Spinoza, whose philosophy had been explored by Hegel's friend and sometime rival Schelling as a basis for historicism, responded to these same early modern dualisms between mind and nature by collapsing God into the world of action and time, traditionally considered a heresy in which the distinction between the sacred and the profane, between the holy and the sinful, is eradicated. Hegel inherits this concept of the immanentization of God in temporal existence, although, as we will consider, his version represents a considerable modification of it. But it does add to his claim that the concept of Spirit has synthesized the dualisms of early modern thought the even bolder claim that it has synthesized both sides in the traditional debate between reason and revelation. Both classical philosophy and modern political thought, despite the other deep differences between them, regarded the claims of reason as incompatible with those of revealed religion. Both classical and modern philosophers had had to dissimulate their own lack of belief in revelation, often with very mixed success – Hobbes and Rousseau, to name two, were widely regarded in their own time as rank atheists. Even when, like Rousseau and Kant, they offered an account of the divine unity organizing nature, no one could mistake Deism for the God of Sinai or Calvary. For Hegel, by contrast, Spirit as the teleological progress of history is nothing less than the "self-actualization of God" as history, specifically the Christian account of revelation. There is therefore no reason for Hegel to dissimulate about where he stands, because no choice between reason and revelation is possible or necessary. Moreover, for Hegel, the synthesis of reason and revelation was emphatically not meant to imply the subordination of the latter to the former – they were two ways of representing the same truth. Hence, among his many influences, Hegel helped found the study of religious ethnography and, as Leo Strauss put it, was the first modern philosopher to elevate the study of religion to a branch of philosophy.

The general tenor of German historicism is captured by Hegel's sometime ally Schelling, although Hegel came to criticize Schelling for flinching from the darker aspects of human strife and power-seeking. For Schelling, nature develops and expresses itself as the world-artist, rising out of the primordial depths and flowering throughout the millennia, like an enormous symphony made up of many cultural and artistic achievements. History unifies self and world. For the classics, the soul achieves unity by rising toward and approximating, through the cultivation of the moral and intellectual virtues, the eternal harmonies of the cosmos. For German Idealism, by contrast, nature as genesis unifies the human self by enveloping the self in its mutable, time-bound processes, and expresses itself by rising to culture through the human self. As Schelling describes the ages of mankind, the history of the world mirrors Homer's *Iliad* and *Odyssey*, a modern period of struggle, mastery and the emergence of human subjectivity, individuality and autonomy, followed by the current era in which this liberated individual, longing for a reconciliation with nature, history, culture and an organic feeling of unity with other people, embarks on the journey home to Ithaca.

As Hegel would have it, for we moderns, the place occupied by the soul in the classical understanding of political community is replaced by history – or, as Hegel terms the historical process in a deliberate assimilation of theological terminology, by *Geist* or Spirit. History is the phenomenology of the (Holy) Spirit. Plato had understood the ascent up the Divided Line from sense-experience toward wisdom to be a recurrent and uncompleted journey, available at any time and place in principle. For Hegel, the Divided Line as an eternal schema of the ascent to wisdom is replaced by the actualization of wisdom in time, accomplished by and for the entire human race. The key to understanding Hegel's conception of Spirit is his argument in the *Phenomenology* that "truth" is the unity of Subject and Substance, or, as he otherwise expresses it, the unity of Understanding (*Verstand*) and Love, echoing Schiller's distinction between Understanding and Beauty. By the former, he means (as does Schiller) the cold analytical thought premised on man's alienation from nature and growing power to master it through scientific knowledge and technique. Understanding is "the most astonishing and greatest of all powers." In its power to rend the world, to dissolve things and recombine them, it is the subjective engine of historical action. The political parallel of this analytical dissection of nature's parts came with liberalism's vision of human beings as isolated individuals impersonally represented by the state. Indeed, for Hegel, the category of *Verstand* comprehends the whole complex of phenomena that we identify with modernity – the interlocking modalities of rights discourse, behavioristic reasoning, and the derivation of empirical observations in a logically necessary manner from Newtonian general laws.

Love, on the other hand, boded our feeling of unity with our fellow human beings and with nature. History reconciles these two dimensions of existence. For Hegel, history is a double-sided quest for unity and fulfillment by means of scientific rationality. The pursuit of Understanding (including political rights and scientific power) itself unexpectedly brings about the reign of Love. Mankind pursues its freedom outwardly through the conquest of nature, including warfare and revolution, such that history can be viewed as a "slaughter-bench" of ambition and domination, as he put it in the Introduction to the *Philosophy of History*. But the Spirit of all history simultaneously embarks on an odyssey of fulfillment that it pursues through its locus, mankind. The result is the "end of history" – the embodiment of reason, freedom, beauty and forgiveness in the present age, specifically in the form of the nation-state with its representative institutions, personal liberties, tolerance, cultural and religious communities and its recognition of human dignity whether it is expressed through our autonomy as individuals or through our overlapping memberships in the various communal contexts that are open to us.

Viewed subjectively or from a strictly secular perspective, this historical process is the human pursuit of freedom beyond the contradictions placed on it by the present. However, viewed more comprehensively and therefore more adequately from the perspective of Spirit, the progress of history is Spirit's *own* development as it supersedes itself through the agency of man. Because of this double-sided "negation of the negation," history can be viewed as the cumulative progression through an ever-richer series of mediations. In this way, the Hegelian dialectic tries to provide a way of understanding social and political existence that gives fair weight to both the communitarian longing for repose and reconciliation and to the more aggressive and transformative aspects of modern autonomy – the "labor of the negative" in history, embracing mankind's pursuit of political, economic and technological mastery over nature. For Hegel, both dimensions – Subject and Substance, Understanding and Love – are essential for a stance toward political life that is both humane and realistic. Guided by this synthesis, we can steer between the extremes of, on the one hand, Jacobin fanaticism – the attempt to impose from above, by revolutionary fiat, a single global pattern for rational political and economic organization – and, on the other hand, the Romantic retreat from the muck of politics into a purely apolitical realm of aesthetic bliss as well as the politicization of Romanticism as a folk nationalism of tribal belonging and instinct. Hegel's successors, as we will see, tend to exaggerate one side or the other of the synthesis of community and autonomy – communitarian spontaneity bereft of purposive rationality, or, at the opposite extreme, the limitless reconstruction of the world.

Hegel's phenomenology is, among other things, an attempt to moderate the hubristic modern assumption that the past has nothing to teach us about freedom or culture, an arrogance wonderfully captured by Flaubert in his fictitious artist Pellerin's masterpiece – a giant canvas depicting Christ piloting a locomotive through a virgin forest, entitled "Progress." Although Hegel does present a historical chronology tracing the history of self-consciousness through such "shapes" as mastery and slavery, stoicism and skepticism, Christianity and the Enlightenment, this phenomenology, to reiterate an earlier observation, should not be viewed so much as a straight arrow pointing forward as a series of circles rippling out from and back toward their origin, evolving into more complex patterns as they intermingle. Although, for Hegel, we cannot literally return to any past civilization, or restore it in the present, the positive contributions of past epochs to the deepening of Spirit (and therefore of the human spirit) remain with us as an organic heritage that can be raised to consciousness through the dialectic of recollection. Phenomenology is not only the philosophical recollection of these multiple historical moments, but their actual therapeutic crystallization in the life of the present. We cannot literally revert to being Stoics or Epicureans, cannot experience tragedy precisely as the Greeks did, but we carry in us as a collective heritage residual experiences of Stoic nobility, Epicurean skepticism and tragic resignation that form the wellspring of experience and culture from which we derive our moral energies as citizens and human beings in the present. In this respect, Hegel was arguably the last great philosophical friend of modernity, precisely because he believed its narrow account of human experience needed supplementation from a friendly outside source, the organic communitarianism that would ground liberal rights within a shared culture that might approximate, for the citizens of modern representative states, the pedagogical political community extolled by Aristotle.

That Hegel believes his account of history demonstrates that human happiness will come about by way of bloodshed and violence, ushered in by the French Revolution and Napoleonic wars, constitutes another decisive break with Schiller, for Schiller's embrace of a purely cultural and aesthetic revolution was a reaction to his disillusionment with political struggle. Like many of his generation, he had at first welcomed the French Revolution as bringing freedom to mankind, only to be horrified by the excesses of the Jacobin Terror. Hegel, by contrast, believes that one must not flinch from the violent side of history in grasping how Spirit's purpose is being accomplished. He believes that the Terror was a necessary if regrettable stage toward that end, although he also believes it will not have to be repeated. Why that is so will emerge as we examine the argument of the *Phenomenology* more closely.

THE CONCEPT OF SPIRIT

As we have observed, a central feature of Hegel's philosophy is that it does not embrace a strictly unilinear conception of historical existence. Hegel's historicism is not the optimistic liberal account of a Condorcet, the belief that history is marching steadily forward. Hegel does not embrace a stage theory of history in which one era is seen as manifestly and decisively outmoding its predecessors in a relentless and triumphant advance. Instead, Hegel believes that, at present, we live in an age of uncertainty and even despair in which reason can often appear to support nothing but arid materialism, while nobler feelings are incapable of finding rational grounds for their conviction. Indeed, although differing from them profoundly in other respects, in his evocation of the historical present as a series of sharply contrasting and apparently irreconcilable alternatives, Hegel's historicism has an initially apocalyptic quality that more closely resembles that of his successors Nietzsche and Heidegger than the textbook liberal progressivism. Mankind in 1807, Hegel argues in the *Phenomenology*, stands at a fateful crossroads. Modern reason has delivered us to a troubling threshold in which the old world is passing irrevocably away while the new world is not yet visible. Only this future, whatever it may be, can redeem the alienation, drift and frivolity of the present. Out of this tension, the concept of Spirit emerges.

This tension takes the form of a cultural battle between science and Romanticism. We could also characterize it as a contest between Kantian rationality and Schiller's espousal of the love of beauty. I am going to dwell on it at some length because it conveys the unique tenor of Hegel's reasoning, as well as how his philosophy functions on multiple levels.

Hegel sets forth the origins of both standpoints in a remarkably rich passage that offers a telescoped three-stage history of the world, both intellectually and morally [8]. The earliest stage was the belief in a higher transcendental God or metaphysical truth, spanning ancient and medieval times:

Formerly they had a heaven adorned with a vast wealth of thoughts and imagery. The meaning of all that is hung on the thread of light by which it was linked to that heaven. Instead of dwelling in this world's presence, men looked beyond it, following this world to an other-worldly presence, so to speak.

But at length, man's attention turned from this absorption in the transcendental Beyond to the world of the here and now, the beginning of the Age of Reason and the Enlightenment:

The eye of Spirit had to be forcibly turned and held fast to the things of this world, and it has taken a long time before the lucidity which only heavenly things used to have could penetrate the dullness and confusion in which the sense of worldly things was enveloped, and so make attention to the here and now as such, attention to what has been called "experience," an interesting and valid enterprise.

Today, however, having immersed ourselves for a couple of centuries in the study of observable empirical reality, we are experiencing the Romantic craving to somehow return to the first age of divine transcendence:

Now we seem to need just the opposite: sense is so fast rooted in earthly things that it requires just as much force to raise it. Spirit shows itself as so impoverished that, like a wanderer in the desert craving for a mere mouthful of water, it seems to crave for its refreshment only the bare feeling of the divine in general.

We once had knowledge of, and a feeling of union with, the "Immediate Being" of the eternal, with which the earthly realm was connected by a "thread" of light. The "heavens were adorned" with the "thoughts and images" generated by this fertile union of what we moderns now experience as the divided standpoints of science and beauty. Spirit develops itself historically by generating such distinctions. Following the thread of light by which mundane phenomena were able to participate in the eternal truth, mankind looked back down at the profane world and saw it for the tawdry and chaotic morass it was. The diminution and stigmatization of the apparent world in contrast with the shining purity of the real world of celestial truth caused mankind to flee from the former and cling to heaven. As a consequence, the thread of light that began by providing a solid connection between the apparent world and the real world – by showing how the eternal truth is instantiated in the transient phenomena that participate in the higher archetypes – ends by draining the apparent world of any connection with the divine, reducing it to a realm of ignorance, woe and oppression. But then, Hegel tells us, "the eye of Spirit had to be forcibly turned to the things of the world and held there" so as to reintroduce the "order of thought" into the "dullness and confusion of the earthly."

With the rise of modernity, then, mankind veered to the opposite extreme of the first epoch, from excessive otherworldliness to an excessive immersion in the realm of earthly "experience." Modernity began as a great quest to retrieve the wealth of thoughts and images previously fenced off from human existence in the divine incorporeal Beyond and bring them down to everyday observable reality. In its fixation on the earthly and the empirical, however, modernity has progressively impoverished those treasures of speculative theorizing and sublime art connecting us to the celestial thread of light, cutting human experience off from the transcendental. Bringing the wealth of heaven down to earth has in the long run robbed it of its spiritual significance by reducing it to the materialistic and measurable.

Hegel is clearly alluding here to the images of the Cave and of the Divided Line in Plato's *Republic*. In the Image of the Cave, Socrates argues that the philosopher must be compelled to forsake the happiness that he finds when he climbs out of the Cave of ignorance into the Sunlight of the Good, sacrificing a measure of his own happiness out of a sense of duty to his fellow citizens trapped by their ignorance in the gloomy recesses below. Likewise, Hegel is suggesting, with his plain references to the Platonic imagery, that "Spirit's eye" had to be "forcibly turned" from its fixation on the Divine and its attention redirected to the earthly and "held there."

But there is a crucial difference between Hegel's allusion to the Image of the Cave and the Platonic original. It is revealed by the small but telling detail that, whereas for Plato in the Image of the Cave, the potential philosopher must be forcibly "turned" in order to face upward from the bottom of the Cave toward the sunlight, for Hegel, the eye of Spirit must be understood as being forcibly "turned" to *forsake* the celestial realm of eternal light that it has *already* attained. In other words, whereas for Plato, the philosopher must compromise his ascent to the truth in order to be philanthropic toward those left behind in the Cave, for Hegel, the spirit of philosophy must return to the Cave out of both philanthropy and a pursuit of the truth. For Plato, the summons toward the Good forcibly turns us away from our commitment to the Cave; later, having achieved a measure of transcendence, we must compromise our happiness and effect a partial return to its twilight recesses. For Hegel, by contrast, in order for Spirit's odyssey to be fully actualized, the "turning" must be viewed as a summons *downward* from the heaven of reified metaphysical transcendence into the wellsprings of historical action out of which the metaphysical realm originally developed.

To expand upon an earlier observation, for Plato, the philosopher's ascent toward the sunlight of happiness and his return to his philanthropic duty to his fellow citizens in the Cave is a recurrent cycle under the aspect of eternity. Moreover, only a very few people, the true natural aristocracy comprised of the lovers of wisdom, are equipped to make this ascent and return, with little hope offered that the philosopher's dutiful return to the Cave will result in any widespread or permanent transformation of the benighted conditions of everyday life for the majority. In contrast, Hegel is arguing that the entire human species makes this ascent from fleshly and sensuous experience toward the light of the truth. Moreover, this ascent is not reenacted recurrently under the aspect of eternity. Instead, the ascent is enacted one time only, and it entails not only the intermittent achievement of transcendence by the philosophic few, but the actual transcendence of past ignorance and oppression by the collective progress of mankind as a whole. The teleological ascent from becoming toward the eternal Good is replaced by the teleological progress of history. Everyone will emerge from the Cave "into the spiritual daylight of the present" [177].

Hegel's claim that the mind must be "compelled" to turn away from the Good and return to worldly experience explains the transition from ancient wisdom to modern science. Heaven, having drained the apparent world of a permanence that is now entirely other-worldly, floats away from the earth and leaves it bereft of order and purpose. Because heaven has drained the world of transcendence, leaving only matter-bound "experience" in its wake, knowledge is subsequently reduced from celestial contemplation to the unencumbered Cartesian subject, which becomes the sole criterion for sure and certain knowledge, a knowledge restricted to the representation of sense-data. Science saves the world from the chaos resulting from heaven's departure through an "order based on thought." Today, however, we thirst for a reascent to the celestial. The realm of sheer feeling, it is hoped, will begin to restore a sense of wholeness lost in the dissection of life empowered by science.

Spirit is the oscillation between wholeness and differentiation prefigured by ancient wisdom and modern science. These reflections lead us back to the contrast between the Hegelian ascent and the Platonic one whose pedigree it purports to assimilate. For Plato, the Good draws us – as Diotima puts it in the *Symposium* – "on up." We want to remain in the empyrean heights, but we have a duty to go back down. For Hegel, on the other hand, the historical process – Spirit – generates the distinction between heavenly and earthly knowledge as one epoch-making way station in its exploration and development of itself. This divide between the divine and the profane constitutes a stupendous gain in the deepening and spiritualization of the human pursuit of freedom. Indeed, the tension between celestial perfection and earthly fallenness reveals in outline the future goal of all historical striving: freedom for mankind will bring heaven down to earth. For these reasons, therefore, if we are Hegelians, we cannot *want* to remain permanently in the sunlight. Indeed, we cannot even wish for there to be a sunlight in the Platonic sense of the eternal truth. We don't merely have to return to the Cave, we must want to return. Going back down is not a sacrifice of our satisfaction, but a return to its source. Philosophy must return to the dynamic origins out of which Spirit develops itself in order to reinvigorate the ideals that otherwise tend to ossify and float off into an abstract realm of the unattainable Beyond. In this respect, if certainly not in others, Hegelian wisdom is prospectively more like the wisdom of Nietzsche's Zarathustra than it is Platonic or Socratic.

Hence today's cultural battle between Science and Romanticism, which appear to glare at each other across a battlefield, the rigor of science versus the sublimity of the poet. Both have serious limitations in trying to explain the whole of existence: the "empty breadth" of empirical rationality faces the "empty depth" of vague Romantic sentimentality [10]: "One side parades the wealth of its material and the intelligibility of its ideas; the other pours contempt on the latter, and makes a parade of the immediate intuitive rationality and divine quality of its content."

Whereas Romanticism possesses depth of feeling and infinite longings for wholeness, science (as Hegel puts it) has spread, extension, and is concerned only with the finite. Like Romanticism, therefore, it too is superficial and one-sided. However, Hegel observes, of these two opposed interpretations of reality, it was Romanticism that first provoked the struggle between them because of its longing to escape the barrenness of modern scientific rationality by opening up the spigot of religious and artistic passion [7]:

The "beautiful," the "holy," the "eternal," "religion," and "love" are the bait required to arouse the desire to bite; not the Concept, but ecstasy, not the cold march of necessity in the thing itself, but the ferment of enthusiasm, these are supposed to be what sustains and continually extends the wealth of substance.

Romanticism seeks to recapture the lost wholeness of the first age, when the world of the here and now was connected to the realm of divine transcendence by a celestial thread of light. The difficulty, however, is that whereas in the first age, reason itself led us from the here and now to the transcendental and immortally true, during the modern age, the meaning of reason was identified with empirical science. That means that in order to recover a sense of the divine in life today, Romanticism must concede the place of reason to its opponent, and embrace its own longing for the divine as sheer emotion and intuition – in other words, embrace it *as* irrational.

The price we pay for modernity is that we "wander in the desert" of empiricism, a realm of dry facticity bereft of inspiration, wholeness and repose. Romanticism betokens an ever more intense longing for a recovery of that lost sense of solid being now banished to a celestial realm whose reality modern empiricism appears to have refuted decisively and irrevocably. In our inchoate longing to find a road back to the lost richness of heaven stirs an eros for the recollection of our vanished riches. Romanticism yields to the "uncontrolled ferment of substance," achieving a rapturous "intensity without content." It reacts to the spiritual poverty of modern science by opposing to its empty flatness an equally false extreme of empty depth, "sheer force without spread." Science, on the other hand, breaks life up into a multiplicity of concrete phenomena, thereby sacrificing the "force" of their underlying unity, in this way counterposing to Romanticism's empty emotional depth an empty empirical breadth. But in so brutally ranging the defects of these two "shapes" alongside one another, Hegel also limns their respective virtues, and prepares the ground for his argument that the "power of *Geist*" must draw upon both – Spirit must have spread as well as depth. For it is precisely the impoverishment of symbolic experience relentlessly pursued by empirical science that provides Romanticism with, as Hegel puts it, "the bait that arouses the desire to bite." In other words, empirical reductionism and its crass creed of utility provides the "bait" that goads Romanticism to "bite" back, energizing it to fulfill its contrarian yearning for the divine and the sublime by trying to recapture the fading civilizational conglomerate of the Great Chain of Being. Romanticism fulfills its longing to escape the arid utilitarian "desert" of the modern present through a hermeneutical openness to the past by "recollecting" the whole rich panoply of "thoughts and pictures" that crowd the premodern era [13].

Modern scientific rationalism has dissolved the old world. Romanticism heralds the advent of the new, but only as a vague and contentless yearning. Typically, Hegel does not tell us specifically what or who he means by Romanticism. He is not interested in a detailed intellectual history, or in the biographies of individual poets and artists, but in the general *mentalité* variously expressed by such figures as Schlegel, Schleiermacher and Novalis, to whom we can add English poets such as Wordsworth and Coleridge, who were influenced by the German Romantics. According to Hegel, the Romantics possess an authentic intimation of the higher spirituality that modern rationalism has turned its back on. But because the realm of evidence, experience and content have been conceded to that specifically modern form of rationality, the Romantic counter-reaction cannot reclaim the totality of experience for itself, but is reduced to floating alongside the modern world like a disenchanted specter. Viewed from across the steely barrier erected by empiricism, the old world of communal heritage seems to be cut off from us forever, as we venture into, on the one hand, ever more desiccated reaches of isolated individualism, materialism and profit and, on the other, the search for purely personal aesthetic escapes so as to anaesthetize our immurement in an anxious, crass and philistine age. The Romantics, Hegel observes, equate knowledge of the whole with a *feeling* about the whole, a rapture over the way in which the whole always eludes complete empirical specification.

The Romantics try to recapture the richness of past, originally unified ways of life in order to oppose the barrenness of the world as it is progressively stripped of its enchantments by science. Fretting that modern mankind has forgotten the divine and is mired in the "dirt and mud," the Romantics want to tear people away from their preoccupation with the "sensuous" and with their private affairs as liberal individualists. Left to itself, however, their effort is doomed to mere archaizing, atavism and nostalgia for moonlit abbey ruins. Because they reject the canons of evidence and causality, the Romantics, having begun by rebelling against the barrenness of the scientific worldview, end up with a "feeling" about the divine that is equally barren. Repudiating his own earlier writings on the disjunction between scientific understanding and an openness to the divine, Hegel now argues that to separate God from rationality reduces God to an arbitrary caprice, no more or less valid than any other spontaneous effusion [10]:

When this non-conceptual knowledge of substance makes a pretense of having drowned the self in the depths of sheer Being, and of philosophizing in all holiness and truth, it hides the truth from itself. Instead of devotion to God, on the contrary, by spurning all measurable precision and determinateness, it merely gives free rein to the contingency of its content, and lets capriciousness be lord.

The attempt to rescue faith by insulating it from the claims of reason ends up paradoxically undermining faith in the eyes of thinking people by reducing it to a mere "enthusiasm." Hegel had made precisely this rescue effort in his own early theological writings. The *Phenomenology of Spirit* constitutes a decisive break with that position, and, as we have observed, with that of Schiller. The cultural battle Hegel surveys between modern rationalism and Romanticism was crystallized in the one-sided responses of Kant and Schiller to Rousseau's evocation of the contradiction between reason and nature. The Unity of Subject and Substance is the conceptual outline of Hegel's attempt at a synthesis of the two opposing worldviews.

Romanticism claims to possess "depth" and "divinity," meaning that it yearns to transcend the finite, concrete and merely empirical. Its polar opposite is "science" (*Wissenschaft*). This is a term that, in this context and for much of the time in the *Phenomenology*, Hegel identifies with a specifically modern canon of rationality – the Hobbesian and Cartesian subject who begins by doubting all received opinion and tradition, and who seeks clear thinking through mental representations that are strictly correlated with the evidence received through the senses, unclouded by what Hobbes derided as the "powers invisible" of piety, Aristotelian teleology or other instances of "absurd" and "insignificant speech" whose existence cannot be verified. But Hegel also identifies *Wissenschaft* with its broader meaning as knowledge in general, whether scientific or not, including such humanities as philosophy, literature, art and religious studies and also with what the classics took to be the study of the cosmos as a super-sensible realm of eternally perfect archetypes that endured beyond all transitory becoming, and in which transitory phenomena participated to achieve whatever degree of solidity and integrity of which they were capable. Hegel quite deliberately plays upon the ambivalent meaning of *Wissenschaft* because one of his major claims is that his phenomenology relieves us of the harsh necessity of rejecting the older kind of knowledge in favor of the newer scientific rationality. *Geist* embraces both and does justice to both.

Spirit must at the same time instantiate itself in the "measurable precision and definiteness" of the empirically observable world. Otherwise, Spirit will be packed off into a pure but groundless ethical ideal or a religious or poetic transport floating above reality. The Romantics believe that by simply turning away from science, they attain a "holy" revelation and an unreflecting, spontaneous union with the transmundane [6]: "The Absolute, on this view, is not to be grasped in conceptual form, but felt and intuited. It is not the conception of the Absolute, but the feeling and intuition of it, that determine what is said and find expression."

Romanticism tries to evade the power of science by conceding its validity so long as it is confined to the realm of the finite – the essential compromise between reason and faith or beauty developed by Schiller in his critique of Kant, and echoed by the early Hegel. According to the mature Hegel in the *Phenomenology*, Science and Romanticism must each reclaim what they have conceded to the other. But it would be fair to say that Hegel is more sympathetic to Romanticism in the sense that, while it stands in need of the heterogeneous content and articulation that only science can provide, it possesses an intimation of the scope and breadth of Spirit that science altogether misses. Romanticism requires scientific supplementation in order for Spirit to become fully conscious of itself. But science, left to itself, cannot even fathom what it lacks.

As we have seen, Hegel evokes Platonic images of the simultaneous ascent of the mind and the passions toward their joint objects of longing – a progressive ascent that actualizes our capacity for happiness by sublimating the passions as energies for cultivating our moral and intellectual virtues as we rise toward the eternal Good. Plato characterizes this ascent as an erotic one – not in the sense of carnal desire, but in the sense that eros, properly understood, is a structured longing, a longing for immortality, in the pursuit of which we aim to perfect our virtues of character and, through achieving that inner harmony of the affects, achieve the fullest and most lasting kind of satisfaction. By attributing to Romanticism the hunger to bite at the bait of the modern world's impoverishment, Hegel selects it as the contemporary avatar of this erotic longing for a completion not yet at hand. This is another reason why it is fair to say that, in diagnosing the merits and liabilities of both science and Romanticism, for Hegel the Romantics come out a little ahead of the game. It is in Romanticism, Hegel implies, that we will today find the traces of that erotic longing for completion through union with the beautiful and the good that Plato identified as the motive both for wisdom and for aesthetic and emotional fulfillment. When Hegel writes that Romanticism's desire to "bite" is provoked by the "bait" of empiricism's reduction of human experience to crass utility, it is possible that he is alluding to Alcibiades' likening in the *Symposium* of Socrates' speeches to an "adder's bite" when they infect a young soul with philosophical madness.

As these two opponents (Science and Romanticism) continue to stare each other down, Hegel goes on, in the meantime, the thrust of history is actually bringing about their resolution, in a way as yet barely to be glimpsed on the horizon [11–12]:

Besides, it is not difficult to see that ours is a birth-time and a period of transition to a new era. Spirit has broken with the world it has hitherto inhabited and imagined, and is of a mind to submerge it in the past, and in the labour of its own transformation. Spirit is indeed never at rest but always engaged in moving forward.

The new era will emerge with a jolt from an at times apparently placid status quo:

But just as the first breath drawn by a child after its long, quiet nourishment breaks the gradualness of merely quantitative growth – there is a qualitative leap, and the child is born – so likewise the Spirit in its formation matures slowly and quietly into its new shape, dissolving bit by bit the structure of its previous world, whose tottering state is only hinted at by isolated symptoms. The frivolity and boredom which unsettle the established order, the vague foreboding of something unknown, these are the heralds of approaching change. The gradual crumbling that, left unaltered in the face of the whole is cut short by a sunburst which, in one flash, illuminates the features of the world.

The modern spirit, Hegel says, has now definitely "broken with" the old feudal and classical conglomerate. It turns against the world and relentlessly subdues it, "dissolving" one remnant after another of the Great Chain of Being. As the comforting contexts of traditional faith, authority and culture "gradually crumble," there is widespread cultural malaise, a feeling that we are adrift in a world increasingly bereft of its moral moorings. By the same token, however, our anxiety over the disintegration of the inherited world of tradition bespeaks our tacit awareness that "something unknown" is "approaching." Just as a child gestates over a long period of nutrition in silence, so mankind has enriched its organic heritage through its long odyssey from ancient to modern times. But, just as a child is suddenly thrust into a strange new world and must struggle for breath, so must the approaching new epoch undergo the trauma of birth. The work of the Enlightenment in dissolving traditions, carried out gradually over two centuries, is suddenly interrupted by a sharp jolt. The "flash" of the "sunrise" brings the form and structure of the new world into view at a single stroke. Hegel's imagery here evokes the French Revolution and the spread of the doctrines of the social contract and the rights of man to the rest of Europe by the Napoleonic wars. The sunlight of the Enlightenment, *la Lumiere*, whose rays have spread gradually for decades, is suddenly concentrated into the "flash" of torches and gunpowder. The gestation of the new epoch requires a sharp pang of revolution, war and terror.

Having sketched the two opponents in the cultural battle and identified their coming resolution in a new dawn, Hegel now shifts the argument to a discussion of Schelling (unnamed), who in my view Hegel believes presented the best philosophical case for Romanticism as a whole, thereby moving the argument to a more purely theoretical plane. Here we should recall that Schelling considered himself to be restoring the importance of Spinoza's critique of modern dualism in the mode of Descartes and Hobbes. Instead of unjustifiably positing a hardened distinction between the self and the world, between the human mind and the irrational happenstance of nature as matter in motion, Schelling's Spinoza argued that nature as understood by modern science evolves continuously into its higher end-states of human civilization, culture, art and learning, all among the "infinity of attributes" of God. Although distinct products of the life-world's evolution, they need not be mutually exclusive: one can be a poet *and* a scientist; a philosopher *and* a lens-maker. We can sample their respective satisfactions in the noble pluralism of "the kingdom of spirits."

To an extent, Hegel approves of this ontology of the life-word, which collapses God into secular time and matter. Schelling's characterization of existence as a "self-originating wealth of shapes," in Hegel's view, "comes about as near to fulfilling what is wanted" philosophically to date, and "self-origination" remains the fundamental ontological premise of Hegel's own historicism. Moreover, Schelling's formula whereby the concept of the life-world can be represented as A = A, which can also be rendered as I = I – including by implication God's spontaneous distinction of himself from himself as "I am what/that I am"– enables us to see how Spirit distinguishes objects or other selves from itself and then reunifies them in its overarching holistic movement. This process, according to Hegel, is the common underlying basis for both the subjectivism of modern analytical rationality as it distinguishes empirically between the self and the rest of the world and Romanticism's exploration of the inner feelings of the self in its experience of the rest of the world, a common origin that has been forgotten as the two cultural standpoints have become frozen in their opposition. However, the problem with Schelling's vision of the life-world is that is remains a "monochrome formalism" in which distinctions and contradictions are too rapidly swallowed back into the formal self-identity of the Absolute [16]:

Dealing with something from the perspective of the Absolute consists merely in declaring that, although one has been speaking of it just now as something definite, yet in the Absolute, the A = A, there is nothing of the kind, for there all is one. To pit this single insight, that in the Absolute everything is the same, against the full body of articulated cognition, which at least seeks and demands such fulfillment, to palm off its Absolute as the night in which, as the saying goes, all cows are black – this is cognition naively reduced to vacuity.

In Hegel's view, Schelling envisions a life-world where everyone and everything is instantaneously reunified, where everything is at one with everything else. (As Hegel jokes, "the night in which all cows are back," apparently a Swabian sidesplitter.) Schelling thereby prematurely leaps beyond the world of strife, conflict and contradiction, fleeing the unedifying and messy contingencies of life, including violence, war and political upheaval. By contrast, Hegel's own conception of the historical dialectic will inject into Schelling's Spinozistic quietistic life-world the belligerent modern thrust of Machiavelli, Bacon, Hobbes, of revolution and the conquest of nature.

We have to return to the dynamic interplay of opposites out of which both the modern physics of matter in motion and the Romantics' restless alienation from the world have emerged, for historical action was the underlying source of their original emergence, and the prospective source of their coming reconciliation. If we follow Hegel up the Ladder to the Absolute, we will be forced to part ways with common sense and cease seeing culture in terms of combatants glaring at each other across a battlefield. The modern view of nature as matter in motion – as a happenstantial flux bereft of purpose – is as necessary to the moody sentimentality of modern poetry as it is to the capacity of modern physics to subsume nature under anthropocentric, analytically self-referential structures of causality and lawlike necessity and thereby repudiate classical metaphysics. Science and poetry, Hegel argues, are battening off of the *same* modern understanding of nature as motion, which is grounded at a deeper ontological level in the principle that history is "self-origination." The simple premise of I = I sums up Spirit's capacity to distinguish itself from itself and to reunify the distinction. It informs both modern reason's corrosive analytical power to break nature down and reconstruct it and the Romantics' ability to experience our alienation from nature and our longing for aesthetic reintegration with it.

According to Hegel, the implicit common ground between the two worldviews is the basic principle of intelligibility, or, more generally, Understanding (*Verstand*), the principle of identity and difference, which enables man to distinguish himself from the world. Both modern science and Romanticism claim to have understood the whole. Both lay claim to the emerging new era, glimpsed so far only as a "bare abstraction." Both claim that their insights possess universal validity and can be universally grasped. Understanding is the seemingly frail tendril that, as Hegel puts it, continues to link the "scientific and the unscientific consciousness," and at least holds out the prospect that each can enter the other's domain.

And this brings him to announcing his own position, one which subsumes the two opposed standpoints of Science and Romanticism, now recast as the polarity within Spirit of Subject versus Substance [17]: "In my view, which can be justified only by the exposition of the system itself, everything turns on grasping and expressing the True, not only as Subject, but equally as Substance." Taken to an extreme, according to Hegel, the realm of Substance "submerges" self-consciousness in its tidal wave of sheer emotionalism, swallowing up everything into God. On the other hand, taken to an extreme, the realm of Subjectivity preserves self-consciousness through the abstractions of modern dualism and its imposition on nature of a contentless rationality, "simplistic" and "undifferentiated." In the concept of Spirit as the Unity of Subject and Substance, both polarities are preserved and their extremes mediated through their interaction and tension with each other.

In Hegel's formulation of the concept of Spirit as the Unity of Subject and Substance, under the pole of Subject is located the modern project for the conquest of nature and human nature typified by Machiavelli, Bacon, Hobbes and modern natural science, whose political concomitants are individualism and liberalism, culminating in the Kantian morality of the Categorical Imperative (the internalization of the conquest of nature as the self's repression of the inclinations). Under the pole of Substance is located the counter-longing for reconciliation, love, beauty and harmony between man and man and man and the world, the longing for community and fulfillment typified by ancient philosophies like that of Plato, but also including religious revelation and the modern Romantics including Rousseau, Schelling and Schelling's antecedent in the formulation of the life-world, Spinoza. Their tension and interaction constitute the nerve of Spirit. A series of related pairings can be grouped as tending toward the Subject side or the Substance side of the interaction: consciousness versus self-consciousness; the particular versus the universal; the striving for freedom versus its current embodiment in civilization; the drive for political mastery versus cooperation; the "labour of the negative" in transforming existence in the pursuit of freedom versus "forgiveness" and the longing for "infinity"; modern analytical rationality (*Verstand*) including natural science and the privileging of the rights-bearing individual motivated by appetitive self-interest versus the longing for Love and Beauty through the aesthetic experience. While they are tensions, however, they are not outright contradictions or antinomies, like that between nature and freedom in Rousseau's thought. History is progressively reconciling their claims. To sort them out for the sake of heuristic clarity is an act performed by the Understanding itself, but the Understanding is always already enfolded in Spirit.

But Spirit, Hegel continues, cannot just be an equipoise between these two polarities. Spirit must develop itself. Hence, as between Subject and Substance, Hegel identifies the aggressive Subjective side of the interaction as the driving force of history, that which galvanizes substance so that it is "living" [18]: "The living Substance is being which is in truth Subject ... is in truth actual, only in so far as is the movement of positing itself, or is the mediation of its self-othering with itself. This Substance is, as Subject, pure simple negativity." With this prioritization of the Subject side of the dialectic as the impetus for its progress, it is as if, through Spirit, the static and impersonal Platonic account of the whole has assumed personhood, gotten up on its hind legs, and begun to walk. We now have before us nothing less than a conceptual outline of the meaning of the entirety of existence [25]: "That the truth is only realized in the form of system, that substance is essentially subject, is expressed in the idea which represents the Absolute as Spirit – the grandest conception of all, and one which is due to modern times and its religion. Spirit alone is reality."

Armed with a view of history that incorporates both its bellicose outward drive and its longing for inward wholeness and repose, each dependent on the other, Hegel is now able to offer a final riposte to Schiller and the Romantics, who cling exclusively to the latter dimension [19]: "Thus the life of God and divine cognition may well be spoken of as a disporting of Love with itself, but this idea sinks into mere edification, and even insipidity, if it lacks the seriousness, the suffering, the patience, and the labour of the negative." Hegel (in a way anticipating Marx) depicts the spirit of modernity as a revolutionary, corrosive and destructive dynamic whose powers of analytical dissection break down and cast aside all previous traditions and customary bonds. Hegel gathers these powers together under the term *Verstand*, the analytical understanding that accompanies the modern ontology of "consciousness" (more about this shortly). It might therefore seem as if what Schiller lamented about the modern era Hegel willingly embraces. But however much he may appear in the first instance to be embracing the modern project for the conquest of nature as against the Romantic protest against it, his long-range aim is to bring these two "shapes" (*Gestalten*) together. Hegel's "shapes of consciousness" are, I would suggest, the historicized analogy to the Platonic Forms, a term which in Greek (*eidos*) literally means the visible "shape" or "look" that we glimpse through the accidental or perishable aspects of a phenomenon. The purpose of the dialectic of Spirit is to show how the permanence of self-identity that, for the classics, resided in a realm of eternal metaphysical archetypes, for Hegel descends into the realm of becoming and develops its permanence immanently and progressively through – and embodied in – time. The "absolute *Wissenschaft*" of Spirit is not, as is sometimes suggested, a pan-logistic attempt to impose conceptual formalism on the diversity of phenomena, but rather an attempt to show how the world's evolution out of the passive cycles of nature into self-expression through its human intermediaries in the realms of culture, thought and civic life reconciles the eternality of classical metaphysics with the time-bound processes of modern physics, so that the visible presence of the (now historicized) Forms as "shapes of consciousness" is the "result" of a dialectic of self-development.

Hegel goes on to liken the "labour of the negative" – the subjective pole of the Unity of Subject and Substance – to the power of Death, both literally and figuratively. Whereas in his view, Schiller and the Romantics fled from death in order to preserve the pristine purity of Beauty, including the corrosive power of modern Understanding to kill the sentiments on behalf of analytical clarity, Hegel's historicism unhesitatingly embraces the living fiber of life shot through with negation and finitude. Only by subjecting itself to Death will Spirit be revitalized and reborn through its "magical power." The language here is heavily redolent with the Christian symbolism of crucifixion and resurrection [32]: "Death, if that is what we want to call this non-actuality, is of all things the most dreadful, and to hold fast what is dead requires the greatest strength. Lacking strength, Beauty hates the Understanding for asking of her what it cannot do." But when Beauty flees from Death, it is reduced to but a glistening bubble ready to burst, sacrificing the robust regenerative power of Spirit:

But the life of Spirit is not the life that shrinks from death and keeps itself untouched by devastation, but rather the life that endures it and maintains itself in it. It wins its truth only when, in utter dismemberment, it finds itself. It is this power, not as something positive, which closes its eyes to the negative, as when we say of something that is it nothing or is false, and then, having done with it, turn away and pass on to something else; on the contrary, Spirit is this power only by looking the negative in the face and tarrying with it. This tarrying with the negative is the magical power that converts it into being.

Hegel's hermeneutic of educational "recollection" plays a crucial role in the dynamic of Spirit. As I observed earlier, by using this term, Hegel surely means to recall Plato's *Meno*. In that dialogue, Plato asks how it is that a person comes to learn anything (81b–e). His answer is to speculate that before we were born into the realm of mortal becoming, perishability and impermanence, our souls – the only immortal aspect of our otherwise finite natures as humans – resided with the other eternal beings and thereby possessed perfect knowledge. Being born human amounted to almost, but not quite, severing that link. The soul retains a fragile and attenuated but still reliable connection to the immortal beings that were its first home. When we study and learn (for example, a Euclidean proof), we are in effect "remembering" a part of that perfect knowledge that the perfect part of us possessed before being immured in our bodily shells.

Hegel is suggesting that, in effect, his teleology of historical progress more successfully and plausibly demonstrates the actualization of this doctrine of "recollection" than the Platonic original. It is no longer necessary to posit the existence of a transcendental empyrean realm beyond time and change, and further to posit a particle of this immortal realm in ourselves (the soul), in order to explain how finite beings can participate in a knowledge of the infinite. If all phenomena are time-bound, then our knowledge cannot leap beyond the limits of time, change, variability and perishability. From a Platonic perspective, Hegelian knowledge resides entirely within the realm of becoming: the sunlight is confined within the Cave. But, Hegel would argue, the decisive superiority of the dialectic of Spirit resides precisely in this collapse of the infinite into the finite, and the resultant immanentization of the telos in the temporal currents of accident and mutability. Now, at the end of the process, it is possible for us to understand retroactively how the entire human species – not just the privileged philosophic few – are now poised to "remember" the infinite wisdom they have currently "forgotten." This wisdom is not merely speculative: It is the concretely actualized outcome of the entire previous eons-long pursuit of freedom, enlightenment and happiness, embodied in the living structures of the modern state, culture, education and religion.

What began as Romanticism's desire to "bite" at the "bait" of the current impoverishment enables it to evolve beyond itself toward Spirit through this process of the recollection of the whole vast panoply of past shapes of consciousness, raising them to self-consciousness and thereby reclaiming them as the organically integrated personality of the coming "sunrise." When the consciousness of the modern individual is sparked by the impoverishment of the present divide between science and the divine to remember this heritage, Spirit will complete its own evolution by breaking through the final crust dividing itself as scientific rigor from itself as love. This is the fuller implication of education as recollection. Viewed from the side of the individual, the learner "acquires what lies at hand as ready for him, making its inorganic nature organic to himself." But looked at from the side of Spirit, recollection is Spirit's own self-cultivation through its human participants. The spirits of all human beings, mediated by the states and cultures in which they live, will join the Spirit of all existence in which they are enfolded, and the wisdom they raise to consciousness will not exist across a divide between the mortal and the immortal, nor will it remain an incompletable quest. Wisdom will fully reside, and will be fully grasped and lived, in the dawning new era. In Hegel's famous phrase "the end of History," he is not so much pointing to a terminal point in time as to the fulfillment of history through the actualization of reason.

Unlike the static archetypes of classical wisdom, moreover, the emerging wisdom of the new era will continue to pulsate with the underlying indeterminacy and dynamism of Spirit, a Heracleitean whole that has been eidetically articulated by the time it reaches the end of its teleological development. Spirit is a dynamic equilibrium shot through with contingency, in which the difference between entities is what establishes, through their mutual tension of resistance, the achieved identity of each. For we must continue to bear in mind that, in trying to demonstrate how historical phenomenology synthesizes Platonic Being with Heracleitean becoming, Hegel insists that the full scope of both realms must be preserved without diminishment.

THE STRUCTURE AND CONTENT OF HEGEL'S
PHENOMENOLOGY OF SPIRIT

The Unity of Subject and Substance is the core concept of the Preface to the *Phenomenology*, which serves as an introduction to the entire Hegelian system in all his writings. However, in the Introduction to the *Phenomenology* properly speaking, Hegel introduces a second major concept without which the Unity of Subject and Substance would not be a complete explanation of the dialectic of historical progress. He terms this concept "determinate negation." It means that, as mankind strives to overcome the current civilization in order to advance its freedom, the new outcome will contain – be determined by – a residue of what has been overcome, which will in turn shape what steps can next be taken [79]. Progress, in other words, is always a matter of two steps forward and one step back, a kind of dialectical cha-cha. The shaping of our future freedom by the residue of its previous manifestation is what imparts teleological purpose to history as well as an element of moderation, not unlike Burke's view that progress should proceed according to precedent and prescription rather than the wholesale, revolutionary overturning of the status quo.

Without the direction for progress that determinate negation provides, according to Hegel, history might be viewed as a pointless cycle of the rise and fall of civilizations and beliefs, a meaningless whirligig akin to ancient skepticism that would constitute a "highway of despair." This possible allusion to Saul's conversion on the road to Damascus underscores Hegel's belief that the dialectic of Spirit is symbolized by the "absolute religion," Christianity, the reinvigoration of freedom through its "death" or negation. Hegel stresses that past historical actors themselves may well have been completely unaware that their ambitions and struggles were serving any such arc of progress: Julius Caesar crossed the Rubicon only to defend his *dignitas* as a Roman nobleman, with no conscious plan to end up as the de facto monarch of the entire world empire, laying the basis for the Augustan principate. It is only "we phenomenologists," as Hegel puts it, standing at or near the end of Spirit's odyssey, who grasp the necessity of how those stages have progressively unfolded – understandably considered one of Hegel's most paradoxical and controversial arguments, inasmuch as the rationality of historical progress emerges only retroactively from the privileged standpoint of the present, enabling us to project that teleological pattern back onto past actors, while the actors themselves experienced history as sheer accident with no clear foresight as to what would result.

A final general note on structure: Spanning the progress of history as it unfolds in the *Phenomenology* are two fundamental stances toward reality that remain fixed points arcing throughout it, crystallizing the poles of Subject and Substance. One is *Sittlichkeit*, the "sphere of ethical life," as one translation has it, or, one might also say, customary and communal being, first emerging with the chthonic and Olympian gods of the ancient Greek polis and developing and reemerging under the pole of Substance in the concept of Spirit. Its representatives include, again, Plato and the ancient philosophers, along with moderns including Spinoza and Schelling, as well as the openness to religious revelation. The other fundamental stance is the realm of "morality" (*Moralitat*), the will of the individual to master his own nature so as to achieve autonomy, emerging under the pole of Subject, whose clearest representative is Kant. These two standpoints are in a tension with one another, but they also interweave as history moves toward its completion.

Altogether, then, the principles of the Unity of Subject and Substance and of determinate negation provide us with the conceptual pie crust, so to speak, which the rest of the book will supply with the phenomenological pie filling of how history has actually unfolded. In broad strokes, here is how that happened. The emergence of Greek philosophy through Socrates and his successors the Stoics established, at the level of principle, the freedom and equality of all human beings through their possession of a soul. However, the reality of archaic Greek life – the primacy of the family, the clan, the ancestral polis, and a morality of mastery at every level of society – stood as the negation of this theoretical assertion of universal equality. The negation of this negation – the universalistic empires of Alexander the Great and Rome – was the first attempt to actualize the equality of human beings established in principle by classical philosophy. However, the reality behind the claim to recognize the right of every Roman to the protection of the law was contradicted by the severe inequalities of wealth and status, the distinction between citizens and noncitizens, and the unfettered despotic power of the emperors. So the earlier inegalitarian ethos characteristic of the archaic Greek world continued to mediate the result of the first attempt to institutionalize universal human equality. The stark contradiction between the Roman Empire's embrace of the Stoic teaching that every citizen is equal before the law and the actual tyranny and injustice of society under the emperors leads mankind to seek a freedom altogether beyond the world, with God in the divine hereafter. Unlike the emperors, God is the "Lord" or "Master" who is truly deserving of our obedience. Thus the civilization of medieval Christendom, devoted to the protection of the City of God through its outpost in the City of Man, the Church, is established on the ruins of the collapsed empire.

Yet the inegalitarian conditions of medieval feudalism contradict the attempt of the Church to establish the equality of Christians in the eyes of God. In this way, residual ancient pre-Christian inequality and oppression "mediate" the new epoch through feudal hierarchy, national rivalries and the competition for preeminence between frequently despotic kings and the authority of the Church, itself not always an unsullied moral authority. Because of this yawning contradiction between our equality in the eyes of God and the brutal social and political reality of the Middle Ages, God must come down from Heaven to Earth and be internalized in every individual Christian in the form of Lutheran conscience. Each believer can now worship God as he sees fit and act as a beacon for God in the world of the here and now without need of priestly intercession or the sacraments of the old Church. But the socioeconomic reality of feudalism still must be transformed if freedom is to have a home in the world, so that the inwardness of Lutheran conscience is now turned outward to transform the world through the spread of Enlightenment. Yet, in the familiar pattern, the epoch of the Enlightenment is contradicted and mediated by the rise of "enlightened despotism" and a still powerfully entrenched aristocratic caste system. That sparks the drive to literally impose pure freedom and equality overnight, through terror, in the French Revolution. The Jacobins' struggle to impose Rousseau's doctrine of the General Will, in which every citizen is an interchangeable integer with every other citizen submerged in the collective, leads to a permanent war on human nature because of the constant danger of the recrudescence of lurking bourgeois, religious or royalist sentiments. Accordingly, forgiveness and a return to faith must mediate the purely political attempt to achieve freedom by force, such that the *Phenomenology* ends with an exploration of the history of religion.

The *Phenomenology* is not a chronological work strictly speaking. Instead, it explores the same "shapes of consciousness" from earliest times to the present, first from the perspective of Consciousness, then a second time from the perspective of Spirit. To clarify this sequence further, we can map onto its stages the three-stage overview of history supplied by the *Introduction to the Philosophy of History* – the government of one, of "Lordship," culminating in the Roman Empire; the government of the few, meaning ancient aristocracy and medieval feudalism; and finally the government of many, the modern constitutional state with its representative institutions and civil society.

Hegel first leads us through the progress of history from the perspective of Consciousness, which always means the consciousness of something – of an object or another self. This is the distinctively modern perspective on knowledge, privileging the individual subject epistemologically as well as socially and politically, and Hegel begins with it because that is what forms the horizon of his readers. The first installment is an analysis of the debate in modern theories of knowledge between Idealists and materialists. The former category is often said to include Locke and Kant, while Hobbes and Gassendi are often identified with the latter, although opinions differ as to who fits where and degrees of synthesis between the two positions abound. It is important to note that what is termed the "epistemological idealism" of, for instance, Kant only maintains that reason organizes the empirical correlates of experience. It is not the full-blown Platonic position (sometimes termed "objective idealism") that the cosmos as a whole is rationally structured independently of the human mind, which for Kant would involve the misleading assumption that we can have knowledge of the "thing in itself" – that is to say, Plato's Ideas. I see both sides of the modern debate as inheritors of the paradox originating in Hobbesian dualism whereby human reason is inexplicably equipped to make sense of an irrational cosmos. The Idealists argue that reality is virtually constructed by the causal categories of the human mind, whereas materialists believe our minds are passively determined by their bombardment with sense data. Both positions are, for Hegel, one-sided and eschew any possibility of an underlying third term that might unite subject and object in certain knowledge. As he has already established through the principles of the Unity of Subject and Substance and determinate negation, there is no method for understanding existence that is not already living within it; we are always already enmeshed in the dialectic of Spirit.

As it happens, however, in Hegel's view the most up to date modern physics, by embracing the concept of Force, transcends the epistemological cul-de-sac of the debate between the Idealists and materialists because it transcends the concept of nature as matter in motion in which its contending versions of dualism were grounded. The concept of force, which referred both to Leibnitz's philosophical principle and actual scientific research, maintained that certain forces like electricity and magnetism were not substances that *have* the power of electricity and magnetism, but simply *are* the forces of electricity and magnetism. The distinction between substance and expression is merely analytical – in actuality, they interact as one. The concept of Force heralded an inroad against the physics of matter in motion – not particles clashing, but quanta or waves.

For Hegel, Spirit, like Force distinguishes between itself and itself and simultaneously collapses the distinction. While consciousness remains trapped by the subject/object distinction, Spirit first reveals through the concept of Force that it is a process that opposes itself to itself and overcomes the opposition – a sheer dialecticity and freedom from fixity that Hegel likens suggestively to entering "the Holy of Holies," a characteristic assimilation of Spirit to divine revelation that arguably connects the physics of Force to God's mysterious pronouncement that "I am what/that I am" – which is to say, completely mutable. We now can progress from consciousness to self-consciousness, which emerges between or among at least two separate selves. At bottom, the self of which self-consciousness is conscious is Spirit. The unity of self and other through their simultaneous division and reconciliation expressed scientifically as the physics of Force has all along been worked out by the historical process.

We should note in this connection that when Hegel refers to the longing for "infinity," he does not so much mean the longing for what is immortally and eternally true, as in Plato's Idea of the Good or the Scholastics' eternal now (*nunc stans*), but rather Spirit's freedom from any fixed or finite entity in its dynamism as an ever-mutable process of division and reconciliation. This is one of the senses in which, for Hegel, Spirit is symbolized by the God of revealed religion and the way in which God cannot be conceptualized as a specific entity or static being. In sum, the concept of Force as the interplay of opposites ushers in the emergence of Spirit, the interplay of self and other, and the historicization of philosophy's ascent up the Divided Line and out of the Cave [177]:

With this we already have before us the Concept of Spirit ... I that is We, and We that is I. Consciousness first finds its turning point in self-consciousness, the Concept of Spirit, where it leaves the shimmer of the sensuous here and now, passes from the empty night of the super-sensible beyond, and steps into the spiritual daylight of the present.

The most advanced modern science hurtles us back to the most distant period of the past, where a struggle between primitive individual selves to master nature – initially for the sake of survival, but opening up the prospect that one's freedom might be verified by the recognition of another whom one has enslaved – leads to the establishment of Lordship and Bondage, which corresponds to the primeval origins of the Government of One from the *Philosophy of History*. The process of Spirit, first ushered in conceptually by the contemporary physics of Force, we now grasp has been at work all along from the earliest origins of man's emergence from the primordial prehuman origins through his pursuit of freedom. Only now that the odyssey of Spirit is nearing the fulfillment of its course is Hegel in a position to set it forth explicitly as a concept.

To continue with our overview of how history unfolds: The Master's inability to achieve a satisfactory recognition of his freedom from the Slave, who is not his equal and whose recognition therefore does not count, leads to Stoicism, the internalization of Lordship through the mastery of the world by the intellect

(Marcus Aurelius is alluded to), and Skepticism, which internalizes the Slave's terror over the complete insecurity of his life at the hands of the Master as a corrosive inability to believe in any lasting truth. These shapes of consciousness correspond to the aristocratic ethos of Greco-Roman antiquity. Christianity emerges with the Unhappy Consciousness, which internalizes two pagan standpoints: We now worship the true Master, God, who dwells within us, yet we are tormented by his infinite distance from us as we are prisoners in a fallen and meaningless world. The belief in the God of revealed religion, with his capacity to stand entirely outside of nature and create and recreate it, is transferred to human agency in the form of modern reason – the will to master nature through natural science and human nature through its pacification by a doctrine of rational self-interest. Having been hurtled back from the forefront of the physics of force to the earliest origins of human history, we are now hurtled forward to the Age of Reason and Enlightenment.

Although we will be discussing Marx's relationship to Hegelianism in its proper sequence, because so many readers are introduced to the *Phenomenology of Spirit* through the Left Hegelian reading developed by Kojeve whereby the Master–Slave dialectic is presented as its major premise, it is useful to observe in this context that it contains no such prominence in Hegel's own text, where it takes up no more than a few pages and is but the first of a series of "shapes of consciousness" including the Master, Slave, Stoic, Skeptic and Unhappy Consciousness. Moreover, I would argue that within this sequence of experiences, if one of them is to be singled out for its importance it would be the Unhappy Consciousness. For Hegel, in my view, the internalization of the Master–Slave encounter within the Unhappy Consciousness as the inner calling from God (the true Master) to man (trapped in a fallen world) is a deepening and sublimation of self-consciousness that transcends the merely outward struggle between opposing selves resulting in the Master and Slave, and points to the emergence of modernity as God's power to transform nature is eventually transferred to human agency. Furthermore, this whole sequence of "shapes" is presented by Hegel at this stage in the *Phenomenology of Spirit* as still largely from within the viewpoint of "consciousness" – that is to say, from the viewpoint of the modern Cartesian self that assumes the priority of the individual. That viewpoint, we now learn, is not adequate.

Having absorbed the many layerings of history to date, and the breakdown of all seemingly fixed oppositions within the mutability of Spirit, we are now in a position to begin all over again and examine this same sequence of standpoints explicitly from the perspective of Spirit, which is freed from the limitations of subjectivity and is accordingly far wider and richer in its sweep. Indeed, it transpires that "all previous standpoints" are mere "abstractions" from Spirit: "Reason is Spirit when its certainty of being all reality has been raised to truth, and it is consciousness of itself as its own world and of the world as itself" [438]. We must observe that Hegel's term for "reason" here (*Die Vernunft*) is not to be confused with the "Understanding" that, as we earlier observed, is characteristic of modern analytical rationality and its drive to break phenomena down into separate and opposed elements, a view that Hegel shared with Schiller. Now that we have grasped the Concept of Spirit, we are able to ascend to a higher kind of reason, an integrative and reflective process that mirrors Spirit itself in reconciling what are merely apparent contradictions, and enables us to develop ourselves.

For Hegel, Spirit alone is truly self-conscious, progressively so as history teleologically unfolds. To reiterate: At bottom, the self of which I as a human being am conscious is the self-consciousness of Spirit operative through me. Only now are we in a position to penetrate those layerings fully. When viewed from within the limited perspective of Consciousness, the shapes of historical experience took the form of individual human actors – the Master, the Slave, the Stoic and so on, a series of "Mr. Selves." Now we learn that they were pulled out of a much broader social, cultural and religious context that alone can explain them properly.

Hegel now reveals to us that Lordship and Bondage was but one authority pattern abstracted from the society of the ancient Greek polis, which, with its bonds between the individual citizen and the community, is the first concrete historical embodiment of Spirit itself with its interchange between self and other; between particular and universal. In Hegel's cumulative presentation, we now learn that the "Master," properly considered, was never an individual – a Mr. Self – but emerged originally as a communal historical force from ancient Greek religion, both chthonic and Olympian. The archaic polis was characterized by lordship and bondage at every level – children served their fathers, wives their husbands, the family served the clan, the clans served the king, and the king served the gods. The cosmos as a whole, according to Aristotle in the *Politics*, is made up of ruling and ruled parts. The conflict between this older natural law centering on the veneration of the ancestors, hearth-worship, and the chthonic gods and a newly emerging human law that saw the displacement of family and ancestral authority by the "daylight" of public life in the agora – leading to a taste for popular self-government, debate and the assertion of young talent, accompanied by the fully realized human qualities of the Olympian gods and crystallized by Platonic philosophy – sounded the death-knell of the old tribal society of the polis and the emergence of the cosmopolitan Alexandrian and Roman empires. Now we learn that the Lord in the fullest sense from the earlier Lordship and Bondage motif was the Roman Emperor with his godlike and terrifying authority, "Lord and God of the World." The philosophical schools of Stoicism and Skepticism grew up around the Augustan principate, with the emperors claiming to uphold Stoicism's teachings about the superiority of the life of the mind to base passion and the need to cultivate moral virtue. The Unhappy Consciousness now emerges in fuller outline as the emergence of early Christianity during the late Roman Empire as a revulsion to the real-life tyranny of the emperors (contradicting their profession of Stoic virtue) accompanied by a spreading disillusionment as people came to see the pagan religions as mere rituals devoid of spiritual satisfaction. In a characteristic layering that defies straightforward chronology, however, in addition to the notion that in principle if not in practice the Augustan principate protected the individual citizen from lawless treatment in conformity with its official patronage of Stoicism, Hegel also alludes to the modern concept of "Right," meaning the idea of the social contract being instituted to protect individual "personhood," and perhaps even to the absolute monarchical power of the Hobbesian Sovereign and the danger it posed of tyranny. Hegel's Roman Empire was in this respect rather protomodern.

Hegel is explicit that this second account of the sequence Master–Slave–Stoic–Skeptic–Unhappy Consciousness is the fuller one, because the opposed selves of the earlier sequence are now thoroughly contextualized within the realm of the political community and ethical and customary being (*Sittlichkeit*) [483]:

What was for Stoicism only the *abstraction* of an *intrinsic* reality is now an *actual* world ... Earlier we saw the Stoical independence of pure thought pass through Scepticism and find its truth in the Unhappy Consciousness ... If this knowledge appeared then merely as the one-sided view of consciousness as consciousness, here the *actual* truth of that view has become apparent.

The emerging predominance of the Creator God of Christianity through the Unhappy Consciousness as paganism faded takes us hurtling forward, just as happened in the first rendition of the shapes of consciousness, through the transfer of God's mastery over nature to human agency and to the modern age. But the treatment is now expanded from modern natural science and the Enlightenment to include the rise of Protestantism, the concept of conscience, and the French Revolution.

With this, we now come full circle to Hegel's own lifetime and the starting point in the Preface, the cultural battle between scientific empiricism and political individualism on the one hand (the realm of Subject) and aesthetic and communal Romanticism on the other (the realm of Substance). The Terror of the French Revolution for Hegel represented the extreme working out of the purely secular, political attempt to master human nature on behalf of the General Will. With Kantian moral philosophy, that struggle against human nature is internalized as the Categorical Imperative's struggle to repress the natural inclinations [584]: "Absolute Freedom leaves its self-destroying reality and passes over into another land of self-conscious Spirit, where freedom has the value of truth...There has arisen a new shape of Spirit, that of *moral* Spirit." In effect, through Kantian moral philosophy, each of us has a little guillotine inside his head, ready to summon the passions before the tribunal of judgement. The emergence of Kantian morality as the internalization of Jacobinism gives rise to the cultural conflict between modern rationalism and Romanticism. Kantian morality, which claimed a rational basis in the metaphysics of morals, is embedded in the human character as "conscience."

Growing up alongside the stern antinatural voluntarism of Kant's Categorical Imperative is the "beautiful soul" of Romanticism, epitomized by Schiller and Goethe. The modern conscience, while it has evolved out of the earlier concept of conscience in Christianity – particularly Protestantism – contrasts with it through being entirely this-worldly and pragmatic. As it sets about to perform its duty in all actions, conscience comes to accept no contradiction between duty and reality – nature must be subdued by the dictates of morality. Hegel is suggesting by implication that although Kant might have been satisfied with a permanent equipoise between the realm of nature and the realm of freedom, Kantianism in action inevitably militated toward the progressive transformation of nature in accordance with the dictates of freedom – the radical Fichtean strain lurking, as we observed earlier, within Kantian ethics.

However, conscience begins to grow smug in its insistence on its purity of intention, and begins to find fault with others for professing to do their duty while secretly having "interested" motives (to use Kant's term of disapprobation) like ambition, happiness and self-admiration. By setting a standard for morality so purely "disinterested" as to call into suspicion the motive behind any action, even of those professing to follow the Categorical Imperative, Kantian morality turns on and consumes itself. Some humbly confess their imperfections to those who presume to judge them. But that opens the judges themselves to accusations of hypocrisy, inasmuch as their own hidden venality is liable to exposure, along with the concealed emotional satisfaction they derive from their self-righteousness in condemning others.

In Hegel's presentation, does the emergence of Romanticism alongside Kantian morality help mitigate the severity of its dictates? Although Romanticism may contribute to softening the judgmental side of the modern character, according to Hegel, the Beautiful Soul, that is to say Romanticism's protest against Kantian moral rigor, does not offer any prospect on its own for the reconciliation of Kantianism's internal conflicts, in contrast with the hopes held out by Schiller in his view that "aesthetic education" could reconcile the demands of duty and sentiment. The reason it cannot be the direct source of this reconciliation is because the Beautiful Soul is too delicate to commit itself to anything. It keeps its heart pure by fleeing from contact with the harsh realities of life, and so becomes a series of insipid sentimental generalities, as Hegel originally diagnosed it in the Preface. It refuses to judge and act at all, and so wastes away in ineffectual maundering.

Therefore, although Romanticism may contribute to a place for natural sentiment in contrast with the dictates of moral duty, the reconciliation of the war within morality between the purity of its duty and its inevitable lapses from enacting that duty can come only when the conscience of the sternest Kantian relaxes his strictures, confesses his own inadequacies, and admits that he shares them with those whom he presumed to judge. Only when the strict moralist learns to forgive others for failing to live up to the inflexible demands of duty, and therefore forgive himself for his own frailties and imperfections in trying to do so, is reconciliation possible. This new burgeoning of forgiveness, the final interweaving of Substance with Subject, constitutes nothing less than the reappearance of God in history, and, in the final section of the *Phenomenology*, the return to an even deeper immersion in the history of religion as Spirit's own history. The whole "wealth of shapes" including Master, Slave, Stoic, Skeptic and Unhappy Consciousness are crystallized in the cultural battle between science and Romanticism that will, once sublimated, usher in the reemergence of God in history in a new era of mutual forgiveness. The exchange of identities between the once fixed opposition between the uncompromising moralist and those who confess their failings mediates the contradiction between them, thus replicating the mutuality and mutability of Spirit, the I = I of selves unified through their distinction from one another, which is to say, of God.

HEGEL ON THE ANCIENT POLIS AND ITS OVERCOMING

Because a major theme of this book is how the thinkers under consideration envision the ancient Greek polis, and how those judgements are both shaped by and contribute to their critiques of modernity and their visions of a future alternative to it, we should dwell in some further detail on Hegel's understanding of the polis and its role in the progress of history. As we will see especially in the cases of Nietzsche and Heidegger, their own evocations of the ancient world and its implications for the present and future are explicitly aimed at Hegel's writings.

Hegel views the ancient Greek polis as the first concrete historical embodiment of Spirit because of its living interplay between the individual citizens and the organic community they made up, an interplay between particular and universal that mirrors Spirit's own dynamic. What held the polis together was *Sittlichkeit*, the realm of ethical being that also has the connotation of customariness. This ethical realm of the polis, Hegel tells us, had two dimensions: the divine law governing the family and ancestor worship, and the human law whose sphere was the "daylight sway" of government and public life. Both laws participated in the ethical realm, but the divine law did so only in an elementary and unconscious way, in contrast with the conscious ethical being of public life.

The conflict in Greek tragedy between the divine law of the archaic gods governing family life and the more properly ethical human law of public life was, for Hegel, the first historical actualization of the interplay between Subject and Substance that he argues provides the structure of historical progress and moves throughout all subsequent historical developments. The human law, which carries forward the pursuit of freedom, tends toward the Subject side of the interaction, whereas the divine law tends toward the realm of Substance. The divine law of the old hearth religion and "the community of the dead" wells up and evolves out of mere nature or "life" into the archaic religion, reminding us that, for Hegel, "life" is not the inert fodder for transformation by the Machiavellian and Baconian project for the mastery of nature, but is more akin to the organicist life-world of Spinoza and Schelling. The welling up of life as the oldest chthonic religion of the ancestors displays a continuous evolution from nature into civilization, the wider and more adequate account of the evolution of the Master–Slave encounter out of the prehuman struggle for survival limned in the first rendition of the shapes of consciousness. The divine law forms the earliest civilization of the polis, of the worship of the earth and the dead venerated in the hearth-religion in which the Greek household formed a kind of family church in which the ancestors, literally buried beneath the hearth-fire, were "fed" by the food the family members cooked. As an organic evolution out of life, the realm of the family and the ancestors is a passive form of Spirit in which the individual is submerged in a chain of immemorial custom and deference to the past.

Emerging out of this shadowy realm into the daylight of the agora, by contrast, is the human law, the new sphere of what will become the classical age, with its emphasis on civic life, philosophic culture and the emergence of anthropomorphic Olympian gods. At first, although its element was the open daylight of the agora, the human law remained rooted in the underlying loam and darkness of the divine law, battening off its ancient traditions to maintain its sense of community: "The publicly manifest Spirit has the root of its power in the nether world. The self-certainty and self-assurance of a nation" is bound "solely in the mute unconscious substance of all, the waters of forgetfulness" [474]. Hegel sees a symbiotic interdependence between the newer realm of reason and the older realm of passive immersion in unreflecting tradition and lack of self-awareness, symbolized by his allusion here to the waters of Lethe, a river running through Hades.

But from the outset, there is a tension between the two realms, which grows ever more acute and finally reaches an open clash. The divine law revolves around the household and the family, but the human law is primarily about public life and political affairs, "because it is only as a citizen that the individual is actual and substantial; insofar as he is not a citizen but belongs to the family, he is only an unreal impotent shadow" – surely a reference to the Kingdom of the Shades in Hades. Further: "The *Community*, the upper law whose validity is open to the light of day, has its real vitality in government ... Government is the reality of Spirit ... the simple *Self* of the entire ethical substance" [451, 455]. In contrast with the passivity of the divine law, the newer human law was active and aggressive. It freed younger talents to outshine their elders. Hegel may have in mind as an example the conflict Thucydides presents between the daring young imperialist Alcibiades, who convinced the Athenians to mount the ill-fated Sicilian expedition over the objections of the older and more moderate Nicias. For Hegel, Spirit expresses itself in the essence of the polis *both* as the divine law and the human law, although they are not in harmony. The communal dimension to history's unfolding represented by the divine law is of no less importance than the "labor of the negative," emerging with the human law, that transforms nature outwardly in the pursuit of freedom, an immanent communality that continues to reemerge down to the present.

For Hegel, Greek tragedy is the crossroads where the conflicting forces of the divine and human law intersect, clash and tear us apart. Characteristically, Hegel's discussions of the tragedies are no more than allusive, since, like every other dimension of the history of Spirit, a strain of tragic consciousness remains with us even now, making his treatment of it not exclusively historical or chronological. Only Oedipus is named, but there are clear references as well to Antigone and Orestes. In the tragic view of life as Hegel depicts it, man is existentially guilty. His will and his intentions are of no consequence compared to the cycles of fate, and his heroism consists of bearing up nobly under this insuperable necessity. Oedipus believes Apollo is his patron because he triumphs through the use of his mind, but he goes down as Dionysus, blinded by his own hand, for his overweening pride. His blood sacrifice enables Apollo to reemerge fresh and reinvigorated.

Aristotle's theory of tragedy in the *Poetics* focuses on the flaw in the main protagonist's character, leading to a disastrous error of judgement or a mistaken perception of the situation. Although open to interpretation, the concept of a flaw does seem to imply that such errors can in principle be avoided – that we are capable of assessing a situation accurately rather than inaccurately, and also of moderating our passions so that they do not carry us away in our actions. Nietzsche is usually credited with being the first thinker to go behind Aristotle's assumption of our capacity to take responsibility for our judgements and actions and suggest that a tragic protagonist like Oedipus is really at the mercy of powerful forces of necessity and chance in the world at large that issue through him and sweep him into a doomed sequence of events. In fact, the more Oedipus seeks clear knowledge about the murder of Laius, the more he makes his own downfall inevitable. As I have suggested elsewhere, Thebes may need an aggressive, ambitious and brainy ruler like Oedipus to serve its own interests – qualities that make his statesmanship indistinguishable from tyranny. At the same time, Oedipus has to be brought low because his overweening ambition offends the gods and makes him a danger to his fellow citizens, especially his dynastic partners in power led by Creon. There may be no way out of this dilemma, and no way that Oedipus could have stood apart from it. As Plato depicts the soul, it is like a chariot in which the charioteer of the mind can and should steer the horses of passion in order to guide the chariot safely on its journey. But tragedy asks: What if it is the case that what we take to be our minds and our conscious intentions are the mere consequences of what our passions drive us to, and that it is the very clash of these passions with the irrationality of the world at large that maintains their dynamic equilibrium?

In my view, the degree to which Nietzsche's understanding of Greek tragedy is anticipated by that of Hegel has not been sufficiently appreciated. Hegel writes that Oedipus' "guilt is not an indifferent, ambiguous affair, as if the deed as actually seen in the light of day could, or perhaps could not, be the action of the self," in other words a course of action that could be chosen or not chosen once Oedipus fully understood the situation. Nor is it the case that "something external and accidental" was "linked" to Oedipus' action "that did not belong to it," such that the "action would be innocent." In other words, the fact that Oedipus did not know the truth about his own origins did not excuse him from being guilty of patricide, regicide and incest. Destiny "does not reveal the whole truth ... [T]he son does not recognize his father in the man who has wronged him and who he slays, nor his mother in the queen whom he makes his wife." But that ignorance about the truth, even though not Oedipus' fault, nevertheless does not enable him to "deny the crime or his guilt." His guilt is inseparable from the totality of his actions, regardless of his lack of foreknowledge. Through his ambition to solve the murder of Laius and thereby preserve his reputation as a great ruler, "what was unmoved has been set in motion, and what ... was locked up in mere possibility has been brought out into the open," linking "the unconscious and the conscious." Like the symbiotic relationship between the divine and the human law, Oedipus' action is brought out from the darkness of destiny "into the light of day," but it is still rooted in the dark and unable to escape its grip [468–469]. He is guilty because he exists.

Greek tragedy is a manifestation of the civilization of the polis in its pre-Platonic epoch, before the emergence of the Platonic and Aristotelian conception that each of us has a soul that can be governed by the mind, and that therefore we have the ability and responsibility to choose right over wrong actions. According to this new perspective, the philosophical crystallization of the Ethical Law, Oedipus could have controlled his rage and thereby avoided killing his father, just as we are told in the *Republic* that spiritedness properly educated in civic virtue can be the ally of reason in the defense of justice, and is governed by it. This capacity for choosing virtue over vice through deliberation is the basis for the possibility of civic virtue and the political community. According to Hegel, the divine law must inevitably be circumscribed by the self-consciously ethical human law; the primacy of the household and clan supplanted by the primacy of citizenship.

Hegel intersperses his allusions to Greek tragedy with possible references to what was actually happening historically during the classical age. The clash between the ethical and the divine at the core of tragedy was also being enacted in reality: Sophocles' *Oedipus the Tyrant* is simultaneously a parable for the ages and arguably a veiled portrait of the great imperial statesman Pericles, or an allegory for the hubris of Athens' rise to empire and its tragic nemesis through the catastrophes of the Plague and the Sicilian Expedition, followed by its eventual defeat by Sparta. On the other hand, Hegel observes, the government "must from time to time shake" the devotees of the realm of the divine law "to their core by war." Otherwise, they get "rooted and settled" in their households and ancestor worship and resist participation in the ethical realm of public life, "submerged in a merely natural existence ... in the realm of the nether world," another reference to the Kingdom of the Dead [455]. This passage is sometimes cited out of context as evidence that Hegel was a militarist who believed that war was a healthy experience for modern society, forcing people to overcome bourgeois self-interest in the name of patriotism. But in my view, it refers only to the era of the Greek polis under consideration, and in all likelihood refers specifically to the Persian wars or the Peloponnesian War. Speaking in the historical present tense, Hegel is arguing that at this period of Spirit's unfolding, the placid submergence of the individual in the community of the dead needed to be galvanized by war, which summoned from the city-states a new emphasis on individual and often youthful merit in military and political leadership, bypassing more moderate elders like Nicias in Athens and Archedamus in Sparta, both of whom feared the destabilizing effects of war on society's internal ordering.

When Themistocles built the Long Walls to insulate Athens from a land attack by Sparta, it involved bringing people in from the countryside. The overcrowding may have led to the outbreak of the Plague in 430 BC, but it also disrupted the old hearth religion in the village homesteads of Attica, and many people believed the Plague was the gods' punishment for Athens' injustice in provoking the war. This is a clear illustration of what Hegel means by the radicalizing effects of war, and how technological improvements demanded by the public sphere constituted a direct assault on the old chthonic morality. It is likely that Hegel has the Plague in mind when he says that when the right of "the dead" is denied by the disruption of the hearth, they "find instruments of vengeance" when the altars have been "defiled" by corpses eaten by dogs or birds: "They rise up in hostility and destroy the community that has dishonored ... the sacred claims of the Family" [474]. The clash between the divine and human laws being carried out in real life in this era is perhaps most clearly crystallized in the *Antigone*, where Creon "passes from the divine law, within whose realm he lived, over to the human law. The sister, however, becomes, or the wife remains, director of the home and preserver of the divine law" [459]. As the ruler, Creon must execute her brother for treason to the state. As his sister, she must seek the burial rites for him prescribed by the old morality by returning him to the womb of the earth with the other ancestors. The tragedy is that both are justified.

We have observed that Hegel's portrayal of the symbiotic interaction between the divine law and the human law strikingly anticipates Nietzsche's presentation of the relationship between the Dionysian and the Apollonian, which we will consider in detail in Chapter 3. In both cases, the realm of rationality and freedom wrenches itself out of its dependence on the realm of tragic passion and fate and seeks to dominate it. In both cases, the triumph of reason, which is inherently universalistic, sounds the death knell for the tribal society of the polis. But whereas for Nietzsche this is cause for regret over the loss of the tragic age of the Greeks in its heroic splendor, for Hegel it is a development that must take place if history is to advance. As Spirit develops itself, it also undermines itself. As Spirit "in itself," life in its earliest phase was a repeating cycle of mere passive happenings, the currents of coming into being and ceasing to exist. As it finds a locus within the midst of life to wrench itself out of those passive cycles of nature and custom and assert its negating energy, it becomes Spirit "for itself," the engine of historical progress. Within the limitations of the tragic experience of the Greeks, the clash between Antigone and Creon is irresolvable, an existential conflict between the claims of the family and the claims of the state. For Hegel, however, the progress of history has to resolve that conflict in favor of the authority of the state, in favor of Creon over Antigone. As the world states of Alexander and Rome supersede the old clan society of the polis, the family is increasingly confined to the private sphere, while public life becomes paramount. As always in Hegel's dialectic, however, the sphere of private family life and its emotional attachments are never simply erased, but enrich the quality of our lives and bolster our incentive to promote the common good in the present.

As his insights into Greek tragedy illustrate, Hegel had a deep admiration for and understanding of classical literature, which he regarded as indispensable to a liberal education. Moreover, his interest in the religion of the ancient Greeks, especially in its archaic form, was something that set him apart from Enlightenment *philosophes* such as Voltaire and Diderot, whose interest in the ancients centered on the rationalism of Socrates, Plato and Aristotle. However, it is also unambiguously the case – in a way that it is not for his successors Marx, Nietzsche and Heidegger – that Hegel identified himself as a believing Christian, and pronounced Christianity to be the "absolute religion" of the modern age. He regarded the "art-religion" of ancient Greece (tragedy and comedy) as the highest religion possible short of revealed (that is, Abrahamic) religion, which he ranked highest. The progression from art-religion to revealed religion paralleled the progression from a view of life centered on the individual self-consciousness as it evolves toward Spirit to an awareness that, as religion, Spirit becomes fully conscious of itself through its human participants. But he ranked Christianity as the highest among the three Abrahamic faiths.

Why is this so? We have already observed that the equality of man before the Creator God set the trajectory for historical progress. We also observed that for Hegel, the modern elevation of free will as the basis for moral autonomy would not have been possible without the transference to human agency of God's capacity to stand outside of and oppose his will to nature and transform it. In Hegel's view, however admirable was the classical account of the soul with its harmony of the mind and the affects, it did not strictly speaking include the concept of free will, which in his view is unique to modernity and has a religious source. However, to reemphasize an earlier point, I do not believe Hegel wishes to be taken as viewing modern freedom as the "secularization" of a religious concept into a purely anthropocentric or humanistic one, such that its original religious garb can now be discarded as history moves forward. Instead, as we have seen, Hegel is arguing that *Geist*, the totality of the historical process in its dynamism, unfolds itself as human freedom and constitutes the "self-actualization" of God.

In Hegel's historicism, the world expresses itself as temporal change actualized through its human avatars, transforming nature and human nature, assimilating the will of God to the "self-origination" of the world. Hegel's characterization of existence as a "self-originating wealth of shapes" bears an ontological resemblance, as we saw earlier, to the God who says: "I am what/ that I am." In contrast with early modern thought's reduction of reason to instrumental rationality and self-interest, historicism offered a new basis for the unity of the self with the other, namely the historical community, an organic unity based on the dynamism of the historical origins rather than the eternally given telos of the ancient cosmologies. Thus, to reiterate: By identifying wisdom about the whole with grasping it as self-origination, Hegel collapses the traditional distinction and debate between reason and revelation. When Hegel sketches the Substance side of the Unity of Subject and Substance, while he groups under it a variety of ancient and modern thinkers, significantly it is Spinoza whom he explicitly identifies (although not by name) as the thinker who "shocked a generation" by identifying God with the world, tantamount to destroying the distinction between the sacred and the profane, a heresy in all three of the monotheistic revealed religions, and grounds for Spinoza's "excommunication" by the Jews of Amsterdam. Into the life-world of Spinoza, emerging continuously out of nature toward the aspects of Godhead, and thus repudiating the dualism of Hobbes and Descartes, Hegel introduces the aggressive dimension of progressive outward historical transformation, the introduction of the "labor of the negative" into Schelling's quietistic Spinoza-inspired "Absolute."

Christianity alone of the revealed religions is the Absolute Religion because it is the symbolization of Spirit's dynamic, schematized as the Unity of Subject and Substance, by which Spirit opposes itself to itself and achieves unity through the "death" or negation of that distinction, a process by which it is cumulatively enriched. Christ represents man's alienation or separation from God, but also reveals that God has alienated himself from himself. The Good Friday of the Crucifixion achieves the Easter of resurrection and reconciliation and Christ's return to God, and man is forever changed. As we observed in our discussion of the Concept of Spirit, this "death of death" is powerfully conveyed in the Preface when Hegel characterized the Understanding as "the most astonishing and greatest" of powers, and that although "death" is the most terrible of experiences, only by facing death through negation can "Beauty" emerge into a new and lasting life. Hegel once shared with Schiller the view that there must be an opposition between a love of beauty and the divine and the corrosive power of modern analytical reasoning, but in the *Phenomenology* he moves beyond this position. To reiterate his formulation in the Preface from a Christian perspective [32]: "[T]he life of Spirit is not one that shuns death and keeps clear of destruction. It endures death and in death maintains its being. It only wins to its truth when it finds itself utterly torn asunder . . . the magic power that converts the negative into being." There could not be a clearer analogy between the moments of Spirit and the Crucifixion as the death of God as Christ, "torn asunder" on the Cross, who then rises from the dead and promises us all immortal life through his sacrifice, a "magic" or miraculous power – although, for Hegel, our immortality will not be eternal life after death with God, but instead our complete absorption of the "infinity" of Spirit's ever richer journey toward fulfillment. It would only be another example of the multiple levels on which Hegel writes if we were also to liken the regeneration of life through death in this passage to Dionysus being "torn asunder" by his maenads, thus fertilizing and reviving the world with his sacrifice.

Hegel displayed great respect for both Judaism and Islam and did much to advance scholarly interest in their histories, whatever one may think of his interpretation of them. But he was convinced that, because in his view they posited a permanent and insuperable chasm between the Creator God and the world of man, they could never achieve the synthesis of the human and the divine, the mediating unity symbolized by Christ. There is no way of establishing precisely what kind of believer Hegel was, but there is also no way of knowing for certain that he did not sincerely embrace Christianity as he re-envisioned it, any more than one could say this with complete certainty about Spinoza's understanding of God. While Hegel's Christianity may arguably have been a kind of deism or pantheism that was not in keeping with any traditional understanding of revealed religion, there is no reason to suppose, given his graduation from the Tubingen Seminary, his self-identification as a Lutheran, and his voluminous writings on religion that he did not take it completely seriously.

Before we leave the topic of Hegel's faith behind, a word should be said about the penultimate section of the *Phenomenology*, on Religion. Insofar as the book provides a chronological account of history, Hegel had already completed it in his discussion of Schiller and God's reappearance in our age, coming full circle back to the argument between Science and Romanticism in the Preface. At this point, one might have expected that he would proceed straight to the concluding section on Absolute Knowledge, where he provides a rapid coda stressing the unity of rational Spirit and Christian revelation by arguing that the Trinity is the embodiment of the Concept, whereby the "content" of Spirit "has received the shape of self." Instead, he once again hurtles us back into the most distant past, as he did previously when retracing the progress of history from the perspective of Spirit.

Now we go further back than ever, into the remotest origins of religious history including Persian, Indian and Egyptian sources, and yet another take on the chthonic religion of the polis and its displacement by the Olympians. In this version, however, the external manifestations of the Ethical (Human) Law in the public life of the polis and its tension with the older legacy of the Divine

(Natural) Law are largely left aside, while Hegel attempts instead to plumb religion in its innermost psychic depths, including its relationship to the revelations of art. It is almost as if he is suggesting that religion might be the *most* profound, the deepest source of self-consciousness – which is to say, the world's consciousness of itself, eclipsing even the concept of Spirit. Alternatively, he may be suggesting that religion is the deepest and most profound level of Spirit's own history. Although it is beyond the scope of our inquiry to explore its riches, the peculiar character of this section should be stressed. For it is anything but a conventional history of religion or of theology, despite the exhaustive knowledge of these subjects that Hegel displays elsewhere. Instead, it is an existential mélange of religious, poetic and mythic archetypes and psychological symbolism. I will briefly sketch its main contours as regards the ancient polis.

The tragic conflict between the Ethical Law and the older Divine Law, between the newer Olympian gods and the older religion of the ancestors, is resolved by the supremacy of Zeus in the Olympian pantheon. Zeus is the bringer of peace and justice, the balancer of reason and fate, the king of both gods and mortals, patron of both the civic life of the polis *and* the ancestral family. However, in comparison with the universal supremacy of Zeus, the individuality of the other, lesser Olympian gods is reduced to flaws and vices like those of humans. Tragedy thereby gives way to comedy, which debunks the old traditions and pokes fun at both gods and human beings for falling short of their pretensions to merit. The tragic splendor of Achilles' or Oedipus' clash with divine Destiny is now reduced to a catalogue of merely human passions that can be poked fun at for their foolishness – as Socrates depicts him, Achilles is an adolescent cry-baby and whiner.

Hegel makes it clear that he prefers comedy over tragedy because, by debunking both religious and human affairs, it elevates critical reason over veneration for tradition, pointing the way to the progress of freedom. Meanwhile, because the gods have been debunked, the virtues they were once thought to embody – Athena and wisdom, Ares and courage – are detached from them and become "clouds" (likely a reference to Aristophanes' comedy), in other words, abstract ideas or speeches, leading to philosophy. Comedy, Hegel strikingly argues, points the way to Christianity, which, in its proclamation of the son of God, also equates the divine with the human. The "death of God" – Christ's crucifixion – is not tragic because it is followed by his resurrection, and offers everyone the hope for eternal life. Therefore, while the synthesis of God and man is not exactly comical, it shares ancient comedy's optimism about our ability to transcend the past and aim for a better future. For Hegel, just as for Plato, comedy is relatively more kindred with philosophy than is tragedy.

Still, the reader is left wondering: Why precisely does Hegel complete his phenomenology of history with the theme of religion, whose chronological periods he has already covered (with, for example, his discussion of the

Unhappy Consciousness), and why does he present it in this unusual way, more evocative of art and poetry than a sober exegesis of the biblical and theological content of revelation? The answer may lie in his original evocation of the Romantic countermovement against modern empiricism in the Preface. Although he acknowledged its thirst for profound truths like Love and Beauty to compensate for the arid desert of empiricism, he also lamented the fact that these sentiments frequently lapsed into mere vapidity and sentimentality, because they lacked the richness of content that the empirical stance toward the world could achieve through analytical rationality. Perhaps his vivid, highly "pictorial" sketch of the history of religious archetypes embedded in our collective psyche is aimed at this failing in the Romantic temperament, urging it to find in religious ethnography and symbolism the psychological depth it might otherwise lack or restrict to purely contemporary experiences.

In short, the examination of religion with which the *Phenomenology* ends is arguably the catalyst for education as "recollection" at its most primordial. It is aimed at the frivolity and boredom that he argued in the Preface characterize the present age, and now that God has reappeared in history, it provides an antidote for that disenchantment. The way forward from today's (for Hegel) cultural malaise and recent political violence and warfare is the way back to the essence of religious experience. It lends force to the argument that the *Phenomenology* is above all a pedagogical classic, aimed primarily at cultural renewal as opposed to a pragmatic set of specific political reforms – although, as we will now consider, definite political implications do follow from the Hegelian account of history.

HISTORY AND POLITICAL LIFE

As we began this chapter by observing, Hegel's historicism evolved as a critical response to the dualistic theories of Rousseau and Kant. His argument that Spirit contains within itself all distinctions of thought and action leads to a number of specific criticisms of these thinkers. As against Rousseau, Hegel maintains that we never encounter human nature that has not already been mediated by freedom and political authority, and as against Kant, that we never encounter the will to freedom that has not already been mediated by nature. These distinctions between nature and freedom are valid analytically but, as aspects of the historical process in its entirely, they are one-sided "abstractions from Spirit."

Whereas Rousseau, as we saw in Chapter 1, argued that the social contract limits man's natural freedom, an unavoidable but undesirable compromise, Hegel maintains that there is no historical proof that Rousseau's state of nature ever existed. In reality, there *is* no freedom without the restraint of the state – otherwise life would be sheer brutality and violence. To this extent, then, Hegel endorses Hobbes' view of the state of nature over that of Rousseau – a limited endorsement, of course, since in Hegel's view, Hobbes had no conception of the thorough historicity of human experience, but was limited by the early modern assumption of the existence of isolated individuals as a permanent underlying substratum of behavior. In Hegel's view, Rousseau reads back into an imaginary original condition a capacity for freedom that can only develop progressively through history. Again, for Hegel the Golden Age is not a lost happiness from which historical progress is alienating us but is its final outcome. Because political right only exists in history and not in an alleged original natural condition, it is impossible to introduce a "perfect" constitution of pure abstract freedom and rights severed from a people's historical context. That was the error committed by the Jacobins when they tried to implement literally overnight Rousseau's doctrine of the General Will and return to the Year One.

At the same time, Hegel argues, nothing great can be accomplished in history without passion, self-interest and – frequently – violence. Kant's identification of freedom with a purely "disinterested" stance is therefore completely false as an account of how good can be achieved. Even an ideal must be *my* ideal. For Hegel, Kant's admission that an act fully in accordance with the Categorical Imperative may never have yet occurred in human history is self-evident proof that he sets the bar for ethical purity of intention so high as to define itself out of having any impact at all. Spirit's unfolding is advanced by the passion of human statesmen and conquerors, who expect honor and riches for themselves as rewards for their benefit to others. Indeed, Spirit itself is *like* a passion – dynamic, mutable, changing. "World-historical" individuals effect a general civilizational advancement as they pursue their selfish aims – Caesar made the Republic into a world state; Napoleon spread the moderate Girondist liberalism of the French Revolution throughout Europe by conquest. Spirit uses them, becomes their "master passion," then discards them like husks. According to Hegel, the ethical ideal cannot be an abstraction at a remove from historical reality, as Kant argued, but is embodied in it. Even in the best of worlds to come, there will be pain, hunger, crime, coercion and death. The end of history is not a utopia.

The final form that Spirit assumes is the modern state: This is the end of history. It embodies the unity of Subject and Substance by uniting the subjective, passionate side of Spirit with its substantive completion through civic life. The modern state embodies Spirit as a dynamic whole made up of living parts, the reconciliation of the Is and the Ought. It is not, as the early moderns had argued, a social contract between separate individuals and a government umpire. Instead, law and morality mediate between the individual and the state, and thereby complete our freedom. The state is not a mere instrument for self-preservation, but an organic whole, the living embodiment of the Concept of Spirit. As history unfolds through the rule of one to the rule of few or some to the rule of the many (preferably, for Hegel, under a constitutional monarchy), Spirit overcomes itself repeatedly, absorbing more and more content – Stoicism giving way to Christianity which in turn yields modern liberalism – and so does the state. Within the state, certain activities provide bonds between its legal framework and the people. Through its religion, the people have a perspective on the divine operations of Spirit not only in their own country but throughout the world, which encourages them to transcend their subjectivity. Art – which, like Schiller, Hegel believes the state has a duty to promote – renders the divine in sensuous form, so that a statue can embody the spirit of an entire age, or its access to God. Finally, philosophy, at least for an educated elite, allows us to contemplate Spirit in its whole dynamic, comprehending it theoretically in conjunction with religion and art. Generally speaking, though, it is religion that primarily defines a people; it precedes and informs any political constitution. Hence, for Hegel, a society is unlikely to embrace whole-heartedly the secular values of liberal individualism unless it has already been shaped by the spiritual inwardness of the Reformation. Unlike modern social contract theorists such as Hobbes and Locke, therefore, Hegel does not believe that it is possible to account for liberal contractualism or the rights of man in purely theoretical terms – to be successful, it requires the underlying seed-bed of Protestant character formation.

In the coming synthesis, the nation-state will emerge as an organic mingling of political, aesthetic, religious and cultural bonds. The nation-state will educate and acculturate. It will embody the history and traditions of a people, or of an association of peoples, so as to mediate the abstract, universalistic and sometimes distant relationship between the state's representative institutions and its citizens. The healing force of religion in history, reconciling the sometimes seemingly hopeless antagonism between Understanding and Love – between rights and community, or the Is and the Ought – is the ultimate basis for Hegel's hopes for a renewed sense of civic community within the prevailing world-view of modernity.

Hegel attempts to synthesize what we now term liberalism and communitarianism by arguing that the nation-state embodies the modern universalistic principles of rights and legitimacy in the distinct historical evolution of particular peoples. In this way, the nation-state is the best hope for avoiding the characteristic extremes of modernity – the Jacobin utopianism which tries to destroy all vestiges of traditional historical community, and the tribal nationalism that tries to liberate the existentially authentic "people" by dismantling the overlay of Enlightenment modernity. Accordingly, just as Hegel's successors attempt, as we will see, to dismantle the Hegelian synthesis by deconstructing its polarities and exaggerating either our direct, tacit and unmediated immersion in the immanent wholeness of the life-world (the realm of Love) or our untrammeled subjective power to assert our wills over this life-world and reconstruct it (the realm of Understanding), so do they, as the political and civic corollary of this ontological critique, tend to attack the legitimacy of the nation-state as the concrete embodiment of Spirit, pulling it apart either in the direction of globalizing rationalism or tribal blood and belonging.

TERROR AND DIALECTIC: CONCLUDING REFLECTIONS ON THE
STRUCTURE OF HEGEL'S *PHENOMENOLOGY*

To sum up the pedagogical aim of the *Phenomenology*: Spirit, which can also
be depicted as the mind, returns to its origins through recollection so as to
recapture its original longing for a satisfying account of the whole. It reintegrates the fragmented knowledge of the modern epoch with that immanent
continuum of the organic cycles of life, community and culture. But at the same
time, that immanent continuum is galvanized and energized by the still-
thrusting negativity of the autonomous and skeptical modern consciousness.
Not only does adequate thinking in the present continuously reenact this cycle
of alienation and reconciliation as mediated progressively by the organic heritage of recollected historical shapes, but it unfolds simultaneously as the historical fruition of mankind's ascent, both collectively and individually.

A reader might wonder at this point whether by emphasizing Hegel's enthusiasm for liberal education and the recollection of our classical and religious
heritage, and by stressing that the main purpose of the phenomenological
ascent is pedagogical, I am to some extent defanging Hegel, as it were, by
emphasizing the pacific, conciliatory, Schellingean and Schillerian dimension of
his thinking at the expense of what Hegel himself terms "the slaughter-bench"
of history – the awesome and awful clash of ambitions, passions and selfish
interests, the power to rend and reconstruct nature, that understandably cap-
tivated the Left Hegelian school of Marx and his successors Lukacs and Kojeve.
I have already stressed that the "labor of the negative" deserves as much
emphasis in Hegel's dialectic of history as the teleological result of that process.
In interpreting the *Phenomenology* as a pedagogical classic, one must at all
times bear in mind that, for Hegel, only by seeing history without illusion as an
outwardly violent, often dreadful process of creative destruction can we retain a
realistic basis for any optimism we might entertain regarding the improvement
of mankind and the world. This hard-headedness about the real world of power
constitutes Hegel's respectful but decisive repudiation, as we have observed, of
Schiller's exclusive emphasis on aesthetic cultivation. But it has to be admitted
from the outset that Hegel's educational enterprise makes sense only to the
extent that we are persuaded that the teleological unfolding of history is indeed
gradually healing the modern Rousseauan dichotomy between nature and
reason, or nature and freedom, making possible a return to the classical contention that education should aim at human wholeness without sacrificing modernity's gains in individual autonomy, constitutional government and scientific
knowledge.

Can we be persuaded of this historical teleology today? When Hegel argued
that history was in a sense reaching its culmination in 1807, that was because
he was looking back to the Terror of 1793 and the ensuing carnage of the
Napoleonic Wars. To him, this was the worst kind of violence imaginable in
human history, an episode so terrible that, because of its shock value, would

never have to be repeated. Standing on the other side of the millions of victims of totalitarianism and genocide, this is impossible for us to affirm today. Given the horrors of the two world wars, of Auschwitz and the Gulag, Hiroshima and ISIS, is it possible to see our own world as developing toward the reconciliation of Understanding and Love, of Subject and Substance? The ideological sanctions for sadism implicit in the Jacobin Terror – the methodical, cold-blooded extermination of class and later racial enemies – have expanded and intensified in a way that no one in Hegel's era would have imagined possible. Given that the polarization between the fanatical extremisms of Left and Right that Hegel believed would dissipate during the nineteenth century in fact grew unimaginably worse during the twentieth and have continued into the twenty-first, Hegel himself, as Emil Fackenheim argued, would probably not be a Hegelian were he alive today. Who would dare to argue, as Hegel had about the Jacobin Terror, that the Holocaust or Hiroshima were regrettable but necessary steps toward the consolidation of liberal democracy, in the same way that Hegel had argued that the Terror constituted a necessary albeit excessive moment in the progress of history by expediting the passing of the *ancien régime*?

A literal-minded reading of the *Phenomenology* as nothing more than a chronological history might well prompt us to ask whether the section called "Absolute Freedom and Terror," referring to the French Revolution culminating in the Terror of 1793, is adequate in any way for understanding the horrors of genocide and totalitarianism in the twentieth and twenty-first centuries. After all, the comparatively small scale of the Terror in comparison to the "industrialized murder" of subsequent totalitarian regimes, as well as Hegel's conviction that such terror need not be repeated, might well lead readers to believe the *Phenomenology* to have been outmoded by the actual unfolding of European and global history, which Hegel plainly did not anticipate. But if my interpretation of the book has merit – that it is both a historical chronology and a cognitive map of the mind – the section on absolute freedom and terror is about far more than the specific events of 1793 in France. At a deeper level, it is arguably about a disturbing built-in tendency of modernity. The Jacobin Terror was only the most vivid example to hand. As usual, Hegel keeps the precise historical connection vague. There are allusions to the General Will, the Law of Suspects (in which to be accused of being a counterrevolutionary was tantamount to proof of guilt), and to testing out the guillotine on a cabbage head, but not much more, and no references to individual personalities such as Robespierre. In this way, Hegel is reminding us that this disturbing tendency reverberates far beyond those literal events and may well lurk as one of the darker components of the modern personality even after 1793. As he writes elsewhere: "Nothing vanishes in Spirit."

What Hegel foresees in the Terror, I suggest, is a crisis tendency in modernization that we might term, in light of the ensuing century's horrors, the struggle between the People and the Party – the primordial urge for collectivistic tribalism versus the project for the extension of technological rationality and control over the entire globe. The Party and the People are anticipated by Hegel's analysis of the Terror and what he sees as its attempt to implement literally Rousseau's doctrine of the General Will. Each continually collapses the other – the Terror tries to impose final control, the General Will subverts every attempt at order:

What is called government is merely the *victorious* faction, and in the very fact of its being a faction lies the direct necessity of its overthrow; and its being a government makes it, conversely, into a faction, and guilty ... Universal freedom can thus produce neither a positive achievement nor a deed; there is left for it only negative action; it is merely the rage and fury of destruction.

The drive for "absolute freedom" must obliterate the distinction between the individual and the collective. The title of the section "Absolute Freedom and Terror" is therefore not so much about two distinct political phenomena but about why the second is the inevitable consequence of the first: "Spirit thus comes before us as *Absolute Freedom* ... all reality is solely spiritual; the world is for it simply its own will and this is a General Will." The allusion here to Rousseau's General Will and its aim to make "all reality ... solely spiritual" reminds us that, as we observed in Chapter 1, Rousseau regarded man's faculty of freedom as what distinguished him "spiritually" from all other living beings, enabling him to rise above material self-interest. It is a striking measure of the political conservatism of Hegel's stance that he regards the Rousseauan attempt to make freedom the chief aim of civic life, however well-intentioned, an unmitigated disaster. What is common to Hegel's analysis of the Terror and to later totalitarian and genocidal politics is the drive to eliminate all the mediating bonds of civil society. His analysis of the in-built extremist tendencies of modernization therefore resonate far beyond the actual events of 1793, and could be used to characterize with equal validity the Bolshevik, National Socialist and Khmer Rouge totalitarian projects: "This undivided substance of absolute freedom ascends the throne of the world without any power being able to resist it ... In this absolute freedom, therefore, all social groups or classes ... are abolished ... Its purpose is the general purpose."

As the reference to "the throne of the world," earlier used to characterize the Roman Emperor as the fullest realization of ancient mastery, indicates – along with a reference to the Terror as "the lord and master Death" – modernization through terror constitutes the pure drive for the mastery of human nature from the Subject side of the Unity of Subject and Substance, now run amok, free of all limitations from the Substance pole of the dialectic. The pure autonomy of the will requires the destruction of human nature torn utterly asunder from the customary constraints of *Sittlichkeit*:

The sole work and deed of universal freedom is therefore *Death*, a death too which has no inner significance or filling, for what is negated is the empty point of the absolutely free will ... [It is] pure negation utterly devoid of mediation, the negation ... of the individual as a factor existing within the universal.

A soundly educated (in Hegelian terms) citizen of today must surmount the horrors of genocide and tyranny by absorbing them intellectually and psychologically, sharpening one's sense of ethical condemnation by recognizing that these variants of millenarian extremism are not dead and buried monsters from a past happily left behind, but the dark side of modernity itself when "the labor of the negative," its imperative of destruction and re-creation, exceeds all bounds of moderation, prudence and respect for human beings. Hegel's conception of the modern nation-state that we examined earlier, essentially liberal and pluralistic, is designed as the antidote to the dangerous fantasies of the General Will.

That leads to another question a reader might raise about my interpretation of Hegel. Given the widespread assumption today in the intellectual world that a claim such as Hegel's to have unfolded the "Absolute Knowledge of Spirit" is neither philosophically possible nor politically desirable (for reasons we will examine more closely in the Conclusion), it is sometimes argued that one can set aside the metaphysical and ontological dimensions of Hegel's thinking and extract his pragmatic political prescriptions, which are closely equivalent to the moderate progressive liberalism of Burke, J. S. Mill or Tocqueville. But in my view, one cannot examine Hegel's thought as a whole, and understand the full reasoning behind those pragmatic claims, and above all about education, without attempting to see them within the context of his metaphysics and ontology at their most full-blown, not to say grandiose.

If Hegel had felt capable of expressing his political teaching in a Tocquevillian or Burkean – that is to say, non-metaphysical – manner, he would surely have done so, perhaps reserving his more purely philosophical speculations for a separate presentation. But he did not do so, and the reason for this is tied to his core vision of education as an erotic ascent. Like Plato, Hegel believes that pragmatic questions of justice, virtue and political authority both presuppose and inform fundamental philosophical differences over the structure of reality, the human mind and the longing for wisdom and immortality. For Plato, whatever may be the meaning of human nature and what that implies about justice, human nature is a part of nature, and therefore its place in that larger cosmic order must be reflected upon. Analogously for Hegel, if human existence is historical through and through, it can only be fully understood within the Spirit of the historical world as a whole. Moreover, again like Plato, Hegel does not believe that human beings can live optimally without the longing for transcendence – the transcendence of their bodily and egoistic selves in the direction of the divine. This is one of the crucial differences, in his view, between liberal political philosophy in the social contract mode of Locke and his own Ladder to the Absolute. Hegel is friendly to liberalism and wants to lend it a helping hand. But he is convinced that its individualistic account of man is psychologically barren and all too often leads to political expediency and cultural vulgarity. Hence, he wants to act as a friend to liberalism by coming to its aid on the basis of philosophical principles richer than its own.

Otherwise, he is certain, liberalism will not only tend to degenerate into materialism, but it will alienate the most thoughtful citizens. Every bit as much as for Plato, for Hegel education in the fullest sense is sped by the erotic longing for nobility and immortality.

Hegel is convinced that liberalism must be saved by being grounded in an ontology of intersubjectivity of which, left to itself, it is completely incapable. In his own philosophy, therefore, he is not capable of giving a straightforward practical account of moderate liberalism in the mode of Burke or Tocqueville. The metaphysics are indispensable. It follows from this that in order to encounter the full meaning of Hegel, we have to treat his metaphysics in tandem with his political philosophy, exactly as he does in his writings. That, as I have said, poses serious problems for a contemporary reader. On the other hand, it has become a commonplace that the longing for religious transcendence and communal belongingness is as strong today in the era of globalization as ever, if not stronger, arguably as a reaction against the homogenization of culture and technology's relentless war on tradition, community and an openness to the mysteries of feeling. To that extent, we remain alive to Hegel's contention that modern liberalism more than any previous political philosophy cries out for a link to the divine, to what transcends materialistic individualism, precisely because, more than any previous political philosophy, it appears to undermine or even expel it, leaving it to recrudesce in forms that either alienate people from civic life or drive them into millenarian projects that attempt to divinize politics.

MARX AND THE FIRST ASSAULT ON THE HEGELIAN MIDDLE

Marx begins a series of assaults on what Emil Fackenheim calls the Hegelian Middle, the grand edifice of Hegel's "Absolute Science/Knowledge" of Spirit meant to bridge the chasm between self the other, between the real and the ideal, and to stave off the political immoderation of the demand for radical revolution. These assaults continue in different but related ways by Nietzsche and Heidegger, as we will see in later chapters. All retain the fundamental ontological premise that existence is what Hegel termed "self-origination," a dynamic of all-encompassing historicity. For reasons we will explore, they reformulate this premise as species-being (Marx), Will to Power (Nietzsche) and the ontology of Being (Heidegger). They also agree that historicity expresses itself through and empowers its human avatars. In this way, the Philosophy of Freedom perseveres in its original search for what Hegel called intersubjectivity, a third term synthesizing the Rousseauan contradiction between nature and freedom through historical action.

Where they radically disagree with Hegel, however, is over his concept of the teleological progress of history as the "self-actualization of God" as Spirit. Marx is heralded by Feurbach, who argued that God is the measure of man's alienation from his own creative powers to transform the world for the material betterment of all. We must reclaim these powers by abolishing the belief in God. Politics, as Feurbach put it, must become our religion. An atheist and a materialist, he proclaimed that "compassion is before thought," turning compassion from a Christian duty into a project for its complete political actualization. The school of the Left Hegelians, initiated by Feurbach and Marx and developed by Lukas and Kojeve, agreed that man's creative powers must be taken back from Hegel's dialectic of Spirit, which, after originating with the understanding of history as the dynamic transformation of whatever limited human freedom, had turned in the end into an iron cage of determinism that supported the bourgeois status quo. We should note in this connection that the materialism of Feurbach and Marx is not merely epistemological or centered on the individual, as in the earlier debate between Idealism and materialism – the entire historical process is materialistic as well as collective.

To this, we might add that the Left Hegelian alternative was already lurking in an unresolved difficulty in the thought of Kant, as we touched upon earlier. His philosophy had aimed to establish an equipoise between nature and freedom. The Categorical Imperative was an ethic of intentionality to overcome the inclinations that could only strive to master nature without ever being fully able to do so: a being in which the Is was entirely surmounted by the Ought would be God. Nature, in other words, sets a permanent limiting condition on the exercise of human freedom. But we have already observed that, in the second formulation of the Categorical Imperative, Kant seems to open the door to the gradual improvement of the structure of reality itself, including the natural realm, by the exercise of the moral will, not merely a prescription for aspirational human behavior. Clearly Kant did not envision the unlimited historical transformation of existence. But Fichte took Kant's emphasis on freedom of will a step further and reduced the meaning of nature to "the material of our moral duty rendered sensuous." Nature, in other words, was now to be seen as sheer purposeless fodder for the open-ended reshaping of reality by the human will, in effect assimilating the meaning of reason itself, including the scientific study of nature, to this endless and Godlike projection of the will. Tellingly, when Fichte first published his theory anonymously, many assumed that it was Kant himself who was finally thinking through the radical implications of his own metaphysics of morals for the ceaseless negation of nature and for Christian revealed religion. This despite the fact that Kant's *Critique of Judgement*, in arguing that natural sentiments might be sublimated in the creation of aesthetic beauty, could be taken as distinguishing his position from the extreme voluntarism of Fichte's concept of the will. Hegel believed that his own ontology of the Unity of Subject and Substance in Spirit had anticipated and headed off this extremist voluntarism, which also fed the Jacobin tendency in modern politics to impose a rational pattern on human nature by direct action and revolutionary will, regardless of the constraints of precedent and tradition. Fichte, the ultimate proponent of man's untrammeled will to conquer and reshape nature, with man having no intrinsic or immanent connection with nature, is to my mind in effect the first Left Hegelian. As I have argued elsewhere, he, rather than Hegel, is the authentic philosophical precursor of Kojève.

One perspective on Marx is that he takes Hegel's concept of Spirit as the unity of Subject and Substance – the conceptual outline of the whole, within which we find the strictly human dimension of history embedded – and totally anthropomorphizes it. This involves re-leveraging Hegel's concept into a process entirely driven by the subjective side of the dialectic, and which is located solely in human action. History is then transformed from the kind of organic synthesis of aggressive and conciliatory forces envisioned by Hegel into nothing but the conquest and transformation of nature in the pursuit of freedom and material survival by human beings seeking power. Thus, whereas, for Hegel, the subject–object distinction is mediated within Spirit, because subject and object are both modalities of the unity of Subject and Substance – and because the human transformation of nature is an emanation of the larger, all-encompassing process of Spirit's negation of itself – for Marx, the subject-object distinction is one-sidedly created by man's labor on, and transformation of, nature. Since man's products embody his own creative powers, that labor is, you can say, objectifying, inasmuch as it invests our own creative powers in the products we make. But it isn't necessarily alienating – that only comes about under the conditions of capitalism.

Thus, whereas for Hegel, nature itself, as a dimension of Spirit, is already connected to Spirit as a kind of latent or passive version of the unity of Subject and Substance – what Hegel calls "life" or "Spirit in itself," including the teleology of nature and the emergence of the archaic family and religion of ancestor-worship – for Marx, nature is entirely alien and material stuff, empty of meaning or purpose, until purpose is imposed on it by man through labor (and labor can include art, philosophy and culture, not just material commodities). For Hegel, historical progress has been the cumulative working out of the unity of Subject and Substance interweaving and moving in tandem, the synthesis of the emerging Golden Age and the "slaughter-bench" of war, revolution and oppression. Just as no era of the past has been exclusively oppressive, the coming end of history will not be exclusively liberating. Marx, by contrast, identifies the entirety of history to date with the belligerence of the Subject side, with the labor of the negative to master nature and human nature, and identifies the coming end of history entirely with the Substance side – sheer collective freedom and the withering away of political authority and social inequality, a millenarian transformation.

Marx never embraced – indeed he strenuously rejected – the idea that socialism's appeal would be invalidated by capitalism's success at improving the living conditions of the workers. Reforms of the Keynesian or social democratic kind through the redistribution of income he anticipated and rejected as merely "better payment for the slave." Instead, the core of Marxism's appeal is the yearning for wholeness, for an existence that unites personal and collective satisfaction. In this respect, he is representative of the Philosophy of Freedom as a whole. Capitalism and its economic depredations are the most important symptoms of this lack of wholeness, but they are only symptoms. The collapse and supersession of capitalism are inevitable to Marx not because of a narrowly empirical development that can be predicted like the weather. These breakdowns are inevitable because capitalism must function by robbing man of a wholeness whose lack is, in the long run, unbearable to our species.

Before we turn to the central ideas of Marx's theory, a few words about context. I do not dwell on the biographical details of the thinkers discussed in this book, but they are sometimes relevant to a degree. Hegel was a university professor and his personal life was respectable and largely unremarkable. His audience was confined to the highly educated, and those people were rarely of low socioeconomic status. By contrast, Rousseau's philosophy was almost the chronicle of his tempestuous vagabond life as it unfolded – as I argued in Chapter 1, the core of his vision derived from an intensely personal experience on one of his "walks." Marx's life intertwined with his thought in a different way. Owing to the increasingly anti-liberal atmosphere of German universities, Marx could not find employment as an academic, and had to scratch out a living from journalism while moving between Brussels, France and England, with financial help from his wealthy friend Engels. This is why it is difficult to point to one or a few masterpieces among his writings where his entire political theory is systematically set forth. Instead, one has to look through dozens of occasional journalistic pieces, letters and pamphlets to construct a coherent account. He may have regarded *Capital* as his magnum opus, but I agree with many contemporary scholars that his concept of socialism and its presuppositions cannot be fleshed out without recourse to his early, so-called humanist writings.

We should add that, during the span of his life, the proletarian movement that Marx foresaw came into being. In 1875, the German Social Democratic Party embraced his theory of socialism, even though Marx did not wholly approve of their gradualism with respect to reform and their willingness to work within the parliamentary system. He was actively engaged in the workers' cause, including the prospects for a socialist revolution in Russia. He repudiated what he termed the "utopian socialism" of Saint-Simon and Robert Owen, along with the anarchist views of Proudhomme, dismissing them as naive for believing that small communes that had abolished private property rights would be allowed to exist in peace in the midst of powerful capitalist states with their police and military power, and for failing to see that by attempting to create Rousseau's "mutualist" Golden Age of the state of nature in the heart of modern capitalism, they could not acquire the means of production that would prevent their relapse into a struggle for survival in an economic environment of scarcity in which Marx believed history had originated. To this extent, like Hegel, his account of the origins was closer to Hobbes' state of nature than to that of Rousseau. But also like Hegel, as a historicist thinker Marx did not believe that human beings strictly speaking possessed any kind of fixed nature. Because Marx's socialism was, he argued, derived from an empirical analysis of capitalism, it was "scientific," not utopian.

Finally, we should note that of all the thinkers we consider in this book, Marx was arguably the least nostalgic about or admiring of the ancient Greek polis and its culture. For Marx, history was driven by class conflict, and whatever pretensions the Greek polis had to fostering communal harmony was only an ideological disguise for the exploitation of the ruled by the rulers in a slave economy. His doctoral dissertation was on the Democratean and Epicurean philosophy of nature, not surprising because as a materialist, atomist and (in the eyes of many) an atheist, Epicurus was a dissenter from the school of classical natural right begun by Plato and Aristotle with its enshrinement of the community of the polis, the aristocratic code of the citizen gentleman, and philosophy as a version of the ascent toward the divine – Marx of course was a materialist and an atheist himself. Moreover, in the famous "swerve" of the atoms (a kind of sub-particle rumba) in Lucretius' account of the Epicurean philosophy of nature, Marx saw a way in which human spontaneity could be compatible with materialistic determinism.

The central ideas of Marx's political philosophy concern alienation, the proletariat and the labor theory of value. According to Marx, human beings produce commodities by investing their labor in the materials provided by nature. By labor, Marx means something much broader than the Lockean, utilitarian understanding. Labor embraces the full range of man's creative potential, not only technical but artistic and intellectual abilities. Labor thus entails the means to biological survival but is not reducible to it. By laboring, we express our creativity and embody it in the objects we produce, achieving (his language recalls that of Schiller) a kind of aesthetic unity between our talents and their external realization that we may "contemplate." "Alienation" occurs when I am ripped out of this unity of self and object. This is the state of affairs under capitalism, where the surplus value of my creations beyond their capacity to sustain my biological existence is transferred to another person who controls my access to the means of production. When we live as "species-being," our material needs are integrated with our fullest range of self-expression. Capitalism perverts this *Gestalt* of integrated energies, reducing man's technical, artistic and intellectual capacities to the service of biological existence alone. Species-being declines into "the animal kingdom of man."

For Marx, then, alienation cannot be properly understood apart from species-being, since this latter concept expresses the unified existence that we have lost under capitalism. The meaning of species-being is complex and controversial, but it is perhaps easier to say what it is not. It is not an ideal in the Kantian sense of standing outside of nature and passion, but an existential, integrated, fully lived or "sensuous" kind of being. It is communal, but an immanent communality. By this I mean that, unlike the kind of community that the ancient political philosophers thought might be achieved through elaborate statecraft and a lifelong education in civic virtue, the communality of species-being is released by the removal of capitalism's impediments to it. It is a free, spontaneous association of individuals because there is no need to compel it by political means. But neither is species-being a happily primitive commune like the Golden Age of Rousseau's state of nature. Because Marx is a materialist – though not a reductive materialist – he believes that while people need not be reduced to living for the sake of survival, neither can they transcend or evade the bodily necessities and the productive techniques developed throughout history to serve them. After the socialist revolution, the productive apparatus of the capitalist epoch will be retained to provide permanently for everyone's material needs. To dismantle this technological apparatus would only rekindle the centuries-long competition for economic survival and domination in an environment of scarcity that had culminated in the miseries of capitalism. Species-being, then, is the underlying and still recoverable source of our inter-subjectivity. In this, it bears a family resemblance to Hegel's concept of Spirit, but, unlike that concept, species-being does not develop itself teleologically. As a latent substratum of communality, it also bears a family resemblance to what Rousseau meant by the state of nature but, in contrast with any concept of the state of nature, species-being is historical through and through, and its indeterminate potential for communality can only be forged by human historical actors. Finally, although Marx evinces perhaps the least admiration for the ancient world among any of the thinkers we are considering, his insistence that species-being not be considered an ideal but instead a "sensuous" fulfillment is arguably the residue of his early interest in the philosophical hedonism of Epicurus.

Marx's socialism may be described as the stateless organization of labor without surplus value. Marxism is notorious, especially in light of the Russian Revolution, for its lack of detail about what kind of political institutions and constitutional safeguards should be established after the revolution. This was not an oversight on the part of Marx, who could be a brilliant analyst of political affairs. Rather, it stems from his conviction that the whole subject matter of politics will disappear after a brief (in some versions of his thinking) "transition" from "the dictatorship of the proletariat" to socialism. For to Marx, politics means the monopoly of state power by a predominant class and as such cannot take place under socialism. Until now, every state has been a submerged struggle between two or more classes. Socialism will emerge only when a single universal class of mankind, the proletariat, sweeps away the remaining husk of the bourgeoisie. At that point, there will be only one class, meaning to say no classes at all, and therefore, by definition, there cannot be a political state.

Marx viewed the industrial working class, the proletariat – an allusion to the poorest class of ancient Rome – as the prime sufferer of capitalist exploitation, the prospective majority class of mankind, and mankind's future redeemer. As early as 1843, Marx was sure that this characteristically modern class could be shown to embody the dehumanizing course of modernity as a whole. Believing this critique of modernity to be borne out by the experience of a living group of the worst off gave him a powerful theoretical and empirical fulcrum with which to analyze the workings of the political and economic systems. Marx endowed the proletariat with a concept central to the Philosophy of Freedom, that man is a self-maker, a creator *ex nihilo* enmeshed in the world he has progressively transformed. Hegel had viewed history as a process (Spirit) that continually crucified and recreated itself, centering on man as the locus for its cycles of dissolution and resurrection. Marx transferred this dynamic power from the all-encompassing Spirit of history, Hegel's version of the Platonic whole, to the purely human, flesh-and-blood struggle of the workers. In his vision of the proletariat's development, it suffers (like Hegel's Slave) from the dissolution of all fixity and security, losing its ties to premodern caste and religion, ultimately losing its property and the very means of survival. But in the history of its suffering, it mirrors (again like Hegel's Slave) the creative drive of history itself and will later do freely what it now passively suffers. Rather than suffer the loss of all security, it will experience the freedom of untrammeled creativity.

According to the labor theory of value, the bourgeoisie must progressively impoverish the proletariat in order to finance the expansion of the capitalist means of production. Since the proletariat, ever increasing in size, lacks the income to buy what capitalism produces, the result is an economic crisis of overproduction and underconsumption, leading to further impoverishment until, on the verge of starvation, the proletariat revolts. The proletariat is ready and able to exercise political power to effect the transition to socialism because the experience of factory work under capitalism has taught it how to discipline and organize itself, while the collapse of the capitalist economy has taught it how to exist without private property. This is how the bourgeoisie acts unwittingly as its own "gravedigger." One of the most original features of Marxism is that, whereas the other great exploration of communism in the history of political thought, Plato's *Republic*, concluded that economic self-interest and bodily desire made communism virtually impossible, Marx believes that communism will be brought about precisely by the fullest development of economic self-interest and bodily desire. Socialism, the least competitive epoch, is brought about by capitalism, the most competitive.

This helps us to understand an important paradox in Marx's thinking: his ability to combine a remarkably hard-headed acuity about the power struggles and selfish interests masked by the modern state with an apparent naivete about how people will act after the transition to socialism. Even granting that the proletariat will exercise its dictatorial power during the transition phase only for as long as it takes to dismantle the shrunken remains of the bourgeoisie's control, someone outside the Marxist standpoint naturally wonders why avarice, vanity, competitiveness and a lust for power will not start all over again under socialism. For Marx, as much as it is senseless to expect altruism from people living within the distorting conditions of capitalism, it is axiomatic that, once history has liberated people from the system that functions on alienation and exploitation, people will shed every motive for aggressive behavior. Simply put, Marx (in this respect a follower of Rousseau) believes that people do not *want* to be competitive and ambitious but are *compelled* to be in a dog-eat-dog world. Once they are no longer forced to act this way, the balm of happiness they will experience is one they will never want to give up once these psychological distortions have dissipated. This shows the very limited sense in which Marx's theory is an empirical one, at least in the instrumentalist Anglo-American view of empiricism. It may also be a further indication of his partiality to Epicurus, whose philosophical hedonism held that true happiness is attained when we are free from want due to limiting our desires, another trace of which can be found, as we discussed in Chapter 1, in Rousseau's conception of the state of nature. Epicurus' philosophical hedonism was a private way of life to be achieved by an individual who deliberately avoided the strain and toil of political ambition and public life, staying in his garden. Another distinctive feature of Marx's adaptation of philosophical hedonism is that he collectivizes it as a condition attainable by the entire human race once politics have faded away.

The laws of economics, Marx believed, enable us to understand capitalism. But when the authentic species-being immanent within the repressive system governed by those laws emerges into "social" freedom, those laws and the assumption in which they are grounded of an egoistic, compulsively selfish individual will lose their validity. This is why, to amplify an earlier point, Marx has so little to say about the psychology of political ambition or the dangers of tyranny inherent in a party presuming to exercise dictatorial power after the revolution. Russian Marxists living to see the rise of Stalin, indeed of Lenin, learned through bitter experience how unhelpful Marx was in this regard. For Marx, the traditional concerns of political philosophy with how to identify and condemn tyrannical ambition and distinguish it from true statesmanship were, however well motivated, symptomatic of what stood in the way of man's final liberation from all such oppression. Once the liberation takes place, the need for such knowledge will vanish along with the dangers with which it was meant to cope. Unlike Hegel, Marx saw no need to write his own version of the *Philosophy of Right*. There was nothing redeemable about modern capitalist bourgeois society, so it was bootless to devise principles by which its legitimacy could be measured. Moreover, the coming era of complete human liberation and happiness would have nothing to do with any version of the state. Hegel is the first and last of the great historicist thinkers to see the continuing validity of a theory of political legitimacy, and the fact that Marx, followed by Nietzsche and Heidegger, had no interest in this at all is an important sign of the increasingly millenarian drift of historicist thinking.

The evidence about America furnished for Marx in part through his study of Tocqueville confirmed, he believed, a key principle of his theory. For Marx,

America shows the furthest point to which the political state can advance: the recognition and protection of such inalienable rights as freedom of worship. Since in this "perfected democracy" religion is only strengthened by being disestablished and privatized, and since religion ("the opium of the people") must be abolished before socialism can flourish, religious tolerance as practiced in America reveals the fundamental limitations of the political state altogether: "To be *politically* emancipated from religion is not to be finally and completely emancipated from religion, because political emancipation is not the final and absolute form of *human* emancipation."

The deficiency of liberal democracy revealed by the freedom of worship is borne out, Marx argues, by the other "rights of man" that comprised the basis of the American founding. The state properly speaking reveals its distinct character only in modern times, when it supersedes feudalism by disentangling religious institutions and the power of property from political authority. In a sense, property was more powerful when the wealthy were also dukes and bishops. But in a more important sense, Marx argues, the rights of property are liberated by being privatized and universalized, since people can now pursue wealth undistractedly and limitlessly, without any sense of obligation to others of the kind that the feudal authorities had at least professed to entertain toward their subjects. Whereas feudalism conflated political authority with personal wealth, the modern state claims to represent impersonally a community of free and equal individuals. But the formal equality of rights guaranteed by the impersonality of the liberal state masks the lived reality of liberal society, a "war of all against all" (Marx uses Hobbes' famous phrase) where the inequality of result expands without limit. The possession of rights – the occasion of so much reverence for the American Revolution – Marx believes to be nothing grander than the pursuit of wealth, in which the greediest and boldest triumph. It is not merely a particular interpretation or application of rights, but the very concept of rights – the identification of freedom with rights – that is defective, amounting to the social and political institutionalizing of alienation: "Liberty as a right of man is not founded on the relations between man and man, but rather upon the separation of man from man ... The liberty of man [is] regarded as an isolated monad, withdrawn into himself."

The community of equal citizens that the liberal state claims to represent is thus a ghostly abstraction in contrast with the growing real inequality between bourgeoisie and workers. It is not a life of high-minded public service but the energy and talent of the successful bourgeois that are admired – he "is considered the *true* and *authentic* man." In other words, if we must choose between the life of Gordon Gekko and the kind of citizenship described in civics textbooks, the alienation typified by the Wall Street bandit at least has some guts and style as opposed to the alienation typified by the wan earnestness of PBS. That the existence of the rapacious bourgeois is recognized as, and really is, the most authentic way of life in a liberal democracy shows, for Marx, how far we are from the unity of the ideal and the sensuous that will blossom through "social" emancipation. Behind the idealistic camouflage of the rights of man, the liberal state serves the interests of the bourgeoisie. This is a prime instance for Marx of how our communal capacities as species-beings are reduced to mere means for the perpetuation of man's "partial being" as a producer and consumer of commodities. As Europe and the rest of the world progress toward the form of the state already perfected in America, Marx forecasts, the contradiction between the ghostly, unrealizable "ought" of the liberal ideal of citizenship and the vicious, degrading "is" of the competition for property will become unbearable. America points the way to the supersession of liberalism and therewith of politics altogether:

Human emancipation will only be complete when the real, individual man has absorbed into himself the abstract citizen; when as an individual man, in his everyday life, in his work, and in his relationships, he has become a *species-being*; and when he has recognized and organized his own powers as *social* powers, so that he no longer separates this social power from himself as *political* power.

During Marx's lifetime, European conservatives began to identify America with modernity at its most soulless. "Amerika" came to stand for the corrosive forces of science and industry threatening the fabric of traditions that bound together an ancient people. In contrast, Marx can sometimes sound like an untroubled champion of modernization, unabashedly pointing to America's advances over Europe. Marx detested the romantic conservatives' nostalgia for a premodern Volkisch community as furnishing yet another way for the bourgeoisie to camouflage the real function of the state as the instrument of its economic interests. He professed zero regard for what Hegel had identified as the strain of *Sittlichkeit* in historical existence, the dimension of reconciliation with the past stretching back to the Greek polis and reemerging through Romanticism and a newly founded longing for religion sparked by a dawning era of "forgiveness" and the "reappearance of God." Marx wanted the proletariat to lose any remaining illusions about the compatibility of capitalism with older loyalties to the organic hierarchy of the Great Chain of Being. One of his reasons for regarding America as "the most perfect example of the modern state" was that, with its absence of a feudal heritage to retard or cosmeticize the victory of bourgeois self-interest, the masses could not cling to these nostalgic traces of throne and altar: "The ... American writers all express the opinion that the state exists only for the sake of private property, so that this fact has penetrated into the consciousness of the normal man." When we tear away these shards of the *ancien régime*, Marx argues, we see that capitalism is relentlessly creating a labor force that will be global in extent and whose division of labor is as specialized as possible. This means the end of the old local craft economy, the village commune and, someday soon, the nation-state.

Modern economic progress is good in Marx's view because its corrosion of the old order frees the masses from their centuries-long tutelage to religious and aristocratic authorities. The bourgeoisie tears the workers out of these old feudal contexts to set them in motion as atomized producers and consumers of manufactures. But after the revolution the workers will retain the autonomy initially forced on them by the bourgeoisie for its own selfish designs and enjoy, for the first time in history, freedom from every authority claiming a transhuman source. The future socialist community will thus transcend liberal individualism without sacrificing the Enlightenment's liberation of the human personality and intellect.

Still, one cannot help but notice in Marx's tone a sense of painful loss and regret, at times almost Burkean, over the vanishing *ancien régime* and outrage at the coarseness of the modern age in comparison with it. Because he has abandoned the Hegelian belief in the legitimacy of the present order as the fulfillment of history, his view of the modern world rekindles some of the fieriness of Rousseau's original disdain for the bourgeoisie. This is apparent in one such passage remarkable for its passionate eloquence:

The bourgeoisie, wherever it has got the upper hand, has put an end to all feudal, patriarchal, idyllic relations. It has pitilessly torn asunder the motley feudal ties that bound man to his "natural superiors," and has left remaining no other nexus between man and man than naked self-interest, than callous "cash payment." It has drowned the most heavenly ecstasies of religious fervor, of chivalrous enthusiasm, of philistine sentimentalism in the icy water of egotistical calculation. It has resolved personal worth into exchange value ... The bourgeoisie has stripped of its halo every occupation hitherto honoured and looked up to with reverent awe. It has converted the physician, the lawyer, the priest, the poet, the man of science, into its paid wage-labourers. The bourgeoisie has torn away from the family its sentimental veil, and has reduced the family relation to a mere money relation.

Despite the sarcasm about the "motley ties" of feudalism, I believe that far more is being felt and expressed here than cheerful contempt for the old ways and complacent optimism as capitalism runs its course toward the edge of Niagara Falls. The more pitilessly realistic Marx is in tearing away the veil, the more one senses his struggle to deny himself the consoling evocation of the premodern community. A similar ambivalence informs Marx's criticisms of the modern state. On one level he approves of America's and other advanced states' destruction of all "feudal, idyllic relations." On another level he manifestly deplores the shabbiness and indignity of the bourgeois state – the contemptible hypocrisy of its claims to establish a genuine community – that result from its destruction of these older bonds of substantive obligation and duty.

The "bourgeois republic," then, as Marx called America, frustrates tyranny of the large-scale, terrible kind by routinizing it into a universal, endless series of minor victories over others in commerce. Locke, Montesquieu and the American founders considered this a great victory for liberty because it channels the most belligerent aspects of human nature into relatively benign and negotiable commercial interests and, in addition to the safeguards provided by representative political institutions, allows us to exercise our other freedoms without fear of harm from those around us. But Marx echoes Rousseau's great protest – that the bourgeois era causes this mundane competitiveness to eat into each one of us heart and soul, dominating our existences. We may no longer be in danger of the rack or gibbet for being on the wrong side of a religious zealot or monarch. But we have also been robbed of any feeling of obligation to others or any sense that society respects faith or probity above avarice. Although Marx had zero interest in restoring any version of Greek or Roman virtue, he does, like Rousseau, appeal to those who consider liberal individualism to have truncated the human spirit. Marxism's goal is not the achievement of a good state to remedy the vices of an imperfect state. Its goal is the transcendence of all states through the transcendence of the final state, liberal democracy.

As the foregoing considerations begin to show, Marx's economic analysis, notwithstanding its frequent brilliance, does not adequately explain Marxism's appeal. Already in Marx's lifetime technology was forestalling the need to extract ever more surplus value from the workers' labor by increasing the efficiency of that labor. The redistribution of income through social welfare programs forestalled the crisis of overproduction and underconsumption by providing the workers with more purchasing power. As a matter of strict empirical observation, then, the labor theory of value was refuted by the course of the industrial democracies' development. In a way these forestalling measures were a real tribute to Marx. The bourgeoisie, one might say, was warned and took the warning seriously.

I do not think Marx, were he brought back to life today, would be dismayed by these apparent failures of his theory as a matter of empirical prediction. Marx lived through many of capitalism's permutations and did not view history as a rigidly deterministic sequence. Regardless of these shifts and starts, he remained transfixed by what he saw as the great either/or that the whole course of modern history was preparing and would sooner or later make manifest: intensifying woe and despair as the prelude to the great reversal of unprecedented happiness and fulfillment. This is sometimes misunderstood by those who think that Marxism is primarily competing with capitalism on capitalism's own terms of increasing economic opportunity. The varieties of Marxism do claim that they will triumph economically in the long run. But the core claim is different, more radical, and cannot be disproved by any criterion of measurable economic performance alone.

The core is "socialism," which for Marx means the unity of the sensuous and the ideal; of individual and collective satisfaction; of the private and the public interest – in sum, the unity of nature and freedom. To reach this core, we have to bear in mind Marxism's origins in German Idealism and Romanticism, with which it shares a number of characteristic thought structures. The Enlightenment made a fundamental distinction between man as a natural being motivated by self-preservation and man as a free being capable of willing himself to rise above the natural inclinations and establish his autonomy. In the New World this distinction helped the individual to throw off the shackles of religious and political authorities claiming to integrate the natural and moral dimensions of human life in some objective teleological hierarchy. Americans were, to recall Tocqueville's observation, natural Cartesians even though few had ever heard of Descartes. They were individual Cartesian selves who invented themselves every day in a cheerful bustle of renovation and enterprise. In Europe, however, the split in man between his natural and free sides was considered true but deeply troubling, a sign that modern man was alone in the world, cut adrift from any mooring in the harmonious orderings of nature or tradition. While the American founders were content to encourage a balance of civic freedom and material self-interest, expecting that each would temper the other, the Europeans were scandalized at the lack of a unifying third term and tended to drive the poles of nature and freedom further apart as they reflected on the most extreme reaches of each. Schiller looked for an aesthetic unity between the individual and a larger culture that would avoid both the debased materialism that he believed came with philosophies, like that of Locke, that stress man's natural side and the tendency of philosophies of freedom, like those of Kant and Fichte, that encourage a kind of fanaticism in which the will strives to overcome every natural limitation. This search for unity culminated in the longing for a "third character," as Schiller expressed it, that would unite spontaneity and feeling with will and autonomy. Schiller went no further than prescribing this pursuit of wholeness so as to enrich the lives of individuals living in the bourgeois world, a way of elevating art over commerce. But Marx, Nietzsche and Heidegger transform it, in different but related ways, into a wholesale longing for millenarian revolution.

Hegel had warned that this emerging millenarian longing for the transcendence of alienation, already evident in the French Revolution, had to be tempered by an appreciation for the degree to which human happiness – even in the future, and certainly now – is, in the real world of experience, always intermixed with avarice, vanity and belligerence. Even at the end of history, therefore, a political state with laws and police will be needed to balance the public and private goods. Marx's connection to Hegel is attested to by a long tradition of commentary and by some of Marx's terminology, but it is important to see how very different their philosophies are in this respect. For Hegel, man's pursuit of fulfillment through the progress of history can never be entirely divorced from either the idealistic or the nasty dimensions of human behavior. Precisely because we are free from nature, Hegel argues, we will also experience alienation. This feeling of Pascalian loneliness in an empty cosmos is modern man's cross to bear, but also a sign of our spiritual strength and superiority to ancient peoples like the Greeks who, unlike us, felt entirely at home in the world. At the same time, however, history is permeated with the power of divine forgiveness and reconciliation, preventing the present and even the darker ages of the past from being nothing but struggles for domination.

Marx regarded the Hegelian dialectic as too consoling about the present and too much of a compromise with alienation. He took the belief in God to sum up

all of man's alienated creativity, a force not in harmony with human development (as Hegel believed) but standing in pure contradiction to it. For Marx,
alienation is not (as Hegel believed) a price that a maturely self-conscious
individual knows he must pay for his freedom from the superstitions and
tyrannies of the past, but an agonizing separation from our unity with nature
and our fellow men that must be totally negated. His response, accordingly, is
to drive the poles of the Hegelian synthesis apart and radicalize each one. He
radicalizes the view of history to date into nothing but a power struggle
between masters and slaves, haves and have-nots. He purifies the elements of
communality and reconciliation that Hegel believed had mitigated this struggle
throughout history to date by locating them entirely in the future era of
socialism. After the withering away of the political, the social will flower. All
mankind will then enjoy the unity of will and feeling that Schiller thought could
be approached only through the delicate and gradual cultivation of aesthetic
education. Indeed, rather than a successor to Hegelianism, Marxism can be
more accurately described as the transposition of the aesthetic unity in cultural
life evoked by Schiller to the plane of the actual liberation of mankind through
revolution from all alienating social and political forces. For Schiller, the "third
character" expressed only the hope that cultured individuals could mitigate the
baseness of excessive materialism and the harshness of dogmatic moralism
through their intermittent shared absorption in beauty. For Marx, precisely
the worst excesses of natural desire and fanatical willpower in the present
guarantee the achievement of this beautiful collective existence for everyone,
meaning to say socialism.

The polarity between the political and the social, thematically rooted in the
structure of Marx's thought, is the source of these sharp contrasts. For Marx,
the political is the sphere of willpower, domination, exploitation and the
conquest of nature. The power of creation *ex nihilo*, the power of the
Fichtean self that pursues its freedom through the limitless reconstruction of
nature, Marx traces as history's terrible engine of revolutionary upheaval and
transformation. Beyond this dark night, and because of it, awaits our release as
sensuous beings freely communing through our labor.

The comprehensiveness of these poles and the tension between them helps to
explain why Marx's philosophy, energized by his immense talents as a political
observer, is so flexible and can survive so many specific refutations by events.
Marxism is not an aspiration toward an ideal, such as the "ethical communism" of Duhring, because not only does the real world not stand in the way of
the ideal one, but the worst outcome of the real is *needed* to actualize the ideal.
Thus Marx does not have to appeal to man's higher sentiments to demonstrate
the possibility of socialism, and he can explore the muck of current politics in
the fullest factual detail without endangering the counterfactual goal. To put it
another way, Marx is against liberalism but in favor of modernization and the
unedifying analysis of politics as driven by self-interest. He thus fights what he
understood as political economy and what we might now term behaviorism on

their own ground – their pride in the imperative to empirical and analytical clarity unbefuddled by moralism and sentimentality – without being limited by the liberal-individualist ontology in which these assumptions are grounded. This combination of contraries surely helps to explain Marxism's appeal in the twentieth century in the developing world as a rhetoric of modernization that does not necessarily require political and economic pluralism and is compatible with the priority of community over rights.

The irony here is that Marxism, whose original aim was the complete transcendence of the state, is transformed into a manifesto for Promethean state-building. In the case of Stalinism, the most extreme and tragic variant of Marxism as an imperative to modernization "from above," this involved a horrific inversion of the political and social poles of Marx's philosophy. In Marx's most coherent version of the transition to socialism, by the time the political revolution to establish the dictatorship of the proletariat occurred, the proletariat would already, under capitalism, have swelled to constitute the vast majority of people, while the productive apparatus needed to end scarcity would already have been fully developed. The material and characterological bases for a classless society would thus have been largely engendered during the late stage of capitalism itself. Marx warned that if the political revolution for the transition to socialism was too far in advance of this socioeconomic development, the result could only be the imposition of equality by *force majeure* – the expropriation and extermination of the oppressor classes, as in the Terror of Robespierre. Stalinism fully bore out this warning. According to Stalinism, since the political revolution (the Bolshevik seizure of power in 1917) preceded Russia's socioeconomic maturation, the state must confiscate the peasants' property to finance rapid industrialization (thus completing the economic modernization that would have taken place under capitalism) and simultaneously achieve, by political fiat, the ideal of a classless society. The result was a program of state terror to be equaled only by the Nazis. Stalin's view, however, was that the Soviet Union was only experiencing in a concentrated time-frame the destruction that capitalism had had centuries to carry out as it uprooted the *ancien régime* and assimilated premodern classes into the proletariat.

This is where the inversion of Marx's dialectic occurs. For Marx, the bourgeoisie's conscious exploitation of the workers unconsciously produces the very opposite of its intention, the preconditions for socialism. In Stalinism the state consciously enacts the process that Marx believed history had unconsciously effected: progress toward the greatest happiness by means of the greatest oppression. Since the development of capitalism had, over centuries, caused the peasantry in Europe to vanish, Stalinists reasoned, why not use the state to hasten history forward in Russia by the deliberate liquidation of classes known from capitalism's unfolding elsewhere to be doomed by history anyway? In Stalinism, then, the revolutionary ruthlessness that, Marx taught, had enabled the bourgeoisie to create capitalism and, undesignedly, the basis for socialism is enlisted in the service of designedly creating socialism. The

Fichtean drive to reconstruct nature and human nature is no longer, as it was for Marx, history's dark prelude to the flowering of species-being – to the release of the human personality from the historically imposed compulsion to aggression. It is the will to power of the "builders of socialism" themselves as they carry out the titanic destruction that Marxism had revealed to be the engine of historical advancement. Plainly, therefore, Marx's philosophy is not responsible for Stalinism in a direct causal sense. Indeed, it frequently warned against such a dangerous, deluded path to the classless society. (Frequently, but not consistently, as I discuss below). At the same time, I would argue that Marx's explosion of the Hegelian synthesis of the unity of Subject and Substance – of freedom and community – left his philosophy intrinsically vulnerable to further radicalizations of its purely political pole, the "scientistic" dimension of Marxism (to use Habermas' term) that serves as an imperative for the techno-logical mastery of nature and human nature. By depicting politics as the pursuit of power bereft of any mitigating bonds of communality and obligation in the present so as to preserve the socialist future from any compromise with alien-ation in the present, Marx made his philosophy vulnerable to manipulation by tyrants like Stalin, who could claim to be employing the ruthlessness of politics as uncovered by Marx himself to hasten the transcendence of the political.

EVOLUTION OR REVOLUTION?

Did Marx call primarily for evolution or revolution to bring about socialism? This question is unresolved in his thought and he did not give a consistent answer to it. The evolutionary alternative stresses that the conditions for socialism have mostly matured within late capitalism, so that the transition phase from "the revolutionary dictatorship of the proletariat" to socialism will be brief and limited, a mop-up operation in which a few astonished Scrooge McDucks are chased from their Money Bins. When embracing the evolutionary path, Marx echoes Hegel's criticism of the French Revolution for attempting to impose socialism from above before socioeconomic conditions were mature. On the other hand, the revolutionary alternative stresses that a violent catharsis is needed for the proletariat to bring revolution about. The labor theory of value holds that the bourgeoisie must impoverish the proletariat to the point of annihilation, until it can take no more and lashes back in fury. In this way, it fulfills the role of the Slave in Marx's revamping of Hegel, suffering on behalf of mankind as a whole and finally emerging as its redeemer. In this view, the transition phase may be long and bloody, not a mere mop-up operation, and the violence therapeutic and cathartic, not merely a means to an end.

Marx oscillates between these two alternatives in his shifting views of Russia's potential for revolution. Dutifully reflecting Marxism's claims to be "scientific," Engels replied in 1874 to a letter from a Russian populist who argues that a revolution can take place in Russia even though Russia has neither a proletariat nor a bourgeoisie – can take place, in fact, more easily because it need only bring down the tsarist regime – that anyone who thinks this can happen without the "productive forces" created by the bourgeoisie "has still to learn the abc of socialism." But after this patronizing put-down, Engels waffles: If the Russian tradition of "communal ownership of the land" can be preserved from its complete break-up into bourgeois smallholdings, a process that the full entrenchment of capitalism in Russia would necessitate, a "higher" form of society could be achieved immediately. But "this can only happen if ... a proletarian revolution is successfully carried out in Western Europe" and can extend "the material conditions" created by the previous capitalist economy necessary to carry it through. In other words, revolution could occur in Russia skipping the capitalist stage for now, but only if the material benefits of the capitalist means of production were available after the true revolution in the West. Engels here essentially wrote the script for Lenin – seize power politically by toppling the autocracy, hold onto the new state as a beacon until the true revolution takes place in Europe and the proletariat can extend its assistance to complete Russia's socioeconomic evolution.

In 1882, Marx himself poses the question more sharply in the Preface to the Russian edition of *The Communist Manifesto*: Can Russia's tradition of the communal ownership of the land proceed straight to "the higher form of communist common ownership" through revolutionary action now? Or must it first pass through the same "historical evolution" of capitalism and its impending dissolution now unfolding in the West? In other words, revolution or evolution? His answer: If the Russian revolution becomes "the signal for a proletarian revolution in the West so that both complement each other," a revolution in Russia can serve as "a starting point" for communist development once the proletariat takes over in Europe. A year before his death, Marx is in effect already giving his blessing to what will transpire when Trotsky urges Lenin not to be so scrupulous about waiting for Russia to develop socioeconomically according to Marxism's own economic theory. Roll the dice; give history a push. Then build the conditions for capitalist productivity from above, but without private property or profit. Skip the bourgeois stage and wait for help from the real proletariat in Europe after the revolution, when the advanced means of production fall into their hands. The bloody record of this emendation of Marxist theory began in 1917 when Lenin arrived at the Finland Station. The "transition phase" went on for seventy years until the regime collapsed, and the attempt to build socialism from above through rapid collectivization and industrialization claimed an estimated thirty million lives.

3

The Will to Power and the Politics of Greatness

Nietzsche's Revelation

In a letter to the historian Jacob Burkhardt written in 1889, a year after he completed his final book *Ecce Homo*, Friedrich Nietzsche quipped: "In the end I would much rather be a Basel professor than God, but I have not dared push my private egoism so far as to desist for its sake from the creation of the world. You see, one must make sacrifices however and wherever one lives." Some might choose to see this as a whiff of megalomania symptomatic of Nietzsche's alleged insanity, although the nature of his breakdown and withdrawal has never been resolved. I prefer to view the remark as a part of the lightheartedness and irony that Nietzsche so much admired, although, as we will see, on a certain level he meant it completely seriously. We realize at any rate that we are now in a very different atmosphere from that of Marx's earnest activism. Although Marx had died seventeen years earlier and his influence over the socialist movement was spreading, Nietzsche never mentions him by name, which can arguably be taken as a sign of contempt, although, as I will suggest, their bodies of thought do share some common ground.

Nietzsche inaugurates the second assault on what I have called the Hegelian middle. Whereas Marx's assault was from the Left, Nietzsche's was from the Right. When I employ this term, I am doing so in its older European meaning, whose core was the longing for a restored sense of community characteristic of the Philosophy of Freedom altogether. Whereas the Left's version of this longing was egalitarian and international in perspective, the Right's version argued for a restored sense of aristocratic rank and hierarchy in an age of egalitarian leveling. Although Nietzsche's vision of the future was ultimately not nationalistic but in its own peculiar way also international, he did extoll a conception of life as being rooted in "peoples and fatherlands" as far superior to the rootless, deracinated and vapid cosmopolitanism of both liberalism and socialism.

In his rejection of the Hegelian account according to which history was progressing benevolently toward a better future for everyone, Nietzsche in a sense returns to the fieriness of Rousseau's original critique of the irredeemably detestable character of the bourgeois age, in this respect like Marx. He famously dismissed Hegel's understanding of cultural fulfillment at the end of history as "a banker's night out in Berlin," as a kind of museum culture in which the bourgeois convinced himself that he had refined and elevated tastes and was not merely a money-grubber. This loathing of *haute bourgeois* philistinism also bears a resemblance to Marx's jeremiads, but for Nietzsche, socialism is every bit as much a symptom of base materialism and spiritual degradation as liberalism, along with other reformist movements like the one for women's rights, or what he terms the "anarchist dogs" prowling the back alleys of European culture.

Unlike Marx, Nietzsche to an extent marks a return to Rousseau's admiration for the ancient polis and its virtues of manly patriotism and martial ardor. But like Hegel and Marx, he is a historicist thinker who cannot accept the concept of a fixed human nature, even a very thin substratum underlying our civilized condition in the way that Rousseau portrays what remains of our original nature. Therefore Nietzsche cannot follow Rousseau in longing for the ancient polis and its republican virtue to be restored or at least approximated in some manner in the present, although he certainly believed it provided a foil for measuring the degeneration of the present age as well as a benchmark for what human greatness could achieve. As we will see, Nietzsche's hopes for mankind are entirely future-oriented, which is why he, like Marx, saw no point in writing a theory of what legitimate government would be in the bourgeois present, although for very different reasons – an enterprise that both Rousseau and Hegel, who remained conditional supporters of the modern Enlightenment project, had viewed as still viable.

Like Rousseau and Marx, Nietzsche was not an academic philosopher. While unlike Marx, he had no interest in shaping political life directly (his political impact came mainly after his death), like Rousseau his writings display a strong element of autobiography, in which his thinking intertwines with his own psychological experiences. And so a brief consideration of his life is in order. He began his career as an academic star, a professor at the age of twenty-four and a leading classical philologist. When you consult an ancient Greek text in the Loeb Classical Library, among the emendations made to the Greek text listed at the bottom of the page, you will sometimes find Nietzsche's name. However, he forsook his academic career after the publication of his first major work, *The Birth of Tragedy*, which had disappointed his academic patron Wilhelm Friedrich Ritschl for being overly speculative and was panned by the eminent philologist Ulrich von Wilamovitz-Moellendorf. Although now free to write as he wished, Nietzsche lived in straitened circumstances for the rest of his life – he came from a good background, but not a wealthy one. His fame and success were largely posthumous.

His love of the classics was profound. But as against Hegel's preference for the classical age and for Plato among the ancient thinkers, Nietzsche extolled the tragic age of Homeric heroism along with the pre-Socratics and Sophists. In an early note, he proclaims his preference for Callicles with his creed of the "natural master" over Socrates. That also implied his preference for the pre-Socratic ontology of nature as flux and chance in which Callicles' defense of tyranny is grounded. As I have argued elsewhere, the "great motions" of impulse and force that issue out of nature as origination fueled a conception of the natural life as similarly sped by impulse and force to master others. This preference for the tragic age of the archaic Greeks over the classical age with which Platonic philosophy emerged coevally provided Nietzsche, as we will consider, a fulcrum both for critiquing Hegel's understanding of antiquity and his prescription for life in the present, a rebellion against Hegel's teleology of historical progress continued by Heidegger, who, as we will see in Chapter 4, also preferred the pre-Socratics over Plato among the ancient thinkers.

Nietzsche's writing style is widely admired for its verve, sparkle and biting humor, and many people who otherwise steer clear of German historicism owing to its daunting and seemingly impenetrable jargon of abstractions make an exception for Nietzsche. The apparently aphoristic, improvised, wandering style of his writings was deliberately aimed at what Nietzsche regarded as the ponderousness of Hegel, Kant and other systematic philosophers. But as it transpires, Nietzsche's thought is far less unsystematic than it might at first appear, and it is organized around some fundamental ontological premises, the central of which are the Will to Power and the Eternal Recurrence of the Same. That is why people who believe that Nietzsche can be treated as standing entirely apart from his German predecessors and contemporaries are mistaken. Although a deeply original thinker who can always be read with profit on his own, he shares, as I will argue, the fundamental premise about the meaning of existence that Hegel termed "self-origination." As we saw in the last chapter, Marx modified this premise as species-being. Nietzsche modifies it as the will to power, with profoundly different consequences. In other words, just as was the case with Marx, and as will later be the case with Heidegger, there is no disagreement between Nietzsche and Hegel that life is historical through and through, a matrix of origination. But there *is* profound disagreement with Hegel over whether and how history develops out of that matrix. Like Marx, Nietzsche too believed that Hegel's "absolute science" of Spirit had robbed man of his creative powers and chained him in an iron cage of determinism. Nietzsche's philosophy cannot be fully understood without keeping this broader context in mind.

TRAGEDY AND THE WORLD-ARTIST

Whereas Marx, in contrast with Hegel, had displayed little interest in the meaning of liberal education, and still less in its Platonic origins – regarding the plight of the working class as vastly more important than such rarefied concerns of the privileged few – in Nietzsche's engagement with Hegelianism, the meaning of liberal education in the modern age takes center stage again. One of the first steps in that engagement is Nietzsche's *The Birth of Tragedy*, which in a way characteristic of German Idealism going back to Schiller and Hegel, looks for the path forward by taking the path back to the ancient polis – the recollection of freedom. But for Nietzsche it is a very different path.

In Nietzsche's now famous thesis tracing the origins of tragedy in the symbiotic relationship between the Apollonian and the Dionysian, the Apollonian is the realm of the Olympian gods, form, stability, daylight and fire, the code of the aristocratic warrior, public life and fine art. The Dionysian is the realm of the Gaian and chthonic gods, of flux and impermanence, of frenzied passion, shadow, earth, water, family, the common people and the personal. The Dionysian cannot achieve great art on its own, only the frenzy of the Maenads in song and dance. But the Apollonian cannot achieve anything great on *its* own without its sensuous sublimation by the Dionysian – on its own, it is synonymous with war, force and despotic rule.

The cult of Apollo at Delphi, according to Nietzsche, symbolized their interaction, "in new birth ever following and mutually augmenting one another." We must fill in some of what Nietzsche implies here from mythological sources. Originally a barbaric war god from the north, Apollo came to Delphi and slew the dragon of the earth goddess Gaia, an antecedent of Dionysus, who guarded a spring that issued from the rocks, symbolizing the earth as a kind of birth passage. Apollo took over the site from Gaia, but she magically morphed into his oracle, merging with the dragon, now a snake, and the potent powers of nature that snakes tapped into, becoming the "Pythoness" or "Python Lady." Apollo's fusion with the sensuous powers of the earth made him ever young and beautiful, and he was worshipped as Pythian Apollo, the Apollo of the Python – in all statues of him, a snake lies curled at his feet. He is, as Nietzsche puts it, the "glorious divine image" of art sublimating passion, the hard, individuated Apollonian clarity of a Praxitiles statue of the god glowing and suffused with the Dionysian pulse of life. Apollo and Gaia's later incarnation, Dionysus, shared the temple site at Delphi, a further symbolization of their symbiotic interaction. Every winter, "in a seasonably effected reconciliation," Apollo visited his mysterious northern homeland, while Dionysus and his devotees danced in the meadows nearby, or, in some versions, took Apollo's place in the temple precinct itself.

For Nietzsche, Homer is the most beautiful expression of the symbiotic relationship between the Dionysian and the Apollonian. His metrical verse is the triumph of Apollonian form over the wordless ecstasy and violence of Dionysus, but it is enlivened by the terrible passions it sublimates. In the *Iliad*, Achilles combines the characteristics of the Dionysian and the Apollonian as we sketched them above – he was born from the water (his mother was a sea nymph), he is closely associated with the sunlight that flashes off his armor; when he goes forth to fight Hector to avenge the death of his personal beloved, the common people gather respectfully (as they do for no other Greek warrior), and in a moment of magic, his horse speaks with him. According to Nietzsche, in Homer's poetry, life is the triumph of form and beauty over terror, especially at the prospect of an early death. The harmonious oneness of man with nature that Schiller termed "naive" is therefore not an accurate characterization of Homer's poetry, as Schiller claimed. Homer does not gaze upon the beautiful surface of nature and reflect it passively back. For Nietzsche, this is to view Homer through the Romantic lens of Rousseau's *Emile*, "reared at the bosom of nature," reflecting human nature's innate sweetness and repose. On the contrary: The perfection of form in Homer's art is actually the outcome of a stupendous struggle, overthrowing an empire of titans and slaying monsters, triumphing over "an abysmal and terrifying view of the world and the keenest susceptibility to suffering." Schiller's quest for an aesthetic harmony between man and nature, so admired early on by Hegel, to heal the Rousseauan and Kantian divide between nature and freedom, is for Nietzsche wishful thinking and self-induced superficiality. (It can, of course, be questioned whether this is an accurate interpretation of what Schiller meant by the "naivete" of Homeric poetry, which, as we recall, he distinguished from the "sentimental" Rousseauan quality of Romantic art.)

"Amid the strife of these two hostile principles," Nietzsche continues, the Apollonian and the Dionysian, "Attic tragedy" emerged as "the common goal" of both forces. Oedipus is the crossroads where the two powerful forces of the Dionysian and the Apollonian intersect and clash. Beginning as the self-identified devotee of Apollo, Oedipus goes down in bloody dismemberment like Dionysus, crying out that Apollo has betrayed him. It is a variation of the primeval motif of the god-king sacrificed to re-fertilize nature, and in this case to reinvigorate Apollo. Nietzsche is in effect returning to Plato's tripartite soul, symbolized by the Image of the Chariot, in which the intellect guides us through the eternal heavens, drawing upon while restraining the energies of eros and thumos, and brings it crashing down by freeing the horses from their reins. There *is* no higher Platonic synthesis of mind and the affects, Nietzsche is arguing, only a struggle. Oedipus' fury and lust are both blind; they take him down into the depths, not up toward the eternal good. By blinding himself, Oedipus symbolically finally achieves the wisdom of blind Tiresias, whose maxim was: Best not to know the truth. Blindness as a metaphor for wisdom is directly antithetical to Socrates' likening of the intellect to the eye of the soul – it is impossible to know too much. Going "on up," as Diotima's Ladder put it in the *Symposium*, from the here and now toward the immortal truth is, in Nietzsche's view, altogether an illusion, certainly for humans. Even the gods in Sophocles are distant, grimmer and more impersonal, not the shining, rambunctious, amusing and libidinous superhuman Olympians of Homer who once walked among us. In sum, Nietzsche wants to go *behind* what in *Beyond Good and Evil* he will designate as the morality of intention, the capacity for moral choice ascribed to man by Plato and Aristotle, into the passions that express themselves *through* it.

Nietzsche continues the trend begun by Hegel, as we saw in the last chapter, to peel away the philosophic overlay of Aristotle's *Poetics* and recover the meaning of tragedy in its deepest primordial origins. Aristotle's account assumes that we are capable of exercising responsibility for our actions. The characteristic that distinguishes humans from other animals is rational choice (*prohairesis*), specifically the capacity for choosing virtue over vice, and if we fail to so choose, we are at fault. But Nietzsche asks: *Is* Oedipus at fault? Or is he fated? If so, what does this tell us about the status of reason and morality in the world? Even Aristotle recognized the intimate connection between tragedy and the god of passion and impulse, Dionysus. The word for tragedy (*tragikos*) is cognate with the words for goats (*tragoi*) and goat-singers (*tragodoi*), who chanted while a goat was sacrificed to Dionysus, symbolizing his mythical dismemberment. Tragedies formed a part of the festival of Dionysus and were always performed before his altar. These dramas provided a public education in the relationship of man to destiny. If one assumes that the cosmos is rationally ordered, including the supremacy of the mind over the passions, you might judge Oedipus as responsible for murdering Laius in a fit of rage. But if life is at bottom hostile and dooms us through our passions, then we may be fated to carry out such crimes. This is Nietzsche's perspective, "the tragic view of life." It rejects both the classical and modern (for example, Kantian) assumption of the capacity for rational choice and taking responsibility for our actions as superficial.

Nietzsche's evocation of the contrast between the Dionysian and the Apollonian echoes Hegel's contrast between the Divine Law and the Human Law in his discussion of ancient Greece in the *Phenomenology of Spirit* – but with a significant difference. For Hegel, the contrast between the two kinds of law expressed itself not only on the level of emotion, but more importantly as a legal structure and pattern for social and political authority, of civic life in the agora. Nietzsche, by contrast, descends back *behind* the structure of the law into a more impersonal pair of broad and mighty existential forces, with an emphasis on their contrasting emotional drives, and with little to say about their specific impact on the social and political ordering of the polis. This recessional descent behind the two kinds of law into their more primordial wellsprings is characteristic of Nietzsche's overall attempt to dismantle Hegel's Unity of Subject and Substance as the conceptual overlay of historical existence as "self-origination" and release its underlying sheer spontaneity. The Unity of Subject and Substance, we recall from the last chapter, is how history progresses through the clash of its two poles. On the subject side, we find the conquest of nature, war, ambition and struggle. On the substance side, the contrary longing for community, reconciliation and harmony. The bellicose subjective side progressively brings about the harmonious communal side, resulting in the "end" – the fulfillment – of history. Hegel's Divine and

Human Law are to Nietzsche's Dionysian and Apollonian as the Unity of Subject and Substance is to the Will to Power, which in my view makes an early appearance here as the "world-artist," a passage that is therefore worth quoting at length:

> Insofar as the subject is the artist, however, he has already been released from his individual will and has become, as it were, the medium through which the one *truly* existent subject celebrates his release in appearance ... The entire comedy of art is neither performed for *our* betterment or education, nor are *we* the true authors of this art world ... We are merely images and artistic projections for the *true* artist ... while our consciousness of our own significance hardly differs from that which the soldiers painted on canvas have of the battle represented on it ... Only insofar as the genius in the act of artistic creation coalesces with this primordial artist of the will does he know anything of the eternal essence of art ... he is at once subject and object, at once poet, actor and spectator.

It was Hegel who initiated the search for "intersubjectivity" as the underlying dynamic of the historical process, and Nietzsche is echoing that search in his evocation of the world-artist. By "coalescing" with the primordial life-world, the human artist overcomes the subject/object distinction. Just as for Hegel, the one true historical actor and self-consciousness was Spirit, so Nietzsche now says that the world as a whole is "the one truly existent subject," expressing itself through its human avatar, the artist. Just as Hegel had characterized Spirit as a dynamic of becoming that expresses itself through its human participants, for Nietzsche, the true artist is at bottom not the human artist but the world-artist. The life-world wells up through the passions of the artist, who sublimates and recasts those energies as art, thereby enabling the world to fulfill its own self-expression. Unlike Hegel, however, it is not a dialectic of progress but rather a clash of tensions barely surmounted; not a synthesis but a struggle.

The *Birth of Tragedy* is a notable installment in Nietzsche's deconstruction of the Hegelian science of Spirit. Just as Hegel argued that the Divine Law was supplanted by Human Law, the chthonic religion of the hearth supplanted by the public life of the agora, Nietzsche argues that the tragic age was supplanted by the classical age when the Apollonian wrenched itself out of its symbiosis with the Dionysian and sought to dominate it, chiefly through the rational and universalistic philosophy of Socrates and Plato (Socrates was the "newborn demon" who "scared Dionysus off the stage"). Authentic tragedy was replaced by the moralizing of Euripides, Socrates' mouthpiece. Whereas Hegel had seen the supersession of the Divine Law by the Human Law as necessary and ultimately beneficial, in the *Birth of Tragedy* Nietzsche regards the domination of the Apollonian over the Dionysian as the beginning of a massive spiritual decline, arid rationalism and democratic leveling.

In general, wherever Hegel propounds a synthesis resolving a tension between historical forces in conflict, Nietzsche re-explodes it, arguing that the conflict has only intensified over the centuries and has reached an agonizing pitch of extremity in the present. However, while Nietzsche's preference for the tragic age and the symbiotic interdependence of the Apollonian and the Dionysian perfected in Homer and Sophocles vividly highlights his view of man's decline into democratic leveling, it provides no movement forward into the future, no contribution to what Nietzsche later termed "the enhancement of the type 'man.'" Nietzsche came to recognize this limitation when he wrote a new preface for the *Birth of Tragedy* after the publication of his magnum opus, *Thus Spake Zarathustra*. I will reserve my discussion of the details of this retrospective criticism until its later appearance in Nietzsche's body of work, including a fascinating new view of Dionysus. But to state it in general terms so that we can understand the transition from *The Birth of Tragedy* to his mature works, Nietzsche came to believe that the Dionysian does not merely need to be reestablished as an equal partner with the Apollonian, as he had earlier thought, but that it must be torn apart by the forward thrust of the Apollonian itself – the ascetic ideal – in order to enable a new birth, the Overman. We would not be amiss, I think, in detecting in this trope an echo of Hegel's own characterization in the *Phenomenology of Spirit* of the unfolding of Spirit as analogous to both the Crucifixion and the dismemberment of Dionysus. But the outcome of this rebirth through death will, in Nietzsche's version of the future, be anything but the benevolent flourishing of the modern nation-state as it finds a new sense of religious purpose through mutual forgiveness. On the contrary: The new messianism of Zarathustra emerges from the unraveling of Platonism and Christianity as Platonism for the people, and the prelude for his call to will the Overman is the "death of God."

Before we turn to Nietzsche's view of the future in his mature works, we should first consider his essay *On the Advantages and Disadvantages of History for Life*. Having given an elegiac backward glance to the tragic age of the Greeks in *The Birth of Tragedy*, Nietzsche now hones his diagnosis of the crisis of the historical sense in the present, and deepens his critique of Hegel.

HOW MUCH HISTORY? A HOMEOPATHIC PRESCRIPTION

Nietzsche's critique of Hegel's impact on education is announced in forthright terms in this essay: "I believe that there has been no dangerous change or turn in the German education of this century which has not become more dangerous through the enormous influence ... of this philosophy, the Hegelian." In Nietzsche's view of the spiritual landscape of late-nineteenth-century Europe, people were gradually losing their conviction regarding the doctrine of historical progress – of which Hegel's account was the most authoritative – while retaining or seeing no exit from their belief in the historicity of the human condition. This is Nietzsche's starting point, and since for Nietzsche, as a historicist thinker, man's historical existence still takes the place (as it had for Hegel) of the classical understanding of the soul, Nietzsche's understanding of the "advantages and disadvantages of history for life" is first and foremost a meditation on what liberal education can and should mean in the twilight of our faith in progress. In Nietzsche's treatment of the three modes of historicity and their relationship to life – the monumental, the antiquarian and the critical – we sense an attenuated yet still real link to Plato's and Aristotle's notions of how liberal education must entail a ranking and harmonizing of different states of the soul. Only now, since it is evidently not given to us to experience the soul *sub specie aeternitatis*, the great classical accounts of the immortality of the soul are replaced by a set of active historical stances of the self toward the world it has historically created. It is no longer a question, as it had been for the ancients, of how best to approximate the eternal verities through our moral and intellectual virtues, but rather of how to go on being human in a world apparently devoid of permanent meaning.

Nietzsche is perhaps the greatest philosophical critic of liberal democracy and modernity. Although so far in this book I have concentrated on the way in which the Philosophy of Freedom offered a broad-ranging critique of classical liberalism, by Nietzsche's time, liberalism itself had grown comfortable with the Hegelian notion that the modern liberal age was the crown of all previous historical development. Early liberal thinkers such as Locke and Montesquieu shaped the belief that liberal democracy was the only reasonable regime. According to them, since it is based on what is universal to mankind – individual autonomy and self-preservation – it allows for a truly rational politics. Under its influence, people would give up nonnegotiable strife over religion, nationalism and divine right, and in this sense act more rationally. Liberalism appeared therefore to achieve in actuality the harmony of politics and reason which for Plato had remained a utopia. The early liberal thinkers were convinced they had made a break with the past and done something entirely new They were "moderns" – the "way of today" (*modus hodiernus*) as opposed to the classical and Christian traditions. So successful was the new liberal epoch that it bred the conviction that this most rational of regimes was the final outcome of all previous history, which was reinterpreted as a series of stages and half-successes leading progressively toward the present, liberal-democratic end of history. Tocqueville, for example, thought that democracy was the historically irreversible and inevitable outcome of the struggle for justice over the centuries. Marx, as we saw in the last chapter, believed modern democracy was the inevitable outcome of man's struggle for survival and economic security, as if Hobbes' and Locke's hypotheses about the state of nature had in fact been the guiding force of history all along. Despite its imperfections, for Marx liberalism was also the harbinger of a new society growing out of its ruins, which would supersede democracy in its current flawed bourgeois form by abolishing private property while retaining its prosperity, enlightenment and autonomy – the supersession of "political" emancipation by full "human" emancipation.

Some, including Tocqueville, had doubts that democracy was the only good way of life, even if its victory was historically irreversible. Like Marx – although he did not share Marx's vision of the future – Tocqueville thought liberalism had robbed people of a sense of community and the security of fixed traditional beliefs about religion. With some of the great Romantic novelists like Flaubert – a favorite of Nietzsche's – this dissatisfaction reaches an extreme of intensity, representative of a growing and widespread disgust with liberal modernity. *Madame Bovary* and *Sentimental Education* offer an ultimately hopeless view of modern life. Flaubert shares neither Marx's hopes for the future nor Tocqueville's belief that liberal democracy can modify its own worst tendencies in the present. For the novelist, modern individualism destroys all grand commitments by reducing man to the "barracks-room" of work and competition. There are no dreams or challenges. Art is vulgarized; religion is corrupt or ridiculous in its craven desire for acceptance, as with the priest who writes a treatise on agronomy called *Manure*. Politics is the servant of business, whether it camouflages itself with the propaganda of the Left or the Right. Flaubert thinks the socialists only want to hasten this process of degradation by destroying the remnants of personal liberty in an absolute state that will chain everyone to their lathes (an "American Sparta," as it is envisioned by his revolutionary and would-be Robespierre, Senecal, who ends up as a police agent for the democratic despot Napoleon III). Nietzsche is the first philosopher to think through the principles of liberalism and its faith in history on the basis of this thoroughgoing and mounting disgust. His writings on education are meant, in effect, to save the talented but disillusioned young men and women of Flaubert's novels from their corrosive disbelief.

Rousseau, we recall, had already rejected modern instrumental rationality in favor of "the sublime science of simple souls." He extolled the simplicity of the natural instincts – the unselfconscious individualism of natural man prior to civilization – as against liberalism's anxiety-ridden competition for wealth, power and status. For Rousseau, the nature of the common man is, in its honesty and sincerity, preferable to the rarest glories of reason, which only emerge when our dependence on others – the loss of our natural self-sufficiency – forces us to learn about them and especially how to deceive them.

Nietzsche also rejects a devotion to reason, but not on the basis of some other conception of a stable human nature, as does Rousseau. Instead, he opposes reason on behalf of "life." By life, Nietzsche means the passionate commitment humans experience when they are creating something altogether new in history. Nietzsche is in this sense the first philosopher of commitment, a forerunner of the existentialists. He embodies a new and explosive combination. He rejects reason and the Hegelian belief that the present age is the end result of history's progressive actualization of reason. But he does so on the basis of a more radical historicism than that of Hegel or even Marx. Nietzsche begins the essay by observing that we may sometimes envy the peace and oblivion of the herd in the field, because "the animal lives *unhistorically*." Man, by contrast, "cannot learn to forget but always remains attached to the past." That is why he can on occasion be "moved" by the oblivion of the beast, "as though he remembered a lost paradise." There is an echo here of a view variously expressed, as we have seen, by Rousseau, Kant and Schiller that the natural equilibrium of the desires confers upon pre-civilized man an effortless happiness akin to the unselfconsciousness of an animal. But according to Nietzsche, man cannot return to this paradise, and, except for these momentary episodes of a desire to forget, does not want to. Man is historical through and through, possessing a "plastic power" to "distinctively grow out of itself, transforming and assimilating everything past and alien, to heal wounds, replace what is lost and reshape broken forms out of itself." Rousseau, Kant and Schiller had all expressed a degree of regret that our lost natural wholeness could not be recovered in the present, but argued that a simulacrum of it could be achieved under the conditions of civilization through civic freedom, moral autonomy or aesthetic culture. By contrast, Nietzsche expresses no such regret, and does not believe that any underlying substratum of innocent instinctual happiness exists for man, nor should we want it to. Whereas Rousseau, Kant and Schiller each in his own way tried to strike an equipoise between our natural selves and the selves we had become through the progress of history in order to achieve the only kind of wholeness that was possible given the truth of the modern account of nature, Nietzsche identifies our capacity for wholeness entirely with our historical dynamism and experiences. In this respect, he is more like Hegel. But he understands history and its capacity to enhance life in a profoundly different way.

This is why Nietzsche understands himself to be the antagonist of Platonism. For him, Plato represents the "superhistorical" belief that man's possibilities are naturally fixed and of eternal duration, which is the death of all striving, risk and creativity. Hence, as he later wrote, "Plato is boring." But in a way Hegel represented a graver danger, because he claimed to have reconciled a noble account of human life on the high level of the ancients with an account of existence as time-bound historicity. Since the Platonic view of the whole was no longer thought to be available to us, Hegel had sought to synthesize the modern account of nature as matter in motion with a free and virtuous life that could rise above materialism, with history as the uniting third term. But, Nietzsche argues, it was precisely this Hegelian account of the meaning of historicity that has led to our current spiritual crisis, more so than any atavistic holdovers from classical thought. Man is historical through and through, but the belief in the Hegelian end of history, in Nietzsche's view, *prevents* man from living historically. For the belief that we are at the end of history makes us think that nothing new and great can ever be achieved. It also convinces us that all past creations – which their creators believed were absolutely true and would last forever –were false, temporary and of merely relative value, delusions on the way to a crowning delusion (mankind's satisfaction at the end of history) that we also increasingly no longer believe in.

For Nietzsche, the relativity of values is true, but it is utterly destructive of life. By exposing the relativity of values, history paralyzes our belief in the possibility of absolutes, the possibility of commitment. How, Nietzsche asks, can you worship a god which you know to be a human creation like all other past gods and values? How can you give your life for your country if you know your country's cause is only relatively just, no more so than that of other countries and eras, and perhaps less? Thus the awful paradox: In order to make history, man must not know the truth about history. Otherwise, we give up striving to create anything new and sink into petty materialism and laissez-aller. For Nietzsche, this is the unavowed, insidious connection between liberal democracy and the philosophy of history today: Historicism paralyzes our commitment to anything new, bold and dangerous, and therefore bolsters bourgeois man's absorption in survival and comfort.

According to Nietzsche, the passionate commitment by which past empires, faiths and art were created needs above all a narrow horizon. One must have the illusion that not everything has already been done; that not all values are relative because *my* value is the absolute truth. If history is to go on, first it must stop. We have to have the feeling that the past is dead and buried, that only the present counts, so we can go on from here. At the same time, we must know something about past history and its glories, because if our horizon is *excessively* narrow, that too can make us complacent and unimaginative, like the herd grazing in the field. The study of history shows us that, since there have been great and inspiring changes in the past, there can be again. That is its proper relationship to life. As the title of the essay suggests, Nietzsche is asking: How much history is too much? How much is too little? The answer lies in finding, so to speak, the right homeopathic tincture of its three major modes – the monumental, the antiquarian and the critical – so as to achieve the proper relationship of history to life.

Let us consider them in turn. Monumental history consoles us in our present struggle to change and improve mankind by reminding us of past successes at doing so. The enduring fame of these achievements allows us to hope that we will enjoy such fame in the future if we succeed. But every advantage of a historical education has a corresponding disadvantage. Monumental history, left to itself, isolates glorious deeds from the complex causes that made them possible for their own time and place. It can fool you into thinking that, because something great happened once, it can happen again simply through an exertion of will. In this way, monumental history does an injustice to the full complexity and contingency of events. The literal-minded attempt to imitate Julius Caesar in the modern world will not produce a replica of that complex and brilliant figure, only the homicidal theatricality of a Mussolini. In Nietzsche's own era, Napoleon III's attempt to imitate his uncle Napoleon I led only to the empty parvenu pomp of the Second Empire, while his pretensions to imperial greatness were shattered in a single day by the military sledgehammer of Bismarck's Prussia.

By tempting us to rashness and fanaticism, monumental history can make us blind to the specific limitations and possibilities of the present. According to

Nietzsche, we cannot copy or restore the past. Rather, we study the complexity of past events in order to understand that current historical circumstances have a comparable complexity but a different content. Monumental history can also lead to a hypocritical veneration of the past in order to make excuses for our failures in the present, or to suppress those who want to do great things now on the grounds that everything great has already been done. Hence, Flaubert's artist Pellerin in *Sentimental Education* venerates the old masters as a way of excusing his own failures as a painter and running down everyone else. The buccaneering businessman Jacques Arnoux justifies his coarse trafficking in art, pottery and financial speculation by decrying "modern decadence." There is nothing to be ashamed of in cheapening art or exploiting artists because all modern art is lousy.

Antiquarian history mitigates the tendency of monumental history to see the past as a marble gallery of unending glories. It narrows our horizon by teaching us to venerate a specific culture of the past. The modern age, according to Nietzsche, does not know what to commit itself to because it knows the history of all peoples and cultures. Everything changes and passes away in a "sea of becoming." (Reminiscent of Hegel's maxim that "nothing vanishes in Spirit.) Antiquarian history is an antidote to this sense of dispersal. A narrow, centuries-old attachment proves that it is possible to make a single choice and stick to it. Even if we revere a tradition that is no longer viable for the present, we can look back to it from an inferior age as proof that improvement is possible in the future. Hence, the Italian Renaissance drew sustenance from Greco-Roman antiquity, which it admired as superior in every way to the present, in order to overcome the stultification of the Middle Ages. Although Nietzsche does not refer to it specifically, a good example of what he means by the need for a narrow horizon and an avoidance of being inundated with historical knowledge is the fact that the great neoclassical Renaissance architecture of Palladio and Michelangelo was actually based on a mistaken understanding of what Greek and Roman buildings had really been like. Out of this imitation partly born of ignorance, something entirely new grew from those ancient roots. A Renaissance building like the Palazzo Barberini mirrors its Greek and Roman forebears at every angle, yet it is utterly unlike anything that the Greeks and Romans actually built.

The problem with antiquarianism is that, if it becomes too exclusively fixed on one segment of the past, it can paralyze new creations just as surely as can too much openness to change. While confirming the possibility of a single-minded commitment, antiquarian history can become chained to this one commitment, so that man becomes once again too much like the beast grazing in the field. Reverence for the past atrophies into a kind of museum culture, cutting us off from life as it is now.

The antidote to this excess of veneration for the past is critical history, which reveals that every epoch is only partially just, partially true to its own best vision of itself. When we probe beneath the surface, we find that all societies are in some measure oppressive and all religions intolerant, and that all regimes promote one form of happiness at the expense of other plausible visions of human fulfillment. These defects always come out with time. People think of new desires or hunger for new experiences, and the old ways start to seem empty or illegitimate. When this happens, it is healthier to clear the past away than to cling desperately to the status quo, as does antiquarian history at its worst. For life reasserts itself through this destruction of the old order. It is a springboard to create something new. Nietzsche himself, for instance, abhorred the atavistic or bourgeois-imperial German nationalism becoming more and more prevalent in his era and looked ahead to a liberating new pan-European identity.

But critical history also has its disadvantages. Exposing the stupidity and injustice of every known era of the past can rob us of our faith in ourselves in the present, and paralyze our confidence that we can improve ourselves, since we spring from the very errors we condemn. We want to shake off the past and start over. But what if everything that we are is bound up with this past, as a consistently critical historicism would have to admit? The disadvantages of critical history bear directly on our recent fashionable obsession with demythologizing the past. Nietzsche would agree that, in order to live up to our own highest principles, we have to shake off our smugness about what has been done up to now and realize that there was much suffering and injustice along the way. However, taken to an extreme, this process of critical deflation can lead to a revision of past history as an unremitting horror story of frustrated freedom, persecution and injustice. But if one's regime is entirely corrupt, why even hope to reform it? The current tendency to see injustice as "systemic" is an illustration of what Nietzsche means when he argues that the healthy skepticism of critical history can be pushed to a paralyzing extreme. For it implies, not merely that we have failed to live up to our principles as a democracy (which we have, often and appallingly), but that at bottom we have no principles at all, since they were never more than window-dressing for oppression. If that is so, then we will be unable to appeal to them now as an adjuration to further improvement.

After reviewing these three perspectives on a healthy relationship between the study of history and the fulfillment of life, Nietzsche now asks: What is there about present historical education that prevents this relationship? Contributing his own assessment of a theme we have encountered in the Philosophy of Freedom extending back to Rousseau – the problem of the divided self – Nietzsche characterizes modern education as fostering an alienating opposition between the Inner and the Outer. A profusion of unrelated, contradictory stories makes up our external culture. Yet they do not really belong to us inwardly, and we know that none of them can be lived now. We pride ourselves on catching the latest production of *La Traviata* while rejecting the heart of the opera's human relationships as sexist and patriarchal. Our eyes mist at Ingrid Bergman's agonizing choice between Humphrey Bogart and Paul Heinried in

Casablanca, while professing to wish her character would not view herself as the appendage of a man. We sift through what Nietzsche calls the "indigestible knowledge-stones" of art galleries and concerts, "comparing their effects," while inwardly their themes and the passions that inspired the art have nothing to do with us. Our inner spiritual lives are confused or blank because we are cut off from any goal worth choosing in the external world. Or, if we do resolve to choose what the modern world can offer us, we end up gratifying our basest whims and impulses.

The divide between the inner and the outer seeks a false resolution, according to Nietzsche, in the pursuit of objectivity. For Nietzsche, objectivity is the unwillingness to be touched deeply by anything we study. It masquerades as open-mindedness, but is really a retreat from deciding what we prefer, a disguise for indifference. Hence, in modern philosophy and classics departments, Nietzsche would observe, few can say with any great degree of conviction why they study what they do. A person studies modal logic or Attic Greek during the week and pursues a passion for sky-diving on the weekend. What is the connection? Objectivity disguises what is in truth a petty subjectivity, a desire to profess a love of culture so as to enshrine it and thereby seal it off from interfering with the gratification of our pedestrian whims.

In looking for a way of healing the division between the inner and the outer, Nietzsche reawakens the traditional concern of liberal education with human wholeness. This is a concern he shares with Schiller, Hegel and others who wrestled, as we have seen, with the psychology of the divided self bequeathed by Rousseau and further elaborated by Kant, radically as he may differ with them regarding the solution. Nietzsche believes we have a vague awareness that life has eluded us. He looks to the young, who have the greatest daring and desire for life before they are anesthetized by education, as the hope for the future. But what should modern education and culture be replaced with? There is no clear answer given here. Since man is a creator, since everything truly great is completely new, no clear aim can be prescribed in advance. More than this, the genie is out of the bottle: Modern man has discovered the dread truth that values are indeed relative. He will never be able to escape from this awareness. Not only do we have to create something completely original, but we have to do so in the *knowledge* that it is a value, rather than an absolute truth. Since the goal cannot be predicted or justified according to the canons of eternal rationality, and since we cannot have the blissful illusion of past epochs that we are pursuing the absolute truth, the only way of being sure we are overcoming the present is through the depth, passion and intensity of our commitment. Thus, for Nietzsche, a narrowness of horizon selectively illuminated by historical insight remains the locus of a healthy personality. Knowledge of history must serve a dedication to our current life and strivings. This is why Nietzsche, far from dismissing the study of history, tries to reform it as the servant of commitment.

But a commitment to what? The essay does not provide a conclusive answer or direction, only sketches a kind of homeopathic relationship of the study of history to life in order to establish how much is too much or too little. At this stage of his thinking, although Nietzsche's critique of Hegel's understanding of the progress of history is already firmly entrenched, he has not yet established his own alternative vision for how mankind is to move forward. Although Nietzsche is a historicist through and through in a way that Schiller, who sought a balance between nature and freedom through the mediation of aesthetic culture, is not, in his effort at this stage to encourage human wholeness through the proper balance between historical knowledge and life, his prescription in the essay bears a broad similarity to that of Schiller, and is limited to educational culture with few implications for a broader transformation of modern life. As we will now see, that changes profoundly in later works like *Beyond Good and Evil*, which advance a distinctly millenarian and revolutionary alternative to liberal modernity that is all-encompassing in its sweep – culturally, psychologically, educationally and, as I will argue, politically. With increasing intensity, Nietzsche will argue that, since the truth of historicism has blocked the path back to any restorative conception of a permanent human nature, including from the ancients, while at the same time, in its Hegelian version, paralyzing the possibility of great historical achievements in the present, the only way forward to the "enhancement of the type 'man'" is through a radical futurism.

PRELIMINARY PERSPECTIVES ON NIETZSCHE'S PHILOSOPHY OF HISTORY

I want to outline four interrelated themes that recur throughout Nietzsche's mature writings which will clarify our understanding when we turn to the text of *Beyond Good and Evil*. The first of these we have already encountered: Man needs narrow horizons in order to beautify life and make it bearable through reverence before a higher authority and the striving for nobility.

The second theme is that, according to Nietzsche, the greatest of these horizons in human history to date is Platonic philosophy and especially its metaphysics of the Ideas crowned by the Idea of the Good. Platonism achieves its power by denying that the world we actually experience is real at all, locating what is real in a higher, eternal and invisible realm of immortal truth. Like Hegel before him, Nietzsche conflates traditional philosophy's search for the eternal Good with that of revealed religion – the Platonic Good is synonymous with God, especially the Christian God. This denial of the natural world around us, of the bodily and sensual, turns man inward and leads to a tremendous spiritual deepening, a capacity for self-overcoming and a capacity to transcend the limitations of external nature. It is therefore the greatest expression in history of the will to power so far, and it is primarily a spiritual transformation, not one imposed by force or violence, although it certainly entailed such literal expressions of might as it unfolded into European civilization. For Nietzsche, this greatest expression to date of the will to power, it should be stressed, was unselfconscious. In other words, Plato did not realize he was arguing for the truth of his metaphysics as a way of narrowing horizons and intensifying the will to power. He believed in the absolute truth of what he thought. That is why he could serve it so unrelentingly. (That did not, for reasons we will explore, preclude its presentation as ironic or esoteric to a degree.)

The third theme is that Platonic metaphysics and its Christian ally now stand over against us, dominating all of reality, imprisoning us in a cage of determinism and paralyzing our capacity to will anything new. Once the Idea of the Good (and of God) was launched, it became a relentless project for subjugating the world through its complete rationalization (a dynamic Nietzsche first explored in *The Birth of Tragedy* when the Apollonian detached itself from its partnership with the Dionysian and turned on it, determined to crush its irrationalism and bring it under its suzerainty). The Platonic Socrates was the first to argue that human beings are fundamentally equal because we all possess a soul linking us to the immortal truth. Enshrined in Plato's metaphysics, this drive for equality fuses with the religious version that establishes human equality in the sight of God. These combined drives usher in the modern age of democratic leveling, the eradication of rank and the campaign to end human suffering. As we recall from Chapter 2, the atheist materialist Feuerbach maintained that "compassion is before thought," a perfect Nietzschean example of how modern secular egalitarianism grew continuously out of Christian revelation and Platonism. This is essentially the same process of the path from Platonism and Christianity to modernity that Hegel unfolds in the *Phenomenology of Spirit*, but for Nietzsche it is not mankind's advance toward fulfillment but a disastrous spiritual decline and flattening, culminating in the "herd man" of contemporary democratic morality, the nadir of humanity which in *Thus Spake Zarathustra* he terms "the Last Man":

No shepherd and one herd! Everybody wants the same, everybody is the same: whoever feels different goes voluntarily into a madhouse. "Formerly, all the world was mad," say the most refined, and they blink ... One has one's little pleasure for the day and one's little pleasure for the night: but one has a regard for health. "We have invented happiness," say the last men, and they blink.

For Nietzsche, the whole unfolding of Platonism in partnership with Christianity to create the modern world is crystallized in the concept of the opposition between the real and the apparent world, our fourth theme. It sums up the paradox whereby what is most "real" is what is least available to sensual experience – the Ideas are invisible, imperishable, cannot be felt, touched or tasted – while what we most directly experience through our senses, desires and pleasures is not real at all, merely "apparent." What is most real becomes what is least real; what is least real becomes the truly real. The very absurdity of this inversion of experience – summed up in the saying attributed to Tertullian about the mystery of Christ's resurrection, "I believe it *because* it is absurd" – is the source of its revolutionary drive to remake the world so that it conforms to this dichotomy.

However, in our own age, Nietzsche argues, the distinction between the real and apparent world is rapidly undermining itself. This happens in two ways. The first of these is not unlike the dynamic that Hegel expressed in the images from the *Phenomenology of Spirit* that we discussed in the last chapter: The real world, the realm of God and the Good, is so far elevated above the apparent world that life in the here and now is drained of all mystery and beauty, reduced to mere empirically verifiable matter. But that means there is increasingly no basis *in* the here and now, in life, for *believing* in the higher realm. Socrates had begun the search for the Ideas by observing that there were many beautiful phenomena around us in the here and now that pointed to a universal Idea of the Beautiful in which they all participated through, as Hegel put it, "a thread of light ... attached to heaven." But the world of the here and now, because it has thereby been reduced in comparison to mere matter, no longer offers any beautiful phenomena that would ground our conviction that they must point to that higher Idea. To maintain that we continue to believe in God and the Good in the absence of any evidence for that belief in the earthly life we experience is a species of what Nietzsche means by "nihilism." You cannot accept that the life around us has been reduced to a low realm of mere matter (a process beginning with St. Augustine and culminating in early modern thinkers like Hobbes) yet go on saying that there is evidence in our lives for the existence of God.

The second way in which the distinction between the real and the apparent world is undermining itself is that, as the Idea of the Good and God brings the rest of existence under its sway, it must eventually turn on itself and kill its own divine residue. For the God with which Platonic metaphysics had originally partnered contained too many taints from the "apparent" world of desire and feeling to satisfy the purity of "the ascetic ideal" (as he terms it in *The Genealogy of Morals*), the denial of life characteristic of both Platonic metaphysics and revealed religion. For the God of the Torah was still a person – he walked in the Garden, he was capable of love, jealousy and vengeance, and he had human favorites. In some gnostic sources, he had a consort. All of these traits that made God a person had to be eradicated. In other words, God had to be sacrificed for the Idea of God. Contrary to the conventional liberal understanding of historical progress according to which belief in the God of the Old and New Testaments is undermined by secular rationalism and science, in Nietzsche's view, the "death of God" (to use his famous phrase) was necessitated by the subjugation of the here and now by the Idea of God itself, whose working out included modern rationalism and science. For Nietzsche, Deism, the Enlightenment's attempt at a rational religion which turns God into a mere concept of transcendental morality and order, a bloodless abstraction, far from being the antithesis of traditional faith, is its inevitable outcome. If God is dead, the basis for all morality as it has hitherto been understood – the assumption that we are capable of taking responsibility for our actions and voluntarily choosing virtue and goodness over vice and evil stretching back to Socrates – has crumbled, for that assumption was grounded in the Platonic understanding of the cosmos as structured according to the Idea of the Good. "If God is dead, everything is permitted" – a maxim variously attributed to Nietzsche and Dostoyevsky. Yet even though we know or sense in our heart of hearts that God is dead, we go on professing our belief in the old morality – another species of nihilism.

We should note that, although the process by which Nietzsche argues that the real (invisible) world undermines our capacity to believe in it by draining the apparent world of anything but what is empirically verifiable resembles Hegel's outline of that process in the *Phenomenology of Spirit* – whether because the here and now has been drained of any evidence for transcendence and reduced to matter in motion, or because a personal God who loves and guides us has been sacrificed to the pure Idea of God – in Nietzsche's version, the implications are completely different. In Hegel's presentation of the Unity of Subject and Substance, the divine sphere of reconciliation and forgiveness intertwines with the secular project for the mastery of nature as history progresses. The secular project culminates in the Terror of the French Revolution and puts the divine dimension at its gravest risk. But that divine dimension endures and reemerges through the reconciliation of Kant and Schiller and a new spirit of mutual forgiveness, God's reappearance at the end of history. For Nietzsche, by contrast, the project for the subjugation of existence by reason beginning with Plato and revealed religion are not spheres with different aims – one for the mastery of nature, the other for harmony and reconciliation – that intertwine and reach a mutual fulfillment. Instead, they are two dimensions of a single, relentless drive to bring life under the domination of rationality. And when that process reaches its culmination, God does *not* reappear in history, for that process has culminated in God's death, God sacrificed to the Idea of God, and that death is final: "God is dead," Zarathustra proclaims, "and we have killed him." A new supreme being, the Overman, will take God's place as the horizon for mankind's future reverence and self-overcoming. With these themes in mind, let us turn to a detailed consideration of *Beyond Good and Evil*.

Why am I stressing this particular text? What I earlier characterized as the fundamental premises of Nietzsche's philosophy – the concepts of the Will to Power and the Eternal Recurrence – are set forth at length in *Thus Spake Zarathustra*, which he considered to be his magnum opus. (As he put it: "Among my writings my *Zarathustra* stands to my mind by itself. With that I have given mankind the greatest present that has ever been made to it so far.") However, since it will not be remotely possible to attempt a full exegesis of that astonishingly rich text, there are two reasons for looking closely at *Beyond*

Good and Evil as a preparation for it. The first is that Nietzsche wrote it following the appearance of *Zarathustra* so as to enable the reader to understand the origin of his teaching by providing a *tour d'horizon* of thought, culture, education, art and politics during his own era from which that teaching arose. By reversing chronology and examining *Beyond Good and Evil* first, it will hopefully provide us with a kind of Michelin Guide to European nihilism that might help us make sense of the notoriously pseudo-biblical and pseudo-Gothic, mythological language of *Zarathustra*, in comparison with which its successor possesses, in the words of one commentator, an almost Platonic clarity. The other reason for focusing our attention on this work is that Nietzsche's understanding of both the will to power and the eternal recurrence do make a brief appearance there, and seeing how they emerge from his reflections on the real-life Europe of his time will help us build a bridge to the fuller and more mythic explication of them in *Zarathustra*.

Another preliminary consideration to keep in mind as we go forward is that, in both the literary and the philosophical senses, Nietzsche the author is not necessarily identifiable with his character Zarathustra, and Zarathustra is not the Overman. Nietzsche is, in effect, preparing us for Zarathustra's revelation, and Zarathustra's revelation points the way to willing the Overman yet to come. Revelation is an entirely apt term here, because Zarathustra is a prophet, his name a variation on Zoroaster, the perhaps largely mythological Iranian founder of Zoroastrianism. His was the first religion that set forth a struggle between the forces of light and the forces of darkness, a struggle between good and evil. Man's proper role was to struggle on behalf of the progressive victory of the light over the darkness. As such, Zoroaster's teaching has been characterized as the first example of a Messianic faith and the religious precursor for all doctrines of historical progress. It has been argued that the Messianic content of late Jewish religious scripture – the transition from maintaining a righteous kingdom of God in Israel to a struggle on behalf of God's light throughout the world, preparing the way for the appearance of his Messiah, a new king descended from the House of David who will reunite the scattered tribes and rebuild the Temple in Jerusalem – reflects the absorption of Zoroastrianism by Jews exiled to Babylon after the conquest of Judaea. Zoroastrianism also influenced the Christian belief that Christ will return and establish the Kingdom of Righteousness on earth after defeating the forces of Satan, and the birth of Jesus incorporated a number of Zoroastrian tropes – the visit to Bethlehem of the Three Wise Men (actually Magi, that is to say Zoroastrian priests) guided by the Eastern Star. Nietzsche's choice of Zarathustra as the source of the new revelation of the Overman therefore says a very great deal about Nietzsche's vision for the future, his comparative assessment of philosophy and revelation, and his proclivity for merging the role of the philosopher with the more primary role of the religious prophet motivated more by his compassion for mankind and "the enhancement of the type 'man'" than by the search for wisdom for its own sake. Still – and it is an important qualification – in noting the suitability of Zarathustra as a vehicle for Nietzsche's thought, we must bear in mind that this is, in effect, Zarathustra's "second coming." In Nietzsche's hands, for reasons we will see, he is not simply the duplication of or return to the ancient Iranian. Having discussed these preliminary considerations of Nietzsche's thought, we now turn to *Beyond Good and Evil* to see how they unfold in detail.

BENDING THE BOW AND THE PREJUDICES OF PHILOSOPHERS

The Preface proclaims that today's struggle against Plato and Christianity, which Nietzsche identifies as "Platonism for 'the people,'" has created in Europe "a magnificent tension of the spirit the like of which has never existed on earth: with so tense a bow we can now shoot for the most distant goals." In *Ecce Homo*, alluding to Zarathustra's origins, Nietzsche identifies bowmanship as a Persian virtue. Could it also be an echo of the challenge of the bow in Homer's *Odyssey*, which Odysseus alone is able to string? The magnificent tension is the contradiction between Platonism's paralyzing effect on the will to create anew and the struggle of the will to reassert itself through such new creations. But it was the unfolding of Platonism that engendered the paralysis and today's struggle to shatter it in the first place, because Platonism has undermined its claims to possess the eternal truth by making it impossible to believe in the eternal Good in a world reduced to matter by the Idea of the Good itself. Because Platonism has led to its own unraveling, Platonic philosophy cannot account for itself or for its historical outcome, despite its claim to be motivated by the search for a higher supersensible and imperishable Being.

Accordingly, Nietzsche argues in Part One, philosophy's claim to be searching for the eternal truth has now been exposed as a "prejudice" concealing a deeper motivation of which it is unaware. Beginning with Plato, all previous philosophy asks: What is the truth? Nietzsche claims he is the first to ask: Why truth? Why do we need truth? "Why not untruth?" he demands, "and uncertainty? Even ignorance?" In reality, philosophy is motivated by "the faith in opposite values" – that is to say, the principle of identity and contradiction. Metaphysics is possible because of this faith in "the intransitory, the hidden god, the 'thing in itself' ... in the lap of Being," or, put another way, in the oneness of the truth and its superordinate reality over accident and chance. It is a prejudice because it does not reflect on its own motivation, which is faith in the intelligibility of the world, and is not even conscious of it. Even Hegel, who had identified existence with sheer historical self-origination, sheer spontaneous chance, succumbed to the metaphysical prejudice when he then insisted that its unfolding must be understood through the conceptual distinction between Subject and Substance, the dialectic of Spirit. Philosophy has been based on the faith in opposite values without being conscious of it, because otherwise the chaos of life would be unbearable. Modern materialists like Descartes say that "everything is to be doubted" that is not empirically verifiable, therefore especially metaphysics and religious belief. But they do not extend this to doubting the value of possessing the truth, in this case their own truth, "atomistic materialism." We begin to see why Nietzsche presents the source of his new understanding of philosophy as a prophet – from now on, philosophy will have to be aware of the need to ask: Why does philosophy *need* to believe in truth? Religious conviction, including faith in the principle of identity and contradiction, offers a more profound source of insight into man than philosophical system-building.

Philosophy, or whatever activity it is now to become, must be aware that the value of truth is the enhancement of life: "Without accepting the fictions of logic ... man couldn't live." Renouncing these false judgements would mean renouncing life itself. Our only alternative is "to recognize untruth" – by which Nietzsche means the claim to possess knowledge of the eternal truth – "as a condition of life." Understanding that philosophy's claim to search for the truth, which entails a permanent code of moral conduct, is in reality an unexamined prejudice or faith whose untruth is nevertheless indispensable for forming a horizon in which life is bearable is to venture "beyond good and evil."

Nietzsche discusses ancient Stoicism to illustrate his contention that the new criterion for the value of truth is the enhancement of life. It is absurd, he maintains, for the Stoics to claim that they live "according to nature." Stoicism does not passively meditate upon nature as an orderly and beneficent cosmos. On the contrary: Stoicism tyrannizes over the chaos of nature by imposing reason on it in order to make life bearable. "Philosophy is this tyrannical drive ... the most spiritual will to power, to the 'creation of the world.'" To *genuinely* live "according to nature," Nietzsche mocks, would plunge you into a vortex of horror: "nature, wasteful beyond measure, without purposes and consideration, without mercy and justice ... indifference itself as a power."

Nietzsche's discussion of Stoicism must surely be directed in part at Hegel. He too, as we recall from the *Phenomenology of Spirit*, identified Stoicism with the intellectual mastery of nature. But for Hegel, the orderly cosmos that the Stoic meditated upon was a true dimension of Spirit. Classical cosmology had been correct that the world was objectively endowed with a rational and benevolent orderliness. What it lacked was an insight into how that world departed from the mode of a static rationality and set itself in motion as a historical actor, in other words as Spirit. But the rationality of the classical cosmologies understood something true about the world. For Nietzsche, by contrast, Stoicism imposed a purely human and fictitious rational construct upon the irrational void of nature. We see again how Nietzsche tries at every turn to explode a Hegelian synthesis into a conflict between irreconcilable realities.

Nietzsche makes a similar criticism of Kant's question: How are synthetic propositions a priori possible, meaning to say, how is it that causal rationality, whose categories are formal and deductively necessary, can make sense of the observable world, where sequences of events are never more than probable? In other words, how does a statement like A does not = B, which is contentless and necessary, resemble an observation like the sun rises every morning, which is only probable, since tomorrow the sun could go Nova? Nietzsche's withering response: Such judgements are *not* possible at all, and we have no *right* to them. Only the belief in them is necessary so that life does not fall apart.

The paradox is that precisely the most thoroughly entrenched delusions of metaphysics have led to the deepening of the human spirit. Philosophy has no relationship to objective reality at all: "It is we alone who have devised cause, sequence, for-each-other, relativity, constraint, number, law, freedom, motive and purpose." Therefore the difference, for example, between modern materialistic physics and Platonic physics has nothing to do with which one gives a true account of nature. It is nothing but a matter of taste. Modern "atomistic materialism" is a vulgar taste whose reliance on the sense data that is experienced by everyone corresponds to gratifying the low material desires of modern democratic mass man. Platonic physics, by contrast, is noble in its resistance to the evidence provided by sense data. Its insistence on a higher, transcendent and immaterial truth that cannot be observed or measured is driven by a spiritual taste for mastering the "mob of the senses," for sense experience corresponds to the lowest common denominator of understanding. As we have seen, Nietzsche's historicist predecessors including Hegel and Marx had tried to reconcile the rational unfolding of history with what they took to be the objective truth of the modern account of nature. Nietzsche is the first to abandon this quest altogether, which he regards as a holdover of the prejudices of philosophers stretching back to Plato. In this sense, he is the most radical historicist we have encountered so far, arguing that what masquerades as objective reality is entirely created on impulse by the human will, and is not mediated by any claim to objective truth or science such as Hegel's "absolute Science of Spirit" or Marxist "scientific socialism." That said, there is arguably a congruity between the modern scientific account of matter in motion and what Nietzsche means by will to power, which he considers, unlike all previous truths, *not* to be a prejudice, but the genuine account of all existence. We will consider this congruity in due course.

The unselfconscious instinct for mastery of "the mob" within oneself that was the authentic motive for Plato's physics must, Nietzsche believes, become self-conscious, liberating itself from the Platonic prejudice that its only motive is love of the truth while restoring its noble, hidden motivation. Since philosophy on its own cannot explain what genuinely motivates it, Nietzsche says, we must turn to psychology. In effect, psychology must replace philosophy. But not, Nietzsche cautions, the traditional psychology of "moral prejudices" that tries to restrain the passions. Instead, psychology must "descend into the depths" behind moral prejudices, which requires the "doctrine of the development of the will to power" – its first mention in *Beyond Good and Evil*. The passions are vehicles for the will to power's expression: therefore the new psychologist must "regard even the affects of hatred, envy, covetousness and the lust to rule as conditions of life." This loss of moral orientation may well make us "sea-sick." But if we persevere, we will "sail right over morality" to the deeper standpoint of psychology. (Is there another allusion to Homer's *Odyssey* here?) Psychology is Nietzsche's antidote for the project originating with Plato and Christianity to bring all of existence under the sway of rationality, which achieves its final form in modern utilitarian subjectivism. Nietzsche's interest in novelists such as Flaubert is a reflection of his search for a richer psychological account of human experience to replace this arid Cartesian narrowness. The will to power is the development of an ontology that he first broached, as we saw, with his discussion of the world-artist in *The Birth of Tragedy*. The will to power, which is not primarily the human will but the will of all of existence, is the condition for the possibility of every value issuing through the affects that becomes a metaphysical truth. Yet, as the origin of all such metaphysical claims to truth, it uniquely does not possess the character of a metaphysical truth itself.

THE NEW PHILOSOPHERS?

Having exposed the unselfconscious prejudices of philosophy and reoriented the search for understanding toward the psychology of the will to power, Nietzsche turns in Part Two to "The Free Spirit." Is the Free Spirit therefore a new kind of philosopher, or a replacement for philosophy as hitherto conceived? It seems likeliest that Nietzsche views the Free Spirit as a kind of prelude to "the philosopher of the future," whom he appears to be summoning: "you that are coming ... you *new* philosophers." Interestingly, he numbers himself among "we 'free spirits,'" rather than explicitly as one of the new philosophers. Is this analogous to his role, as I suggested above, as preparing the way for Zarathustra? Who and where are the Free Spirits and the new philosophers in Europe? Nietzsche's subtitle for *Thus Spake Zarathustra* is "a book for everyone and for no one." In other words, there may be no one out there as yet who is ready for it, but on another level, all of mankind is potentially receptive, given the crisis of nihilism that touches us all even if we cannot name it. Nietzsche himself cannot know who or where they are. His books amount to a summons shouted into the void: Calling all Free Spirits! Report to Zarathustra Central! He can only assume that the "magnificent tension" between the self-unwinding of Platonism-Christianity and a reawakening of the will to power has stirred others as well.

Part Two begins by reiterating the need for narrow horizons that he stressed in *The Advantages and Disadvantages of History for Life* so as to be able to create truth. But the elaboration of any such truth into a system, and its claim to absolute and permanent authority, obscures the origins out of which it issued. The tension of striving created by the concentration of all our energies on a narrow horizon is what leads to the refinement of the will to power in its expressions as thought, art, religious faith and statecraft. But the erection of those expressions as final and unalterable truths dispels the tension of striving that gave rise to them in the first place – they become, as we might now say, reified. This is what happened with Plato's metaphysics of the Forms. They emerged from the tension of seeking, against all evidence derived from experience, a higher, invisible and permanent reality in which the changeable here and now could be shown to participate, connecting the world of change to a supersensible beyond. But as the metaphysics of the Forms was elaborated into a fixed doctrine, their relationship to life degenerated from a tension into a flat-out contradiction. The higher supersensible realm drained nature of the enchantment which had made it possible to glimpse the Forms in sensuous and temporal phenomena in the first place, which has now made it impossible to believe in the Forms, since there is no evidence for them in a world they reduced by contrast with themselves to mere matter. The emergence of metaphysics inevitably hardens into the dichotomy between the real and apparent world, which at length makes metaphysics itself impossible to believe in as something rooted in our experience of the here and now. The tension between the real and the apparent world is needed for creativity, Nietzsche argues, but not on metaphysical grounds. By understanding that this tension emerges from the will to power's seeking an outlet for its expression, we are able to understand that creativity is a *process*, not the erection of an allegedly permanent truth – the will to power expresses itself as the distinction between the real and the apparent world as its final outermost manifestation. For Nietzsche, the will to power is a new account of the whole that grounds the will not to truth, but to illusion, as necessary for life. It is the condition for the possibility of what has so far declined into metaphysics.

Nietzsche's initial reference to the doctrine of the will to power at the end of Part One, in conjunction with the need for the prejudices of philosophy to yield to the deeper insights of psychology, is now presented as a fully rounded ontological premise – "will to power" is Nietzsche's name for the whole, the matrix of self-origination out of which issue all of our individual acts of will, our instincts, even the organic processes of procreation and nourishment (non-human as well as human), the source of "*all* efficient force univocally." As he later put it in *The Will to Power*, the entire world viewed from within its deepest originary recesses would be "the will to power – and nothing else! And you yourselves are also this will to power – and nothing else!"

As if to emphasize that the Free Spirit will be mainly a psychologist guided by the doctrine of the will to power, Nietzsche sets forth a miniature genealogy of morals, three stages of morality which telescope the psychological development of mankind to date. The earliest stage was the morality of consequences. It is perhaps best evoked by the tragic age of the Greeks that Nietzsche explored in *The Birth of Tragedy*, the world of Homer and Sophocles. The morality of consequences meant that you acted in harmony with what you *were*. As Heraclitus pronounced, the distinction between master and slave, ruler and ruled, emerged directly from the flux of nature as strife. ("War is the father of all and the king of all; and some he has made gods and some men, some bond and some free.") It was your fate to be one or the other. A "good" man was a master – brave, proud, never stooping to justify his actions. He was good not necessarily in the modern moral sense of treating everyone decently, but in the sense of being hale, strong and beautiful. This is reflected in Greek aristocrats calling themselves "the beautiful and good ones"(*kaloi kagathoi*) and Roman aristocrats calling themselves "the Good Ones" (*Boni*). Because the master ruled unconditionally, inevitably he was capable of violence and cruelty. A "bad" man, by contrast, was born an inferior and therefore had slavish qualities – cowardly, dishonest and ugly; bad in the sense of a rotten piece of fruit. The actions of a tragic hero like Oedipus were the consequences of his destiny, not of introspection and choice. Indeed, these tragic characters were almost more like impersonal forces wearing masks than self-aware individuals (Creon's name, for example, simply means "ruler").

The next stage in Nietzsche's typology, the morality of intention, has been by far the most predominant, stretching from the classical age down to the present – it has come to define what is meant by morality altogether. It assumes that everyone has a soul, and that each of us is capable of using our mind to reflect inwardly on our intentions, and that we are therefore responsible for choosing just over unjust actions. Our outward status, appearance, or the pull of the passions should not interfere with our intention to be good, and if they do, we are to blame. The morality of intention distinguishes between good and evil more than between good and bad. Since we are responsible for our actions, bad behavior is not the result, as it had been for the morality of consequences, of blind chance, fate, or birth. Instead, when we do bad things, we do so deliberately, even though we know them to be bad. That means we are intentionally evil in a Satanic kind of way. It is the difference between Oedipus' blind fate and Iago reveling in his own fiendishness.

For Nietzsche, the morality of intention represents the greatest psychological refinement, inward deepening and spiritualization that man has yet achieved. The transition from the morality of consequences to the morality of intention parallels what Hegel treated as the supersession of the divine law by the ethical law and Nietzsche's earlier presentation of the domination of the Dionysian by the Apollonian. The capacity to choose right over wrong guided by the intellect is coeval with the emergence of Socratic and Platonic philosophy, where justice is a feature of the objective and eternal structure of the cosmos, knowable through our link to the eternal, the soul. It reaches down to the present as Platonism and Christianity, but is now tottering on its foundations due to nihilism and the "death of God."

That brings us to the third and newest stage, the "extra-moral" perspective on understanding morality, coming into view today but only in outline. I suggest that it corresponds to Nietzsche's call for a new psychology at the end of Part One, free of "moral prejudices," which "descends into the depths" behind what we believe to be our moral intentions, and views the passions as vehicles for the discharge of the will to power, even passions hitherto considered vices, such as "the lust to rule." For reasons that will become more apparent as we move forward, the extra-moral perspective is connected to the will to power and the eternal recurrence of the same. Because Nietzsche is sometimes mistaken for calling for a return to Homeric heroism and "the blonde beast," it is important to stress that the extra-moral perspective is not simply a return back behind the morality of intention to the morality of consequences. Nietzsche is no atavist. The inward refinement of the soul achieved by the long sway of the morality of intention constitutes a deepening of man that must be further enhanced by a recessional descent behind intentionality into the roots of becoming where the self coalesces with the pre-self – with the will to power – not evaded by some doomed flight of nostalgia into the ancient world. It is emphatically about the future. As Nietzsche puts it in *The Will to Power*, the Overman will combine "the Roman Caesar with the soul of Christ." The great moral watersheds of Platonism and Christianity will be surpassed, but not jettisoned. There will be no regression from their contribution to the human spirit. Whatever great is to come will build upon them.

Nietzsche ends Part Two with a contrast between the genuine free thinkers, who reject the idea that life is a realm of laws that apply equally to all, and those who are "falsely" identified as such, namely liberal free-thinkers, "levelers" and "slaves of the democratic taste." In an echo of his criticism in *The Advantages and Disadvantages of History* of the excesses of critical history, he says that these fake free-thinkers blame the "old society" for being virtually the sole "cause of all human misery and failure." They work for equal rights and the abolishment of all suffering, the "universal green-pasture happiness of the herd," perhaps another glance back at *The Advantages and Disadvantages of History*, implying that the reduction of human beings to pedestrian materialism will in effect rob them of any historical sense of creativity at all, like the grazing herd of which he wrote earlier. Nietzsche concedes that these liberal reformers possess courage and a "respectable decency," but they are nevertheless "ridiculously superficial."

By contrast, Nietzsche continues, "we" genuine free spirits "think that hardness, forcefulness, slavery, danger in the alley and the heart ... the art of experiencing devilry of every kind, that everything evil, terrible, tyrannical in man, everything in him that is kin to beasts of prey and serpents serves the enhancement of the species 'man,' as much as its opposite does." The genuine free spirits are at "the other end from all modern ideology and herd desiderata." Indeed, they are the "antipodes" of modern democratic ideology, "grateful to god, devil, sheep and worm in us, curious to a vice."

Nietzsche's language here is sulfurous and disturbing, and not for the last time in *Beyond Good and Evil*. This is the first indication of a theme that assumes mounting prominence as the book unfolds: an emerging struggle between the herd man of democratic morality and a coming new aristocracy bent on salvaging a sense of rank and the possibility of greatness, fueled by "everything evil, terrible, tyrannical in man." Are we warranted in identifying this with an inner struggle whereby the Free Spirit refines and cultivates his own psychological finesse, including the capacity for "tyrannical" self-overcoming? Certainly. But are we warranted in assuming that the invocation of evil, tyranny, devilry and the qualities of a beast of prey refer *solely* to an inward process, that they are merely metaphors for a strictly personal *askesis*? There is no justification for this at all. Clearly Nietzsche envisions a process that could take place both inwardly and psychologically *and* simultaneously involve literally tyrannical, evil and terrible historical transformations involving entire peoples or even the entire world. After all, every great historical watershed of which we have knowledge – say, the establishment of the Roman Empire, or of Christendom – simultaneously involved a cultural and spiritual transformation and enormous force and bloodshed. Nietzsche regards these past great transformations as important markers of what the will to power can achieve – he is deeply interested in politics and warfare as well as culture. In other words, there is no reason to assume that in this respect Nietzsche does not entirely share Hegel's view that history is a "slaughter-bench." The insistence that Nietzsche is being purely metaphorical, that he is calling for no more than a personal and internalized care of the self, stems from a wish to exculpate him from the arguably dangerous political possibilities that his view of the future may open up – a motive that should be extraneous to trying to understand his thinking. I raise this now because passages of this kind will come up repeatedly.

THE ADVANTAGES AND DISADVANTAGES OF RELIGION FOR LIFE

The next step in Nietzsche's movement away from the prejudices of philosophy is to consider "What Is Religious." Part Three arguably represents an ascent to the most profound origins of the will to power, deeper even than the psychological finesse of the free spirit – an ascent that is actually a recessional *descent* away from and back behind the foreground current consummation of the will to power as the distinction between the real and apparent world and our modern systems of thought and culture. In confirmation of the notion that what is religious is a deeper source of the will to power than the free spirit, Nietzsche offers another three-part telescoped genealogy of the development of the human type, this time not based (as it was in Part Two) on morality as such, but on the even more primordial phenomenon of sacrifice in which, for Nietzsche, morality is grounded. For the emergence of religion is coeval with the desire to sacrifice man to one's god, "a great ladder of religious cruelty."

In my view, the earlier three-part genealogy of morals discussed in connection with the free spirit in Part Two can be mapped onto this religious genealogy of sacrifice in Part Three, which further amplifies the sources of morality.

I will compare each stage of the genealogy of morals in Part Two with what I argue are their parallel stages in the genealogy of sacrifice in Part Three. The sacrifice of human beings parallels the earliest phase of the morality of consequences: Just as the morality of consequences was based on one's literal, outward status as a master or an inferior bred directly by nature, with no role for introspection and self-examination, the religious impulse at its most primitive reveres God by sacrificing actual flesh and blood human beings to him, with no regard for their inner motivations or goodness, their guilt or innocence. Sometimes this demand takes the form that we sacrifice what is dearest or closest to us, like Agamemnon's sacrifice of Iphigenia. The next phase, the morality of intention, is accompanied, we now learn, by the transformation of religious cruelty from the literal, outward sacrifice of human victims into the believers' *inner* sacrifice, destruction and crucifixion of their *own* natures, instincts, passions and ambitions. Perhaps the binding of Isaac can be taken as a transition from the first phase of sacrifice to the second: God relents on his demand that Abraham sacrifice his son, but Abraham proved ready to sacrifice his natural love for his son if called upon to do so. The literal destruction of sacrificial victims is now internalized as our capacity to summon our fallen natures before the tribunal of the soul, possessed by every human regardless of one's worldly status, and deem them worthy of psychological death through penance and mortification. This combination of the morality of intention and the sacrifice of one's nature has been the predominant epoch in human evolution so far, and grounds the emergence of Platonism and Christianity (as "Platonism for the people") as the most life-denying of all historical forces to date, culminating in today's frozen dichotomy between the real world of God and the apparent world of nature. Finally, we are today entering a new land where we have had to sacrifice God himself, to purge him of any remaining capacity for pity, consolation or love toward us, hopes which stand in the way of the final obliteration of our natural instincts and passions by pure reason. This ultimate sacrifice parallels the beginning of the extra-moral phase of the history of morality in Part Two, the realm of the future, of the new perspectives of the will to power and eternal recurrence that will yield the Overman to take the place of God, the new supreme being before whom man can once again kneel and offer reverence.

As so often in Nietzsche's writings, in his discussion of religion there is a shadowing of Hegel that seeks to unravel his purported resolutions of historical tensions. Whereas for Hegel religion and reason intertwine in the beneficent progress of history, for Nietzsche revelation undermines the claims of philosophy to self-sufficiency in its devotion to reason, exposing the source of its prejudices in a way that it cannot do for itself – by showing how they presuppose faith in the world's intelligibility – while the history of religion itself has been both good and bad for fostering the enhancement of the human type. Indeed, when one considers Nietzsche's argument that the "death of God" results from the need to purge God of his personal traits and feelings in the name of the purity of the idea of God, Hegel could be adduced as one of the main deicides. For Nietzsche, Hegel's claim to have synthesized reason and revelation in the dialectic of Spirit in reality reduces authentic religious revelation to the mere outward "representation" of Spirit, a decorative husk of symbolism drained of its own autonomous claims on our belief and its capacity to shake us to the core, no different in this respect than Deism.

In his consideration of what is religious, Nietzsche veers back and forth between praising Christianity's positive contribution to man's spiritual deepening and the enormous harm it has done, an almost schizophrenic alternation. Again, whereas Hegel presented Christianity as the Absolute Religion, its progressive actualization of reconciliation and communality flowing and interweaving in tandem with the modern project for the mastery of nature and for individual liberty, Nietzsche disentangles these two dimensions of history to show how the secularization of Christianity as modern egalitarian leveling and pedestrian materialism, while originating in Christianity itself, could not help but undermine and eviscerate the profundity of its faith. He therefore must both retrieve from history Christianity's contribution to the authentic deepening of the human spirit and castigate its contemporary degeneration into the religion of human suffering, reminiscent of his approach to historical education in the *Advantages and Disadvantages of History*.

The core of primordial Christian faith, according to Nietzsche, was the injunction to love man "for God's sake," because God loves us. Since, absent God's love, man is self-evidently completely unlovable for his *own* sake, this renunciation of our natural instinct to despise what is merely human for its baseness constituted "the greatest will to untruth" in history for the "beautification of life." Among the expressions of this beautification, the Saint stands out as a tremendous example of the will to power expressed as the morality of intention: His uncompromising denial of human nature and the desire for worldly honor and power on behalf of the completely invisible world of God, his willingness to die at the hands of the rulers of the "apparent" world (the one everyone experiences) rather than renounce "the real world" (the one no one but the believer does), brought the rulers of the world to bow before him "as a riddle of self-conquest and . . . renunciation." The ruler sensed in the Saint "the superior force . . . the strength of will" to face the terrors of torture and death rather than renounce his invisible Master, and they consequently recognized and honored in the Saint "their own . . . delight in dominion" sublimated from the mere physical domination of those under their subjection to a domination of the self on behalf of a higher realm that could not even be seen. They had to ask themselves: What inside information does the Saint possess that kings, conquerors and emperors do not? "The powerful of the world sensed a new power, a strange, as yet unconquered enemy. It was the 'will to power' that made them stop before the saint. They had to ask him. . ." One senses an undertone here of Pilate's conversation with Christ and his curious bafflement over Christ's claims for himself.

For Nietzsche, the Saint is an archetype of the will to power that the philosopher can employ as a means to the end of "education and cultivation" in himself and others. But when religion insists on being not merely a means to this end but the ultimate end in itself, "one always pays dearly and terribly." One might detect a resonance here of the Platonic teaching that philosophy must govern "poetry" (including the making of the gods) in order to educate the soul without succumbing to its enthusiasms. But as we will see momentarily, Nietzsche has a radically new conception of the philosopher and his role as a ruler. Christianity went awry when it insisted on having sovereign sway as the end in itself. Thus, Nietzsche laments that, although one cannot be too grateful for what Christian spirituality has done for Europe, when out of compassion Christianity preserved "all that was sick and suffering," the result was "to worsen the European race." Although the modern age of the Enlightenment fancied that it had repudiated and replaced the authority of Christianity, in fact it flowed directly from Christianity itself as the secularization of compassion through contemporary democratic leveling, the flattening of rank and the pursuit of bourgeois comfort. By jettisoning the primordial Christian claim that man is lovable only for the sake of God, modern secular morality clings to the Christian value of compassion while gutting its rootedness in faith. A question haunting Nietzsche's diagnosis is: If modernity has shown that man is nothing but a system of matter in motion bent on self-preservation, and not uniquely loved by God, why does man deserve compassion? To go on proclaiming compassion toward all while conceding that humans are intrinsically of no higher worth than selfish appetites, why might they not be equally deserving of neglect, cruelty or destruction? Why not Raskolnikov rather than John Stuart Mill? This unanswered question takes us to the heart of nihilism.

As if to suggest another religious path that the will to power might pursue in the dawning age of the extra-moral perspective – rather than its hitherto inextricable interconnection in the West with Christianity – Nietzsche interrupts his diagnosis of Christianity to urge that we think "German pessimism" through to its depths, think our way past and behind it, so as to "liberate it from its half-Christian, half-German narrowness" with "an Asian and supra-Asiatic eye." German historicism was sometimes referred to as "the philosophy of pessimism" because it was widely perceived as implying that all our actions were bound to their historical time and place, that we could not transcend historical determinism to reach a higher and permanent truth, which made all of our actions and beliefs of dubious validity beyond our own era. As we saw in Chapter 2, Hegel concedes this danger when he argues in the *Phenomenology of Spirit* that, without the principle of determinate negation that imparts a teleological and rational progression to history, we might experience history as a pointless whirligig of the rise and fall of civilizations and beliefs, a "highway of despair." For Hegel, it was only from the maws of the crushing power of historical necessity itself – the labor of the negative – that one could retroactively extract a rational roadmap to our future deliverance; absent that roadmap, pessimism was justified. Nietzsche by contrast is arguing that German historicism is pessimistic precisely *because* it clings hopelessly to a role for reason within an irrational kaleidoscope of events against which reason can never prevail. That is its claim to greatness, but also its pitfall.

Instead of trying to rise above that kaleidoscope by denying the world of flux and contingency, "like the Buddha and Schopenhauer," one ought to push right through that pessimism into the underlying wheel of life, and want "to have what was and is repeated into all eternity ... the whole play and spectacle," to grasp that God is a vicious circle. In order to arrive at the current crossroads sketched in the Preface whereby we today experience the greatest "bending of the bow" ever known, the impending clash between the greatest expression of the will to power to date (Platonism and Christianity) in its current ossification and a resurgent will to power that will yield the Overman as the consummation of all the epochs of the will to power's previous development, we cannot want everything that has led us to that crossroads *not* to have happened. Otherwise, we would not be spiritually equipped for the great leap toward the Overman. Whatever has happened previously is "necessary again and again" in order that we can "need" ourselves in our historical role and make ourselves "necessary" for the future. This is the first allusion in *Beyond Good and Evil* to the Eternal Recurrence of the Same. I would suggest that, for Nietzsche, it is another pathway – along with the doctrine of the Will to Power – to the dawning extra-moral perspective on creativity, the pathway beyond the dichotomization of the real and apparent world. Another way of putting it is to say that Nietzsche is urging us to push back behind the entire complex of Christianity and Platonism and what they have degenerated into in the present and free them up as forces that emerge out of and remain in play in the more primordial wheel of life. Not for the first time does Nietzsche attribute to German historicism an unselfconscious "Asiatic" or Vedic underpinning, and that helps to explain the continuing Vedic resonance of the remarkable aphorism that follows on the proper uses of religion as a means toward ruling.

The tripartite hierarchy of rule limned in this passage – rulers, warriors, workers – is one of the most ancient authority patterns in the West, with Vedic origins and famously known from Plato's *Republic*. As an example of the extra-moral perspective, for Nietzsche it illustrates neither an intrinsic belief in religion for its own sake nor a rejection of it, but the use "the philosopher will make ... of religion for his project of cultivation." It does not make the mistake Christianity did when it insisted it was an end in itself; for the philosopher, religion is strictly a means. A peculiarity of this image of a tripartite hierarchy is that it is from the most distant historical past while existing simultaneously in a sort of permanent now as an abiding paradigm for rule, and it can presumably serve as a guide for the future, as the new rulers emerge and finally the Overman. (As we will see in Part Nine, the distinction between the Master and Slave moralities possesses a similar kind of historical endurance spanning past, present and future.) This lack of specificity about its precise historical provenance may illustrate what Nietzsche meant when he urged us to break through German pessimism into the wheel of life and embrace as necessary its "whole play and spectacle." The image descends back behind the prejudices of philosophers, behind the search for metaphysical truth, and therefore behind the Platonic paradigm of the philosopher-king to something existentially more primordial. The hierarchy is not, as was Plato's *kallipolis*, a "pattern in the sky" – it is time-bound and historical through and through. Most strikingly, Nietzsche merges the philosopher as traditionally conceived of with the legislator, the prophet and the "breeder."

The task of the highest class of rulers in Nietzsche's schema is not the pursuit of wisdom (as in the philosopher-king of Plato's *Republic*), but the selective cultivation of the body of the people. The rulers are "prepared and predestined to command," a "governing race" in whom the art of governing is incarnate. In keeping with the historically floating status of the image, approximations of such rulers could reach back to the Homeric master class of the morality of consequences or forward to the new breed of rulers that Nietzsche has told us in Part Two is emerging to combat the current age of nihilism, and it can encompass any number of intermediate examples of imposing real-world aristocratic governance including the ancient republics of Greece and Rome, although these would appear to fall short both of the primordial Vedic prototype and the coming global ruling class. Like the ancient Brahmins, these rulers may choose to stand outside of the "necessary dirt" of everyday politics – making war and inflicting punishment – and devolve such tasks onto a suborder of chiefs, the higher rulers being men who stand "apart and outside, . . . men of higher and supra-royal tasks."

The second highest class in the hierarchy is bred by religion for ruling and obeying, strengthened inwardly through "asceticism and puritanism," perhaps akin to an order of warrior monks or the Janissaries who originally had neither families nor property. In this way, they partly resemble the warrior class of Auxiliaries in the *Republic*, but their characters are bred presumably by religious revelation rather than Platonic "correct opinion" – a code derived indirectly from Platonic metaphysics and a philosophic religion purged of all qualities that do not conform to reason. At the lowest level of Nietzsche's hierarchy are the "vast majority . . . of ordinary human beings . . . laborers and toilers." Religion gives them "contentment with their lot, ennobles their obedience" and justifies "the whole everyday character, the whole lowliness, the whole half-brutish poverty of their souls." Spreading the sunlight of religion over their endless toil "makes their own sight tolerable to them." According to Nietzsche, Christianity at its most valuable as an instrument of rule taught the lowliest how to place themselves "in an illusory higher order of things" under God, which made them content with their wretchedness. This is Nietzsche's only favorable reference to Christianity in the aphorism, and suggests that Christianity's particular concern with comforting the wretched masses might be an important means of ruling to supplement the Vedic or "Asiatic" code of the higher castes. The fact that he can introduce Christianity as a particularly effective means for reconciling the lower orders to their lot into what is otherwise a completely different religious pedigree in this aphorism suggests again how accepting the wheel of life and the eternal recurrence frees all of those forces from their chronological fixity so as to interplay with each other.

CLEANSING THE PALATE AND BEGINNING AGAIN

The Epigrams and Interludes making up Part Four are rather like cleansing the palate before a new set of courses. A series of brief and seemingly disjointed maxims, they remind one of collections of ancient sayings such as Diehl's *Fragments of the Pre-Socratic Philosophers* or modern maxims like those of La Rouchefoucaud. Perhaps they suggest how the world might break up into new, fresh and initially disconnected experiences when encountered by the Free Spirits. One interpreter suggests that they signify a shift from the deepest meditations on philosophy and religion in the first three parts of the book to a *tour d'horizon* of contemporary European morals and culture informed by those meditations, a return to the surface of life – accordingly, therefore, comparatively less demanding and intense. In 146, Nietzsche writes: "When you look long into an abyss, the abyss also looks into you." He may be suggesting that, having plumbed the depths of the most profound and in many ways most subversive interpretations of faith and knowledge and having been introduced to the ontological premises of the Will to Power and Eternal Recurrence, we now need to step back from that perhaps frightening abyss in favor of a more restorative approach, focusing on whatever valuable can be salvaged from the way we live now, including Nietzsche's own life among his contemporaries. Let me summarize the ensuing parts of the book briefly and then examine the details.

In *The Natural History of Morals*, Nietzsche reintroduces the "magnificent tension of the spirit" from the Preface and localizes it as the fruitful tension between European moral sentiment today ("refined, old, irritable and subtle") and our as yet "young, raw, clumsy and butterfingered" effort to extract from it a "typology of morals." He also states again the need for a narrow horizon of centuries-long obedience to an unbending moral code so as to muster the strength of spirit for creating new values today. In *We Scholars*, Nietzsche implicitly includes himself in the group, just as he earlier included himself among "we free spirits," perhaps suggesting that he is still only on the way to fully becoming a free spirit himself because he is still to some degree an ordinary scholar. (Recall his quip to Burkhardt.) *Our Virtues*, whose title implies that Nietzsche shares in them, suggests that not *everything* in the modern age is irredeemably nihilistic and spiritually damaged – there is still something to build on, and we still experience intimations of revival. As he wrote earlier about Critical History, if everything about the present is corrupt and vitiated, we cannot possibly entertain hopes for it as a springboard to a better future.

Peoples and Fatherlands is a survey of contemporary European nationalism which is a similarly mixed assessment of its merits and drawbacks. Although Nietzsche's aim is to stress positive energies in the European present, precisely because those energies are to be a springboard for future betterment, his discussion breaks out into ever more radical motifs about the coming great reversal. Only the final part, *What Is Noble*, marks a departure from this survey of contemporary European manners and morals. Its only titular parallel is *What Is Religious*, suggesting that *Beyond Good and Evil* ends by returning to the thematic intensity of the first three books.

PHILOSOPHERS WHO COMMAND UNCONDITIONALLY: THE COMING BATTLE

Early in *The Natural History of Morals*, Nietzsche depicts Socrates as reducing the grandeur of aristocratic morality to a utilitarianism that "smells of the rabble": If I do bad, I will suffer the consequences of being treated badly in return, whereas if I do good, others will be good to me and life will be "useful and agreeable." Therefore, doing bad is an error about one's own self-interest. For Nietzsche, Socrates' utilitarianism is the emergence of the morality of intention in its most unvarnished *ressentiment* toward the natural master, who will not deign to consider his own safety and comfort in doing what his nobility calls for, whether that entails doing harm to others or not. Socrates wants everyone to be concerned about his own safety. Plato's act of creative genius, in Nietzsche's view, was to refurbish Socrates himself as the new standard for nobility, cladding his philosophy of plebeian *ressentiment* in a sheen of beautification, presumably meaning the Idea of the Good which would launch reason's domination of the West. Nietzsche's evaluation of Plato here reflects the privileged access he believes we have today to the typology of morals through the emerging extra-moral perspective that looks behind philosophy's claim to search for the truth to its own unselfconscious motives. In other words, Plato did not understand himself to be falsifying Socrates by ennobling him in this way, a self-consciousness which would have deprived Plato of the narrow horizon of absolute commitment required for such a mighty will to untruth. Plato believed in his own metaphysical hypotheses. That does not preclude a consummate degree of artistry in portraying Socrates as their source.

Following Nietzsche's assessment of Plato is a brief reflection on the history of the Jews, who effected a "miraculous ... inversion of values" by taking everything the morality of consequences had considered hallmarks of a superior man – conquest, wealth, lordship, sensuality – in short, "the world," and equating them with godless wickedness. By contrast, the poor and the weak were equated with goodness and holiness. In effect, the Jews began the great "slave rebellion in morals" in which the weak were elevated as being preferable to the strong in God's eyes, the beginning of the distinction between the invisible real world and the fallen apparent world. In this way, the Jews paralleled through revealed religion what Socrates advanced through philosophy, the denigration of worldly honor and might.

The history of morals culminates in Nietzsche's apocalyptic vision – reiterated from Part Two, but even more ominously – of a coming struggle between today's "herd animal morality" and an emerging new class of rulers "who command unconditionally." Today's European herd-man is the final despicable product of the slave morality of the religion of human suffering and its secularization as modern democratic politics and culture, a creature who "wants there to be nothing more to be afraid of," a degeneration of the human species now identified as historical progress (whether Hegelian, Marxist or liberal). And the rise of this new caste of rulers stimulated into existence by the ignoble irritant of herd-man morality will bring the herd men themselves the "immense comfort and salvation" of bowing to a master, as happened most recently with Napoleon. For beneath their profession of belief in democratic equality and individual rights, the mass of human beings secretly regard taking responsibility for themselves to be "an intolerable burden." Continuing his assimilation of philosophy as it had been traditionally conceived of to actual historical warfare and rule, to the legislator and the prophet, Nietzsche characterizes this emerging caste as "new types of philosophers and commanders." There could not be a clearer inversion of Hegel's Master/Slave dialectic. In Nietzsche's view, the master and slave moralities have *not* been synthesized as modern bourgeois citizenship; on the contrary, the tension between the master morality and the herd morality is escalating toward an unprecedented conflagration.

Nietzsche's language in describing this coming struggle of the new rulers against herd morality is as dark and disturbing with respect to its violent revolutionary political implications, I suggest, as anything that he wrote in *The Will to Power*, a work composed from his notebooks after his death by his sister, the future disciple of Hitler, and considered to contain some of his scariest prognostications. For in comparison with what "will be necessary" in the coming global battle, Nietzsche writes in *Beyond Good and Evil*: "whatever has existed on earth of concealed, terrible and benevolent spirits, will look pale and dwarfed by comparison." I suggest that Nietzsche envisions "we" free spirits, still themselves in the process of emerging in response to Nietzsche's SOS call to "everyone and no one," as preparing the way for this new ruling caste, responsible for culling them and shaping their instinct for command:

The conditions that one would have partly to create and partly to exploit for their genesis; the probable ways and tests that would enable a soul to grow to such a height and force that it would feel the compulsion for such tasks; a revaluation of values under whose new pressure and hammer a conscience would be steeled, a heart turned to bronze, in order to endure the weight of such responsibility; on the other hand, the necessity of such leaders, the frightening danger that they might fail to appear or that they might turn out badly or degenerate – these are our real worries and gloom – do you know that, you free spirits? These are the heavy distant thoughts and storms that pass over the skies of *our* life.

Based on this passage, we might liken the Free Spirits to educators of a new ruling caste, and to me, Nietzsche's language echoes the "tests" to which the young Auxiliaries are to be subjected by the founders of the best regime of Plato's *Republic* (413b–414a), with the crucial difference that these educators are not shaping the souls of the future citizenry so as to wean them away from the temptation to tyranny, but on the contrary to hone and refocus their tyrannical instincts for domination over both themselves and their subjects. Despite Nietzsche's clear understanding of the cataclysms that could result from such a pedagogy ("the frightening dangers that [such leaders] might fail to appear or that they might turn out badly or degenerate"), these risks are apparently entirely worth taking, and perhaps are themselves tests of one's strength of character, rather than submit to the unspeakably worse cataclysm of herd morality triumphing entirely and swallowing up any chance for renewed greatness on earth.

ALL WILL BE DIFFERENT

In moving on to discuss "we scholars," Nietzsche again confirms that Zarathustra is not his literary alter-ego (to say nothing of the Overman); Nietzsche is only the summoner of the free spirits who will prepare the way for the new ruling caste. He revisits many of his criticisms in *The Advantages and Disadvantages of History* of how modern historical culture divides us into inner and outer selves. The professional scholar's outward profession of objectivity disguises an inner lack of purpose or inspiration for what he studies, like an art historian who visits magnificent cathedrals so as to specialize exclusively in the shaft between the base and pilaster of the columns, oblivious to the rest of the building's soaring sublimity and its architectural symbolization of the soul's journey to salvation. (I actually met such a person at a Humanities institute.) Specialization robs higher education of its role in opening a student to the wonders of existence, converting it into a mechanism for manufacturing new specialists, until it becomes entirely self-referential. In earliest times, Nietzsche writes, philosophy emerged as a fortification against barbarism and instinct. But today, philosophy has become the servant of herd morality. Today's man of knowledge is industrious, patient and an egalitarian, but not noble. He is afraid to say "yes and no," to offer a judgement about the most sweeping issues facing mankind, for fear of being perceived as a dilettante by venturing beyond his specialization. "How," Nietzsche asks, "could such a philosophy dominate?" At its best, the cult of scholarly objectivity preserves a certain decency and good taste born of its narrowness in a culture rife with charlatans – in contemporary terms, the rigor of a modal logician divorced from every other aspect of life compares favorably with a best-selling self-help guru. But true philosophers,

Nietzsche reminds us, must command – they must be legislators, prophets and rulers.

Philosophy's current "paralysis of will" is compounded, according to Nietzsche, by the "absurdly sudden attempt at a radical mixture of classes and races" characteristic of today's Europe, dissolving old loyalties and certainties. What can one choose to affirm amid this dizzying parade? At this juncture, Nietzsche pays tribute to the "noble model" of Kant and Hegel in attempting to subdue this cultural maelstrom through its relentless classification by logic, morality and art into a catalogue of truth. A work like Hegel's *Phenomenology* makes "everything easy to look over, intelligible," a task of compression "enormous and wonderful" in which scholarship can take a "subtle pride." This qualified redemption of Hegel's phenomenology is best seen in light of Nietzsche's earlier introduction of the eternal recurrence. Viewed in that light, Hegel's "shapes of consciousness" might be freed from their dialectical overlay of teleological progress and liberated as a trove of possible values, masks, styles, "the whole play and spectacle" of everything that has been and will be again. Another silver lining in Europe's current chaotic mix of old and new values is that it provokes skepticism "in all its heights and depths": Our awareness that traditional beliefs are of merely relative value, historically time-bound and not eternally grounded, can produce a coruscating nihilism that may paralyze the will but can also be the catalyst for willing a new future. But whatever Hegelian historicism liberated from its teleological chains by Nietzsche's teaching about the eternal recurrence may contribute to this alternative future, genuine philosophers must be commanders and legislators, not classifiers: "Their knowing is creating, their creating is legislation, their will to truth is will to power."

At this moment Nietzsche reveals how essentially and at bottom he is a modern. To equate knowing with creating is to invoke Machiavelli's summons to the conquest of Fortuna in order to create "new modes and orders," refined as Bacon's and Hobbes' maxim that to know something is to be able to make it, thereby improving the human lot, further radicalized as the Fichtean reading of Kant whereby reason is entirely assimilated to our will to master and reshape nature, and Schiller's and Hegel's identification of modern reason with *Verstand*, the Baconian power to tear nature apart through analysis in order to improve upon it. By identifying thought with rule and power, Nietzsche stands in that modern line of succession, however great may be his qualms or even detestation regarding liberal modernity.

According to Nietzsche, just as philosophy originated as an exertion of the will to power to contain the forces of barbarism, the prospect of its revival today lies in the increasing "menace of Russia," in response to which Europe will eventually have to fight back "by means of a caste that would rule Europe," one whose "terrible will" would cast a goal "millennia hence." This is Nietzsche's third evocation in *Beyond Good and Evil* of the new caste of rulers emerging from the dark skies of nihilism. It will, as he puts it, pursue a goal thousands of years into the future, perhaps the ultimate advent of the Overman? Its emergence will be global in scope, liquidating whatever "splinters" of dynastic and democratic politics remain from the former Europe: "The time for petty politics is over." The twentieth century, Nietzsche predicts, will "bring the fight for the domination of the earth." These prognostications bring into view Nietzsche's conflicted judgement about the value of independent nationalities, and while he addresses the issue explicitly in his discussion of *Peoples and Fatherlands* in Part Eight, it emerges from a somewhat different angle here.

Nietzsche makes it clear that he loathes the modern nation-state as the embodiment of the social contract model bequeathed by the Enlightenment – "the coldest of all cold monsters," as he calls it in *Zarathustra* – and shows his preference for the rooted peoples that are the authentic tribal homelands over whom this bloodless and rationalistic bureaucratic construct has been imposed. He notably disliked the German bourgeois-imperialist nationalism associated with Bismarck. But precisely because authentic peoplehood has been so thoroughly vitiated by the modern concept of the nation-state codified by Hegel as the embodiment of the bourgeois end of history, ultimately Nietzsche is not defending the rootedness of unique historical peoples as an alternative to the nation-state. (In contrast, as we will see in Chapter 4, with the early Heidegger.) Instead, politics must vault over the nation-state altogether, even in its comparatively more authentic underlying Volkisch sediment, and seek the rebirth of the will to power on a global level. In aiming for a new order that will span the planet, Nietzsche's political eschatology bears an ironic resemblance to that of Marx: For Marx, the "revolutionary dictatorship of the proletariat" will usher in world socialism; for Nietzsche, the new ruling caste will usher in mankind's new supreme being, the Overman.

Paradoxically, whereas conventional nineteenth-century German Volkisch nationalism regarded any conception of a world political order as a Jacobin and Marxist anathema, or the imposition of the effete materialistic values of the Enlightenment on German manliness, stressing the irreducible uniqueness of the German people's rootedness in its homeland, Nietzsche, while sympathetic to this same view that "the people" is the authentic existential experience that is overlain by the impersonal mechanisms of the state, believes that precisely because the modern nation-state has made a return to authentic peoplehood impossible, the very instincts that lead us to revere "the people" – loyalty, honor, reverence, courage, rank – compel us to conclude that our future recovery of those instincts must emerge transnationally on a world level. Nietzsche's politics are the very antithesis of nostalgic; he is every bit as much a futurist as Marx. "Alas," he warns those unready for the upheavals to come, "if you knew how soon, very soon – all will be different."

DREAMING OF EUROPE: A MELLOW OLD SOUL
AND AN EVER-YOUNG FUTURE

In *Our Virtues*, Nietzsche continues to look for positive signs in the present, again recalling his argument in the early essay on historical education that critical history can go too far in exposing the flaws of how we live now. Reiterating his elevation of psychology over philosophy in Part One, he praises Flaubert as the supreme psychologist of "bourgeois stupidity": Novelists may well tell us more about the human soul today than the narrow academic philosophy of "the theory of knowledge." He provides an extra-moral explanation of Kant's identification of morality with "disinterestedness," revealing what happens when you descend behind a rational rule – the categorical imperative – to the unspoken motive for proclaiming its truth. The "average man," according to Nietzsche, comprehends higher activities like philosophy as "disinterested" because they cannot imagine how it could possibly be pleasurable or profitable. In reality, what genuine philosophers (not today's specialists) do is "exceedingly" self-interested, an entirely selfish pleasure and passion, whether they are aware of it or not. (Presumably even Kant!) Instinctively realizing that this pleasure would be viewed as twisted or even monstrous by the many, they garb their passion in a "seductive and mystical-transcendental expression," perhaps like Plato's Images of Philosophy in the *Republic*. In light of Nietzsche's argument, we could view Socrates' most public speech – the *Apology* – as an attempt to camouflage himself as the proto-Stoic selfless guardian of Athenian virtue as protective coloration for his most private dialogue, the *Symposium*, where philosophy is entirely identified with the pursuit of erotic satisfaction. One must add that even if Nietzsche is correct about Socrates' need for the disguise of "disinterestedness" for public consumption, Plato might have understood it as a salutary public presentation of an eros for knowledge of the eternal Idea of the Good that was nonetheless entirely seriously meant, and ultimately at the service of moral virtue as well. In fact, for reasons already adduced, I believe that Nietzsche would not have attributed to Plato a full awareness of his own extra-moral motivation – the will to power as the will to untruth so as to create a higher realm of eternal Being that would have sway over all existence and immortalize him. As I have written elsewhere, if one can characterize both Plato and Nietzsche as having exoteric teachings that conceal their esoteric teachings, the exoteric teaching will be different in each case, because the truths they are concealing are diametrically opposed.

Another of our virtues, Nietzsche continues, is that the deadweight of historical knowledge paralyzing creativity that he lamented as "indigestible knowledge-stones" in *The Advantages and Disadvantages of History* has now been rehabilitated as a liberating "carnival" of "costumes" because Nietzsche's principle of the eternal return has freed what Hegel termed the "the self-originating wealth of shapes" of consciousness from Hegelianism's iron cage of teleological progress: "With all our dangerous curiosity, our multiplicity and art of disguises ... those of moralities, articles of faith, tastes in the arts and religions ... We ourselves are a kind of chaos." This new age of costumery, disguise and chaos is being stimulated into existence by a growing and profound revulsion for "English morality," the reigning philosophy of utilitarianism extolling a "mediocre" creed of "English happiness" – "comfort and fashion" – which followers of the herd morality embrace. The boredom and irritation induced by English philosophy in the emerging free spirits is therefore only to be encouraged as the catalyst for it being swept away in the great transvaluation of values that is coming.

Nietzsche crystallizes that great transformation by once again invoking Odysseus, alluded to in the Preface through the challenge we face today of "bending the bow" so as to shoot past Platonism and Christianity toward "the most distant goals." This new and "higher" Odysseus (perhaps his second coming through the eternal return), equipped with the new typology of morals, is "deaf to the siren songs" (like Odysseus lashed to the mast) of the "old metaphysic bird catchers." The prejudices of philosophy are yielding to the psychology of the extra-moral perspective, a resistance fortified, Nietzsche goes on, by the blindness of Oedipus (symbolizing the wisdom of not seeking the truth) and the deafness of Dionysus (perhaps symbolizing our imperviousness to the divine Word). An example for Nietzsche of a profound reaction to "flathead" English utilitarianism is Pascal, who sought meaning through faith in a world emptied of God by modern natural science. Characteristically, Nietzsche elevates revelation over reason as the deepest source of the will to power's refinement of the spirit. Pascal shows how the religious will to power need not be relegated to the past history of morals, but may reemerge in strengthened form today precisely through its encounter with a modern materialistic reason that denies every kind of transcendental experience, including both religious faith and the metaphysical transcendence sought by traditional philosophy.

This Pascalian will has two dimensions. The "will to superficiality" dwells on the surface of life, looking for forms, patterns and "masks" that clarify the richness of experience. Alternating with it is the "will to cruelty" – skepticism toward the merely apparent, the enchanting surface, and the drive to burrow beneath it into its "profound" unseen origins. The intellect, according to Nietzsche, needs to crucify itself, to discharge its power by denying itself satisfaction: "in all desire to know there is a drop of cruelty ... those dangerous thrills of cruelty turned toward oneself." It intensifies its "Puritanical" power by denying the apparent world on behalf of the real world, whether it be Plato's denigration of the world of experience as chaotic in contrast with an unseen eternal perfection which then merges with Christianity, or Hegel's conviction that the settled appearances of everyday life are the product of the underlying strife of its ongoing dismemberment and reunification as Spirit.

But, according to Nietzsche, it is precisely that resolution of the two modes of will in a comprehensive metaphysics in which strife is subdued by reason which must be resisted, like Odysseus resisted the sirens' song. This implies that we need to dismantle Hegel's purported Unity of Subject and Substance and re-envision them as the Will to Cruelty and the Will to Superficiality, in dyadic alternation. Hegel's equivalent of the will to cruelty – the power of the Understanding to rend life apart, to crucify the enchanting surface, to dismember beauty – is what allowed beauty to be reborn through death. But for Nietzsche, the eclipsing of metaphysics by the will to power means that no such dialectical resolution is possible, only the increased tension between these poles as they interact and clash: That alternation should be our guide to interpreting experience. We must resist the siren song both of Platonic and Hegelian dialectic – this the grand Pascalian challenge of staring into the empty void in search of the human.

The title of Part Eight, *Peoples and Fatherlands*, captures how far we have come from Rousseau's *Social Contract*, Hegel's *Philosophy of Right* and Marx's "scientific socialism." Nietzsche jettisons all previous attempts to render a rational account of history, all attempts at permanently legitimizing bourgeois society (in this respect like Marx), and instead reaches behind the modern construct of the social contract to evoke the homelands of particular peoples and the old-fashioned patriotic language of the fatherland as our primordial political experience. Rousseau had retained an equivocal attachment to pre-Enlightenment political existence in his romanticization of the ancient polis, but ultimately embraced the civil freedom with which the modern social contract might ennoble our vestigial natural freedom. For Nietzsche, that attachment to pre-Enlightenment values is not equivocal but unqualified in contrast with the bourgeois present. Even though, for the reasons already discussed, Nietzsche's final position is not conservative Volkisch nationalism, it is little wonder that he was often perceived in this way as his influence spread. Of the two extremes of Jacobin hyper-rationalism and Volkisch tribalism that Hegel tried to contain by synthesizing them as the Unity of Subject and Substance instantiated in the middle ground of the nation-state, Nietzsche fully embraces the Volkisch dimension as the necessary if insufficient starting point for uncovering authentic political existence, even though he exposes its ultimate shortcomings because he is a radical futurist in a way that Hegel's defense of the bourgeois status quo as the near-zenith of the completion of history had attempted to forestall. The "historical school" whose chief exponent was Hegel (arguably with Burke as a precursor) was originally considered to be synonymous with political conservatism, the attempt to combine the valid contributions of the Enlightenment to human progress with a continued reverence for historical tradition and precedent, crystallized in Hegel's understanding of education as "recollection." That seamless identification of historicism with conservatism ends, in different but related ways, with the revolutionary scenarios of Marx and Nietzsche for the future.

In Part Eight, Nietzsche again expands upon his forecast that two human types are evolving out of the encounter between utilitarian herd morality and the liberation of German historicism as an "exhilarating" trove of possibilities. The accelerating "democratization of Europe" involuntarily stimulates as its contradiction – never to be synthesized with its opposite – an emerging elite of strong men free of illusion, "accustomed to masks ... stronger and richer than perhaps ever before." That includes the "cultivation of *tyrants* in every sense,

including the most spiritual" (my emphasis), meaning to say therefore not
excluding the most straightforward and literal kind of domination. (After all,
Odysseus, the object of Nietzsche's praise, was not only the subtle "many of
many turns" who resisted the sirens' song – he also slaughtered his own nobles
for importuning his queen until the floor ran with blood.) Wittingly or unwittingly, Nietzsche performs another inversion of Marx: For Marx, the growth of
the proletariat into a world class compels the bourgeoisie to act as its own
gravedigger by unwittingly preparing the conditions for socialism. For
Nietzsche, the democratization of Europe goads into existence a new master
class that will reign over the herd men, who in this sense are their own
gravediggers.

In a beautiful aphorism on the decline of music from the European to the
merely national, Nietzsche characterizes Beethoven's music as "a mellow old
soul that constantly breaks and an ever-young future that constantly comes," a
"twilight of eternal losing and external extravagant hoping." In other words,
we might say, Beethoven was the musical equivalent of Hegel's understanding
of education as the "recollection" of the shapes of freedom as gathering and
bringing to consciousness the accumulated moral, cultural and intellectual
energies of the past for the coming new dawn of fulfillment. As I suggested in
Chapter 2, Beethoven's Ninth is like the *Phenomenology of Spirit* set to music,
just as the *Phenomenology of Spirit* ends with Schiller's *Ode to Joy*, as does the
symphony. Beethoven's music, Nietzsche writes, was the voice through which
Schiller, Shelley and Byron sang as they "dreamed with Rousseau and danced
around the freedom tree." For all of his strictures against Hegel and his other
predecessors, Nietzsche recognizes in them a nobility and grandeur utterly
absent from the utilitarian mindset of his age, and along with seeing the
potential that might be unlocked from "German pessimism" through the
eternal recurrence, Nietzsche also believes that the prospect of a new supranational Europe which he wants to rekindle previously reached a peak with
Beethoven and his contemporaries. Today, though, we can no longer understand the feeling they shared. German music as "the voice of the soul of
Europe" has now degenerated from the pan-European into the "small" taste
of a Schumann, into "mere fatherlandishness," which is a regression unless it is
the springboard to a new universal aim for man's development.

In contrast with Nietzsche's praise of German philosophy and music,
inspired by Rousseau, he now pounds another nail into what he hopes will be
the coffin of modern liberalism: "They are no philosophical race, these
Englishmen." Bacon, Hobbes, Hume and Locke, he thunders, contributed in
succession to the "debasement and lowering" of philosophy. The greatness of
German Idealism arose as a battle cry against this "English-mechanistic doltification of the mind." Nietzsche's judgements of this kind exceed in radicalism
anything we have encountered so far in the Philosophy of Freedom's critique of
the Enlightenment. Rousseau's critique of Hobbes' state of nature was unspar-
ing, but his tone was civil – he was attempting to improve upon it while

accepting many of its fundamental premises. He revered Locke as *le Sage*. Neither Hegel nor Marx was satisfied with liberalism's limitations, but both regarded it as a necessary stage in the rational progress of history. For Nietzsche, however, it constituted the very death of philosophy, the servant of everything low, of herd morality. He evinces an uncompromising disdain for and wholesale rejection of the Enlightenment that was burrowing its way into the soul of Germany's intellectual and cultural elites during the span of Nietzsche's own lifetime and beyond, captured by Hans-Georg Gadamer's identification of his student days in the 1920s as "the end of the age of liberalism with its belief in progress based on science."

WHAT ENDURES?

Just as the first three, arguably more profound books of *Beyond Good and Evil* ended with *What Is Religious*, the book as a whole ends with the similarly titled *What Is Noble*. Moreover, like the earlier discussion of religion in Part Three as a means to the tripartite hierarchy of ruling past and future, the discussion here of the Master Morality versus the Slave Morality, and how they have intermixed and reemerged down to the present, has a floating pan-chronological quality. It can be taken to refer back to the first stage in the typology of morals, the Morality of Consequences, with its Homeric Master caste, but also to intervening historical examples (such as the Venetian empire). Finally, it can be taken as a guide for mankind's evolution from today's dawning extra-moral perspective as we sail into the coming deliverance of the new global ruling caste and, ultimately, the advent of the Overman. We need to return to the phenomenon of nobility and see how it endures as a foothold against the rising tide of nihilism and herd morality that threaten to engulf us. Moreover, bearing in mind Nietzsche's revelation of the eternal recurrence of the same, perhaps the emerging new global caste of rulers – or perhaps even the Overman – might one day be tempted to embrace the slave morality themselves, just as had the aristocracy of pagan antiquity under the impact of Socrates, beginning the "whole play and spectacle" over again. In that case, Nietzsche's diagnosis of both moralities here could contribute to due diligence regarding the prospect of such a choice in an age yet to come. At any rate, Nietzsche's discussion of the Master Morality is most definitely not a nostalgic return to the "blonde beast," to the tragic age of the polis at its greatest, as in the *Birth of Tragedy*, although it might draw inspiration from its heroism. Like everything else in *Beyond Good and Evil*, it is primarily a pathway to man's future.

We should also stress how far Nietzsche's understanding of the master morality is from the perspective of classical philosophy. For Aristotle, to take a famous example, nobility or greatness of soul is the pinnacle of the virtues of moral character, but because contemplation is a higher form of happiness than moral character, greatness of soul is explicitly subordinated to the higher intellectual virtues of wisdom and prudence. For Nietzsche, by contrast, having (as he sees it) exposed the prejudices of philosophy, including its wish to erect itself as sovereign over all other creative realms including ruling and art, the remaining pinnacle of human achievement is what the classics would have considered as the admirable but still merely sub-philosophic trait of nobility. He liberates pride, as it were, from the tutelage of Old Man Contemplation. That is consistent with Nietzsche's assimilation of the role of philosophy as it was traditionally understood – as *theoria* – into what he proclaims is its true role as commander, ruler, prophet, breeder and now tyrant. What matters ultimately is not wisdom, therefore, but rank. To go a step further, Nietzsche's use of the "what is" locution in *Beyond Good and Evil* solely for the discussion of religion and nobility may point to the fact that, after the collapse of Platonism and all traditional philosophy through its exposure as a prejudice and as having culminated in nihilism, these are the two remaining and enduring peaks of human greatness: faith and nobility. Perhaps now that the frailty of traditional philosophy has been exploded by the truth that the whole is "will to power, and nothing else," these two peaks might also provide footholds in the abyss enabling us not to be overwhelmed and swept away by the chaos at the heart of all existence. If one wants an avenue into the possibility that Nietzsche has an exoteric and an esoteric teaching, it might lie in considering to what extent he considers the history of morals and its highest future possibilities such as "Caesar with the soul of Christ" to be a way of giving us something to hold onto in what would otherwise be a pure maelstrom.

The discussion of the Master and Slave moralities constitutes – unsurprisingly – a systematic uprooting and re-exploding of Hegel's Master/Slave dialectic and his claim to have synthesized these two shapes of consciousness. Whereas Hegel believed that the Master's freedom proved unsatisfying because the Slave was not his equal, for Nietzsche, aristocracy needs slavery precisely *because* of the Slave's inferiority, establishing the "pathos of distance." For Nietzsche, it would never cross the Master's mind to want an inferior's recognition. The primordial expression of the Master morality in the history of morals was, as we saw earlier, the Morality of Consequences, the code of the ancient Greek "beautiful and good ones," who regarded the slave as born to his status and intrinsically rotten. Their predominance, Nietzsche now elaborates, was not primarily based on physical strength, but in "strength of soul" (perhaps echoing Aristotle's word for pride, *megalopsychia*). They have contempt for "the cowardly, the anxious, those intent on narrow utility," and "those who allow themselves to be maltreated" because they do not possess a sense of honor. A trace of this archaic aristocratic stance can be found even in Aristotle's metaphysically driven codification of ethics: He considers humility a vice, because any man who will not claim the honor to which he is entitled suffers from "smallness of soul," the precise reverse of St. Augustine's elevation of Christian humility over pagan vainglory. Nietzsche's presentation of the Slave morality, on the other hand, corresponds to the succeeding stage of the morality of intention – utilitarian, skeptical toward the master's assumption of superiority, which the Master cannot or will not deign to justify by arguments, what Nietzsche earlier characterized as the philosophy of *ressentiment* and "the rabble" led by Socrates. War and struggle are good for the Masters; they need foes to overcome, "a constant fight." Their mastery is not, as Hegel maintained (with echoes of Augustine) a life of vain and empty self-indulgence; on the contrary, the victory over and continuing domination of inferiors is their very lifeblood. An epoch that puts aside the art of war to pursue peace and prosperity is concomitant with the rise of the Slave Morality – it emphasizes the happiness of the common man, the rise of individual preferences, tastes and opinions, and the neglect of rank. This was the path of historical progress for Hegel; for Nietzsche, a manifest decline.

Still – and this is crucial to note – in Nietzsche's final judgement, the superiority of the Master morality is profoundly equivocal. Formerly, irony had been the hallmark of the Master, who treated his inferiors with amused disdain over their inability in their mean station to grasp his glory. Punishing them for this lack of comprehension would be beneath a proud man's attention, equivalent to punishing a dumb animal – such anger was reserved for avenging slights from one's aristocratic equals. This attitude is well conveyed by the story of how an ordinary middle-class man once encountered the Duke of Wellington at a reception and, not recognizing the great hero, innocently remarked: "Mr. Jones, I believe?" To which the Duke amiably replied: "If you can believe that, you can believe anything," before moving on. Irony is the trait of a superior character. But now it passes to the Slave, captured in Socrates' ability to drive his aristocratic interlocutors to wordless befuddlement when asked to explain exactly what they mean by words like nobility, justice, the best, the good. For the slave wants to persuade himself that the master is not *really* happy. Darting wryly in and out of his verbal acrobatics, Socrates made the masters look like big lugs. Precisely because the slave secretly thrives on a morality of mediocrity, safety and vengeance on the great, Nietzsche writes, he must conceal it ironically by fashioning an outwardly seemly lexicon of "measure and dignity and duty and neighbor love," the baits with which he will trap the Masters in his word webs and drag them down. Through irony, Socrates becomes the victor.

Leaving this difficulty of the Master morality's self-sufficiency unresolved, Nietzsche concludes by reiterating the divide within Christianity between the reverence for God that it has inspired over millennia – the source of much of what remains of a sense of rank in Europe – and the nauseating familiarity of people with "modern ideas" of equality to which Christianity also gave rise. Even a peasant, he writes, in a possible echo of Rousseau, might possess more "relative nobility of taste and tactful reverence" in his simplicity and lack of presumption than the "newspaper-reading *demimonde* of the spirit, the educated."

ZARATHUSTRA'S TEACHING: GENERAL REFLECTIONS ON NIETZSCHE'S PHILOSOPHY OF HISTORY AND ITS POLITICAL IMPLICATIONS

Now that we have explored Nietzsche's assessment in *Beyond Good and Evil* of Europe and the modern world as a source of retrospective clarification for our understanding of *Thus Spake Zarathustra*, while we can do no more than approach the threshold of Zarathustra's teaching, let us begin with some reflections on its main themes.

At the broadest level, Nietzsche's introduction of Zarathustra crystallizes the entire transition from nature to history that has been the theme of this book as we have followed the Philosophy of Freedom extending back to Rousseau. At the age of thirty, Nietzsche tells us, having spent ten years in a cave atop a mountain, Zarathustra tells the Sun that his wisdom wearies him: He must descend to man and share it like honey. We pause to note that Alexander the Great and Christ were around thirty when they died, exemplifying the "free play" of historical patterns that Nietzsche opens up for us, but also how very much Zarathustra's destiny differs from theirs. Zarathustra evokes the Socratic philosopher who ascends from the cave toward the sunlight of wisdom, but in striking contrast, Zarathustra's wisdom at the height has *become* a cave, a constriction. To replenish it, he must "go down." His companions in his cave, the eagle and the snake, remind us again that he is not a philosopher in the Platonic way, seeking knowledge of the eternal supersensible truth, but a prophet, a mystic, a shaman. Through these creatures, he taps into the powers of the sky and earth, the Manichean struggle between the light and the darkness, the "Asiatic" tincture that Nietzsche identifies in Part Three of *Beyond Good and Evil* in the proper employment of religion as a means of ruling and breeding humans. Zarathustra's reversal of the Platonic ascent also reminds us of Rousseau's descent from the heights on Lake Brianne toward the waters of becoming that we discussed in Chapter 1. But whereas Rousseau made a solitary descent behind his thinking self to merge with his naturally solitary and instinctive pre-self, Zarathustra wants to re-immerse himself in collective humanity and history: "I love man."

Reaching a marketplace (like Socrates, he is a public-spirited thinker drawn to the town square rather than a solitary like Rousseau) where a display of tightrope walking is about to take place, Zarathustra immediately proclaims his teaching to the people: "I teach you the Overman. Man is something that shall be overcome." Men must give up their "other-worldly hopes" and remain "faithful to the earth." Like the tightrope walker, man is strung between present and future, "between beast and overman" – currently he is no more than a cross "between a plant and a ghost," between subhuman materialism and lifeless transcendence, between the apparent world and the real world as they have been driven apart and rigidified by Platonism/Christianity. As he puts it later: "A thousand goals have there been so far ... The one goal is lacking. Humanity still has no goal."

As the tightrope walker gets halfway across, a figure looking like a jester appears out of the platform door and, rushing across the wire, jumps past the man on the tightrope, who, having been muscled aside, falls to his death. I suggest that the jester is a fake free spirit, one who tries to pass over into the future realm prematurely and creates only a mangled human being. As Zarathustra's rival (he seems to already be aware of Zarathustra's teaching, and is perhaps jealous of his influence), the jester mocks him and warns him to leave town or lose his life, threatening Zarathustra by claiming that he is hated by the just and pious (just as, in a certain sense, both Socrates and Christ were hated by the conventionally and self-professedly just and pious of their times). Zarathustra leaves the town, accepting that there is as yet no place for him there. He carries the tightrope walker's broken corpse, which he lays to rest in a hollow tree (perhaps a Druid allusion again suggesting Zarathustra's reliance on the fertility of the earth). Zarathustra's first fresh encounter with man after descending from his cave reveals that, unlike Socrates, for whom the philosopher must return to the Cave and sacrifice his own happiness out of a sense of "philanthropy" toward the cave-dwellers, Zarathustra's satisfaction comes from exercising his compassion toward man in his isolated frailty and urging him to evolve into something higher. After this first encounter with a broken human life after descending from his cave, Zarathustra's mission now begins in earnest.

At this juncture, let us restate the broad themes of Nietzsche's philosophy of history within which he situates Zarathustra's teaching, amplifying them on the basis of the texts we have explored. The project of the West was launched by Platonism and Christianity as Platonism "for the people." Nietzsche assimilates the idea of God into the Idea of the Good, and together they work to bring the rest of existence under the sway of the ascetic ideal, reducing the rest of existence to mere appearance. The problem is that for a long time there were still too many residual vestiges of the lower realm of the sensual in the God of revealed religion himself – he was jealous, vengeful, took sides in war, chose a people, and could be swayed by prayer. Therefore, the God of revealed religion had to be purged of these traits on behalf of the Idea of God; purged of anything residual in himself that was connected to the human and the here and now – God the father, the son, the bride of Israel: these were all too tainted with the merely apparent world of the passions and had to be sacrificed. The consequence was the abstract, contentless and impersonal God of the Philosophers – of Deism, Locke, Spinoza and Kant – along with Hegel, who, despite his own self-understanding as a Christian, from Nietzsche's perspective could be seen as in reality subordinating revelation to reason, claiming to have synthesized them with no loss to either, but in truth reducing revealed religion to mere outward window-dressing and ritual, the symbolic "representation" of the Absolute. Originally, according to Nietzsche, our faith in the God of revealed religion made the world in which we first encountered God seem shabby and fallen, since God was so far above us. Today, the Abrahamic God is dead, having been sacrificed to the ascetic idea itself. Thus we can no longer believe in the God of revealed religion because the apparent world, reduced to matter in motion, has been drained of any evidence for his existence. To live in a world drained of divine mystery, yet go on claiming to believe in that God, is the essence of nihilism. We cannot go on professing the moral code bestowed by the Abrahamic God while no longing believing that God is present in our lives.

For example, what basis is there for our continuing to feel compassion for man, as the secularized egalitarian version of Christian revelation still holds? The authentic core of Christian faith, Nietzsche says, was to love mankind "for God's sake." In other words, the only reason we have for loving man is that God loves him. The implication is that, absent God's love, modern man himself might not be lovable at all; indeed, he might be utterly despicable, like Swift's Lilliputians. If, given that God is dead, man is now nothing but a system of matter in motion, in effect an animal unsuccessfully "crossed with a ghost," why does he deserve compassion? Why does he not deserve neglect, or even harm? As I put it earlier, why John Stuart Mill instead of Raskolnikov? This unanswerable question is symptomatic of a despair over meaning that will increasingly lead, Nietzsche predicts, either to the anarchistic lust to reduce the world to smoldering ruins or a retreat into Buddhistic withdrawal from the moral filth of society.

That is why, Zarathustra teaches, mankind needs a project, needs hope for the future. That project was once provided by God. Now mankind, Zarathustra ordains, must will the Overman: "You still want to create a world before which you can kneel; that is your ultimate hope and intoxication," as once they had knelt before God – "Before God! But now this god has died." Zarathustra then seems to address what we might surmise is the new ruling caste whose emergence Nietzsche forecasts in *Beyond Good and Evil*, perhaps to be shaped by the Free Spirits. The old God, Zarathustra says, had stood in their way, but now they are free to rise to the supreme station which the death of God left vacant: "You higher men, this goal was your greatest danger. It is only since he lies in his tomb that you have been resurrected; only now the higher man becomes – lord." As we have observed from the outset, Nietzsche's philosophy is arguably more akin to revelation than to reason; his hero is a prophet rather than a metaphysician. Zarathustra has compassion for man's hopes, and man must have some kind of salvation, a future deliverance, to revere. But unlike earlier prophets such as those of Judaism and Christianity, or perhaps even the original Zarathustra (the Iranian prophet Zoroaster), Nietzsche's Zarathustra calls for salvation through a new order premised on the destruction of human equality. Just as mankind had previously experienced hope and intoxication from kneeling before God, it will do so again through kneeling to the God-men in its midst.

ZARATHUSTRA VERSUS THE CRUCIFIED? THE AMBIGUITIES OF NIETZSCHE'S ASSESSMENT OF CHRISTIANITY

In discussing the suitability of Zarathustra as a vehicle for Nietzsche's thought, I should expand upon my remark that Nietzsche's Zarathustra might differ from his Zoroastrian prototype; that this might be, in effect, Zarathustra's "second coming." As we learn from *Ecce Homo*, in Nietzsche's view,

Zarathustra was the very first figure to elevate morality into a fixed metaphysical truth: "the transposition of morality into the metaphysical realm, as a force, cause and end in itself." As such, he was the primordial basis upon which both Platonism and revealed religion were built: "Zarathustra was the first to consider the fight of good and evil the very wheel in the machinery of things ... [it] is *his work*." For that reason, Nietzsche believes, Zarathustra/ Zoroaster possessed a clarity about his own originality that Platonism and Christianity could not match, inasmuch as they were already inheritors of the monumental shift his dualistic cosmology accomplished in the meaning of the world: "He is more truthful than any other thinker," according to Nietzsche, because "his doctrine, and his alone, posits truthfulness as the highest virtue." Zarathustra would never flinch from what he had wrought, the clash between good and evil, by fleeing from the real world – now reduced to sin and baseness by its contrast with the light – into the sterile realm of an "idealist." He would stay in the world and make a stand for its betterment. In sum, he "has more intestinal fortitude than all other thinkers taken together." Therefore, according to Nietzsche, it is only appropriate that the great reversal we are now living through, whose distant author he was – the self-unwinding of Platonism/Christianity, the emergence of nihilism, and the possibility of a noble new future in the Overman – should be vouchsafed to the original creator of the greatest expression of the will to power, and therefore the will to untruth, to date. In his second coming, Zarathustra, through Nietzsche, will fully recognize and understand what became the disastrous consequences of his original cleavage between the real and apparent world, and recognize as well that his new revelation must resist that cleavage and what we now know to be its calamitous consequences so as to remain "loyal to the earth," such that, in Nietzsche's view, the first metaphysical messiah merges in his reappearance among mankind with Dionysus. Zarathustra's unsurpassed truthfulness, Nietzsche concludes in an autobiographical account of why he chose the Persian prophet as his vehicle, would lead him today to the "self-overcoming of morality into its opposite – into me – that is what the name of Zarathustra means in my mouth."

In the coming extra-moral epoch, the psychological and intellectual energies that were once summoned forth by Zarathustra's original teaching, which today may enable us to bend the bow and shoot further than ever before, that original teaching – along with the teachings of his progeny, Platonism and Christianity – will be redeployed along an entirely new trajectory. At this juncture, we should look more closely at the retrospective critique Nietzsche made of *The Birth of Tragedy* after he wrote *Thus Spake Zarathustra*, for it arguably propounds a kind of synthesis of Zarathustra, Christ and Dionysus that had been beyond his reach in his earliest work.

This transformed Dionysus is now "that Dionysian monster," Zarathustra, who dances like a Dionysian cultist, but wearing a rose-wreath crown – an allusion, perhaps, to the blood-drawing thorns of the rose, and the rose in the cross that was sometimes used to symbolize the passion, death and resurrection of Christ. In *Ecce Homo*, Nietzsche sides with Dionysus "versus the Crucified," usually taken to be a straightforward rejection of Christ. But in expanding upon the contrast in #1052 of *The Will to Power*, Nietzsche reveals that the similarities between them are as striking as the contrasts – both are god-men whose death through being torn apart leads to eternal rebirth. In some sources, Dionysus, the son of Zeus and Persephone, is identified as "the young man of the tree" on which he was impaled. One etymology of his name is "Zeus-tree," and he is sometimes depicted in vase art as merged with a tree. Impaled on a cross and impaled on a tree are not far apart. According to Nietzsche, Christ's death signifies a devaluation of life in favor of a preference for an otherworldly beyond, whereas Dionysus' death and re-fertilization of nature signifies his loyalty to the earth. But they share in common the dynamic of rebirth through death, and Christianity's denial of life – of the "apparent" world – in favor of the heavenly "real" world is, after all, what makes it the greatest expression of the will to power, based upon the will to untruth, to date. Instead of seeing Dionysus as being in simple opposition to "the Crucified," therefore, I think Nietzsche (the title of whose autobiography alludes to the passion of Christ, and in which he also claims to have provided Zarathustra with his second coming) means to suggest that Dionysus super-sedes while incorporating Christ and that this synthesis comes together as Zarathustra, who is loyal to the earth, but who is also, we must always remember, a prophet, Zoroaster, and one heavily identified with the origins of messianism. However much the coming new dispensation of the Overman may differ from the past and from the original Zoroastrian teaching, Nietzsche's vision of the future world remains a struggle between the forces of light and the forces of darkness in which our struggle on behalf of nobility might progressively transform the world in its victory over the dark-ness. Its final aim, the Overman, may be one whose contours cannot be known to us ahead of time, but surely if it is to somehow fuse Caesar with the soul of Christ, the synthesis of Dionysus and "the Crucified" might contain a hint of what is to come.

As this complex new pedigree merging Zarathustra, Dionysus and Christ (another instance of the "the whole play and spectacle" of history, to recall Part Six of *Beyond Good and Evil* as it has been liberated by the eternal recurrence) makes very clear, Nietzsche's evaluation of "what is religious" leaves a number of difficult-to-resolve ambiguities in its wake. On the most general level, I would argue, this is mainly owing to the fact that, because he rejects the Hegelian notion that history is a unilinear teleological progression with a beneficent outcome for present-day history, in his view, instead of witnessing the steady resolution of moral, political and religious contradictions, we are witnessing instead their increasing intensification. A new epoch is coming – the Overman – and it will draw upon the spiritual energies accumulated by the genealogy of morals to date. However, it will not constitute a direct and foreseeable dialectical outcome emerging straight out of them today, like Hegel's notion of the end of history, but instead, an apocalyptic revolutionary break aimed at an as yet unspecifiable new order that will bear virtually no resemblance to the current epoch of "herd morality." Mankind as a whole will not advance toward the sunlight, as Hegel had promised. Instead, a new aristocracy will usher in a return to rank which will ennoble even the inferior through their service to it.

As we saw in Chapter 2, Hegel had viewed reason and revelation as advancing in tandem to bring about the end of history after the final violent excesses of the French Revolution and the Napoleonic wars. He distinguished between them as twinned partners in a single movement forward: Philosophy dealt with pure conceptual knowledge (the dialectic of Spirit), while religion (meaning Christianity) provided through the death and resurrection of Christ the symbolic representation of the truth of that triune dialectic. For Hegel, those distinctions, while real, were subsumed within their fundamental unity. To an extent, Nietzsche's treatment of reason and revelation is not dissimilar. He, too, regards reason and revelation as fusing in what we can call Platonism/Christianity, two dimensions of the same dynamic. He, too, does not overlook a sense of how they differ in their contributions to that dynamic. In fact, for him the differences are more robust than they are for Hegel: The Saint (who is motivated by a fanatical belief in the "real" world of God and heaven as opposed to the fallen pleasures of the "apparent" world of sin and the flesh) is a very different psychological type from Socrates (who is motivated by a plebeian *ressentiment* against his betters, although it is outwardly clad in the beautification of Platonic metaphysics), even though they join forces in the ascetic ideal to deny life. Correspondingly, Caesar is a very different psychological type than Christ – the former's nobility and courage must fuse with the latter's compassionate sublimity of soul in whatever the Overman will turn out to be in surpassing them both.

In other words, for Nietzsche, as reason and revelation have unfolded over time, they have become allies, just as for Hegel. But for Nietzsche, the outcome is not the beneficent fulfillment of the *telos* of mankind envisioned by Hegel, but on the contrary the spiritual catastrophe of herd morality and the secularized religion of human suffering. Accordingly, whereas for Hegel, when we explore the past we acknowledge the role of religion in moving history cumulatively forward and accept its continuing validity as a part of the richness of Spirit, for Nietzsche, when we explore the past, the further we go back in time, the less monolithic and oppressive a juggernaut we will find Platonism/Christianity to be, since it is still gathering its forces to subdue the rest of existence and is not yet running inexorably along a single track. Hence, even though Nietzsche is ultimately a futurist and not a traditionalist, in lieu of the total transvaluation of values awaiting us through the rise of the Overman, we are likely to find the past more appealing in its archaism than the present. As we have observed, the new world to come will be global, meaning that distinct "peoples" will eventually be superseded. But in the meantime, while the Last Man is still predominant, we will find in the rootedness of "peoples" a more authentic and robust kind of existence, a real if attenuated link to premodern and hence superior (albeit doomed) experiences of patriotism and honor, than the shallowness of liberalism and socialism. Analogously, he tells us that what remains of the primordial experience of Christianity can still arouse in us a feeling of awe, a feeling that we have touched the deepest origins of faith and, standing behind those origins, of ancient philosophy and its originally beautiful search for a higher world. In some respects like Rousseau, Nietzsche is trying to square the circle of an account of history that advances toward modern civilization while losing ever more authenticity. But whereas Rousseau could never entirely resolve the contradiction between the pure natural happiness of the lost origins and various attempts to lessen modern man's alienation, for Nietzsche that combination of progress with the loss of everything noble in life might be redeemed by the complete apocalyptic reversal of the human condition to come.

Nietzsche's ambivalent evaluation of religion flows from these paradoxes about the forward movement of history. On one level, in his view, modernity has issued from the alliance between the otherworldliness of both Platonism and Christianity, apparently initiated by the former's metaphysical assertion of an incorporeal "real" world, subsequently popularized as Christianity. Yet the further we go back in time, the alliance between these two forces – as exemplified by the contrast between Socrates and the Saint – appears to be more tentative or not yet fully resolved. Nietzsche sometimes suggests that current Christian belief, in its alliance with rationalism and modern egalitarianism – that is, with the working out of Platonism – has forsaken an earlier, more primordial version of its own experience, our wordless awe and terror at the divine presence, as well as our fundamental motivation for faith, which is reverence and sacrifice for God and love of man for God's sake. In other words, for Nietzsche, the truth about Christianity in its pristine origins seems much closer to the quasi-mysticism of Augustine than, say, the rationalized Aristotelian theology of Thomas. In his treatment of what he regards as the real Jesus, moreover, Nietzsche appears to want to rescue Jesus' own sense of his mission from its institutionalization by what became the Church. According to Nietzsche in *The Anti-Christ*, Jesus was concerned only with "inner realities": We were already with God, all of us, including children. For Jesus, the Kingdom of Heaven, Nietzsche wrote, "is a condition of the heart – not something that 'comes upon the 'earth' or after 'death.'" What for Jesus were only external symbolizations of his inner relationship with God, the Father and Son are hypostasized by his successors into eternal truths.

We can infer, I think, that for Nietzsche the mystical and numinous experience of revelation in which Christianity originated was at length subsumed under the pure otherworldly transcendentalism it shared with Platonism and its mysteries gradually reduced in their joint pursuit of the ascetic ideal in the denial of life and nature – of the merely apparent world – on behalf of the real world of invisible eternal truth. And there is historical evidence from outside of Nietzsche to confirm that something like this is what actually happened. From the time of Paul onward, the revelation of Christ did begin to merge with Hellenistic rationalism (In the beginning, "the Logos became flesh," to cite the famous opening of the Gospel of John), culminating in the systematic theological Aristotelianism of Thomas, and, according to Nietzsche, joining Platonism in the subjugation of the rest of existence under the yoke of reason. At length, as we have seen, that project culminated in the rational transcendentalism of this fusion between Platonism and Christianity turning on and purging whatever remained in our experience of God as mysterious, numinous and intimate, bringing about his "death" today. So in this sense, like Hegel, Nietzsche's account of the relationship between reason and revelation overcomes the age-old conflict between them in the forward movement of history toward the bourgeois democratic present, with the all-important difference that, unlike Hegel, for Nietzsche the contemporary outcome of that movement is entirely baleful.

And yet, because Nietzsche, for reasons we have attempted to set forth, cannot view the past as a series of cumulative dialectical building blocks toward the modern Enlightenment and liberal present, outmoded but still worthy of respect, something in him cannot entirely embrace the eradication of the debate between reason and revelation. He cannot accept it happily, as does Hegel, precisely because, for him, the outcome of the progress of history altogether has not been happy, but has culminated in nihilism. Indeed, as we have seen, Nietzsche often appears to favor revelation over traditional philosophy as a more primordial account of how and why we seek knowledge, and he sometimes claims that the Europe of his own day is witnessing a religious revival that wants to return to the mystical existential origins of faith and liberate it from its debilitating forced marriage with secular liberalism and the wanness of Deism.

These paradoxes are only complicated by the fact that when Nietzsche uncovers what for him is the *earliest*, the *most* authentic experience of what will become the fusion of Platonism and Christianity, its originator, Zarathustra – who in Nietzsche's view was the first to posit a metaphysical account of morals in his division of the cosmos into the realms of light and darkness, and summon us to bring about the progressive triumph of the light – is emphatically a religious founder, a prophet, appearing to confirm the implication of Part Three of *Beyond Good and Evil* that religion provides a deeper source for what motivates the search for philosophical transcendence than can philosophy itself. I conclude that, in Nietzsche's thought, there can be no final resolution of the question of whether and to what extent Platonism and Christianity comprise a single force, albeit still distinguishable from one another, which can be jointly identified, as Hegel did, through an overarching concept of the objective truth of historical progress such as Spirit, because for Nietzsche there can be no final resolution of history's contradictions available to us in the present modern epoch as the actualization of wisdom. Moreover, since for Nietzsche philosophy presupposes faith in the intelligibility of the world and therefore cannot refute revelation, the contest between reason and revelation arguably culminates in the victory of the latter, or at a minimum in a dead heat between the competing accounts.

THE FUNDAMENTAL PREMISES OF NIETZSCHE'S HISTORICISM

Having dwelled at some length on Zarathustra's early emergence in *Thus Spake Zarathustra* and the cascading implications of the relationship between his teaching and both philosophy and revelation, we are now in a position to make a more general observation about the structure of Nietzsche's thinking. As we have observed, Nietzsche's philosophy of history has two main, and equally fundamental, ontological premises – the Will to Power and the Eternal Recurrence of the Same. Let us consider the relationship between them more closely. As an account of the whole, the will to power has the same ontological status as Hegel's view of history as self-origination: "Everything is will to power, and nothing else." As we saw, it was prefigured in Nietzsche's early conception of the "world-artist." The world is a field of forces that radiate through human creativity and issue forth as great faiths, philosophies and civilizations. The will to power is the condition for the possibility of what has hitherto expressed itself as the finished products of these great watersheds of culture, which in their pretensions to lasting immortality at length become reified as the hardened distinction between the real and the apparent world. Through understanding human creativity as issuing from the underlying onto-logical principle of the will to power, we can free it up as a process, not viewing it as a completed doctrine or dogma *sub specie aeternitatis*, as had been the case with the prejudices of traditional philosophy.

Above all, we must realize that the will to power is not the expression or projection of an individual subject – instead, the will to power expresses itself through the passions and the affects, *resulting* in a self and in individual action as the last stage in its emergence. Moreover, the greatest of those creations, while sparked by individuals of genius, will sweep up entire peoples and epochs, an inegalitarian collectivism. Anticipating Freud and Jung, Nietzsche suggests that the creativity of the individual taps into a well-spring of shared subconscious archetypes that will be transmuted in their outward historic expression. The fact, for instance, that certain mythical and symbolic motifs are, so to speak, hard-wired in us as a collective unconscious does not preclude the fact that I, as an individual, can interpret, work through and make meaningful for myself those motifs in a way that is com-pletely unique to me, while inspiring numerous others who may follow my inspiration. That is how Nietzsche believes the will to power underlies all human volition and expression without curtailing individual creativity. In his unique way, through his ontological premise of the will to power, Nietzsche is faithful to the intersubjectivity, to use Hegel's term, characteristic of the

Philosophy of Freedom as a whole, in contrast with the premise of isolated individualism on which early modern political thought was founded. The greatest creators fashion horizons for entire civilizations, uniting the individual with the community.

This is the place to address the criticism sometimes leveled at Nietzsche that while maintaining that there are no universal truths, he claims precisely this status for the will to power, a formal self-contradiction that makes him just another metaphysician in spite of himself. I do not believe this is a fatal objection. Nietzsche is arguing that the will to power is the condition for the possibility of any philosophy premised upon the thing in itself or the eternal truth – which, for Nietzsche, is all philosophy to date – along with other expressions of the will to power including art, faith and music. It is therefore the condition for the possibility of metaphysics but is not itself metaphysical. That is to say, the will to power (meaning the world) intensifies itself by focusing itself as the illusory pursuit of a permanent truth issuing through its human conduits, the philosophers and other creators, but the philosophers "forget" or were never aware in the first place of their authentic motive, genuinely believing themselves to be animated by a love of the permanent truth. So, although one can say that Nietzsche regards the will to power as true, it is not true in the same way as all philosophy to date has claimed to be true, or possibly not true in the same way as any kind of philosophy at all. As the spontaneous source of the impulse to find the metaphysical truth, it cannot itself be understood in metaphysical or "thingly" terms. To me, the possibly fatal objection to the doctrine of the will to power is that Nietzsche is trying to revitalize philosophy and faith by making its creators self-conscious about what they are doing and what motivates them, which is not love of the truth. But how can one will a value that one knows to be a value without it losing the power of the beautiful illusion of the permanent truth? There can be no will to power without reverence, Nietzsche tells us, but how can man experience reverence bowing to a god which he knows himself to have created? This is a problem stretching all the way back to *The Advantages and Disadvantages of History*: Man cannot "learn to forget" the relativity of values.

Even if I am right in arguing that Nietzsche's doctrine of the Will to Power is exempt from the charge of formal self-contradiction – it is a universal truth that there are no universal truths – because, as the origin of all such truths, it is true in a different way than any previous truth because it makes no claim to be an eternal essence, there is, nevertheless, another sense in which one might argue that the Will to Power *does* make a claim to objective truth as did past philosophies. I mean to say, the congruity I mentioned earlier between the Will to Power and the modern account of nature as matter in motion, as a field of spontaneous happenstance out of which all phenomena, human and nonhuman, emerge. Nietzsche ascribes this same universal scope to the will to power – all phenomena, both human and nonhuman, issue from it.

In *Beyond Good and Evil*, we recall, Nietzsche argues that every concept of nature, every system of physics, whether ancient or modern, Aristotelian or Baconian, was nothing but an expression of higher or lower tastes, possessing no claim to objective reality – which was nothing more than a purely human imposition of causality. But his own doctrine of the Will to Power does seem to be congruent with a specific account of physics – the modern one – and thereby implies the claim to a kind of objective reality itself. At first blush, this might surprise us, because no one is more withering in his criticism of the "doltification" of English "flathead" utilitarianism, which is intrinsically grounded in the modern scientific account of nature. But at bottom, Nietzsche's main objection to that version of the modern account of nature is the chasm it created between man as an isolated individual driven by appetitive self-interest and utility and the rest of existence. If one considers instead the alternative account of nature as "life" proffered by Spinoza and Schelling in order to break down the Hobbesian and Cartesian chasm between the isolated human mind and nature as matter in motion, and to argue instead that what originates as the spontaneous emergence of nature evolves continually into the heights of human achievement, then we are already not so far from the connection that Nietzsche is propounding between the Will to Power and nature as a spontaneous origination of forces. (This helps explain Nietzsche's claim that Spinoza was his "precursor.") And, upon consideration, it is clear that this is the only account of nature that Nietzsche could have found amenable to his own doctrine, because the Platonic and Aristotelian understanding of the whole utterly precluded man's ability to create and recreate historical existence: Nature does not change.

We have already observed that Nietzsche's historicist predecessors, while rejecting liberal individualism and its concomitant of a materialistic and mechanistic Baconian understanding of nature, were open to finding a way of merging their historicist accounts of existence with the substratum of matter in motion in a Spinozist kind of synthesis. Hegel, for example, did not deny the validity of the modern account of nature, but characterized it as a primitive, undeveloped variety of Spirit – Spirit "in itself," which through historical evolution acquired selfhood through its human avatars as Spirit "for itself" – and his debt in this regard to Spinoza's notion of the life-world was transparent. Hegel was even more enthusiastic about the concept of Force, because he believed that it grounded his dialectic of Spirit in the latest cutting-edge developments in physics, which were arguably supplanting the atomism of early modern natural science. As for Marx, he was happy to try and absorb the utilitarianism of the Philosophical Radicals and economic theories of capitalism such as those of Smith and Ricardo into his own historical dialectic, whose outcome would nevertheless be their complete shattering through the victory of socialism over capitalism. And now we find that Nietzsche, too, whom we had first supposed to be the most radical historicist in jettisoning all and any claims to be grounding his philosophy in such an allegedly objective scientific account, insisting that all accounts of nature were fictions created to enhance life, is only too happy to find a wider validation for his theory of human creativity in the modern physics of matter in motion. In this respect, once again, as we observed with respect to his equation of knowledge with power in Part Six of *Beyond Good and Evil*, Nietzsche is a throughgoing modern. In *The Will to Power*, for example, Darwinian biology gets a partial endorsement: Darwin understands that life is premised on ceaseless struggle, but he concludes that it is motivated by what is materially advantageous to the victor. Whereas he should have realized, Nietzsche says, that "the feeling of increase, the feeling of becoming stronger, is itself, quite apart from any usefulness in the struggle, the real *progress*; only from this feeling does there arise the will to struggle" [#649]. We don't struggle in order to survive, we survive so as to go on struggling.

Now to the second of Nietzsche's fundamental ontological premises, the Eternal Recurrence of the Same. It has long perplexed interpreters because, read in a certain way, it appears to suggest that everything that has happened to date will happen forever in the identical way. This would surely amount to an utter paralysis of the belief in the possibility of creating anew, a coruscating determinism, indeed fatalism, of the kind that Nietzsche from early on resolutely resisted in the claims of Platonism and Hegelianism to have established the fixed and unalterable truth about the world and human psychology. Indeed, as I will show in the next chapter, this is precisely the way in which Heidegger interprets what Nietzsche means by the eternal recurrence, enabling him to present Nietzsche as the very consummation of Platonic metaphysics (to my mind, an egregious misinterpretation). Because, in my view, it would have been absurd for Nietzsche to establish the eternal recurrence as a fundamental – perhaps even *the* fundamental – principle of his historicism if he intended it to result in this kind of fatalism, constituting the refutation of his entire body of work, we need to interpret it in a different way, one that he regarded as indispensable for liberating creativity.

Here is my suggestion: To arrive at today's "magnificent tension" between Platonism/Christianity and the next stage in the enhancement of the human type – the Overman – we must *want* what has happened to date to have happened; we cannot want it *not* to have happened, including even its downside – its culmination as the religion of human suffering, nihilism and the Last Man. The Overman will not be a regression behind such great expressions of the will to power's aim as "Caesar with the soul of Christ"; he will leap over that greatest spiritual combination to date in ways that cannot be anticipated. What the Overman fully will be cannot as yet be known. Only *after* the leap forward has been made will we know in retrospect the full story of what "the same" has been, of *what* will eternally recur. Only then will we be fully able to appreciate why the earlier stages were necessary. Until then, the full meaning of the past will be as closed to us as the full meaning of the future. For now, we only know what had to happen to bring us to the present crossroads, and since we cannot *not* want the advancement of "the type 'man'" to overcome nihilism, we must want to have reached this crossroads over and over again, so as to bend the bow and prepare us for the running leap toward the open future. Therefore, the eternal recurrence cannot possibly mean that we want everything that has happened to date literally to happen in the same way forever. That would amount, as I have stressed, to the paralyzing fatalism born of the Hegelian deadweight of history that Nietzsche fought throughout his life, evoked in *Thus Spake Zarathustra* as "the isle of tombs." If it were simply the case that the world as we know it to date will repeat itself forever, the truth about eternity would be synonymous with the truth of our own epoch, for we would already know in full everything that can be. To know all that can be, in what order and how it progresses, would be to destroy chance, and therefore creative spontaneity. The eternal recurrence is not an iron cage of determinism; it is an open circle rather than the closed circle of Hegel's Absolute Science of Spirit.

After the leap, only then being in possession of the *complete* story of what went before, will the Overman be able to create with the full knowledge of what has occurred that is as yet denied to us, meaning that he will be able to strike forward in new directions that will not even be available before that future epoch – and which means that the Overman will want *another* cycle of events than the previous pattern to recur eternally, for not only will the Overman's emergence change retroactively his understanding of what went before, revealing its full significance in light of the advancement, but his epoch will establish a new crossroads for aiming further. Only now, for example, will the Overman realize *why* he had to combine the Roman Caesar with the soul of Christ to become what he is, whereas before his advent we only knew that whatever he was to be, it could not be less than this combination of greatness. But now the Overman, starting with that combination having been brought to completion as his beginning point, will be at a new crossroads for aiming further. In other words, we will *never* have a complete account of what it is that is to eternally recur; it will be retroactively altered forever. Again, it is an open circle, not a closed one, and a ceaseless source of hope. "For the earth is a tablet for the gods and trembles with creative new words and gods' throws," Zarathustra proclaims. "How should I not lust after eternity ... and the ring of occurrence?"

In my view, the eternal recurrence compensates for a fatal flaw in the will to power, and that is why they are linked. Left to itself, as Nietzsche sees it, the will to power wants to destroy the past in order to take revenge on the weight of history for stifling our creativity. That is why, Nietzsche believes, the anarchistic drive to blow up the world and rebuild it will be succeeded by moral absolutism. Its revenge is to impose a new, never to be altered absolute of its own so as to crush the former absolutes, which paradoxically results in its own creativity being paralyzed: Revenge, Zarathustra says, "is the will's ill will against time and its 'it was.'" Revenge is a poisonous motive for historical change, the "adder's bite" of *ressentiment*, the "spirit of gravity" that "wants the highest values, the thou shalt, to be permanent," and regards any threat to its own permanent truth as a "tragedy." The eternal recurrence frees us from the grip of revenge against the past and our purblind clinging to our own triumphant code. As Nietzsche puts it in *Beyond Good and Evil*, by saying "yes" to all that has been, we descend behind the pessimism of Hegelian determinism enshrining the status quo into the "play and spectacle" of the wheel of life. This colorful and invigorating chaos does not prompt tragic moaning about the loss of certainty, but laughter over its evanescence: "Not by wrath does one kill, but by laughter," Zarathustra, the dancing Dionysus, proclaims. "Come, let us kill the spirit of gravity." For Zarathustra, the eternal recurrence vindicates everything has ever existed as preludes to our joy: "To redeem those who lived in the past and to create all it was into a 'thus I willed it' – that alone should I call redemption."

In sum, we should envision a whole that eternally attains consciousness of itself as Nietzsche, who reveals Zarathustra and the Overman, and wills another turn of the wheel. The only way to survive nihilism is to surpass it by embracing this most utterly meaningless of all possible worlds – ours – and affirming it as good. The eternal recurrence is an immanent this-worldly eternality, the unending stream of earthly life's events and adventures, not the repetition of static phenomena solicited recurrently by eternal ideas. The eternal recurrence will dissipate the spirit of gravity in an eros for all that can be. We are as much causes of the past and future as we are caused by them, so we have no need for permanence, which is the outcome of the spirit of gravity in its desire to put an end to new willing. Each moment of the "vicious circle made God" is wholly creator of and created by everything in between. The will to power cannot be freely expressed without the eternal recurrence; otherwise, it is in peril of being twisted by the motive of revenge. This prompts us to wonder whether the two ontological premises are truly codependent, or whether the eternal recurrence – Nietzsche's historicist recasting of the longing for immortality sought by traditional philosophy – is not Nietzsche's most profound truth, more profound even than the revelation of the Overman that it makes possible.

A connected series of aphorisms from Part Two of *Thus Spake Zarathustra* perhaps best illustrate how the Will to Power and the Eternal Recurrence interrelate. The first is *The Night Song*, which captures Zarathustra's despair over how much light his disciples have sucked from him, leaving him isolated in a world of perpetual darkness (a Manichean dichotomy that recalls the original Zoroaster). They have feasted on the "honey" of the teaching he brought down from the mountain, that of the Overman. But he is left with nothing, only the blinding light of his own truth. He "does not know the happiness" of those who long for his wisdom. One is reminded of Socrates' remark that although he can carry to term the souls of young men with an eros for wisdom, he himself is always left barren. The last of these aphorisms is *The Tomb Song*. Zarathustra takes leave of his achieved wisdom in a gloomy retrospective, in which he surveys the graves of his previous teachings, now dead. (Perhaps Nietzsche is making an autobiographical reference to discarded past enthusiasms like *The Birth of Tragedy* or Wagner's music.) But he is saved from despair by the realization that underlying and generating them all was his will to power, and it remains as strong as ever.

The link between the despair of the first aphorism and the stirring reaffirmation of the last is provided by an intervening erotic aphorism, *The Dancing Song*. In it, Zarathustra dances with Life, personified as a woman, and out of this encounter emerges another woman, his Wisdom, who very much resembles Life, to such a degree that Wisdom grows jealous and reproaches him for wanting to cast her off and return to her predecessor. But that prompts Life to remind him that it is she who is the source of his wisdom and she who summons him to the dance once again when he leaves his acquired Wisdom behind. Here I think we see a cycle by which Zarathustra's love of life produces the offspring of his attempt to encapsulate Life permanently as his own wisdom, but must eventually shed that current settled wisdom and return to the dance with Life in an eros for wisdom renewed. The song has a Dionysian resonance (in keeping with Nietzsche's synthesizing of Dionysus with Zarathustra, as we earlier observed), and Zarathustra's relationship with Life might well put one in mind of Socrates and Diotima – the major difference being that Diotima is a seeress through whom Socrates is introduced to the eros for eternal truth, whereas Zarathustra's dance with Life is a cycle of fecundity which generates a temporary Wisdom that must eventually be entombed and fresh wisdom sought. Zarathustra's dance with Life is in the dusk, in a verdant setting, and its alternation between a current wisdom and the summons to create new values I think expresses the eternal recurrence as a wellspring of ever new possibilities in the "play and spectacle" of the world. It enables us to see how Zarathustra, faced with the truth that his past wisdoms must now be entombed, does not react with resentment and rage against the instability of existence and succumb to the adder's bite of wishing to destroy all past wisdoms and replace them with one final, true and unalterable teaching – the "will's ill-will against time" – but gives himself over to the ever self-replenishing impulses of the Will to Power. It is not the Platonic eros through which beauty draws us on up toward the eternal truth, but a Nietzschean eros that is empowered by the unquenchable richness and variability of existence. One final thought haunts: In *The Dancing Song*, does Life *already know* about Zarathustra's teaching of the Overman? Is the Overman his current Wisdom, the enticing woman he tends to confuse with Life? And does that mean that even the teaching about the Overman has begun to separate itself from the open possibilities of Life and harden into one of the "tombs" of a settled teaching, or the "painted thoughts" in the final aphorism of *Beyond Good and Evil*? Is this the last handrail to cling to before we plunge into the endless vortex of the abyss, having gazed into it until it gazes back?

Having attempted to clarify the two main premises of Nietzsche's philosophy of history – the Will to Power and the Eternal Recurrence – let us proceed to a more general comparison with his predecessors discussed in this book. To reiterate an earlier observation, Nietzsche's historicism does not take issue with Hegel's principle that existence is a "self-originating wealth of shapes," an intersubjective basis for human communality meant to resolve the contradictions inherited from Rousseau between nature and freedom, the is and the ought, the real and the ideal – an underlying unity of temporality to replace the third term between self and other, between self and world, once provided by Platonic transcendental cosmology. As we have observed, the debate with Hegel among his successors, inaugurated by Marx, is over the meaning of *how* history unfolds, along with an assessment of the present, what should happen in the future, and an assessment of the ancients as a foil for modernity. Hegel's successors, including Nietzsche, want to unlock the Pandora's box of sheer becoming, possibility and spontaneity, creative forces that were repressed by the finished teleological outcome of the Hegelian progress of history. From the perspective of his critics, Hegel's authentic insight was the principle of self-origination. But he betrayed that authentic grasp of the radically historical and time-bound character of existence by chaining it in a metaphysical cage of determinism, a philosophical failure of nerve. The underlying matrix of strife in Hegel's historicism gradually hardened into the finished doctrine of "the end of history," a rational progression that happens one time only and in one way only. Instead, Nietzsche is saying: We must dismantle the grand edifice of the Hegelian system, go behind the teleological progress of history, behind Spirit, behind the unity of Subject and Substance, deeper into sheer origination and take back the freedom of human creativity from Hegel's reified dialectic of Spirit, so that the will to power can re-enchant life, so that the mystery and wonder of life can flood back.

History still matters for Nietzsche, a point sometimes lost on contemporary interpretations that want to assimilate his thinking to sheer anarchism or decisionism. But history is no longer to be seen as a unilinear Hegelian progression in which each stage of history contributes cumulatively to ever greater material, ethical, cultural and political improvement. As we have seen, wherever Hegel sees the synthesis of a contradiction, Nietzsche wants to re-explode the contradiction. Master versus slave, the human law versus the divine law – whereas Hegel believes history has progressively reconciled these tensions, Nietzsche believes that the tensions have gained in intensity over time and are more acute than ever in the present. This is what he means by bending the bow so as to shoot further than anyone has before.

History matters, because the will to power has expressed itself in a series of powerful archetypes that have lent incomparable depth to the human spirit and deepened us with a vast range of psychological nuance and subtlety. Again, the grand arc of history to date can be summed up as Platonism and Christianity as Platonism for the people. The belief in the Good as God has been the most fantastic denial imaginable of appearance on behalf of a higher reality. Instead of a teleological unfolding, historical existence today is the gathering of an enormous crisis, an apocalyptic contradiction between the positive achievements of the will to power to date and the yearning for a new leap beyond its constraints. At every stage, therefore, the unfolding of the genealogy of morals has both a positive and a negative dimension – Christianity leads to spiritual deepening and ascetic self-overcoming, but also to democratic flattening and vulgarization. The original inner spiritual deepening has been overtaken by greater and greater frivolity, leveling, materialism and philistinism. Instead of the Master/Slave dialectic being progressively resolved by the evolution of liberal democracy and bourgeois civil society, Nietzsche sees a coming planetary struggle between the forces of the modern democratic herd man, on the one hand, and, on the other, a new elite of potential masters whose souls are being tested and deepened by their revulsion for herd morality and their intense desire to escape its narrowness, baseness and conformism. So past historical archetypes matter for Nietzsche, but only as benchmarks for a totally new reality for what man might yet become, a "spectacle and play" of moral and psychological energies, finesse, passion and subtlety that can fuel the leap forward to the Overman.

A final word about Nietzsche's significance for nineteenth-century political philosophy. Although Nietzsche has a millenarian vision of the future almost certainly involving tyrannical rule, violence and the use of power, strictly speaking there is no Nietzschean political science. For Nietzsche, the coming epoch of the Overman is beyond politics, every bit as much as socialism is beyond politics for Marx. Even though their views of the future are diametrically opposed – broadly but not misleadingly put, Marx anticipates the victory of the slaves over the masters, while Nietzsche anticipates the reverse – neither is able to provide institutional or constitutional details about the coming epoch because it is *not* a political state at all but more akin to an ongoing revolutionary transformation.

Moreover, since for Nietzsche we cannot know in advance what precise form either the Overman's character or authority might take, speculation about it is pointless, if not downright destructive by attempting to chain it to the irredeemable conditions of the bourgeois present. For Nietzsche just as for Marx, there is no best regime, no concept of political legitimacy. From opposite extremes, both oppose the *Burgerlicher Gesellschaft* of Hegel's *Philosophy of Right*, the quintessence of what Marx means by the liberal nation-state's conversion of us into "isolated monads" and of what Nietzsche calls "the beast with the thousand eyes." We should add at once that the trans-political character of Nietzsche's thought did not prevent political theorists and analysts from drawing upon its themes for their own diagnoses of modern politics, nor did it prevent political actors from claiming to be carrying out Nietzsche's project, both of which we will consider shortly.

While there is no Nietzschean theory of the state, no political science of the Overman, Nietzsche does provide us with an unfolding sequence of the possible stages toward the Overman's advent, which we can piece together from *Beyond*

Good and Evil and *Thus Spake Zarathustra*. They can be no more than suggestive or provisional motifs, because the forces of the future are gathering in ways that cannot yet be clearly identified, and no outcome is guaranteed – herd morality may triumph once and for all. The Free Spirits, among whom Nietzsche includes himself, are those who are emerging to bear witness to a more distantly emerging new master class. The Free Spirits, I have suggested, are the addressees of *Thus Spake Zarathustra*, "a book for everyone and no one," because no one can as yet know who and where they are, but they are arguably Zarathustra's disciples in the book. They are the recipients of Zarathustra's teaching on the Overman and, as we saw in *Beyond Good and Evil*, they may act as the educators of the eventual master caste who will battle for the earth against herd morality in the twentieth century. Whether this new caste emerges directly from the free spirits themselves, who would therefore be their preceptors in the same class in a manner analogous to the relationship between the Guardians and the Auxiliaries in the *Republic*, or whether they are a completely new caste of future planetary masters, is impossible to tell. Altogether, then, the pathway to the future is by way of Nietzsche and the other free spirits, who receive Zarathustra's teaching on the Overman, and assist in breeding a new generation of rulers, who are either themselves the Overman, or will prepare for his (or their) final advent. Beyond that, once man has been "redeemed from revenge" by the eternal recurrence, all we can glimpse is "the bridge to the highest hope, and a rainbow after long storms." No one can know what will happen when we cross that bridge.

The further one reads into *Zarathustra*, the greater the evidence is for the provisionality of this pathway to the Overman. In Part Four, we learn that "Zarathustra's kingdom" may last for "a thousand years" in its own right, still working toward "the higher man." Zarathustra also gathers a collection of "higher men" from the past – religious, political, philosophic, artistic – in his cave, an allegory for the way in which aiming for the Overman will draw upon the energies of earlier greatness without being restricted by it. And yet, once gathered, Zarathustra repudiates them as too distorted by the past, "crooked and misshapen." They are not the "clean, smooth mirrors" he needs for his "doctrines." But then, having almost entirely repudiated the past heritage they embody, he reintegrates them as "bridges" over whom "men higher than you stride." Although they are not now the ones "to whom my heritage and name belong," a "genuine son and perfect heir may yet grow from your seed, even for me." Nietzsche's ambivalence toward the past – wanting to escape it, yet wanting to affirm it – only deepens as the book unfolds.

I also argued in this chapter that it may be impossible to resolve definitively which of Nietzsche's two fundamental principles – the Will to Power and the Eternal Recurrence – is the primary one, although a case can be made that it is the latter. As *Zarathustra* unfolds, we receive the impression that the work never resolves this question, but instead presents a constant dyadic alternation between the yea-saying acceptance of life symbolized by the Eternal Recurrence and the heavens-storming mastery of life symbolized by the Will to Power. Hence, in *At Noon* Zarathustra appears to have attained a feeling of blissful oneness with the world: "O happiness! O happiness! ... The world is perfect ... O happiness, how little is sufficient for happiness!" This could be taken to mean that the yea-saying of the Eternal Recurrence is truly the highest experience. Yet a few pages later – preceded by his repudiation of the higher men to date – the Will to Power comes roaring back as Zarathustra stridently proclaims: "Whoever belongs with me must have strong bones and light feet, be eager for war and festivals ... The best belongs to my kind and to me; and when one does not give it to us, we take it: the best food, the purest sky, the strongest thoughts, the most beautiful women." If I may be permitted a degree of levity, it is as if we have suddenly shifted from a stay at the Esalen Institute to an episode of *Vikings*.

THE POLITICS OF GREATNESS

Nietzsche's fame began to spread after he went silent in 1888. By the time he died in 1900, he was something of a household name in Germany, his works republished and translated into other European languages. A sign of this delayed recognition was the fact that Germany's greatest living composer, Richard Strauss, composed a tone poem for *Thus Spake Zarathustra*. This would be very roughly the equivalent of W. V. Quine being made the subject of an opera by Andrew Lloyd Weber, or a Broadway musical about Stephen Hawking ("Hawking!"), although the terms of comparison are not precise. Nietzsche's influence on philosophy, literature, aesthetics and psychology would take pages to list, and he is still one of the world's most written-about thinkers. His influence on politics is of course the most controversial part of his legacy, and the one most relevant to our concern in this book with the dangerous longing for political wholeness. But even if philosophies such as the ones we have been considering do arguably have negative consequences for political practice, one can draw upon them for theoretical, psychological and aesthetic insights into other spheres, setting aside the question of their political impact, and those insights can also fertilize other reaches of political theory, philosophy and culture. In other words, in studying these thinkers we have to pursue a balance between not flinching at or trying to candy-coat the illiberal political implications of their works and not reducing their significance to nothing but an extremist political ideology.

Among Nietzsche's positive contributions to intellectual and cultural life arguably not compromised by the illiberal political implications of his thought we can include his influence on the field of psychology through Freud and Jung; his influence on classical studies (his interpretation of *The Birth of Tragedy*, derided on its first appearance, is now widely regarded as credible); his influence on cultural studies, for example Camille Paglia's bracing romp *Sexual Personae*, based on Nietzsche's distinction between the Apollonian and

Dionysian; his influence on literature (Thomas Mann's *Death in Venice* also brilliantly employs the Dionysian/Apollonian motif from *The Birth of Tragedy*); his influence on existentialism, literary criticism and postmodernism. To this I would add that Nietzsche's search for a pre-rational, psychological incentivization for philosophy, his claim that philosophy's professed pure search for the truth is a "prejudice" that cannot account for itself, opens up a whole new way of reading Plato – considering, for example, the extent to which Socrates' wonder at the phenomenon of eros, or of the holy, might have provided him with an anterior motive for his elaboration of a philosophical understanding of the cosmos in terms of the Ideas. Concomitant with this, the implication that revelation might, as we saw in *Beyond Good and Evil*, be a more profound source for understanding human existence than philosophy, including understanding philosophy itself, opened the way for the revitalization of the debate between reason and revelation, viewed once more as unresolved, that gathered even greater force with Heidegger by way of Kierkegaard. Nietzsche believed he was witnessing in his own time a growing impatience with attempts to reconcile reason and revelation and the emergence of a new thirst for authentic faith: "It seems to me that the religious instinct is indeed in the process of growing powerfully – but the theistic satisfaction it refuses with deep suspicion." In other words, the sacrifice of the biblical God to the purity of the idea of God was rekindling a craving for the authentic original experience of divine revelation, now drained by Deism and the assimilation of Christianity to the modern democratic project of its original wondrous qualities.

Finally, we can point to Nietzsche's own predictions about the emergence of what would become fascist politics as positive contributions to political analysis. His characterization of Napoleon's success as Europe's last great slave rebellion, suggesting that the herd men flocked to him because they secretly craved to be dominated by a master to relieve them of the burden of their atomistic individualism and isolation, arguably foresaw the coming appeal of fascist "strong men" and "Caesarean" politics (to use Spengler's term). In this regard, perhaps the most authentic example of Nietzschean political analysis would be Ortega's *Revolt of the Masses*, which argued that fascism arose from modern democratic mass man's resentment of the high demands for restraint, civility and learning placed on them by the *haute bourgeois* culture of the late nineteenth century, sparking their urge to smash it through "direct action" led by Caesarian demagogues – in short, a slave rebellion. This comports with what I interpreted earlier as Nietzsche's suggestion in the episode of the tightrope walker in *Thus Spake Zarathustra* that, in the coming transvaluation of values from the death of God toward the Overman, a "jester" decked out in the costume of the fake free spirit might superficially ape Nietzsche's teaching in order to promote himself, forcing man to rush across too soon toward the Overman, plunging him to his destruction – a Last Man who, like Hitler and Mussolini, sported the slogans of the master race.

Now that we have stressed Nietzsche's positive contributions, ones that are comparatively unsullied by the controversy over the extremist political consequences of his thought, let us face that controversy directly. In examining Nietzsche's thought for its politically dangerous implications, we will turn to some rather chilling passages from *The Will to Power*, a work his sister began compiling from his *Nachlass* after Nietzsche ceased writing in 1888, and published after his death in 1901. (I will address the question of its provenance momentarily.) In one of the most disturbing examples, Nietzsche welcomes the attempt to create "socialism" precisely because he foresaw what a disaster it would be, and therefore a "great experiment" whereby life could "negate itself" and "cut off its own roots." In other words, it is not the Hegelian or Marxist belief in the rational outcome of the struggle for historical progress in which we should invest our hopes, but the liberating creative and violent forces of that underlying strife itself. He continues: "The earth is large enough and man still sufficiently unexhausted, hence such a practical instruction and demonstration *ad absurdum* would not strike me as undesirable, even if it were gained and paid for with a tremendous expenditure of human lives." There are plenty of expendable people and territory to experiment with before they run out, so the likelihood of mass bloodshed from the creation of socialism need not deter us. For Nietzsche, the violent struggle to create such a patent absurdity as a classless society (we remember that the greatest will to power issues from the greatest will to untruth) will be "something useful and therapeutic: it delays 'peace on earth' and the total mollification of the democratic herd animal; it forces the Europeans to retain spirit, namely cunning and cautious care, not to abjure manly and warlike virtues altogether, and to retain some remnant of spirit, of clarity, sobriety and coldness of the spirit." Nietzsche's implication would appear to be that the struggle to create socialism would hone a new hardness and cruelty among both its supporters and its enemies.

This call for the destruction of herd morality through revolutionary struggle resonates directly with what we have already encountered in *Beyond Good and Evil*. The genocidal violence necessitated by an exercise of the will to power on the scale of socialism would itself provide new rulers, those liberated from the history of morality and embarked on the extra-moral perspective, with a test for inner self-overcoming and spiritual deepening: "To gain that tremendous energy of greatness in order to shape the man of the future through breeding and, on the other hand, the annihilation of millions of failures and not to perish of the suffering one creates, though nothing like it has ever existed!" We note in passing the echo here of Nietzsche's earlier characterization of rulers in *Beyond Good and Evil* as breeders. In other words, for Nietzsche, if we are to be concerned about anyone perishing in this scenario of the future, it is not the victims of the genocide, but the inner toll this mission will take on the psyche of those who carry it out. This notion that political mass murder provides an inward spiritual test for those who carry it out, that *they* are the ones to be pitied because they must sacrifice every traditional moral scruple and impulse to decency in order to serve the coming new age, is a familiar trope from the annals of both Bolshevik and Nazi genocide. In general, Nietzsche welcomes every sign of mounting political tension in Europe. Although, as we earlier observed, he rejected nineteenth-century bourgeois-imperialist nationalism in favor of a supranational battle for the earth in the century to come, he entirely approved of the militarism it engendered as way stations to that coming struggle: "Personal manly *virtu*, virtue of the body, is regaining value, estimation becomes more physical, nutrition meatier. Beautiful men are again becoming possible. Pallid hypocrisy (with mandarins at the top, as Comte dreamed) is over. The barbarian in each of us is affirmed; also the wild beast" (an echo of *Beyond Good and Evil* #44). Kant's ethic of disinterested and egalitarian morality has been exposed as "a scarecrow," a rickety barrier against a rising tide of barbarism reminiscent of how in *Beyond Good and Evil* he welcomed the invigorating effect the rise of barbarous Russia would have on making German philosophy once again fit to "command."

This coming epochal struggle, Nietzsche argues, is why "philosophers have a future," recalling his identification in *Beyond Good and Evil* of the new philosophers with rulers, prophets, tyrants and breeders. He intensifies as well the argument he made in the earlier work that the emergence of the extra-moral perspective and the free spirits as heralds and shapers of a new global ruling caste portends an apocalyptic and millenarian reversal in which everything will be transformed: "This is the time of the great noon, of the most terrible clearing up. ..." It will be "the greatest of struggles," and for it, "a new weapon is needed." It must "provoke a fearful decision, to confront Europe with ... whether its will 'wills' destruction. Prevention of reduction to mediocrity: Rather destruction!" This necessity for a "decision" also flows directly from *Beyond Good and Evil*: Because of the magnificent tension between Platonism/Christianity as it unravels as the death of God and the fearsome undirected energies unleashed by nihilism, enabling us to shoot our bow further than ever before, the coming struggle will be no mere reversion to any previous value system, but a world created anew. Out of this either/or struggle between our complete annihilation by herd morality or the triumph of the Overman there are now emerging:

[M]ore favorable preconditions for more comprehensive forms of dominion whose like has never existed ... the production of international racial unions whose task will be to rear a master race, the future "masters of the earth"; a new tremendous aristocracy, based on the severest of self-legislation, in which the will of philosophical men of power and artist-tyrants will be made to endure for millennia – a higher kind of man who, thanks to their superiority of will, knowledge, riches and influence, employ democratic Europe as their most pliant and supple instrument for getting hold of the destinies of the earth, so as to work as artists upon "man" himself. Enough: the time is coming when politics will have a different meaning.

It is sometimes argued that these passages cannot be taken as representative of Nietzsche's considered views. For one thing, *The Will to Power* was published by his sister after Nietzsche went silent, and while it is known that he had contemplated writing such a work, he left behind no such completed manuscript. She and Nietzsche's friend Peter Gast assembled the aphorisms according to one of Nietzsche's outlines for it. It is also argued that the extremist views expressed there differ significantly from the political implications of his published works, suggesting that they were a symptom of his breakdown. To my mind, neither objection is compelling. While it appears to be the case that Nietzsche's sister arranged the order of the aphorisms, there is no solid evidence that the individual aphorisms were not written by him. Moreover, the extremist views expressed in *The Will to Power* differ – if at all – only in degree and amplitude from the disturbing views we have already encountered in *Beyond Good and Evil* about an emerging new master class, new tyrants and a coming century of struggle for the domination of the earth. To take another example, already in the *Genealogy of Morals* Nietzsche had written: "the sick are the great danger of man, not the evil, not the 'beasts of prey.' Those who are from the outset botched, oppressed, broken, those are they, the weakest are they, who most undermine the life beneath the feet of man." Finally, one of Nietzsche's major (albeit controversial) interpreters, Martin Heidegger, regarded *The Will to Power* as an entirely legitimate part of Nietzsche's corpus, and cited it freely. All in all, then, there is no reason for treating his scarier political prognostications in that work as representative of some kind of mental decline or distortion of his real views. And there is no denying that his views could easily be – and were – interpreted as proto-fascistic. The similarities between tropes from Nietzsche's thought and Nazi ideology are transparent: the Will to Power (evoked by Leni Riefenstahl's *Triumph of the Will*), the Superman, the master race, the Lords of the Earth, a new epoch to endure for millennia, the elimination of the unfit. Nietzsche's sister, whom Hitler honored on several occasions, wrote that "if my brother had ever met Hitler, his greatest wish would have been fulfilled," fusing Nietzsche with the leadership cult of the Fuhrer, and while that claim is transparently absurd, there is no denying that the more inflammatory aspects of Nietzsche's political vision for the twentieth century could have given rise to it in people's minds. We now have to consider whether the view of Nietzsche's thought as intrinsically inspiring elements of Nazi fascism was justified, and if so, precisely how and to what degree. Or did the Nazis merely cherry-pick among inflammatory passages in Nietzsche that they could shape to their own purposes?

I begin by suggesting that the relationship of Nietzsche's thought to fascism is analogous to the relationship of Rousseau's thought to the French Revolution that we discussed earlier: Nietzsche may well not have intended to have such an influence, but his immoderate, extravagant and inflammatory rhetoric – which we have sampled throughout our analysis of his texts – lent itself to being selectively employed by such an extremist political movement. In other words, as Rousseau was to Robespierre and the Jacobins, Nietzsche was to Hitler and the Nazis, who mined his writings for slogans to extoll the Third Reich. In neither case did the thinker cause, or necessarily foresee, those political projects, but they did fuel the revolutionary expectations and passions that drove those movements. Regardless of Nietzsche's intentions for his own future impact, it could have been predicted that the irresponsible extremism of his language was bound to attract revolutionary nihilists who claimed to be his disciples. It was arguably a perversion of the overall intention of Nietzsche's writings, but they left themselves wide open to being perverted in this way. The philosophies of Locke, Hume and the other specimens of what Nietzsche contemptuously termed liberal "English-mechanistic doltification" could never have been perverted in the same direction.

That said, it must be admitted that any conclusion about the negative political implications of Nietzsche's writings, especially their fascistic implications, can be no more than conjecture. We cannot know with certainty that he would have embraced any extremist movement, or what kind. During his lifetime, a growing number of nationalist intellectuals including Julius Langbehn, Paul de la Garde and Moeller van den Brucke developed a vision of the future German Reich that foresaw Hitler's projects for *Lebensraum* in the East, the revival of Teutonic martial ardor and the rejection of the effete values of liberalism and the Enlightenment. We know that Nietzsche admired Langbehn's essay on the origins of Christianity, and he spent some time with Paul de la Garde because the latter thrust himself into Nietzsche's circle in a bizarre attempt to "rescue" him after his collapse. But there is no record of Nietzsche's enthusiasm for or endorsement of this growing trend of Volkisch nationalism.

We also cannot know with certainty to what extent his hoped-for changes leaned more toward the psychological and spiritual side as opposed to a literal and violent political transformation. But I still maintain, as I argued with respect to *Beyond Good and Evil*, that we cannot exclude considering the dangerous real-world political implications as a part of his legacy, nor can we assume that his hoped-for changes would be *purely* inward and confined to the development of the individual's personal character. Clearly Nietzsche is on one level talking about such an inward spiritual self-development. But nothing in his writings entitles us to conclude that he is restricting the meaning of the will to power to an entirely personal lifestyle askesis, just another boutique of private fulfillment within an otherwise unchanged liberal democratic status quo. Nothing warrants our reading of the scarier, darker prognostications about the coming resurgence of the will to power directed toward the advent of the Overman as being merely metaphorical, symbolic of a purely inward psychological development. To do so is to defang Nietzsche in an attempt to make him respectable.

This would be a useful moment to review the ongoing theme of the beautification of modern life that we have traced in this book extending back to Schiller and his adaptation of the Romantic dimension of Rousseau. For Schiller, aesthetic education was meant to be a source of repose for the individual living in an age otherwise dominated by utility and self-interest. While Schiller believed it would make us better citizens by refining our characters, he never envisioned it extending to the beautification of political life itself. His concept of what he called "the third character" between nature and freedom, meaning the aesthetic experience, was entirely innocent of the millenarian political expectations ultimately summed up as the Third Reich of National Socialism. It did point to a coming new age, but only in the benign sense, shared with Schelling, of a purely cultural completion of mankind's journey "home to Ithaca." As we observed in Chapter 2, the belief that mankind's collective political experience could itself be made beautiful through revolutionary violence began with Marx, who conceived of socialism as achieving for all mankind the aesthetic wholeness of a work of art.

Nietzsche advances his own variation on this longing for the aestheticization of politics. We observed in our discussion of *The Birth of Tragedy* a certain affinity between the early Nietzsche and Schiller – an affinity which Nietzsche might have deprecated – insofar as Nietzsche was searching for a restored equipoise between the Apollonian and the Dionysian, or between form and emotion. Whatever the degree of that early resemblance may have been, by the time of Nietzsche's mature writings it has entirely vanished. Nietzsche is not solely advocating a mission of spiritual and aesthetic cultivation by an elite of academics, students and artists safely back-stopped by liberal civilization, and presupposing the stability of constitutional representative government. He really does foresee a coming planetary struggle that cannot possibly be said to preclude literal and violent transformation. Like Marx, he is not willing to settle for the individual's contemplation of aesthetic beauty. He wants to beautify the human race through struggle; not through the liberation of the masses, but through their subjugation to lords worthy of respect. His vision of the future is one in which, as he puts it, the "higher" men will "get hold of the destinies of the earth, so as to work as artists upon 'man' himself." We have come a long way from Nietzsche's depiction in the *Birth of Tragedy* of the world-artist expressing itself as the symbiotic interaction of the Dionysian and the Apollonian in the work of art. That passive receptivity of the human artist to the welling up within himself of the life-world has now been transformed into an omnipotent lord who will literally use man as his clay. We are not far here from the temperament informing Mussolini's admiration of Lenin as a "sculptor of human souls" – a compliment paid by the Fascist to the Bolshevik that underscores their underlying similarities. Of a similar temperament are Nietzsche's chilling remarks about socialism, that its inevitable cost in millions of lives might be worth it as an interesting experiment in human improvement.

In order to arrive at "the new Nietzsche," one has to tiptoe through his texts as one would a minefield, cherry-picking a few shards completely out of context in order to make Nietzsche into a friendly democrat, liberal, feminist and environmentalist. A current example of this is to enlist Nietzsche posthumously as a supporter of the European Union and an opponent of Brexit secessionism on the grounds of his denigration of mere nationalism in favor of a supranational vision of the future, conveniently ignoring the fact that, as we observed, for Nietzsche that future will not culminate in anything remotely resembling the bureaucratic politically correct capitalist European superstate run from Brussels, but in a coming battle for the lordship of the earth between the new ruling caste and the herd-man. For Nietzsche, the EU would represent nothing more than a multinational iteration of "the beast with the thousand eyes, that coldest of monsters."

If it is true that any direct link between Nietzsche's intentions and the rise of Nazism must remain conjectural, any reservations we might entertain on Nietzsche's behalf against such a tyrannical project must also remain conjectural. For instance, it is sometimes argued against the connection between Nietzsche and Nazism that someone of Nietzsche's background and refinement would have been appalled by the petit-bourgeois coarseness of a self-made rabble-rouser like Hitler and would have despised the vulgarity of the Nazis. But can we really believe that someone with as transgressive and iconoclastic a mind as Nietzsche would have rejected a man like Hitler on conventional class and aesthetic grounds alone – that he was not a gentleman? Throughout his writings, Nietzsche takes an endless delight in *epater le bourgeois*, and holds up as exemplars of the will to power men from the lowest rungs of society – the sly plebeian Socrates consumed with *ressentiment* against his betters; the despised, penniless and ragged Saint; the Corsican putschist and parvenu Napoleon; the "pale criminal" in *Thus Spake Zarathustra*, sometimes likened to Dostoyevsky's Raskolnikov. Is it really to be believed that snobbery among the upper middle class about Hitler's background as a former corporal and house-painter would have been decisive for Nietzsche had he witnessed it, especially since he had himself renounced respectable society to live apart in his untimely meditations? The deeper problem with assessing Nietzsche's connection to Nazism is that it is difficult to find binding ethical criteria in his philosophy that would enable and oblige one to condemn such extremism in principle before it achieved political power and enacted its full monstrousness. On the contrary, the tenor of Nietzsche's attitude to such threats of open-ended revolutionary transformations, as evidenced by his assessment of "socialism," seems akin to: Let's roll the dice and see what comes of it.

While Nietzsche displayed no interest in the Volkisch Right of his day because, I would argue, he spurned nationalism in favor of a grander global aim, it is worth remembering that the Nazis were not conventional German nationalists either. Their aim was world domination to usher in the utopia of "the National Socialist world-blessing," to gather in the Aryan peoples everywhere and destroy International Jewry. The Waffen SS formed an international brigade as a step toward this coming global new order. It is true that, as Ortega may have learned from Nietzsche, fascism could be seen as another version of European mass man's secret longing for a "master," as Nietzsche had said of

Napoleon. But to the extent that Nietzsche might have foreseen future herd-man rebellions like socialism, surely he would relish the prospect as intensifying the contradictions of nihilism and thereby advancing the coming planetary struggle. Nietzsche may have regarded the French Revolution as a "slave rebellion," but he also regarded its culmination, the rise of Napoleon, as the happiest interval known to mankind in at least a century. Could he therefore have been hostile in principle to a fascist "revolt of the masses," to use Ortega's famous phrase? I have argued that the tightrope walker episode in *Thus Spake Zarathustra* might demonstrate that Nietzsche foresaw how his teaching could be distorted by a herd-man tricked out as a member of the emerging new master caste trying to force the pace of events. But consider the sequel: When the jester causes the man to plunge from the tightrope by forcing him to cross over, Zarathustra rescues his broken body and pronounces that God is dead. It is this very failure born of a premature leap across that enables Zarathustra to carry man, so far only "a cross between a plant and a ghost," to the next level. In other words, had Nietzsche witnessed the attempt by what he regarded as a fake Superman like Hitler to force history forward, can we be sure he still would not have approved? Based on his writings, it seems that even given every prospect that a movement like Nazism would result in a catastrophe of destructive madness and depravity, Nietzsche might still believe the risk was worth taking, the experiment worth making, even at the cost of "millions" of lives, in order to replenish man's fighting spirit and stave off the paralysis of pacifism, exactly as he wrote in *The Will to Power* about experimenting with socialism. Maybe the outcome would be better the next time. (Already in *Beyond Good and Evil*, he had warned that the Free Spirits must risk "the frightening danger" that the coming new master class "might fail to appear or that they might turn out badly.") It is rightly observed in Nietzsche's favor that, in contrast with much of the nationalist Right, he despised anti-Semitism as born of petit-bourgeois jealousy toward an extraordinarily accomplished people. This is sometimes advanced as evidence in and of itself that Nietzsche could never have embraced the programmatic anti-Semitism of Nazism, culminating in the Holocaust, meaning that he would have rejected its central project from the outset. But given his willingness to engage in an experiment with political catastrophe potentially costing "millions" of lives on the grounds that the outcome could be some kind of step forward for the advancement of the human type, or a run-up for another try, can we be certain that his objections to anti-Semitism would have constituted an absolute ethical bulwark against Nazi genocide? Or might the risk of mass murder simply make the battle for the future of the planet more acute and complex, a spiritual challenge to the perpetrators to steel themselves, to deepen their will to power, at the risk of "perishing" psychically through carrying out the terrible tasks imposed on them by destiny? I do not see how this possibility can be excluded. Nietzsche's language in section 964 of *The Will to Power* bears a chilling resemblance to Himmler's secret speech at Posen.

Without question, Nietzsche regards the great watersheds of religious faith, philosophy and artistic creation as incomparably superior and more spiritually intense expressions of the will to power than mere physical force, conquest and power-seeking – superior to any form of ordinary power politics. Nevertheless, those spiritual high-watermarks of the will to power were themselves the catalyst for major upheavals of war, revolution and imperialism. Think of the vast conflagration set in motion by the spiritual victory of Christianity over paganism, entailing (if you are a Gibbonian like me) the collapse of the Roman empire and Greco-Roman civilization through its inner moral disintegration and its replacement by Christendom, riven in turn by centuries of strife between Church and Emperor, the slaughter of Christian sects by one another, the strife between Rome and Luther strewing Europe with carnage; think, too, of Napoleon's career of glory and bloodshed, smashing the *ancien régime* on behalf of the Enlightenment in an avalanche of corpses. In other words, to reiterate an earlier observation, there is nothing that Nietzsche would have disagreed with in Hegel's pronouncement that history is "a slaughter-bench." After all, it is hardly likely that the politically most liberal of historicist thinkers among those we are considering would take a more hard-headed view of the violent dimension of historical change than one of the least liberal. Given Nietzsche's expectation of and longing for a coming eschatological reversal, a battle for the mastery of the earth in the approaching twentieth century, he was inevitably embracing the prospect of real-world violent conflict, perhaps on an unprecedented scale.

The heart of the matter is that Nietzsche rejects all forms of a transhistorical ethic, from Aristotelian to Kantian, that would equip us to stand outside of events and make a moral judgement about such movements ahead of time, before they ran their course. For Nietzsche, willing the Overman is a leap into a future whose outcome simply cannot be known in advance, for good or for ill. Perhaps I am wrong about this. Perhaps some such ethical standard lurks in Nietzsche's apocalyptic futurism – the notion, perhaps, that the Overman will combine the Roman nobility of Caesar in the soul of Christ, and therefore could not result in a coarse brute like Hitler or entirely forsake the value of compassion. I am not convinced of this for the reasons stated throughout this chapter: For Nietzsche, compassion toward mankind need not exclude its domination by a master race, nor can we know ahead of time exactly what tincture of either Christ or Caesar will survive in the Overman. But even if Nietzsche's thought does contain an ethics of some kind, I still do not see how, on the basis of everything we have considered in his writings, this ethical judgement could be rendered until *after* the leap across had been made, entailing who knows how much destruction along with the possibility of complete failure.

I conclude by reiterating that the potential fascistic implications of Nietzsche's thought must at the end of the day remain conjectural. We cannot know with certainty whether and to what degree he might have embraced political movements that he did not live to see. The analogy between

Nietzsche's relationship to fascism and Rousseau's relationship to the French Revolution is not, we should add in this connection, a balanced one. Robespierre and the Jacobins explicitly invoked Rousseau's General Will as their ideal; Hegel considered Rousseau to have written the script for the Jacobin Terror. By contrast, Hitler and the Nazis drew upon a whole panoply of extremist thinkers and ideologues besides Nietzsche. While Hitler was presumably pleased enough to be linked with Nietzsche's Superman by his sister, he never identified himself as Nietzsche's disciple in the way that Robespierre did with Rousseau. By the same token, any reservations we might entertain on Nietzsche's behalf against a fascist movement like Nazism must also remain conjectural. We cannot be certain he would have been an opponent. But even if, *per impossibile*, we could be absolutely certain that the implications of his thought were meant by him to be entirely apolitical, entirely for the sake of personal self-care or entirely tolerant of liberalism and democracy, his imprudent and immoderate rhetoric was destined to be misunderstood or distorted by actual political extremists out for blood.

In my parents' day, Nietzsche was taken to be without question a proto-fascist. That was a distorted interpretation. In recent years, by contrast, the "new" Nietzsche is presented as a feminist, democrat and environmentalist. That too is a distortion. The difference is that the old distortion can be corrected by a close reading of Nietzsche's texts. The new distortion is not so easily corrected because it is based, not upon a one-sided interpretation of the texts, but their bowdlerization, comparable to those redacted CIA documents in which 90 percent of every page is blacked out. That is why, of the two most prevalent distorted interpretations of Nietzsche, I prefer that of my parents' day. If you begin with the distortion of Nietzsche into nothing but a Nazi prophet, you can reason your way past that to the vastly more nuanced core with its negative and positive potential. But if you begin with the defanged, tranquilized new Nietzsche, the Nietzsche of easy-going mandarin self-fulfillment, it will be very hard to think your way through to the danger, and therefore to the nuances. The truth is somewhere in between the two distortions, but to grasp Nietzsche fully, you have to veer initially more to the Hitlerian reading, because that is a distortion that can be corrected by a careful reading without flinching from its grain of truth, whereas the view of Nietzsche as a democratic pluralist requires an outright and conscious falsification of his thinking.

4

The Distant Command of the Greeks

Heidegger and the Community of Destiny

"Because we have embarked on the great and long venture of demolishing a world that has grown old and of rebuilding it authentically anew ... our knowledge must be stricter and more binding than all the epochs before us, even the most revolutionary," Martin Heidegger wrote in *An Introduction to Metaphysics*. "Only the most radical historical knowledge can make us aware of our extraordinary tasks and preserve us from a new wave of mere restoration and uncreative imitation!"

This essay was based on a lecture course Heidegger gave in 1935. Presumably he said words much like these to a group of rapt students, perhaps some of them wearing the swastika. German university students had gone over to National Socialism in large numbers. Their professor, an ardent supporter of "the revolution" himself, was summoning them to action, to fulfill a commitment to the destiny of the German people that was in fact already underway. As he had put it in his *Rectoral Address* in 1933 upon assuming the Rectorship of Freiburg University, "But there is no need first to awaken this following. Germany's student body is on the march." We are compelled to ask: How did the arguably greatest thinker of the twentieth century find himself serving one of history's most murderous dictatorships? As George P. Grant suggested, if we could answer that question, we would understand a great deal about the twentieth century itself.

Heidegger's philosophy of Being is, following Nietzsche, the second assault from the Right aimed at Hegel's Absolute Science of Spirit and its teleological view of historical progress, an assault that includes the continuing denigration of liberalism. It also continues the fascination with and admiration for the civilization of the ancient Greek polis that, as we have seen, had been a continuing motif in the Philosophy of Freedom stretching back to Rousseau and Hegel. Like Nietzsche, Heidegger's vision of the polis favors the archaic horizon of tragic grandeur and pre-Socratic ontology over Hegel's admiration for the classical age of Periclean democracy and Plato. Whenever Heidegger speaks of "the Greeks," he means pre-Platonic and pre-metaphysical – in other words their authentic primordial historical existence.

That said, there are several ways in which Heidegger differs from all of his predecessors. Hegel, Marx and Nietzsche all granted the importance of the unfolding of history to date as a benchmark and guidepost for what must come next, whatever shortcomings they find in modernity. Despite other profound disagreements, Marx agrees with Hegel that history has been a rational process, and that its bourgeois liberal stage is inevitable for further progress. Even Nietzsche, while rejecting any conception of the rational progress of history, identifies major benchmarks in the psychological deepening of man through the genealogy of morals ("the Roman Caesar in the soul of Christ"; "the Saint"; "the three metamorphoses") that will serve as an inspiration and a springboard for willing the future Overman.

In Heidegger's thought, by contrast, we encounter the furthest extreme yet in the denigration of historical progress in his rejection of virtually every phase of history since the ancient polis as irredeemable. For Heidegger, the history of Being is synonymous with the history of our loss of and alienation from Being. In this respect, his elevation of the ancient Greeks as a point of departure for diagnosing the crisis of modernity is far more radical than that of Hegel and even Nietzsche, unmediated by any intervening historical watersheds. Heidegger displays virtually no interest in individual human psychology or biography. Nietzsche's admiration for great music and literature, including modern figures such as Montesquieu, Goethe, La Rouchefoucauld, Tolstoy and Emerson, as windows into the human spirit is largely absent from Heidegger's ontology of Being, with the exceptions of his deep interest in Sophocles' *Antigone* and Holderlin's *Der Ister*. Whereas Nietzsche identified Goethe as one of the free spirits and "magnificent" for being a true European rather than only a German, Heidegger dismissed his work as "mere cosmopolitanism" in contrast with Holderlin's immersion in the German soul (he was described by an admirer as "the most German of Germans"). As for Roman thought and the civilization of Christendom with its monumental philosophical theologies such as Thomism that attempted to synthesize Christian revelation and classical natural right, Heidegger largely passes over them as obfuscations. As he puts it in *An Introduction to Metaphysics*, only Greek and German, "the most powerful and spiritual of all languages," offer a direct pathway toward Being.

The greatness of the Greek origins, he proclaims in the *Rectoral Address*, stands across a chasm from us as it issues its "distant command" to reawaken our destiny today. Everything between the Greeks and their enduring command to us today deserves to be "demolished" as "a world grown old," paralleled by the call in *Being and Time* for the "destruction of metaphysics." Each of Hegel's successors we have examined sought to unleash historical existence as "self-origination" from the conceptual cage of Hegel's dialectic and restore its underlying energy of sheer becoming and spontaneity to man's own creative powers. Heidegger goes further than any of them in summoning forth the originating matrix of history as an "overpowering power," as pure unmediated strife. In the saying of Heraclitus, which he cites approvingly, *physis* is *polemos*: Being is War.

There is another way in which Heidegger's philosophy of history differs from his predecessors. In the philosophers we have considered up until now, the intrinsic connection between their thought and later extremist political movements has been speculative, ranging from implausible in the case of Hegel to plausible as regards Rousseau, Marx and Nietzsche. With Heidegger, by contrast, it is an incontrovertible fact: He was a committed National Socialist. Hence our consideration of his thinking must proceed somewhat differently. In the case of Rousseau, Hegel, Marx and Nietzsche, we attempted to explicate their thought as much as possible from within, and then in conclusion examined whether and to what extent it lent itself to an extremist political project. We will endeavor to follow the same procedure with Heidegger. But, inevitably, our consideration of the intrinsic philosophical content of his works of the 1920s and 1930s will veer into a chronicle of his growing commitment to the Nazis along the way, with which his consideration of the Question of Being is inextricably interwoven.

Moreover, although any commitment to an explicit political party or movement such as National Socialism vanishes from his works after the 1940s, Heidegger continues to explore retrospectively what that commitment had meant – sparking, as we will see, intense controversy – while opening up new vistas for the ramifications of his later thought for other reaches of political theory, culture and action. Like Nietzsche, his influence on contemporary thought, literature and art was multifarious, from Robert Musil's *A Man Without Qualities* to David Reisman's sociological classic of the Pax Americana era, *The Lonely Crowd*, to say nothing of his impact on the Frankfurt School, postmodernism, deconstructionism and political theorists including Arendt, Strauss, Gadamer, Derrida and Foucault. Therefore, just as with Nietzsche we pursued a middle path between turning a blind eye to the extremist implications of his thought and reducing him to a protofascist, in Heidegger's case we must pursue a middle path avoiding the two distortions of, on the one hand, explaining away his commitment to National Socialism as a personal enthusiasm with no intrinsic grounding in his thought and, on the other, reducing his significance for philosophy to nothing but an ideology of fascism.

Like Hegel, Heidegger's career was spent as an academic philosopher at Germany's ancient universities, unlike the outsiders Marx and Nietzsche whose work found no welcome in their august precincts. Recognition and respectable accolades came early for Heidegger. Even before the publication of *Being and Time*, according to Arendt, Heidegger was the "secret king" of German thought. Unlike Nietzsche as well, who had tried to free philosophical speculation from academic jargon, Heidegger's thought is saturated with the terminology and formal philosophical problematics inherited from Hegel, Schelling, Kant and Fichte. And yet, ironically, through placing his intellectual stature at the service of Hitler, appearing on reviewing stands with Brownshirts and Party officials taking the Hitler salute, Heidegger was more of a direct political actor than any of his predecessors. In the aftermath of that political commitment, Heidegger spent the rest of his life dedicated to living close to nature more devotedly than Rousseau's stagey gestures of rusticity, inhabiting a primitive ski hut in the Black Forest without electricity or heating, chopping wood and drawing his own water. But he was no solitary: like other famous modern intellectuals, he travelled, gave talks, made TV and radio appearances.

That brings us to a final striking feature, Heidegger's close proximity to us. Heidegger died in 1976 – just yesterday, so to speak. Other notable events that year (depending on your perspective) included my first year as a PhD student and the release of Led Zeppelin's *The Song Remains the Same*. Although Heidegger hearkens back to the entire accumulated legacy of German Idealism and is steeped in its oldest, most venerable sources, he brings the Philosophy of Freedom right into our own clamorous age, until under his sway it finally crashes and splinters into pieces, bringing to an end the whole fateful narrative of German historicism's encounter with the contradiction between nature and freedom bequeathed by Rousseau.

Our examination of Heidegger's works will concentrate first on *Being and Time* and *An Introduction to Metaphysics*, which, together with his *Rectoral Address*, detail his ontology of Being and its intrinsic connection to the emerging National Socialist movement. Although the *Rectoral Address* intervened between *Being and Time* and *An Introduction to Metaphysics*, we will reserve our consideration of it for a separate analysis of what precisely may have appealed to Heidegger about the National Socialist movement, since it was the most outrightly politically engaged of these works. We will proceed from there to considering Heidegger's writings after he leaves National Socialism behind – sometimes characterized as "the Turn," a phase already decipherable in *The Origin of the Artwork* and extending into *The Letter on Humanism* and *The Question Concerning Technology*. Although on a certain level unpolitical, these later works have profound reverberations for Heidegger's critique of modernity and a vision for its overcoming. First, however, let me suggest a general perspective on what Heidegger means by the Question of Being that can serve as a guide for all of these works.

THE BEING TREE: INTRODUCTORY REMARKS ON HEIDEGGERIAN ONTOLOGY

Several times in this book I have referred to Diotima's description of the Idea of the Beautiful in Plato's *Symposium* as the paradigmatic classical understanding of Being:

[It] is always being and neither comes into being nor passes away ... It is by itself and with itself, always being of a single form ... For this is what it is to proceed correctly in erotics – beginning with the beautiful things around us, always to proceed on up for the sake of beauty itself, ending at that study which is the study of nothing other than the beautiful itself.

With Heidegger, we reach the complete reversal of this paradigm. As he puts it in *The Origin of the Artwork*: "Origin here means that from which and by which something is, and what it is and as it is. What something is, as it is, we call its essence. The origin of something is the source of its essence." Instead of the Platonic ascent from becoming toward eternal Being, Heidegger offers us the descent into the temporal origins – the *Ursprung* – as the source of all that is. Being (*Sein*) as origination is the source of "the beings" (*Seiendes*) visible all around us. The Question of Being opens up the ontological realm, from the ancient term "the speech about Being," while the realm of the multiple distinct phenomena issuing from (as we might put it) big-B Being as origination is the realm of the "ontic," or small-b beings.

As an avenue into his new way of posing the Question of Being according to which "the origin of something is the source of its essence," Heidegger invites us to consider an oak tree in full bloom at the height of its growth. Classical metaphysics, according to Heidegger, takes this moment of the visible "presence" of the tree and extrapolates from it a supersensible realm where the oak tree remains this way eternally – the Idea, Form, Substance or Essence of the tree. This perfect higher tree never comes into being or decays, never grows, blossoms or withers away – in effect, it is the most perfectly thingly kind of thing of which we can conceive, with all elements of chance, accident and mutability banished from its pure stability.

This is the realm of metaphysics, the higher imperishable, invisible, immaterial eternal sphere that philosophy has traditionally identified as our sole valid point of entry into understanding Being. It recalls Aristotle's well-known example that the telos or final purpose of the acorn is to develop into the fully completed oak tree. But why, Heidegger asks, are we entitled to isolate this *one* moment of the full temporal cycle of the tree's existence as it comes into being and passes away, and privilege its visible completion at the expense of its hidden roots, which burrow deep in darkness under the earth and are as great in extent as the visible tree in the sunlight? Why, instead, do we not envision the Being of the tree as a process of emergence out of the hidden origins into a transitory moment of visible completion followed by its gradual decline and return into the origins whence it emerged?

The path to Being as a process of origination is the core premise of Heidegger's philosophy. By contrast, in his view, metaphysics posits a hardened chasm – akin to what Nietzsche called the distinction between the real and the apparent world – between the perfection of the eternal tree and the perishable, mutable dynamic of its emergence from and decline back into the roots. In comparison with the eternal endurance of the perfect tree, the tree we actually experience comes to seem shabby and flawed, a failure to achieve its own end, and appearance is therefore increasingly denigrated as "mere" appearance, a condition in which the visible tree falls short of its own perfection, riddled with accident and chance. In this way, metaphysics gradually becomes the project to remedy the flawed realm of the apparent world and transform it in the image of its own pure rationality, the complete domination of one moment of Being, that of perfect thinghood or "presence," over the entire rest of the process of coming into being and passing away. (Akin to what Nietzsche termed the ascetic ideal, whose early formulation was the domination of the Dionysian by the Apollonian.) For Heidegger, this classical imperative to erect "the yoke of the Idea" over the rest of existence, as he put it in *Plato's Doctrine of the Truth*, is the distant inception of modern technology.

Heidegger's ontology of Being therefore stands in a symmetrical relationship to Plato's metaphysics of the Ideas in the sense of positing its antipodal opposite: Whereas Plato searches for the eternal causes of the whole, Heidegger seeks to uncover the roots of the whole. Because Heidegger's "fundamental ontology" is the unconditional opposite of Plato's philosophy of the whole, it paradoxically possesses a parallel with Platonism's abstract quality – not the abstractness of a transcendental account of the whole in which our understanding of the here and now sheds all concrete particularity as it rises toward pure reason, but the sheer indeterminacy of Being as origination, empty of all "ontic" content. Although Hegel also transposes our perspective on Being from the eternal truth to existential "self-origination," he is in a sense closer to Plato inasmuch as his dialectic of Spirit develops historically into the middle realm of everyday life, the multiple "shapes of consciousness," corresponding to Plato's understanding of the "participation" of the world around us and our opinions in the Ideas. By contrast, because Heidegger rejects altogether any study of the "ontic" realm of "everyday life" as valuable for its own sake – the realm of concrete ideas, debatable opinions, customs, public life, culture, institutions and formal intellectual disciplines – on the grounds that it is an obfuscation of fundamental ontology, covering over the process of Being's unfathomable self-emergence with a project for rational control, his relationship to Plato's philosophy takes the form of its *total* inversion. For Plato, conversational debate about everyday opinion, virtue and the good life is the beginning of the search to elucidate the truth about the whole. For Heidegger, in stark contrast, to become lost in such "everyday talk," chatter or blather (*offentliche Gerede*), is the beginning of our drifting *away* from the roots of Being in pursuit of an illusory reasoned clarity. In fact, for Heidegger, Hegel's claim to have identified a rational and teleological pattern in history – the "Absolute Knowledge of Spirit" – is merely one of the final culminations of a metaphysical agenda for the subjugation of Being stretching back to Plato. Even more startlingly, he regards Nietzsche's philosophy of the Will to Power as the last stage of Platonic metaphysics in its full actualization as global technological mastery. Heidegger's way of exploring the Question of Being has profound consequences for our understanding of politics and morality, including, as we will see, the politics of the future. Let us turn now to an overview of some key terms from *Being and Time* and then examine them more closely with respect to their broader political implications.

AUTHENTICITY, COMMITMENT AND RESOLVE

As Heidegger observes at the beginning of *Being and Time*, Being is common to all things, and the fact that we specify all things as "being" demonstrates that we as humans are already involved with the whole of life in which the things that we identify as being take their place. But when we try to talk about Being itself, apart from all concrete things, it seems vacuous and empty. This is because all previous philosophy has searched for Being in terms of a higher, permanently true "actuality," from Plato's Ideas to Kant's metaphysics of morals to Hegel's teleology of history. Heidegger, by contrast, will be the first to pose the Question of Being in terms of "possibility" [38]. Because it is closest to Being, "possibility stands higher than actuality." In this way, the vacuousness of the metaphysical account of Being is filled with the rich loam of indeterminacy, the roots of the tree.

Among all the beings that come into being and pass away, *one* of these – man – is aware of the impermanence, the finitude, of all beings. Man alone has a relationship to the whole. For man is not just a thing, but a thing which questions the life in which all things occur, a gateway for the question of life as a whole – "the being (*seiend*) for whom Being (*Sein*) is an issue" [8–12]. Man's openness to doubt about his purpose is at the deepest level what Heidegger means by "existence." Man *is* this process, a way of being, not a fixed entity, and it is the specific dimensions of this openness to doubt that constitute what Heidegger calls fundamental ontology. Dasein, the distinctively human mode of Being, is the "there" (*Da*) of Being (*Sein*), the place where the question of Being unfolds. The core of Being – impermanence – touches Dasein through our moods in our awareness of our own death, which is to say our awareness of our finitude. Moods such as anxiety and care disclose our innermost connectedness to Being as such, to impermanence, and these moods are wordless intimations, prior to rational articulation – the "call" of Being at its most profound level is "silent" [271–272].

The openness to change and doubt which constitutes man's existence is directly conditioned by the mutability and impermanence of Being as such. Dasein is the only being aware of the Question of Being because of our awareness of death. By this, Heidegger does not merely mean our physical death – although it includes it – but our not being any fixed entity, in other words, sheer possibility. Initially, our insight into our own finitude and that of everyone else is deeply disturbing: Entering the Question of Being is not a mere intellectual exercise, but courses throughout our whole existence. "Care" (*Sorge*) burdens man with an insight into the temporality of all things (preeminently his own), an "anxiety" (*Angst*) which is thrust upon him by the mutability of Being itself [188–189]. But when we grasp that finitude means that nothing is fixed, nothing is permanent, finitude can be the wellspring of new possibilities, of becoming that which is not yet. Facing the prospect of death is, it turns out, in reality liberating, enabling us to live "authentically." First experienced as terrifying, anxiety can be turned around into the "resolve" to face our finitude and recommit ourselves to the destiny in which we are involved. Fundamental ontology is the set of active conditions by which a world is generated through man's encounter with Being, and by which man lets Being issue in this historical world. Fundamental ontology does not deal with *what* man is according to some conception of his permanent nature, but *how* he is what he is in any particular historical world. "How" has priority over "what."

In order to understand Heidegger's conception of historical change, we must look at what he terms "everyday" life, the way in which he believes we experience life "first of all and most of the time." Within the everyday world, the stable aspects of beings as they have emerged – the "present-at-hand" – is elevated into their sole and absolute reality. In other words, Being, the generative origin of all things present-at-hand, is reified as a higher presence or actuality that solicits the visible beings to emerge according to the principles of logic, mathematics and the empirical sciences. The search for Being in the "reflected" image of "the looks of the world" – likely an allusion to the literal meaning of a Platonic form (*eidos*) as a "look" – is, Heidegger asserts, the flaw in all traditional metaphysics from Plato to Hegel. The search for metaphysical clarity likens thinking to the clarity of sight; hence Socrates' metaphor of the mind as "the eye of the soul" in its drive to classify all beings according to propositional speech and reasoning. But for Heidegger, our attunement to Being should be by way of its invisible roots.

According to Heidegger, wherever we ordinarily encounter human beings, they are inextricably involved with a historical "world" which they share with "others." Typically, however, everyday life is profoundly "alienating," blocking the restorative energies of Being that underlie it. In order to remedy this alienation, man must achieve authenticity through "freedom-toward-death." By resolving to face his finitude, man opens it up to become anything in particular – at the most fundamental level, the historically unique epochs of peoples and worlds which their members share. The struggle to be free in the face of man's overwhelming impermanence establishes the "clearing" for man's "historicity." Paradoxically, Being needs this one being, man, to resist its overpowering originary power to engulf it, and thereby act as a channel or medium by which the power can radiate into what is, including man himself in his conventional attitudes and traits once the epoch-founding struggle has settled down into the stable appearance of everyday life.

That will suffice for an overview of the basic themes of fundamental ontology. Now we must examine them in more detail as they relate to Heidegger's vision of an authentic political community. How precisely does Heidegger claim to be able to uncover the structures of possibility that underly every "factical" Dasein, that is to say, every historical world as it actually exists? According to Heidegger, when we encounter human beings first of all and most of the time, they are enmeshed in the particular world which they have already opened up, but whose momentous origins they have forgotten as that world has assumed an appearance of unshakeable stability. We feel as if we have been "thrown" into a world not of our own choosing. Heidegger wants to demonstrate that man's need to question his world, which leads back to the upheaval of its origins in a rediscovery of authenticity, is already actual *in* man's experience of his ordinary, everyday world, but as something unselfconscious and merely implicit [44]. Man's questioning and doubt about his world is, as Heidegger puts it, "pre-ontological" – a vague but strong feeling that creeps into everyday life. Heidegger wishes to raise this feeling to consciousness, to make it clear and explicit. This can only be done, he argues, by generalizing and formalizing the ways in which man experiences everyday life, abstracting from the multiplicity of worlds and their distinct chronological histories, customs and cultures. Fundamental ontology, he says, must be sought in "the existential analytic of Dasein," meaning the generalization of everyday experience [13]. Another way of putting this is to say that if the true meaning of human experience lies in its primordial origins rather than in a substantial end, that truth can in no way transcend ordinary experience, but most somehow reside *in* it organically.

Fundamental ontology, to reiterate, does not deal with what man is, but how he becomes what he is in any particular historical epoch – the recurrent structures of possibility of any possible world. Its aim is to uncover the set of active conditions by which a world is generated in the struggle between man and Being. Heidegger maintains that every historical world as it actually exists – every nation with its specific politics, morality and culture – has these "ontological foundations" as its origin and basis [16–22, 28, 118–120]. In this connection, we must stress an important feature of his argument. Heidegger repeatedly emphasizes that these underlying structures of possibility do not imply a universal substratum of pre-civilizational human nature, the "primitiveness" of a universal anthropology akin to Rousseau's state of nature. Nor do they imply a universal ideal yet to be achieved, analogous to Kant's Categorical Imperative or the "end of history" in Hegel's *Phenomenology of Spirit*. There are only the unique and independent worlds that have grown out of local encounters with Being. In other words, man has no pure freedom *beyond* the particular world to which he is committed, and his commitment takes place nowhere except in the midst of this world, its people and their heritage. This heritage, a people's "ownmost distinctive possibility," discloses the fixed possibilities within which human beings move, and within which their future will move. (Hence his play on the interconnectedness of "historicity" [*Geschichtlichkeit*] and "fate" [*Schicksal*].)

As the one being for whom Being is an issue, Dasein has a "foreknowledge" of its finitude through its moods, an "ontic" situation that grounds and anticipates the ontological Question of Being. In this way, for Heidegger, human experience and the longing for wholeness are still central to philosophizing as they had been traditionally going back to Plato, but in a completely new way – man is a *who*, not a *what*. Man is not "in the world" in the same way that water is "in a glass." But Dasein's being-in-the-world is the existential and pre-reflective ground for the possibility of subsequent propositional statements like water is "in a glass." Similarly, only because I am always already in the world is it possible for me to view myself detachedly and on reflection as an entity living "on this planet." The care with which the wearing on of time burdens us as an intimation of our mortality is always care for *this* world, the heritage we already live within, and the ontological question of Being emerges from our always already being engaged with the "ontic" world of actuality, the composite structure of Dasein as being-in, being-with, being-in-the-world, being-with-others and being-with-one-another. Care, anxiety and resolve are how Being touches us in the midst of everyday life and discloses our finite choices – not a flight from finitude, but an authentic embrace of it. It is important to stress here that, for Heidegger, Dasein is *never* an individual subject, but a complex of forces that is intersubjective and collective at the deepest level. The modes of Dasein are inseparable from Being, they constitute its "there." Dasein does not possess discrete properties such as being with others: Those forces always already express Dasein "equiprimordially" as the presence of Being [54–57, 118–120].

When Being touches us through our finitude, making us aware of the primordial possibilities that the everyday world, in its anxious search for security and control, tries to "dim down" and paper over, it acts as the spur to authenticity. But that resolve to recommit ourselves to the authenticity of the origins can *fail*. In answering the call of the Question of Being, Dasein can "cut itself off from its ontic roots" in the ontological question, freeing itself from anxiety under the illusion that it is recovering its authenticity, while in reality floating away into the mere traditionalism of the security of the "old thinking" of metaphysics or religion, or reducing authentic commitment to a mere ideology justifying a particular choice of values in the current everyday world – for example, the Hegelian doctrine of the progress of history, Marxist dialectical materialism, or liberal reformism. Standards for what constitutes authenticity inevitably conflict, and the relapse back into inauthenticity mistaken for the way to break out of it is the rule rather than the exception.

Because most of the time the world has assumed an appearance of all-embracing permanence and solidity, this bewitching appearance "tempts" us to regard the world as a finished product [77]. We stand passively before it, mindful only of how it might be preserved as it is, including by modifying or reforming it in superficial ways that do not break out of its ambit of officially prescribed choices. The need to get along as best we can in a world for which we no longer bear any active responsibility alienates us from others and, since we are involved with others at the very core of our being, alienates us from ourselves. We grow "unsociable" as the primordial relationship of being-with is covered over, well-nigh obliterated, by what Heidegger calls the "they-self" (*Man-Selbst*), a coinage that collectivizes the impersonal pronoun for "one" and "they," corresponding to *on* in French. The spurious permanence of the they-self is the public authority which orders our lives as fearful conformists or efficient managers of the surrounding environment. Heidegger's evocation of "the dictatorship of the They," a dictatorship that includes but goes beyond the seemingly self-perpetuating and disembodied mechanism of public opinion, has made a powerful contribution to the sociology of alienation from bourgeois "mass" society [125–127]. For, despite the abstract quality of Heidegger's presentation, it points clearly to what has been widely perceived as the hectic self-interest, hypocrisy and loneliness of contemporary liberal individualism. The they-self is a creature of isolated "ones" which reinforces its members' fear of failing to conform to the world as it now exists by impersonally prescribing what "one" may or may not do. "One" does what "they" do. The they-self's desire to manage and fortify the world's power to remain as it is serves to "tranquilize" human behavior and prevent a reemergence of those risks which lie concealed at the origins of the world. It transforms, for instance, the simple tools of agrarian living close to the earth into the economic and managerial behemoth of industrialized urban society [121–130].

In the they-self's world, the people's "heritage" is trivialized, forgotten or treated as irrelevant so as to obscure any heterodox challenges that might spring up out of the past to challenge the illusion of a perfectly self-sufficient, timeless and ongoing present. The politics of everyday life is thus reduced, as Heidegger puts it, to a utilitarian "reckoning and balancing of claims" among egoistic individuals. In this connection, Heidegger derides the social welfare programs of modern states and the public morality of "empathy" they promote. These conventional links of empathy (sustained, presumably, by legislation and public opinion) take for granted the existence of fundamentally isolated individuals who have already come to view one another as static, self-contained objects like the everyday world altogether, and can only reconnect with one another through the bloodless artificial mechanisms of state management.

The radical alienation from Being summed up as the dictatorship of the They and its apparatus of the modern state helps us to understand the insistently nonempirical character of fundamental ontology, a disdain for measurable evidence outpacing even Nietzsche, and explicitly at odds with the claims of Hegel and Marx to have offered empirical evidence for their theories of history. The problem, in Heidegger's view, with the conventional human or social sciences (*Geisteswissenschaften*) such as political science, psychology and anthropology is that they start by observing the everyday world in its appearance of objective permanence, and then devise methodologies to organize these observations. In other words, the social sciences presuppose a particular, independent world without realizing that their evidence is true for this world alone. The "ontological foundations" of all such worlds can never be approached through "hypotheses derived from empirical materials," since these hypotheses can never be valid for any world other than the one from which they are derived – a world which is unique and, therefore, substantively incomparable with other worlds. The social sciences, having been elaborated in terms of the empirical actuality of the everyday world, are incapable of reaching behind and uncovering the grounds of their own possibility. Put another way, unlike Hegel, Marx and Nietzsche, Heidegger rejects the very concept of a horizontal universality, of a science of history or a genealogy of morals of "the type 'man.'" We encounter only the vertical universality of irreducibly unique collectivist monads, of "peoples." In Being, "nothing touches." Every phenomenon, human or nonhuman, is a singular revelation [55].

To be a captive of the they-self is to live "inauthentically." But – and this is a crucial point – to live authentically, or, more literally, to become real (*eigentlich*) in no way means to transcend or withdraw from the world out of which everyday life has emerged. For everyday life is merely the "dimmed down," fossilized and devitalized form of an original encounter with Being. The "temptation" to live inauthentically is thus "constitutive" of man in the depths of his being-there. It is neither a "sin" which can be redeemed, nor a "fall" from a natural or biblical golden age. There is, in short, no exit from one's world, its people and heritage. To live authentically, therefore, consists in "seizing upon" the vital origins, the struggle out of which the everyday world has issued, and reenacting those origins afresh [138, 194–195].

Authentic commitment can take no other form than self-consciously "choosing to make this choice"; "coming back" to the "definite possibilities" of this one world beneath the encrusted "actuality" of everyday life [144, 268]. The alienation that characterizes everyday life at its most typical and fully developed acts as the spur to this coming back. Subverting our mere "fear" (*Furcht*) of failing to conform and get along, this anxiety bespeaks a sneaking consciousness of everyday life's groundlessness – its vaporous, "rootless" quality as it floats further and further from the "house" (*Heim*) of our primordial interaction with Being. Anxiety dispels the illusion that we have been "living concretely." On the contrary, we feel "uncanny" (or literally "unhoused" – *unheimlich*), "floating" and "fallen" in the midst of the familiar and customary [175–180]. This very anxiety is a disguised blessing because it is an intimation of the underlying impermanence and mutability of Being. Our intimation of the necessary fragility of all attempts to build a permanently satisfying world brings us face to face again with that struggle with life's "overpowering" challenge to build a world. In order to reenact the origins of our world, we must be liberated from the they-self's delusion that the everyday world can remain as it is forever. We can "choose to make this choice" only when we recognize that it is the impossibility of our choice lasting forever that makes it possible and necessary to choose again. Anxiety reveals, at bottom, the consciousness of our finitude, that innermost recess where we are touched directly by Being.

To sum up: The condition of human beings "first of all and most of the time" is to live "inauthentically" in their conformity to the status quo. The belief that the world can be managed according to the canons of the metaphysically present-at-hand, that our fear of death can be postponed by technology and social planning, that ambiguity and doubt can be kept at bay by the anesthetizing dictatorship of public opinion, protect us from confronting the initially terrifying reality of our impermanence. When we break free in our recommitment to our destiny, in that moment of resolve (*Entschlossenheit*) – and then alone – we live authentically. However, this resolve upon the origins is as much a blind sally into the future, for it involves the rejection of everything customary and familiar as we take over the "basis" of our community's destiny. When the death of our community's current historical possibilities is faced with resolve, when a people "goes under the eyes of Death," new possibilities open up that draw upon the deepest roots of our collective destiny, a past *behind* the conventional interpretation of the past (such as received tradition, a political ideology, or a doctrine of progress). These choices, as Heidegger puts it, guide our individual "fates ... in advance" as the destiny that comes down to us as the community's unique historical existence [384]. Confronting the finitude, arbitrariness and particularity of our world dispels the complacency of everyday life, enabling us to see ourselves for what we really are. Suddenly vanish all the frivolous distractions and superficial diversity which mask the emptiness of inauthentic existence.

The implicit political implications of fundamental ontology now begin to take shape. "Resolve" is the active expression of the inner strength mustered through "care." As the one being who wonders about the source of all beings, care is thrust upon man by the mutability of Being. For, as the generative origin of all beings, the matrix from which they emerge and into which they pass away, Being *is* Nothing. Resolving to face the finitude which surges through all things establishes man's "freedom-toward-death" or "finite freedom." Because he can face the necessity of his world passing away, he can grasp the possibility of regenerating this world. As a participant in the destiny which shapes each people from its origins, man can join his "time" and "generation" in rechoosing that destiny [382–385]. This frees him from the inauthentic delusion that the world will always exist just as it is now. Members of the everyday world have forgotten their participation in the creation of their historical world. It has been reified as an objective realm standing over against them as subjects. They can accept this world passively or exert their control over it; both responses presuppose the cleavage of the world into subject and object – the self versus the other selves; the self versus the rest of existence – and therewith the "alienation" of man from Being.

What Heidegger means by an "impassioned freedom toward death" is precisely the means by which man is to recommit himself with new energy and clarity to the people and heritage in which he is already engaged, but whose full possibilities have been forgotten in the listless routinization of everyday life. Far from being a call to the mere acceptance or conservation of a cherished tradition, Heidegger's understanding of freedom as "seizing upon" the destiny we share with others is therefore a call to the most thoroughgoing revolutionary transformation of everyday life – an impassioned recommitment to our heritage which is paradoxically "against it, and yet for it"; for it *by* being against it [383–386]. Resolving upon its "finite freedom" enables a people to shatter the dictatorship reared out of their own alienation. They give themselves over to their historical destiny, which enables them to vault into the future rooted in a past so primordial as to bear little if any relationship to the reified present. As the people push forward into their future – unknown, since the inauthenticity of the present and of received tradition cannot be relied upon to provide any guide for it – only then in fact will its past, purged of everyday life, reveal itself fully in retrospect "in its genuine essence (*Wesen*)." Its true "heroes" and authentic folkways will rear up out of the deepest roots of the past, where they were trapped by the they-self's official history of the past designed to repress any heterodox alternatives and enshrine the present as the Panglossian best of all possible worlds [178, 266, 307–308, 385].

Consequently, the community's reassumption of its destiny requires a new kind of radicalism that is both backward and forward-looking, what I have elsewhere termed atavistic futurism. It requires the rejection of all existing political, social, cultural and moral bonds in the name of a contentless communitarianism; a wholly abstract notion of the people rooted in a past so primordial as to bear little if any resemblance to what is regarded in everyday life, by custom, public and intellectual opinion, *as* the people's past history. To repeat: We must seek a past *behind* the past. In order to be "for" our heritage, we have to go "against it." To resolve upon a past so totally unfamiliar requires the most radical futurism. Because the emptiness out of which the everyday world is projected is indeterminate and substanceless, the world which each people builds up in this void is, to stress an earlier point, unique and arbitrary. Man cannot, as Heidegger says, get back "behind" this void and fill it once and for all, nor can he transcend it. In the absence of any such guide for specific, limited goals, the reenactment can only take on the character of audacious daring (power, struggle, resolve, violence), a tremendous negative energy purging everyday life in the longing to reexperience what Heidegger calls the "ecstatic moment of vision" when the community's world sprang into being. Consistent with his rejection of everyday life and the metaphysical "ontic" kind of reason characteristic of it as standards for guiding the community's recommitment to its destiny, Heidegger cannot define authenticity in any concrete way. He can only evoke it negatively as that "*by the neglect of which*" we are inauthentic [268].

Because Heidegger's vision in 1927 of an authentic political community, actualized for him six years later (as I will argue) as the National Socialist revolution, has often been castigated for its lack of ethical standards, and for his refusal during the rest of his career to ethically condemn what the Third Reich had done, it bears emphasizing here that at the very outset of fundamental ontology in *Being and Time*, the existential analytic of Dasein is incompatible in principle with any variety of formal ethic such as Kant's categorical imperative. Kant's chief value for Heidegger is that his philosophy of freedom emptied the concept of selfhood of its "soul-substance," that is, of all historical and substantive psychological content, received tradition, the "perfectionism" of the classical account of the soul, or what Hegel later termed shapes of consciousness [319–320]. Kant's failing is that, having emptied selfhood of its "ontic" content, he still clung to a metaphysical concept of individual selfhood as something "present-at-hand," hovering at the brink of Dasein without having the radicalism to go over that brink and descend still further behind that fixed individual self into the power of sheer possibility disclosed through Dasein's collectivized, pre-individuated structures of "equiprimordial" engagement. For Heidegger, historical events cannot be judged according to any transcendental or transhistorical standpoint – including a historicist one such as Hegel's doctrine of teleological progress – purporting to enable us to detach ourselves from our destiny, for nothing can transcend Being. Heideggerian "decision" can only be judged by the intensity of its opposition to "inauthentic everydayness," including the rule of law, political deliberation, human rights, the progress of history, ethics and either liberal, conservative or socialist values.

Although *Being and Time* is ostensibly setting forth the "pregnant structures" of possibility that underlie the emergence of a community and a people at any time and place in principle (beginning with the ancient Greek polis [27]), there are unmistakable references to the kind of alienation widely associated in cultural critiques on both the Left and the Right with modern life in an industrialized mass society like Germany in Heidegger's own era. In this respect, Heidegger continues the Philosophy of Freedom's critique of bourgeois materialism stretching back to Rousseau. But he is carrying this critique to a new pitch of comprehensiveness requiring the jettisoning of all traditional beliefs, canons of rationality and moral psychology, which his predecessors in varying ways and to varying degrees had accepted. In *Being and Time* the world of everyday inauthenticity at its most alienating – greedy, conformist, despiritualized – clearly evokes a twentieth-century urban setting. Authentic existence open to Being, by contrast, is invariably invoked by bucolic metaphors drawn from the countryside – the farm, the earth, the village. These had been common tropes of German Volkisch nationalism since at least the 1880s. Moreover, no reader of *Being and Time* could have been unaware of the frequent identification of "big city" greed and corruption with Jews and other "foreign" minorities, although this did not necessarily go further than a prejudice.

Given these contemporary resonances, can we envision in *Being and Time* what recognizable political form from Heidegger's own era the people's return to its destiny would take? What exactly is the community's "ownmost distinctive possibility"? Because of the radical abstractness of fundamental ontology, as we have seen, the existential analytic of Dasein can offer no guidance in advance about concrete goals – "what Dasein factually resolves" as it takes over its "factual basis" [383]. But several things are clear, I believe, about what this recommitment *cannot* include. It cannot include the mere reform of the existing conditions of everyday life. Ordinary political controversies over changing some specific institution, policy or morality are not radical enough, since the very familiarity of the disputes and their objects keep us chained to everyday life. Heidegger makes clear his disdain for any compromise with the conditions of ordinary political dispute and party politics with his dismissal of the whole question of justice as a "mere balancing and reckoning of claims," part of that "everyday chatter" by which the they-self manages its affairs. By conceding the meaning of justice to utilitarian haggling, Heidegger appears to conflate justice with the lowest and most materialistic version of the liberal social contract, with the consequence that the need to understand justice is not a dimension of what is highest and noblest in human life – a point of departure not only from Plato and the classics, but from moderns such as Rousseau, Kant and Hegel.

Heidegger is equally emphatic that, despite what strikes many readers as the conventional Volkisch overtones of *Being and Time*, the people's "return" to Being is not meant to encourage conservatism in the sense of restoring or bolstering cherished traditional or premodern ways of life. For Heidegger, a tradition is inauthentic if it in any way buttresses everyday life, and traditional elements residing in everyday life do buttress it even if they seem to cut against it, since they do make up a part of its totality. (Heidegger, like Marx, would presumably view a Burkean account of conservatism as valuing tradition only insofar as it was a way station to the inevitable triumph of the modern state, an accomplice in fortifying the they-self.) For Heidegger, a return to Throne and Altar *Junker* conservatism or the Wilhelmine Reich was no more to be sought than bourgeois capitalism or socialism. The origins which a people reenact must stand across a chasm from everything familiar, whether they be past or present institutions and customs, and their resolve is therefore by definition revolutionary. What exactly Heidegger means by a community's return to its destiny – "inherited yet chosen" – will continue to loom large in what follows.

Finally, it is clear that the community's return to Being cannot embrace historical progress in the Hegelian or Marxist sense according to which man is progressively transformed through the objective conditions of social and economic life in which he is engaged. As we saw in Chapter 2 in the discussion of determinate negation, for Hegel each advance in the pursuit of freedom is shaped and limited by the previous historical epoch that it overcomes, imparting a teleological structure to the progress of history as well as moderating the excessively radical drive for freedom by precedent and prescription. For Heidegger, by contrast, freedom is the return to a protean, indeterminate nothingness that overturns all existing conditions without either developing them or being developed by them, altogether dispensing with precedent and prescription along with moderation.

The theoretical move in *Being and Time* enabling this transformation is Heidegger's explicit rejection of Hegel's principle of determinate negation. For Heidegger, the indeterminacy and lack of fixity that characterizes Being as "possibility" is not what Hegel means by "negation." In his view, Hegelian negation already implies its pairing with an object in the "ontic" realm of everyday life to be negated and mediated, chaining freedom to inherited traditions, convention and ordinary political squabbling. In other words, although Hegel understands that Being is dynamic, he nonetheless converts it into an absolute subject which progressively overcomes its contradictions, logicizes itself and completes itself. Ultimately, therefore, even Hegel mistook Being for being, that is to say, interpreted it metaphysically. Heidegger rejects Hegel's whole conceptual overlay of the Unity of Subject and Substance that, when paired with determinate negation, enables Hegel to present history as a rational progression. Heidegger descends behind this, for him, inauthentic overlay of rational control into the sheer nothingness, the sheer "notness" (*Nichtkigkeit*), at the core of Being, a nothingness that cannot be "filled up" with the positive content of progressive historical change [285]. Our return to Being is not intended to "negate" the present-at-hand so as to cumulatively improve it while being mediated by it. Instead, "the people" is summoned by "the call" of Being to recommit itself unreservedly to this underlying vortex of destiny. All positive accounts of the outward course of history such as that of Hegel are merely reinforcing doctrines for the "dictatorship of the They."

As we recall from Chapter 2, applied to the events of history, the Unity of Subject and Substance explains Hegel's argument, for example, that the Master/ Slave relationship, after its pagan morality has been superseded by Christianity, continued to mediate the new morality as the Unhappy Consciousness of the believer who cannot bridge the distance between his spiritual master God and his bondage to the world of the flesh. To take another example: When Protestantism supersedes Catholicism, the salvation previously confined to heaven is brought down to earth as the faith within the individual believer. But the previous, literal otherworldliness is preserved in a mediated form, inasmuch as the internalized salvation of the Protestant is still unable to transform the external world (a development that must await the French Revolution). Hegel's dialectic interprets history as a cumulative progress through an ever richer resolution of contradictions. When the outward transformation of the world has run its course in tandem with the inner reconciliation of man with himself and with his fellow human beings, Spirit will be absolutely manifest. Although Marx rejected what he regarded as Hegel's idealism for mediating the world's actual conflicts out of existence into an imaginary, wholly "inner" reconciliation, he preserved the dialectical method in his examination of how the starkly opposed "positive" antagonisms of the modern world had emerged from the cumulative conflict between labor and capital.

The contrast with Heidegger in this regard could hardly be more striking or instructive. For Heidegger, we may say, the negation of the present-at-hand by Being develops neither one nor the other. The "notness" underlying beings cannot be conceived of in a determinate way, as the absence of a being. The negation is, so to speak, absolute rather than determinate, leaving no "mediated" residue. Hence Being is not, as it is for Hegel, embodied in the "ethical life" (*Sittlichkeit*) of the state, a synthesis of legal, religious, aesthetic and personal mores, providing an empirical benchmark for further advancements. Nor does the everyday world reveal, as it does for Marx, the current level of development of the antagonism between labor and capital, furnishing empirical evidence for an emerging final conflict between the bourgeoisie and the universal class of the workers.

Heidegger believes that to conceive of history as a mediated dialectic serves only to reify the historical process itself, lifting it out of its generative origins and objectifying it as a record of man's outward, rational transformation of the environment. For Heidegger, this record can only be a catalogue of the varieties of inauthenticity into which peoples "fall" from their primordial encounters with Being. Those who look to such a "world-historical" record for a solution to human alienation are, instead of reorienting themselves more closely to Being, "floating" further away from it as they rummage among "exotic and alien cultures" [20–23, 175–180]. For Heidegger, rather than a dialectic of historical progress, there is a titanic opposition between the awesome negative "power" of Being resurging as the people's destiny and the "rootless" inauthenticity of everyday life. The "power" of destiny is in no way mediated – that is, mitigated or qualified – by existing socioeconomic and cultural conditions. Instead, freedom-toward-death "revokes" those conditions and sweeps them away [383–386]. As earlier with Marx and Nietzsche, we see how a theoretical critique of Hegelian historical progress intertwines with an implicit political critique, each reinforcing the other. For Heidegger, Hegel's doctrine of progress was at bottom nothing more than a way of shoring up modern bourgeois liberalism by depicting it as the sole rational outcome of all previous historical development.

THE INNER TRUTH AND GREATNESS OF NATIONAL SOCIALISM

An important context for understanding the huge impact of *Being and Time* upon its publication was the widespread conviction that the catastrophes of world war, revolution and economic depression had rendered a Hegelian (or even a Marxist) account of rational historical progress untenable because it had been so utterly refuted by the course of events. Hans-Georg Gadamer, one of Heidegger's students at Marburg, later recalled the 1920s as "the end of the age of liberalism with its belief in progress based on science." What had transpired for that generation was not the fulfillment and flowering of history, but unprecedented carnage, upheaval and destruction, far outstripping the French Revolution and Napoleonic wars which for Hegel had been the worst examples of the "slaughter bench" of history. By jettisoning Hegel's dialectic of teleological progress, Heidegger was arguably able to revive historicism with his existential analytic of mood, care, heritage and community that grounded the Question of Being directly in Dasein's finitude and insisted that Dasein "is nowhere able to transcend it." In this way, Heidegger hastened the rescue of historicism from its earlier philosophical displacement by neo-Kantianism, which had renounced an interest in psychology or speculative ontology in the manner of Hegel – a movement itself now on the wane. In short, in Heidegger's transformation, historicism minus Hegelian progress gave us existentialism, among whose principal founders Heidegger is counted. Hegel, by contrast, likewise grounds transcendence in finite historical experience, but believed that the teleology of historical progress would eventually transcend finitude: Time culminates in the actualization of wisdom at the end of history. Faced with the crisis of German and especially Hegelian historicism, which appeared to have been completely invalidated by how history had actually turned out, Heidegger is saying: We must go *behind* Hegel's metaphysical concept of the Truth (the Unity of Subject and Substance) and return to his original authentic insight identifying existence with sheer self-origination. But, as we have seen, Heidegger absolutely resisted the contraction of existentialism to a purely personal creed of self-cultivation in the manner of Kierkegaard or, later, people influenced by him like Sartre. The rational progress of history might be dead and buried, but a collective political choice still had to be made.

In *Being and Time*, the finitude from which a people seeks to hide in everyday life finally compels it, through anxiety, to resolve upon the recovery of its destiny. Although the "dictatorship of the They" was clearly meant to evoke the conformism and egoism of bourgeois modernity specifically, the aim of fundamental ontology was to generalize the ways in which worlds come into being at any given time and place, notwithstanding the fact that the content of each such destiny would be unique. By 1935, however, Heidegger believed that Germany faced the unique peril of its literal as well as spiritual finitude or destruction – a peril which, if properly heeded, could expose the groundlessness of bourgeois modernity for itself and the West as a whole. In *An Introduction to Metaphysics*, Heidegger seeks to begin philosophy anew by linking Germany's destiny to the original Greek experience of Being as *physis*. Moreover, the history of the West begins to assume a prominence in *An Introduction to Metaphysics* which it lacked in *Being and Time* as providing the "determinate" account of man's alienation from Being. We are constituted, Heidegger now argues, by a determinate concrete historical relationship to the indeterminate dynamic of Being. For Germany today, this determinate relationship to the indeterminacy of Being goes back to the Greeks, largely unmediated by later watersheds such as Rome, the Middle Ages, and the doctrine of historical progress, which only obscure it. Posing the question of Being through directly reengaging the Greeks uncovers "the source of our hidden history," a destiny that holds all history and politics under its sway down to the present. In order to recover its destiny, Germany must rethink this hidden history in order to understand exactly how the "fall" from Being came about. Only in this way will Germany's contemporary struggle be able to redeem the West as a whole.

This history has, indeed, a kind of dialectic – but not in the Hegelian sense of freedom progressing gradually through mediated stages to supersede our alienation from the world and from one another. On the contrary, the provenance of this history will remain hidden as long as it is viewed in such a benignly teleological light. It must be seen instead as a dialectic *only* of alienation, as a steady, regressive development away from freedom. And yet, the very persistence and strength of this alienation are necessary, in Heidegger's view, to compel "modern man" to face his peril with a clear-sightedness unknown since the "violent ones" who founded the Greek polis. This negative dialectic, in which man must undergo the extremity of the alienation from Being in order to realize just what has been lost, remains at the core of Heidegger's understanding of history even as the political context of the 1930s passes from view.

While it may still have been the case in *Being and Time* that community might take forms other than the Volk – for example, a scholarly community engaging with the history of metaphysics – by the time of *An Introduction to Metaphysics*, Heidegger is arguing for the self-evident primacy of the German people among all other varieties of community and of all other peoples, and identifies philosophy entirely with serving its destiny, including its political destiny [8]. A meditation on Being combined with a call to revolution, its archaeology of the history of the West may also have been Heidegger's way of compensating for the abstractness of the existential analytic of Dasein in *Being and Time*, which, because it set forth the general structures of possibility for any time in principle, was sometimes confused with the transcendental analytic of Kant, despite its unmistakable identification of Dasein as collective rather than an individual self and its critique of Kant for clinging to a metaphysical conception of selfhood.

Heidegger's initial aim in *An Introduction to Metaphysics* is to demonstrate that metaphysics cannot deal with the main question that he says philosophy must ask: "Why are there beings rather than nothing?" Aristotle, by contrast, would have asked: "What *is* it? What is the purpose?" But Heidegger conceives of Being in terms of the ground of all beings, as genesis rather than telos. Being cannot be understood in terms of the properties of things, or through causes and variables. We must forsake the visible surface for the invisible depth. Nor does the attempt to rank beings illuminate the meaning of Being. Man is not significant as one being among other beings, as Aristotle argued when he identified the capacity for reasoned choice as the trait that distinguishes the human animal from other organisms. According to Heidegger, man is only notable as the site for the question that wants to know why anything is.

The question of the origins opens up the possibility of authenticity because it is coeval with the shattering of security. By asking why there are beings rather than nothing, we return to the indeterminacy of the origins. *Thinking* about the origins is the existential enactment of *returning* to the origins. The question implies that what *now* is *need not be*. The presence of the question, Heidegger goes on, cannot be determined objectively by the existence of a particular set of institutions or cultural circumstances. For the question concerns the whole historical movement of a people. Being and man reciprocally interact in the "storm" of existence. Being challenges man and man challenges Being; man must make a stand or be swept away. Out of this strife issues the greatness of a people. The people is the historical setting wherein we might recognize the question, meaning that philosophy is the organ of the people's destiny. It is useless in the everyday sense of solving problems.

As in *Being and Time*, in *An Introduction to Metaphysics* the problem with traditional metaphysical thinking is that, because it takes objectivity to be "self-evident," it cannot deal with nothingness, which is to say Being. (As he put it in *Being and Time*, "The Being of beings 'is' not a being" [6].) Metaphysics tries to go "beyond beings" *by way of* beings. Thus, it can conceive of their source only as "another and higher kind of thing" – a supersensible Form or Idea. Its paradigm is logic. But the limitation of logic is that it cannot deal with the Nothing, with nonbeing, meaning origination. For it can only conceive of nothing as the absence of a concrete being. Logicians say that dwelling on the mysteriousness of the Nothing when it is conceived of apart from concrete beings leads to nihilism, to a lack of faith in reality. On the contrary, Heidegger argues, nihilism is *caused* by reducing Being to thinghood. If one identifies Being with the most thing-like of things (like Plato's Idea of the Good), then Being, which is general and universal and lacks such concreteness, is reduced to a "vapor," an empty abstraction. But when Being is understood as origination, its "nothing" is not a vapor of absent beings or empty concepts, but a well-spring of fecundity, the roots of the tree.

Traditional epistemology senses this problem, according to Heidegger, when it asks: What is Being *apart* from its properties and attributes? What is its "is-ness"? (I will resist referring to an American president). What underlyingly holds a bundle of properties together, setting off one such bundle from another? But because, following the lead of metaphysics, epistemology identifies Being with thingliness, it has no answer. When the attributes of a being are stripped away to uncover its unity, it appears to vanish into an empty "vapor," like Kant's unknowable thing-in-itself or Locke's "something I know not what." This vapor is none other than the looming "destiny" of Being altogether, dammed up by metaphysical thinking in its thralldom to ontic being. Far from saving us from nihilism, the reduction of Being to thinghood through the reign of logic increases nihilism. The despair of nihilism is caused *by* the reduction of reality to the empirical, which drains the world of its mysteries. If logic itself derives from a particular approach to Being, valid within the limitations of its premises but not beyond them, it cannot, Heidegger argues, be the judge of all such approaches. Philosophy includes but is not reducible to the empirical, scientific or logical. Poetry and revelation may rank higher than science because they reveal Being more richly and primordially than analytical rationality. It is the difference between the poetic evocation of the storm in the mountains and a weather report. The meteorological exactitude of the weather report can be derived from our attempt to explain the poetic evocation, but the reverse is not true: the weather report will never yield the poetic account.

So was Nietzsche right, Heidegger asks, that Being is a fallacy? Or can the extreme loss of Being lead to a new recovery of Being? Heidegger links the loss of Being to Germany's political and cultural decline, and Germany might redeem all of human history if it is the site of this question, a redemption stretching all the way back to the ancient Greeks. The reduction of Being (*Sein*) to beings (*Seiendes*) is concomitant with the economism, empiricism, technology and egalitarian mediocrity that characterize the modern state. Liberal modernity as such is nothing less than our total alienation from Being. For Heidegger, the surest historical precedent for understanding an authentic relation to Being is Greece in the age of the great pre-Platonic poets, thinkers and statesmen. As he unfolds it, in the original Greek experience of *physis* or nature, the relation between man and Being is a reciprocal one. *Physis* is cognate with the verb *physein* (to grow). Being, as the literal meaning of *physis* suggests, "grows" out of nothing to reveal itself. Statesmen, poets and thinkers make a stand against this "overpowering" force. Through the "creative violence" of their own "power" and "struggle," they enable Being to accomplish its revelatory urge by issuing in a world with man as a sort of midwife: Being "presences" as poetry, thought and the polis.

Heidegger identifies the original pre-Socratic evocation of the Greek word for "appearance" (*apophainesthai*) as a "shining forth" of "glory," including divine glory, not the realm of irrational chance, becoming and perishability in comparison with the eternal Ideas to which it was reduced beginning with Plato. Heidegger's pronounced preference for the pre-Socratics over Plato stems from their view of existence as strife, war, ceaseless becoming, chance and necessity. This was the road not taken in the destiny of the West, supplanted by the "yoke of the Idea." Yet metaphysics, however distorted a perspective on Being it may be, *is* our history down to the roots. Because metaphysics has culminated in modern rationalism, it must be saved through a recessional movement behind its thought systems to the conditions for its own possibility. Ontology must account for metaphysics as one aspect of the "presencing" of Being – that aspect of the process of Being which is reified as a permanent essence – without succumbing to its bewitchment. Man is the conduit for Being happening historically, emerging into a transitory presence. But that aspect of permanence seduces us into a greater and greater pursuit of reasoned clarity. Beginning with Plato, metaphysics becomes a project for bringing all existence under the hegemony of the permanent, which launches technology. And yet the very tyranny of metaphysics might goad us, even terrify us, into reopening the infinite possibilities at the core of Being, to recommit ourselves to our collective destiny as a people.

Common to both *Being and Time* and *An Introduction to Metaphysics* is the idea, earlier discussed, that the prospect of destruction, by revealing the finitude of a people in all its precarious fragility, dispels the complacency of everyday life and convinces them of the need to risk the recovery of their destiny, if need be by going "under the eyes of Death." Expressed in *Being and Time* as one of the formal ways in which fundamental ontology acts as a guide "back to one's factical 'there,'" it comes to life here in what Heidegger sees as Germany's dire situation pressed from both sides by the two superpowers.

"Our people," he says, are caught between the "pincers" of America and Russia, which are dominated by "the same dreary technological frenzy, the same unrestricted organization of the average man." Germany, he goes on, must "wrest" its destiny from within itself, and thereby "move the history of the West" out of these pincers. "Metaphysically the same" despite their superficially different ideologies, America and Russia oppress Germany not only figuratively but literally as technological behemoths. The "inner truth and greatness" of National Socialism thus emerges from "the encounter between global technology and modern man" – the possibility that, having experienced alienation from Being to its depths and being threatened with destruction by the two superpowers, Germany has no alternative but to recover its destiny and lead the West as a whole out of these pincers.

For Heidegger, man's relation to Being is not a question of a human subject exerting its will against an objective environment. It is rather a reciprocal interaction in which man assumes the passive role of "letting-be" (*Seinlassen*) – acting as a conduit for Being's revelation through assuming the role of "resolve" against the "care" that Being's protean power to generate all things imposes on him. Heidegger now plays on the word "resoluteness" (*Entschlossenheit*), a key term in *Being and Time*, to let it suggest "unclosedness" (*Ent-schlossenheit*). He thereby doubly stresses that resolve is not a kind of subjective willfulness, but rather a simultaneous passive openness to Being and opposition to it – modes by which Being "has" man to accomplish its own presencing. In other words, resolve is as much a surrender as an act of will. The people's surrender to its "fate" and "heredity" already limned in *Being and Time* constitutes our openness to the overpowering power of Being, a surrender that empowers our choosing to recommit ourselves to the community's destiny. In founding the polis, a statesman "administers" the power of Being by interpreting it for his people as their norms – their laws and mores. The "greatness" of the founding – its spontaneous magnitude – occurs only at the "beginning," when it is "closest to Being." Later, laws and mores degenerate into listless routines. At this point, Heidegger says, when they become "ethical" in the sense of being taken to possess a timeless validity (like Aristotle's *Nicomachean Ethics*): "Being has gone out of them." *Physis* is separated from the originary sway of history and becomes "physics," the logical articulation of a static account of the whole [46–49, 117].

For Heidegger, the rise of empiricism and positivism since the seventeenth century is coeval with the steady reduction of Being to metaphysics, which began with Plato. The history of the West, not only philosophically but politically and socially, is the working out of this alienation from Being. Germany, as the only people besides the Greeks through whom philosophy has spoken, is today accordingly the locus both for the consciousness of the most acute alienation from Being and for harboring the greatest possibility for reopening an authentic relation to Being. The "greatness" of German Idealism, Heidegger suggests, rested in its partial recognition of, and struggle against, this accelerating process of decline. Seeming to evoke Hegel, he uses the term Spirit (*Geist*) to describe the confrontation of man and Being embodied in the dynamic unity of a historical epoch like that of the Greeks. Indeed, Heidegger's presentation of the reciprocal interaction between man and Being closely resembles the reciprocity of self-consciousness and Spirit found in Hegel's dialectic, where man, by pursuing his own freedom, also accomplishes Spirit's self-actualization. The crucial difference, however, is that for Heidegger, the "greatness" of this interaction lies in its creative origins, not in its subsequent working out. Hegel's error, in Heidegger's view, was to assimilate the power of Spirit into the rationality of a completed historical "system."

Today, as a consequence, he argues, Spirit has alienated itself from its creative origins and has been reduced to the "intelligent" manipulation of beings. Because Marxism is devoted to "the exploitation of the means of production," it shares this same worldview, common to positivism, capitalism and liberalism alike. The identification of Spirit with "intelligence" presupposes the splitting up of the world into what is empirically verifiable and the conceptual "vapor" of what is logical, ideal or a value. In restricting itself to managing the tasks of economic productivity or state bureaucracy, Spirit confesses its contemporary impotence to change the world fundamentally. It allies itself with positivism to organize all experiences, flattening them so that they can be shared by the average man of all countries. The consequence is a spiritual wasteland. In the modern world, thus given over to mediocrity, prize fighters are considered heroes and a symphony concert in Tokyo can be experienced simultaneously with an assassination.

Philosophy and art now become activities of merely derivative, relative worth. They do not shape the lives of whole peoples, but are banished from the "real" world into the "pure" realm of values that are pursued "for their own sake" because they cannot explain or alter empirical reality, which is now regarded as synonymous with Being per se. We are reminded of Nietzsche's critique of modern museum culture; the inner versus the outer; the cult of objectivity. Art is now reduced to "aesthetics," a game of taste, and divorced from great historical and political achievements. From Heidegger's perspective, Homer was a legislator; T. S. Elliot is merely a diversion for the cultured. In the university, spiritual cultivation has been reduced to a series of "holiday ornaments."

In *Being and Time*, Heidegger had criticized the Hegelian idea of world-historical progress as the degeneration of authentic historical existence into a catalogue of varieties of "inauthentic everydayness" stitched together in a spurious reconciliation. In *An Introduction to Metaphysics*, he develops this critique as he assesses the specific historical situation of Germany in the 1930s. The mention of Spirit and of Marxism as allies of positivism suggests that, for Heidegger, German historical philosophy as a whole has degenerated into a set of methods for pursuing what are, at bottom, the same technological goals as bourgeois liberalism. The "everyday world" and "the dictatorship of the They" from *Being and Time* are now located predominantly in America and Russia, which take themselves to be the spearheads of historical advancement, but which Heidegger believes have raised the organizing powers of inauthenticity to an unprecedented zenith.

For Heidegger, I would suggest, the "greatness" of Spirit and of German Idealism lay in Hegel's original insight into existence as "self-origination," an insight from which Hegel flinched, taming it and dimming it down with his positive doctrine of teleological historical progress and his qualified endorsement of the Enlightenment values of liberalism. Whereas for Hegel, the Unity of Subject and Substance reconciles history and reason, for Heidegger Being is not synonymous with the universality of logic, science, or of "thought systems" – it grounds and precedes all of these. Philosophy as the primordial questioning of the history of Being precedes all positive historiography or any outward account of progress like that of Hegel, which only serves to ratify the status quo of everyday life. For Heidegger, the decline of Spirit is coeval with the rise of empiricism. Spirit had been the confrontation of man and Being embodied in an age, a dynamic unity. Now the two poles of Hegel's dynamic interplay between Subject and Substance are split into the static dichotomy of the "real world" versus the world of "values." Heidegger wants to salvage the original promise of greatness in Hegelian Spirit, but without Hegel's dialectic of progress; to go behind the dialectic of progress into the strife of the origins. Heidegger aimed to open the underlying Pandora's box of creative chaos, dismantling the metaphysical edifice of Hegel's Absolute Science of Spirit, and he believed "the revolution" of 1933 could be the spark. But that revolution could be truly far-reaching, tearing up modernity by the roots, nay, even the premodern as it has come down to us retrofitted as a mere stage in man's progress toward the present only if it was grounded in the History of Being.

The Question of Being, Heidegger announces in Part Four, is synonymous with the History of the Question, which provides Being's *own* history, still unfolding. There have been four chronological pairings in this history from earliest times down to the modern age. The first two pairs, Being and Becoming and Being and Appearance, are the oldest, corresponding to the pre-Socratics and the ancient poets. Although in Heidegger's view, even the pre-Socratics' distinction between Being and becoming and Being and appearance may be a harbinger of the metaphysics to come, these two pairs are much more closely linked than the two subsequent pairs, Being and Thinking followed by Being and the Ought. The distinction between Being and Thinking is introduced by Plato and Aristotle. But it becomes "actual" only in the "modern era" as Being and the Ought. Through the German Philosophy of Freedom, Plato's Ideas become the Ought of Kantianism. In bare outline, Heidegger's stages of the History of Being are not dissimilar to Nietzsche's genealogy of morals, in which modernity emerges continuously out of Platonism through the ascetic ideal. The crucial difference, however, is that Heidegger's genealogy is absolutely bereft of moral and psychological content. The implication is that understanding the History of Being cannot be sidetracked by mere "ontic" and "everyday" considerations.

Originally, for the Greeks, Being "shone forth" (Heidegger's rendering of *apophainesthai*) as appearing. Truth was coeval with appearance, not a separate category. Being and becoming easily merged into the second pair, a "reciprocal relation" of Being, becoming and appearance. The inner tension within this complex of forces created a world, the polis, whose "power" and "glory" are modes "of the highest being." The third pair is ushered in when Plato and Christianity achieve the demotion of appearance to "mere" appearance by erecting a "suprasensory realm" over it (echoes here of Nietzsche's distinction between the real and apparent world). Thinking is therefore not in the same relation to Being as becoming and appearance, with which Being had originally coalesced. Thinking "represents" or "transposes" Being, forcing a division of Being into "forms," the rise of logic, technique and a corresponding decline of a people's original glory and rank. Hence (and one might again picture Heidegger addressing the "movement" students in his class) the struggle against "intellectualism" today as we answer the distant summons of the polis to the recovery of our destiny as a people. We need to free logos from the chains of logic. In its authentic earliest meaning, Logos "collects" the presence of Being, precedes and grounds all mere intellectual discourse (including logic). "Rank and domination" are "implicit" in Being as the gathering of conflict, tension, unrest and strife.

The polis emerged as the violence of "power against the overpowering," a "poetic outline of extremes." Our comprehension of it is therefore not reducible to metaphysically narrowed academic disciplines such as history, psychology or anthropology. History is a drama without transcendence. It is at its greatest only in its origins, not in its subsequent course of events, where you increasingly get "not development, but flattening." The clash of forces that issues in a world is the violence that "creates states." Authentic speech such as Homer's "administers the overpowering power." But as the authentic polis declines into everyday life, the creative violence of the founding degenerates into mere "versatility," the skillful defense of the world as it is.

Heidegger now confronts a problem that will preoccupy him throughout his postwar writings as his political commitment to National Socialism fades from view. If *logos* and *physis* were originally so close, how did they ever get separated? Astonishingly, modern man, he writes, by erecting Thinking and the Ought over becoming and appearance, can *stop* the interplay of these forces through the reign of metaphysics; can "decline all openness to Being." This is "the supreme act of violence" against the overpowering power of Being itself as man makes his stand. The "secession of logos" from authentic historical existence and its reduction to logic and the routinization of ethics is a "victory over Being." Hegel's teleology of history is the culmination of this Platonization of existence. Being is reified as the Idea in which beings participate. Being as such therefore also becomes a transcendent and transhistorical Ideal, because no perishable being can live up to its purity. But the meaning of man's essence, Heidegger stresses, is *never* a metaphysical answer, it is always a question. Man's proper role and destiny is not to achieve victory over Being, but to be its "historical custodian." And the key to this is to persevere in understanding that the underlying reality of Being is *me on* – what is *not*.

LET US COMPARE ETYMOLOGIES

Let us pause briefly for an etymological interlude. As I have observed, *An Introduction to Metaphysics* veers back and forth between the purple prose of a political tract and rarified musings on the History of Being that employ novel etymologies in support of Heidegger's claim that the ancient Greek language (uniquely along with German) offers a direct path into the Question of Being. These etymologies are widely contested; in my view, some are plausible, others less so if at all. A couple of examples must suffice. The first strikes me as plausible. The second is more open to question, but stimulating.

The first of these is Aristotle's famous definition of man as a rational animal – in Greek, *zoon echon logon*. This is rendered in Latin as *animal rationale*. In the Latin transliteration, the two nouns – animal (*zoon*) and reason (*logon*) – stand in simple apposition to one another, their interconnectedness implied. But in the Greek, the middle term providing the explicit connection between animal and reason is the participle of the verb "to have" (*echon*), literally "animal having reason." According to Heidegger, this verbal link offers a clue to the mystery of how two objectively distinct entities – a living organism and reason – could be connected, and the connection is temporal, a fluid historical process. This in turn points us to the underlying existential relationship between Dasein and *Sein*, Dasein's existential intimation through finitude of the meaning of Being as such. As he put it in *Being and Time*, "man is the being for whom Being is an issue."

Only on the basis of this always already existing primordial engagement between man and Being is it possible to make a propositional statement to clarify that engagement by specifying its two component elements of a living organism and the mind. The metaphysical formulation is not inaccurate, but if we are not aware of their underlying temporal connection, which the Latin apposition of "animal" and "reason" occludes, we will forget the Question of Being which prompted us to wonder what that relationship was in the first place, and instead begin by assuming a dualistic conception of the human in which its biological and rational components are stacked on top of one another, each one to be further explored and classified in separation from the other, carrying us further away from their joint temporal roots. In the original Greek formulation, by contrast, Aristotle could not even express the definition of a rational animal without that underlying temporal connectedness slipping in between, prompting us to question its adequacy and reminding us of its existential origin.

The second example of the way in which, according to Heidegger, Greek etymologies point to fundamental ontology is a phrase Heidegger cites from Aristotle's *Metaphysics* [VII.4]: *to ti en einai*. Aristotle takes the infinitive of the verb "to be" (*einai*) and by placing an article in front of it (*to*), turns it from a process of becoming into a substantive, in other words "the Being." This turns Being as the temporal process of coming into existence out of the origins and passing back into the origins into "another and higher kind of thing," which as we have seen Heidegger characterizes as the perspective of classical metaphysics altogether. Aristotle further modifies this thingly reification of Being as "the Being" by modifying it with the particle *ti* – meaning "what" or "it" – and *en*, which is the third person imperfect of the verb "to be," the tense signifying action continuing in the past or, as one commentator put it, an action taking place in a timeless present, because the imperfect tense conveys the idea of an action without a beginning or an end. Hence, translated literally, the phrase means something like "The (what it was continuing to be) Being." This complicated evocation is simplified in Latin by flattening it into the single word *essentia* or essence. Like a Roman road paving over a countryside of wandering lanes and byways with a single concrete band, Latin drains Aristotle's Greek of its nuances and subtleties. In a certain sense, Heidegger implies, Aristotle would have preferred to express his metaphysics in Latin had it existed for him, because it lent itself readily to the kind of contraction of the meaning of Being to the one moment of privileged metaphysical essence he and Plato were aiming for, whereas when Aristotle tries to wrestle Greek into conveying this monistic entity, it wriggles and undulates at every turn to evade such exactitude.

* * *

I will conclude my discussion of *An Introduction to Metaphysics* with some general observations about its politicality. Heidegger is often called one of the founders of existentialism, a philosophy of commitment, resolve and authenticity. The intensity of the commitment is the criterion for its authenticity, not the objective validity of the outcome. Because there is no transhistorical perspective on existence whereby the mind can rise above events, thought is another mode of action. To think is to engage with life and the world. The Question of Being is not an abstract intellectual exercise, but an engagement in the cycles of life, death, destiny and fate. Hence, at the deepest level of principle, Heidegger's philosophy of the 1930s was inseparable from his politics and his politics were inseparable from his philosophy. We cannot understand one without the other. It is not possible to read a work like *An Introduction to Metaphysics* for its philosophical content alone. The philosophical and the political interweave. Heidegger's most fervent jeremiads about the crisis of the 1930s alternate with some of his most illuminating insights into metaphysics. In the 1930s, Heidegger is swept up by the notion that existential commitment might be exercised collectively by the German people. The German people might, through National Socialism, pose the Question of Being on an active level, resolving upon their collective destiny, returning to the underlying potency of their historical possibilities so as to throw off the shackles of global technology pressing in on them in the shape of the two metaphysical superpowers. When that hope fades, Heidegger's philosophy ceases to be overtly political, although it never loses its relevance to the reality of the modern world and ways of reconnecting with Being despite the ever greater predominance of global technology.

A violent resoluteness to sweep away a world infected with the economistic and managerial politics of modern times; the vision of a pure and unified community that will broach no compromise with ordinary political squabbling and interests; the conviction in the signal importance for the West as a whole that Germany lead this revolutionary reencounter with Being: It is on the basis of these considerations that we can grasp the openness or vulnerability of Heidegger's philosophy to the kind of political alternative offered by National Socialism. As George Steiner observed, the language of 1927 was already the language of 1933. In *Being and Time* in 1927, Heidegger called upon Dasein to "choose its hero" [385]. In 1933, he found the hero he had been looking for. The dismissal of all concrete political issues as a self-interested "reckoning and balancing of claims," as he put it in *Being and Time*, could well induce one to view the boldest and least programmatic of political movements as the authentic voice of the community in its underlying, protean vitality. Moreover, if nothing transcends the historical community, and if such a movement is spreading everywhere, representing itself as the "anti-Party" aimed at sweeping away the selfish interests of both the traditional left and right (as the Horst Wessel song proclaimed, "against the Red Front and the Reaction"), might one not embrace it as the legitimate harbinger of that destiny which is true for one's own people and it alone? In my view, Heidegger saw in the Nazis a great national revival that rejected the selfish values of liberalism, bourgeois materialism and the Enlightenment for the sake of patriotism, courage, passion and daring. This is why it is clear in *An Introduction to Metaphysics* as it had been in *Being and Time* that the people's return to Being is not a return to conservatism, but a revolution. Heidegger decries the "campaign against ... today's intellectualism" on the grounds that it is not sufficiently radical. For, by restricting itself to combating recent intellectual culture, it appears to justify those who advocate a proper use of the traditional intellect, content to jettison Freud and restore Goethe. In order to be truly effective, such a campaign, he implies, would have to uproot not only the intellectualism of today but the "spiritual reaction" (*Reaktion*) that hopes merely to rescue a relatively more old-fashioned kind of intellectualism from contemporary decadence. He warns against this defense of what is presumably Germany's pre-Weimar intellectual culture as "the feeding ground of political (reaction)." The kind of uprooting Heidegger has in mind is far more revolutionary than any such "mere restoration."

THE POLITICAL IMPLICATIONS OF HEIDEGGER'S EARLY THOUGHT

The career of the allegations about Heidegger's responsibility for fascist politics has been the reverse of that for Nietzsche. In Nietzsche's case, a purblind identification in the Anglosphere of his thought with fascism led in time to a more balanced approach that finally veered to the opposite extreme of viewing his political influence as entirely benign. In Heidegger's case, after the initially scratchy postwar response he received from critics such as Lowith and Arendt on the grounds of his political stance in the 1930s, as his fame spread in Europe and the Anglosphere, his commitment to the Third Reich was at first almost completely omitted from scholarship about his work, banished to an occasional footnote about this "unfortunate interlude" and variously ascribed to his political naivete as an ivory tower academic or the ambitions of his wife to climb the Nazi social ladder. Characterizations of his existentialism at times approached an exercise in Zen Buddhism, apolitical and restricted to the private individual.

Then, beginning with a few isolated figures like Karsten Harries, a determined effort to explore the intrinsic connection between Heidegger's fundamental ontology of the 1920s and 1930s and his embrace of Nazism gained more and more ground, eventually flipping to the opposite extreme from the earlier ostrich-like avoidance of this topic to identifying Heidegger's entire philosophy as nothing *but* an ideology for fascism, leading a French scholar to argue that his books should be removed from the philosophy section of the library and shelved under Nazi Studies. Whereas Nietzsche went from being excessively blamed to being excessively exculpated, with Heidegger it was the reverse. We therefore have to seek out the same middle ground as we did with Nietzsche so as to find the correct balance between understanding without flinching how Heidegger's Nazism was grounded in his philosophy without reducing the significance of his thought to nothing other than this.

Without wading too far into the reeds of the details of Heidegger's collaboration with the Nazis – exhaustively documented elsewhere – let us consider in broad outline what he did and why he may have done it. Already considered by many to be Germany's greatest thinker, Heidegger's assumption of the rectorship of Freiburg University in 1933, followed shortly by his joining the Party, lent his prestige to the Nazi regime and provided a public platform for his commitment to it. Storm troopers appeared at his inauguration; he began and ended his lectures by exchanging the Nazi salute with his students, declared that "the *Führer* himself and he alone *is* German reality and its law," and supported Hitler's withdrawal of Germany from the League of Nations. His openness to the radical alternative presented by National Socialism, indeed his search for it, is, as we have observed, already manifest in *Being and Time*, which was on one level a work for the ages – unearthing the recurrent structures of possibility from which communities emerge at any time and place – and on another level replete with standard critiques of modern mass society from the Left and Right: the "dictatorship of the They" and the alienation, impersonality and corruption of big city life frequently associated in Volkisch ideology with the Jews. This critique of modern life was redolent of Fritz Lang's *Metropolis* (a film adored by Hitler) and of Volkisch ideologues such as Moeller van den Brucke.

Heidegger's two main explorations of what "the revolution" signified for him are in *An Introduction to Metaphysics* and his earlier Rectoral Address. The Address was his most detailed and explicit act of public commitment to the regime, which is why we have elected to treat it out of sequence with *Being and Time* and *An Introduction to Metaphysics* as fitting more squarely under the heading of the political implications of Heidegger's thought, aside from the fact that, for reasons we will discuss, Heidegger's ardor may have cooled somewhat by the time of the later work. But the Rectoral Address is far from being a mere political tract. Like *An Introduction to Metaphysics*, it seamlessly interweaves Heidegger's political commitment to National Socialism with his philosophical meditations on Being, and is a legitimate part of Heidegger's philosophic *oeuvre*, testifying to his growing interest in Nietzsche and the evocation of modern man as "homeless in the world." But the political implications of what has been called the "anarchist commune" of *Being and Time* and *An Introduction to Metaphysics*, where the people is empowered by the "overpowering power" of Being's upsurges, are more transparent in this work than any other. The German people's recovery of its destiny opens a Pandora's box of all the forces of havoc formerly suppressed by the political establishment: "Nature, history, language, people, custom, state, poetry, thought, faith, disease, madness, death, law, economy, technology."

In the Rectoral Address, the three classes or "bonds" of Heidegger's vision of the university and of Germany as a whole – labor service, armed service and knowledge service – closely parallel what the National Socialist movement actually called for, vividly evoked in its propaganda: Everyone – workers, soldiers, intelligentsia – must serve the People. They have also been likened to the tripartite structure of the city and the soul in Plato's *Republic* of artisans, warriors and philosophic guardians, a parallel Heidegger surely intended. For him, Nazi Germany was the historical actuality of the best regime. But like his philosophy as a whole, Heidegger's tripartite structure represents the complete inversion of the Platonic city. For Plato, the rule of philosophy over spiritedness and desire in the soul – "writ large" as the Philosophers, Guardians and Artisans in the city – is a reflection of the orderliness of the cosmos. Indeed, the division of labor among the three classes is premised on each nature remaining at one with itself, an order internalized in the soul, and an anticipation of the selfsameness of the Ideas. Spiritedness, the seat of courage and zeal in the soul, is firmly reined in by the rule of wisdom as it polices bodily desire. In this way, the division of labor in the city and the soul points to a "pattern in the sky," a way station to the philosophic life, and not a project for political actualization. By contrast, the three classes of Heidegger's vision of the Reich and the university literally spring from the German earth, from their "joint rootedness" in Germany's destiny. What had been a myth in the *Republic*, the autochthony of the best regime, is now a historical reality. The task of the "knowledge service" is synonymous with their commitment to the fate of the German people. Arguments made by Socrates in the *Republic* with a degree of irony and playfulness are inverted and applied quite literally and humorlessly by Heidegger. One wonders whether the collapsing of wisdom into existence, so that no standpoint independent of our destiny is possible, makes irony impossible. In Platonic terms, Heidegger employs philosophy to liberate thumotic boldness, aggression and zealotry from any boundaries whatever. Indeed, inasmuch as for Heidegger, philosophizing is synonymous with action on behalf of the people, he assimilates philosophy to a variety of *thumos*. In the *Republic*, reason rules thumos in its policing of desire because, left to itself, the patriotic vigor of spiritedness could spill over into fanaticism and zealotry, even turning on the wise themselves for being disloyal or impious (the real-life fate of Socrates). Heidegger removes any such restraint. It is as if Socrates, rather than trying to instill moderation in the soul of Callicles to cure him of his mad fantasy of becoming the revolutionary tyrant and master who plunges the conventional order into destruction, joins the young man and eggs him on. If nothing transcends the people's destiny, including wisdom and God, then service to it is indistinguishable from fanatical zeal.

Much of what Heidegger appeals to here in extolling "the movement" can be described as an attempt to restore German manliness, to rescue it from the softness and effeminacy widely felt to have been instilled by bourgeois materialism, hedonism, political jobbery and effete cultural pastimes. Hence his praise for "still youthful students who at an early age have dared to act as men, and who extend their willing to the future destiny of the nation." This critique of the loss of manliness was a widespread feature of the Volkisch critique of Weimar and of the Enlightenment altogether. But Heidegger can only restore manliness by perverting it into a caricature of violence and coarseness bearing no resemblance to the traditional understanding of manliness as gentlemanliness, and hence, just like all of fundamental ontology's evocation of the past behind the past, in reality it calls for the creation of a "new man" comparable to the claims of other totalitarian regimes like the Soviet Union, akin to the dream of Ernst Junger (with whom Heidegger corresponded) of a German warrior-worker, a right-wing Stakhanovism. By identifying the meaning of rationality with modern instrumental utilitarianism, and even tracing this back to classical metaphysics as its inevitable working out, Heidegger cuts himself off from the Platonic conception of manliness as an ordered harmony of reason over the passions sublimated as virtues like courage and honor-seeking. In other words, for the classics, there was a role for courage within the order of nature crowned by wisdom, suitably limited to the service of civic virtue. Heidegger overturns it, inviting his young listeners to abandon themselves without restraint to the furthest extremes of spontaneous boldness and impulse in the service of a fanatical collectivism. These students will not comprise an aristocracy but something more akin to the Red Guards, not a guardian class of the wise and liberally educated, but an elite of Raskolnikovs whose task is to serve the German destiny by guarding against relapses into bourgeois scruples about the impartial rule of law, parliamentary democracy or freedom of speech.

This helps us to understand exactly what Heidegger means by the "self-overcoming of the German university," the title of his address. It has nothing to do with traditional liberal education, but is about facing with resolve "the most severe endangerment of human being in the midst of the overwhelming of what is," similar to the encounter between Dasein and *Sein* in *An Introduction to Metaphysics*. This explains the peculiar and baleful way in which Heidegger purports to revitalize higher education and restore its unity of purpose. That unity of purpose is not provided by the governance of all branches of human learning by the philosophic quest, as it was for the classics, but by the shattering of philosophy so conceived. It will not be the unity of transcendence oriented toward the eternal truth, but of origination and rootedness, of the encounter between Dasein and the "war" of Being linking Germany to the greatness of the Greeks: "If we submit to the distant command of the beginning, science must become the fundamental happening of our spiritual and popular (Volklisch) existence."

Heidegger, an extraordinarily erudite scholar himself, will not teach these students so much as summon forth their untutored energies, to channel their fervor into serving the larger national destiny by using his authority to disabuse them of any bourgeois scruples about the impartiality of scholarship and its supposed detachment from politics. The purpose of questioning is not to advance knowledge, but to recover our roots in Being: It "shatters the encapsulation of the sciences in separate specialties, brings them back from their boundless and aimless dispersal in individual fields and corners, and directly exposes science once again to ... all world-shaping powers of human-historical existence." Recalling his argument in *Being and Time*, Heidegger says that the "ontic" social sciences and humanities drift away from Being as origination in their search for a rational clarity leading to an excessive narrowness and specialization that covers over the wonder originally stirred in us by Being. Now the aim is to shatter their compartments and return them to the ground of their origination, the inversion of the Platonic view that knowledge of the arts and sciences are routes toward their dialectical transcendence by the overarching Idea of the Good. Today, accordingly, "academic freedom is being banished from the German university" because it is a mere negative freedom indifferent to the fate of the people. The disarray of academic specialization, each pursued in isolation from the rest, must be submerged in a common "bond and service" to the people. The leaders are "themselves led" and "grow strong from" their "rootedness" in "the fate of the German people," gaining "clarity, rank and power." Academic freedom is no more to be desired than individual freedom of choice. For the choice has already been made: "The young and the youngest strength of the people, which is already reaching beyond us, *has* already *decided* the matter."

In a final riposte to Plato, Heidegger ends the address by quoting a proverbial saying from the *Republic* [497d]. Usually translated as "all great things are precarious," Heidegger renders it (questionably) as "all that is great stands in the storm." Socrates is arguing that all beings decline from their approximation of stable perfection into becoming, and that even the city of perfect justice and reason, were it ever to come into being, would eventually succumb to the corruption of its ordering principles and its decline into inferior regimes. By rendering it as "all that is great stands in the storm," Heidegger reverses Socrates' meaning that even great things do not last into the sense that whatever can withstand the "storm" of Being thereby emerges from its struggle as "great." This is in keeping with his core premise that the strength, form and perdurance of any "presence" derive from its tension and struggle with the "overpowering power" of Being out of which it issues – that *physis* is primordially akin to *polemos*, not *eidos*. This misinterpretation of Plato flows necessarily from the status of Heidegger's ontology of Being as the antipode of Platonic reasoning, and it is characteristic of all of his often very illuminating exegeses of Plato. From Heidegger's perspective, it does not actually matter what Plato intended or how he understood himself, because the voice of Being as "possibility" breaks through Plato's metaphysics even as he attempts to bring it under the "yoke of the Idea." It is not so much that Heidegger interprets Plato as that he uncovers the way in which Being – which "speaks" Greek – reveals itself through his words.

THE ATTRACTION AND THE CULPABILITY

The apology sometimes made for Heidegger that he was a naive ivory tower academic who stumbled into National Socialism as a political innocent is unconvincing. The character of his commitment to the regime in the Rectoral

Address and *An Introduction to Metaphysics* is fervent, entirely self-conscious, and offers a detailed prospectus for "the movement" as he understood it. The Nazis at this time did not exercise the same degree of pervasive surveillance of every possible sign of discontent or even lukewarm loyalty regarding their aims, as the Soviet Union did under Stalin. As long as you were not one of their designated victim groups, you could go on much as before as long as you did not actively oppose or criticize the regime. This included academics. However, when it came to appointments to prestigious cultural institutions such as heading a symphony orchestra, a theatre, or a major university, the Nazis demanded Party membership and openly proclaimed loyalty. Heidegger had to know that in the very act of accepting the rectorship of Freiburg, he was crossing that line.

The debate goes on about the degree of his perfidy. At the risk of oversimplifying, I would say his behavior was worse than some, better than others. It was worse than that of his student Hans-Georg Gadamer, who avoided the Nazis and was associated with the circle that plotted the attempt on Hitler's life in 1944 – and who defended universal civilization in stark contrast with Heidegger's single-minded devotion to Germany – to say nothing of other cultural icons like Thomas Mann, who emigrated and made anti-Nazi broadcasts to the German people through the BBC. On the other hand, Heidegger's behavior was better than that of Carl Schmitt, who supported burning books by Jewish authors, demanded that German law and science be "cleansed" of "the Jewish spirit," and celebrated the Nuremberg Laws as the "return" to "German constitutional freedom," and thus had blood on his hands in a direct kind of way that Heidegger did not. Indeed, if it were not for Heidegger's fame as a philosopher before the Third Reich and afterward, his collaboration would merely be one story among hundreds of others, the story of "Professor X," of interest mainly to historians of the period, and would not have provoked a fraction of the attention it has received.

It is clear that Heidegger was not an ideological disciple of official National Socialist doctrine. Even in the Rectoral Address, his major act of public commitment to the regime, he made a point of defining loyalty to the leadership of the movement as containing an element of "resistance" so as to keep it authentic, mirroring the strife at the root of the reciprocal interaction between Dasein and *Sein* – an anarchistic tinge. In general, Heidegger proved not to be loyal to the regime in the way that it wanted its spokesmen to be loyal. Indeed, there is no trace in his writings or utterances of the biological racism which was the core Nazi doctrine (again in contrast with Schmitt), especially with regard to the alleged subhuman character of the Jews, nor is there any call for their specific persecution as a group. In my view, the absence of biological racism in Heidegger's writings was completely consistent with the fundamental ontology of *Being and Time*, inasmuch as for Heidegger, biological racism would have necessarily been a distortion typical of science as a whole, the reduction of the meaning of existence to a set of empirical claims, just like Marxism and positivism. It was not so much its falsity that excluded it for Heidegger as its flawed materialistic perspective. There is also no hint in Heidegger's endorsement of the regime of a call for the German conquest of Europe. At this period, Hitler constantly touted Germany's desire for peace, and many believed him, including foreign governments and observers. As for withdrawing from the League of Nations, it is quite possible that Heidegger believed Hitler's presentation of it as Germany leading the way in summoning *all* authentically-rooted "peoples" to liberate themselves from its cosmopolitan hegemony and service of the Great Powers, with no hostile intent beyond that. Many at the time believed this as well, and even Hitler's claim to be the protector of the Sudeten Germans' autonomy had a Wilsonian ring to it. As late as 1935, Hitler's greatest adversary Winston Churchill himself remained uncertain whether Hitler would prove to be catastrophic for Germany or a statesman who only wanted to restore its dignity.

Beginning with what was later published as *An Introduction to Metaphysics*, drawn from a course he taught two years following the Rectoral Address, Heidegger stressed "the *inner* truth and greatness of National Socialism" (my emphasis) as "the encounter between global technology and modern man." As early as 1935, in other words, there are hints of the contrast between this original inner potential and the outward course of what National Socialism was becoming. For Heidegger, certain features of the regime such as its mass rallies suggested it was falling short of its "inner truth and greatness" and lapsing back into an inauthentic, conformist everyday "they-self," with no trace of the "resistance" he called for in the Rectoral Address. When Heidegger argues that Spirit has been "emasculated" by Marxism and positivism into the manipulation of economic productivity and the empirical ordering of things, he includes "the management of ... the race of a Volk." While he does not name National Socialism as the source of this management, clearly it is what he means, and for him it is another component of the juggernaut of technology. For these reasons, the regime grew to distrust Heidegger (his classes may have been spied on); he resigned the rectorship after a year. Even though Heidegger's public commitment to the regime was unreserved, the Nazis disapproved of the *way* in which he supported them.

Despite these possible reservations and an internal critique of the regime, we must hasten to add that at no point afterward did Heidegger apologize for his collaboration, express regret for it or for the worst of its horrors including the Holocaust. Moreover, nothing in his possibly dissident version of the movement's "inner" greatness could have precluded in principle the political employment of mass violence, whether he approved of a specific policy or not. Even if it is true that Heidegger had originally envisioned a nonexploitative version of National Socialism whose mission was to lead in freeing all "the peoples" from the "pincers" of global technology and the Enlightenment values of individualism and materialism behind it, in my view nothing in that vision could have excluded in principle either Nazi imperialism (to free "the peoples") or genocide, since Heidegger recognizes no ethical standards of a Platonic or Kantian character that stand outside of the "overpowering power" of Being as "war." That openness to violence on the level of ontological principle is clear in *Being and Time* and *An Introduction to Metaphysics*. These factors must weigh heavily against him. While we saw in the last chapter that we can only speculate about the degree or type of political extremism that Nietzsche might have tolerated in a future movement for the "mastery of the earth" and can reach no firm conclusion, there is no way around the fact that Heidegger *did* tolerate Auschwitz after its full horrors had been revealed. Moreover, as we will consider when we turn to his postwar works *The Letter on Humanism* and *The Question Concerning Technology*, his later oblique attempts to explain why he would not apologize for Nazism or condemn its atrocities in retrospect can only compound our inevitable dissatisfaction with his account of his actions.

So what originally drew Heidegger to National Socialism? The Nazis possessed a Mephistophelean capacity to shift shapes in order to appeal to different kinds of potential converts. In my view, Leni Riefenstahl's propaganda film of the 1934 Nuremberg Rally, *The Triumph of the Will*, presented the face of the movement that appealed to Heidegger. The film constantly alternates between the Third Reich as the cutting edge of advanced modern technology and its restoration of Germany's ancient primordial destiny. This alternating dyad is conveyed by the film's opening, where we see Hitler in his airplane above the clouds, solitary in his greatness, accompanied by Wagnerian-sounding musical strains. The plane then descends like a Valkyrie, the clouds part, and below we see the ancient Gothic spires of old Nuremburg, festooned with swastika banners. This paradox of what Geoffrey Herff terms "reactionary modernism," the notion that the dynamo of German modernization and, implicitly, military might will restore the most cherished traditions of the Fatherland is consistent with the backward and forward-looking stance, the atavistic futurism, of Heidegger's vision of the German people's recommitment to its destiny that we observed in *Being and Time* and *An Introduction to Metaphysics*, a revolution that is "against" its heritage inasmuch as it is futuristic and modernistic, and yet "for it" inasmuch as it will release the suppressed energies of a past *behind* the past currently tranquilized and suppressed by liberal modernity. In the case of the Third Reich, this paradox will eventually work itself out as the utopian mission of Nazi imperialism to create in the East an agrarian paradise of soldier-peasants, a new order of Teutonic Knights with missile launchers, served by inferior races.

In Riefenstahl's film, scenes of peasants and farmers in quaint traditional garb presenting their wares to the Fuhrer alternate with the increasingly enormous rallies of massed identical marching formations, suggesting the eradication of all regional, social and class barriers as the regime achieves Germany's total unification – once again, atavistic futurism. The famous rallies staged by Albert Speer synthesized the two strains: square blocks of hundreds of thousands of identically uniformed bodies, the warriors of the future, are contained and ornamented by a phantasmagoric spectacle of burning tapers, Roman legionary standards, eagles and horns, a weird mélange of ancient and Viking tropes.

Finally, Riefenstahl constantly stresses the youthful character of the Nazi movement, and its spirit of comradeship and solidarity. The Hitler Youth are always running, marching – they stay up all night. They are presented as a new generation trained to a Spartan standard of discipline so as to be always ready for war, but resolved that by being prepared, they will never have to engage in one. The spirit of martial ardor is instilled in the young mainly to inculcate a sense of service to the nation and the sacrifice of the individual to the collective. Taking all these elements together, the evidence suggests that it is this presentation of National Socialism as a tremendous national resurgence of self-sacrifice, duty and honor, rising above crass materialism and petty political bickering to serve the people, that Heidegger found inspiring along with so many others, reflected in his praise of young German manhood in the Rectoral Address. In keeping with the new regime's intended image of peace, harmony and reconciliation, there are virtually no racist references in the film. Strikingly, at the same time, Hitler's lexicon of terms in his speeches like destiny, commitment and resolve – at one point suggesting that the movement might strike outsiders as "uncanny" – bears an eerie resemblance to Heidegger's own.

The Triumph of the Will, whose Nietzschean-sounding title we remarked upon earlier, is considered not only a propaganda masterpiece but also a milestone in the history of cinematography, because Riefenstahl created many technical innovations that subsequently became standard. Throughout this book, we have discussed the motif in German Idealism suggesting that membership in a political community could somehow be as aesthetically and emotionally satisfying as experiencing a work of art. This trend began benignly with Schiller, who never crossed the line from believing in the cultural value of the individual's aesthetic experience for a more fulfilling kind of citizenship – that Freedom could be approached "through Beauty" – into believing that political life *itself* could be an aesthetic collective experience. But later thinkers did move toward that step. Hegel took the aestheticization of civic life a step further when he extolled the "aesthetic democracy" of classical Athens with its blend of civic freedom and high culture, although he never suggested that citizenship could be wholly synonymous with beauty and nobility, eschewing the need for institutions, laws and coercion. But Marx did cross the line. As I suggested in Chapter 2, he believed that the socialist community of the future could literally be akin to a work of art. The private intervals of aesthetic rapture that Schiller regarded as one component of a balanced modern life is transferred by Marx to a collective bliss through the complete submergence of the individual in the social whole through revolution. The aestheticization of violence, originating in the virtue festivals of the Jacobins and Sergei Eisenstein's idealization in film of the Bolshevik Revolution, reaches an artistic culmination in Riefenstahl's film. As the political vision of the future from Hegel to Heidegger becomes increasingly more counterfactual and millenarian, less and less moored in the here and now of liberal modernity and its institutions, the more fantastical that vision of the future becomes.

* * *

Along with other thinkers, scholars and artists who declared their allegiance in 1933, Heidegger evidently saw in Nazism not the vulgar ravings that actually characterized its doctrine, but the prospect it harbored for the long-awaited "German Revolution" against the debased materialism, philistinism and selfish individualism thought to have been imposed on authentic German culture by liberalism and socialism. Heidegger shared many of his contemporaries' distaste for the compromises, juggling of interests and chronic disunity of parliamentary democracy.

And then the disillusionment set in. In an essay written in 1945 but published only posthumously in 1983, Heidegger explains more fully what he had thought to be promising about National Socialism:

I saw in the movement that had gained power the possibility of an inner recollection and renewal of the people and a path that would allow it to discover its historical vocation in the Western world. I believed that, renewing itself, the university might also be called to contribute to this inner self-collection of the people, providing it with a measure.

His rectorate was an attempt to find in the revolution that had come to power, beyond all its failings and crudities, something that reached much farther and that might someday bring about "a gathering of what is German unto the historical essence of the West." He came to realize, however, that the Nazis embodied the most radical version of the will to technological domination that he had already decried in America and Russia. He had not realized, he writes, the degree to which the German spirit had already been vitiated by this technological will; how little there remained of a resonance between people and Being that might be evoked to restore a sense of collective wholeness. He continues:

Unimportant as it is in itself, the case of the rectorate of 1933/34 would seem to be a sign of the metaphysical state of the essence of science, a science that can no longer be influenced by attempts at its renewal, nor delayed in its essential transformation into pure technology. This I came to realize only in the following years.

He concludes: "Taken by itself, [the rectorate] is as unimportant as the barren rooting in past attempts and measures taken, which in the context of the entire movement of the planetary will to power are so insignificant that they may not even be called tiny." Terrible as the destruction and carnage unleashed by the war had been, according to Heidegger, they are as nothing compared to what is coming, a mere introductory phase, "only a fleeting appearance on waves of a movement of our history, of whose dimensions the Germans have as yet no inkling of the catastrophe that has engulfed them."

That catastrophe remains, as it was in *An Introduction to Metaphysics*, global technology. As we will shortly consider, Heidegger's subsequent disillusionment with National Socialism and with any expectations from a political movement provided an important theme for his later philosophy. In his work on Nietzsche begun in the late 1930s, and in such postwar works as the *Letter on Humanism* and *The Question Concerning Technology*, he elaborated the idea of the technological will to power as the chief crisis of the modern age, exemplified both by liberal and socialist internationalism and by nationalism such as that of the Nazis. If there is to be a deliverance from this crisis, it can only take place globally, not nationally.

But let us dwell for another moment on what he wrote in 1945. Bluntly but not misleadingly put, Heidegger is telling us that he failed to see that National Socialism was just another version of the superpower "pincers" pressing in on Germany in *An Introduction to Metaphysics*. It had failed to live up to the promise of its "inner truth and greatness," becoming "metaphysically the same" as America and the Soviet Union. In other words, he had failed to see that Hitler was every bit as bad as FDR! It is hardly surprising that many find this explanation to be both astonishingly obtuse and self-serving. One cannot help but wonder: If the Third Reich had not been defeated, would Heidegger have regarded it as a failure? If Being is strife, and if no ethical standards transcend historical action, then what criterion can there be for authenticity other than the "glory" and "violence" of victory (to recall his language in *An Introduction to Metaphysics*)? But we must postpone our full assessment of his explanation until we have traced it further in his postwar writings.

The political potency of Heidegger's early philosophy might, I think, be summed up in this way. Like the earlier German thinkers we have considered, he rejects the concept of human nature in favor of an active, historical conception of man. At the same time, he frees the historical definition of man from any need to demonstrate or embody itself in the concrete conditions of everyday life, culture and politics, a rejection of Hegel's teleology of history outstripping that of his anti-Hegelian antecedents Marx and Nietzsche. He attempts, in other words, to reject entirely the progressive notion of history without abandoning an entirely historical definition of man. The radical cutting edge of the demand for freedom and community thus comes close to lopping away every restraint of circumstance, unloading the burden of empirical demonstrability which Hegel and Marx had believed essential to their conceptions of historical change. Fundamental ontology attempts to elucidate the permanent conditions of human impermanence. Such a standard, always underlying everyday life but never mediated by or absorbed into it, can stand forth as a critique of everyday life that is recurrent, radically pure and beyond compromise.

ESCHATOLOGICAL REVERSAL: THE SHEPHERD OF BEING AND THE DELIVERANCE OF THE EARTH

We should pause, for several reasons, to consider Heidegger's essay *The Origin of the Artwork*. It signifies, already in the late 1930s, Heidegger's withdrawal from any overt political commitment, and foreshadows his increasing preoccupation with the saving power of art to mitigate the domination of technology. It continues the shift in orientation already observable in *An Introduction to Metaphysics* away from a focus on the human side of the dynamic interaction between Dasein and *Sein* – the "existential analytic" of *Being and Time* – to a focus on how specific forces of history issue through Dasein as "the creators." To me, this is not a "turn" in the sense of repudiating *Being and Time* but rather amounts to turning the encounter between man and Being around and examining it from the reverse perspective: the encounter between Being and man. Whereas some scholarship finds a transition from the historicity of Dasein in *Being and Time* to the historicity of Being as such after the "turn," to my mind the historicity of Being is already present in outline in that first work, prompting Heidegger's exposure of the false path already taken by the ancient Greeks seduced by the logical interpretation of the world, the critiques of Hegelian Spirit and the bewitching power of the present-at-hand. In *Being and Time*, Being as a whole always touches Dasein through our finitude, opening up the prospect of Dasein's "wholeness" [233–235], making us aware of the primordial possibilities that the everyday world in its anxious search for security and control tries to "dim down."

The *Origin of the Artwork* attempts to render a poetic, noncausal account of art, recalling the argument of *An Introduction to Metaphysics* that Being is neither final nor efficient cause, but self-origination. We cited its opening lines at the beginning of this chapter as one of the most succinct statements of Heidegger's inversion of Platonic metaphysics: "the origin of something is the source of its essence." Plato's understanding of poetry is clearly the subtext for Heidegger's discussion of the artwork. According to the famous teaching of Book Ten of the *Republic,* poetry is nothing but the image of an image. A cobbler makes a shoe guided by the Idea of the shoe – it is thus a mere "image" of the true, eternal shoe, corresponding to the second lowest level of the Divided Line, that of empirical observation. A poet, by depicting an image of the artisan's image, is third in distance from the Idea of the Shoe. Poetry is therefore lower in rank even than craftsmanship (corresponding to the lowest level of the Divided Line, that of imagination), and must be governed by Philosophy, which studies the Ideas directly. Since Socrates likens virtue to a craft, an implication of this argument is that the fantastic imaginings of Homer must initially be clarified through the basic reality of everyday observable experience, better comprehended by the arts and the division of labor. For example, the poet tries to make us believe in a centaur. But because of the craft analogy, which establishes that every nature is self-identical and performs its distinct "job," and is therefore guided by logos or reason, we who know that the arts understand reality better than the poets in their intoxication with imaginary appearances realize that there is no such thing as a half-man, half-horse. The poet creates that illusion by mixing a shadow of a horse with a shadow of a man in the shadow-show he projects on the back wall of the Cave.

However exaggerated or ironic the *Republic* may be in ranking poetry as further away from true philosophic knowledge than humble crafts like carpentry, it set the terms for debating the meaning of aesthetics down to Kant and Schiller. This is the conception of the artwork as subordinate to metaphysics that Heidegger wants to dismantle. For Heidegger, Being is the originary source of all beings, the roots of the whole. Poetry and art are just as valid a perspective on Being as metaphysics, perhaps – as we observed in *An Introduction to Metaphysics* – even more so, because they are less reductive. In this way, Heidegger continues and extends a theme we have followed since Hegel first identified existence as a "self-originating wealth of shapes." If Being is origination (or, put another way, revelation), then art, if not sovereign over philosophy, at least reigns equally with it: As Holderlin put it, through art, "everything first steps into the open," welling up in "the symphony of the world's course." Even before the emergence of historicism as the solution to Rousseau's antinomy between nature and reason, the contrast between the richness of our natural sentiments expressed through art and the arid formalism of modern rationalism began to move poetic revelation and reason closer being equal partners, reflected in the merger Schiller proposes between them through aesthetic education to mitigate the harsh dualism between one's free self and one's natural self entailed by Kant's Categorical Imperative.

In the *Origin of the Artwork*, Heidegger reverses the Platonic rule of philosophy over poetry through two striking examples. The first is a painting by Van Gogh of a pair of peasant boots. Rather than being at a third-order remove from the Idea of the boots, ranked below the product of the bootmaker, according to Heidegger the painting of the boots is *more* revealing, *more* true than a display of actual boots or a photograph of the same. The artist's depiction of the gnarled and time-worn peasant's boots connects us to the peasant's enveloping environment of soil, wind and labor. By artificially evoking the "presence" of the boots, in other words, the painting is as close as can be to their source in Being as origination, closer than the actual boots themselves: "Truth happens in Van Gogh's painting."

As usual, the analogy to Being is bucolic. The painting of the peasant's time-worn boots is more "real" than the gleaming polished uncreased boots we see neatly displayed in a shoe store, just as he observed in *Being and Time* that the axe embedded in the tree stump in the forest is, through being organically connected to its environment, more real than when we encounter it gleaming and neatly arranged in a toolshed. He writes here: "As long as we only imagine a pair of shoes in general, or simply look at the empty, unused shoes as they merely stand therefore in the picture," we shall never discover the *being* of the equipment of the shoe.

From the dark opening of the worn insides of the shoes, the toilsome tread of the worker stares forth ... the accumulated tenacity of her slow trudge through the far-spreading and ever-uniform furrows of the field swept by a raw wind ... Under the soles slides the dampness and richness of the soil. In the shoes vibrates the silent call of the earth.

The second example are the remains of an unnamed ancient Greek temple. The temple is the place where an equipoise of tension emerges from the strife between Earth (Being as origins and possibility) and World (Being as presencing, form, lighting): "World and earth are always intrinsically in conflict, belligerent by nature. Only as such do they enter into the strife of lighting and concealing. Earth juts through the world and world grounds itself on the earth in so far as the truth happens as the primal strife between lighting and concealing." I can amplify Heidegger's evocation of the temple by drawing on Vincent Scully's topographical interpretations of sacred Greek architecture, which display a clear indebtedness to Heidegger's essay. As Scully describes the temple of Apollo at Delphi, the marble of the temple gleaming in the sunlight, framed against and holding at bay the looming mass of mountain behind it and acting as a focal point for the sunlit valley spreading out from it below, opens what Heidegger describes as a site for Being where "truth happens."

Because of the influence of Plato's elevation of metaphysics over art, we are accustomed to thinking that the temple, in its geometrical symmetry, is an architectural representation of the orderliness and proportionality of the eternal cosmos; that it symbolizes a higher supersensible truth and the division between the real and the apparent world (an impression aided by their remains being pristine white, suggestive of the supersensuous and transcendent, although in reality they were brightly, even flamboyantly colored). But according to Heidegger, the temple doesn't "represent" anything: "[It] does not mean that something is correctly represented ... but that beings as a whole are brought into unconcealment and held therein." It is truth as "unconcealment." (In another contested etymology, Heidegger interprets the first letter in the Greek word for "truth" [*aletheia*] as privative, meaning *a-leitheia*, the unhidden.) The temple opens up a world, and its Being is nowhere but there. The contentless structures of fundamental ontology in *Being and Time* and *An Introduction to Metaphysics*, whereby Dasein, by making a stand in the midst of *Sein*, issues in a historical clearing are now rounded out, concretized and historically embedded as the tension between Earth (Being as the ground of origination) and Sky (the "presence" of Being as the work of art).

The *Origin of the Artwork* also enables us to continue our ongoing examination of the relationship of the Philosophy of Freedom to ancient Greek art as a fulcrum for diagnosing and curing the ills of modernity. We observed how, beginning with Hegel, historicism rejected the rational analysis of tragedy tracing back to Aristotle, wherein the tragic hero was seen to possess a "flaw" which might have been avoided by prior reflection – assuming, therefore, that humans are capable of exercising ethical choice – in favor of seeing tragedy as a clash between primordial forces of destiny and necessity. We also observed how Nietzsche's Dionysian/Apollonian distinction was a modification of Hegel's contrast between the Divine and the Human laws whereby Nietzsche recedes behind Hegel's linkage of that opposition to the specific political and cultural institutions of the classical era, including statesmanship, civic life and war, to a more generalized interaction of and clash between broad and impersonal historical forces, at whose crossroads the tragic hero was torn apart, conveyed through allusions to tragic poetry including Homer and Sophocles.

Heidegger takes this recessional movement back behind the positive historical record even further than Nietzsche. His modification of Nietzsche's Dionysian/Apollonian distinction as the tension between "earth" and "world," evoked by the ancient temple, turns them into even more impersonal forces with no precise social, moral or political linkages to the history of the polis, no detailed interpretation of the birth of tragedy, and no consideration of human agency. It savors of the pre-Socratics' cosmologies of sweeping, purely impersonal forces like "chance," "necessity" and "strife." Throughout Heidegger's thinking, chronological history and individual psychology matter little in comparison with his concern with their underlying ontological roots. Time and again, he brings us to the very edge of that historical specificity – as in his throwaway remark in *Being and Time* that we cannot understand the emergence of Being in the ancient polis without knowing Thucydides, then just leaving it at that [39] – but without crossing over into the realm of the everyday "ontic" world with its bewitching allure of permanent knowledge, and thereby covering over the existential experiences of Dasein with metaphysical (including psychological) fixity. In my view, the *Origin of the Artwork* is an example of a rich contribution by Heidegger to the philosophy of art that stands on its own and is not ethically compromised by his political commitment.

THE WRONG EXISTENTIALISM

Now let us explore how Heidegger's understanding of modernity unfolded after World War II. Heidegger wrote the *Letter on Humanism* in 1947 in order to clarify the differences between his philosophy and the existentialism of Jean-Paul Sartre, one of whose sources had been *Being and Time*.

According to Heidegger, the reduction of Being to beings has meant that throughout the history of philosophy man's reality has characteristically been conceived of as that of a biological "animal." One must then try to explain what qualities make man distinctively human by piling a soul, mind, or free will on top of this biological being. Existentialism's contribution to this metaphysical catalogue is to affirm the radical freedom of the human subject in the face of empirical contingency, introducing his own meaning into a meaningless cosmos. It is thus, in Heidegger's view, part and parcel of "the destiny of Western history and of all history determined by Europe" against which it purports to rebel. Sartre's existentially free self is in truth the "tyrant of Being" who reacts to his imprisonment within empirical reality by striving to manipulate and exploit it.

Like all metaphysical definitions of human being, Sartre's affirmation of radical freedom stands apart from Being. But man, Heidegger reiterates, is not an entity like other entities. As the *zoon echon logon*, he is the temporal gateway for the Question of Being. The existentialism of Sartre, in Heidegger's view, is a code for individual autonomy with no organic relatedness to the world. It is thus squarely within the modern epistemological prioritization of the isolated self, a mere liberal lifestyle credo for a Cartesian subject. As we have seen, for Heidegger, by contrast, existentialism arises from the interaction of *Sein* and Dasein in a historical clearing, always already embedded in its "equiprimordial" complex of being-in-the world and being-with-others within a "heritage." Plato had argued that essence precedes existence: the order of the world determines my place within it. Sartre reverses this so that existence precedes essence: I determine my place in the world. But according to Heidegger, in flipping Plato in this way, Sartre preserves the divide between existence and essence as objectively distinct entities, and therefore remains entirely within the trammels of the metaphysical.

Heidegger also takes this opportunity to provide a retrospective view of German politics. What he termed in *An Introduction to Metaphysics* the "encounter between global technology and modern man" is, it transpires, in his view at the heart of the crisis of the West every bit as much in 1947 as it was in 1935. Now, however, he makes a pointed distinction between what he terms "nationalism" and the longing for a "homeland (*Heimat*) . . . near to Being." As Heidegger uses the word, "nationalism" is a collective subjectivism bent on the "lordly" domination of external reality, thus completing "subjectivity's unconditional self-assertion." As such, nationalism is what we might term a rational construct, the modern state, reifying the longing for a homeland, or of what was earlier called a "people," into a bureaucratic entity. "Internationalism" is no better an alternative, since it is a mere yoking together of otherwise unrelated national subjects under a cosmopolitan veneer aiming for an ever more dreary, alienating and oppressive world-state. (There can be little doubt about how he would have assessed the EU.)

Citing the poet Holderlin, Heidegger now offers what appears to be a considerably modified view of the German destiny from the one he expressed in 1935. The message of Holderlin's poetry, he argues, is not for Germans to transform the world (as Heidegger himself seemed to expect in 1935), but to return to their "fateful belongingness" to the West. In linking Germany's destiny to that of the West as a whole, Heidegger is consistent with his earlier view. But the belligerent lexicon of "resolve," "violence" and "struggle" now fades from view in favor of a more purely passive openness to Being by "letting-be" one's own people and other peoples. At the same time, however, this suggestion of a kind of irreducible pluralism of autonomous peoples is not to be confused with the assumption of universal values. Holderlin's evocation of the homeland in its uniqueness is favorably contrasted with the "mere cosmopolitanism" of Goethe. This recalls Heidegger's criticism in *Being and Time* of searching among "exotic and alien cultures" for evidence of a universal humanity. On the whole, though, the criticism of nationalistic "self-assertion" predominates. We should recall here that even in *An Introduction to Metaphysics* there were a few critical allusions to a predilection in Germany for mass political rallies and the heedless pursuit of scientific and technological prowess. If we put them together with the forthright critique of nationalism given in 1947, perhaps we can surmise that Heidegger wished to distinguish between the flawed, merely nationalistic (or "everyday") actual outcome of National Socialism and its "inner truth and greatness" – the promise it originally embodied for reviving a "homeland."

The heightened emphasis on "letting-be" one's own homeland and other homelands – on the passive mode of a people's relation to Being as opposed to the active mode of resolve – is accompanied by a markedly more ambivalent view of America and Russia, the two "pincers" of 1935. Now, as before, "Americanism" and "communism" are presented as the major spearheads of global technology's advance. But whereas they were earlier depicted as enemies of a prospective German "struggle" to redeem the history of the West, now, in the absence of any such prospect, they are given more weight in exposing the "determinate" content of the contemporary historical situation. They are not, we are admonished, to be seen as mere "world views" erected to defend some arbitrary and superficial value preference. Rather, they contain an "elemental experience" of the destiny of the West, which is now working itself out as technology. In *An Introduction to Metaphysics*, the rather contemptuous descriptions of America and Russia as promoters of "dreary" mediocrity contrasted with the incipient authenticity of the German mission (though the German people too, of course, would be poisoned by the same inauthentic trends until and unless it hearkened to its destiny). With the collapse of the German mission in both its original "inner" promise and its vitiated outcome, Heidegger seems to concede that the course of Western history has ceased to provide an either/or choice between an authentic political community and the triumph of global technology. Instead, the course of Western history has settled more firmly than ever into the development of the agenda set by the technological superpowers. Whatever intimations of an authentic relation to Being are now possible, therefore, will have to be experienced within the horizon of a politically already dominant world system. That leads to a new assessment. Marxism, earlier dismissed as an ideology for rapacious economic productivity, is now commended for harboring a "superior" account of modern alienation. This is presumably because, although it conceives of man in the "metaphysical" mode of a subject which objectifies its labor, it also expresses the full historical development and agony of this separation of man from his creative powers. Because it recognizes that history is our foothold in Being, Marxism is in Heidegger's view altogether preferable to the ahistorical subjectivism of the French existentialists, as well as preferable to American liberalism.

The *Letter on Humanism* develops the identification which Heidegger began in *An Introduction to Metaphysics* between global technology as the working out of Western history and the "inauthentic everydayness" of the "they-self" in

Being and Time. Hence, bourgeois modernity is depicted here, just as it was in 1927 and 1935, as a "dictatorship" defending "the habitual somnolence of prevailing opinion." Heidegger is as much as ever against the evasion of this dictatorship by retreating into private diversions. Moreover, it is even more the case than in previous works that the contemporary era has, for Heidegger, a privileged place in the history of Being. By nearly obliterating Being, Heidegger argues, technology has revealed more starkly than ever before the absence of Being from beings. Because Being is absent from the modern world, it is nearer and more manifest than ever before as something overwhelmingly lacked: its absence looms. George Grant's phrase "intimations of deprival" captures this experience. Furthermore, we have been freed from the comforting delusion that the history of our alienation has been, as Hegel believed, a cumulatively benevolent teleological process. Thus, precisely because of technology, Being "has made itself known in the present epoch of world history" after lying "hidden so long in oblivion." By damming Being up, in other words, technology concentrates its forces as never before. Accordingly, although Heidegger no longer speaks of salvation in any recognizably political sense identified with a single people, he believes that "in the future" man may yet emerge into an authentic relation with Being as a whole as its "guardian." As we await the outcome of our destiny and hope for a more open relationship to Being, all we can do is cling to *Die Heimat* as a dwelling place "near to the source."

Before discussing that hoped-for future more fully, there is a final point to note about the *Letter on Humanism*. Heidegger is more sympathetic here than in earlier works to the contemporary yearning for an ethics to "safeguard bonds" in a world where, he believes, virtually all human relationships are coming to serve the imperative of technology, making man "homeless in the world." He still maintains, however, that no binding ethical standards can be derived from Being. The primordial meaning of an "ethos," Heidegger claims, is a "dwelling place," in other words *Die Heimat*, or possibly the work of art, not the metaphysical, ahistorical and purportedly universally valid codification into which it is hardened, beginning with Aristotle, as "ethics," and which is itself, therefore, an adjunct of the juggernaut of technology, feeding the delusion that we can manage it. The poetry of Holderlin evoking a homeland "near to the source" is deeper than any such code. Technology has made possible the "healing upsurge" of Being back into beings precisely through gathering all the forces of Being under its yoke. But that healing upsurge, it transpires, has a destructive counterpart as well, the "malice of rage," presumably directed at the dreary banality and conformism of technological everyday life by "the hale" (a word related to "healing" as well as to a sort of brawny health). The interplay of healing and the malice of rage can perhaps be viewed as Heidegger's attempt to ground the phenomena of what are, in conventional moral discourse, good and evil in the "upsurge" of Being. If so, this does not correspond to an ethical distinction between good and evil, better and worse, or virtuous and vicious conduct. Perhaps the malice of rage can be linked to the role of Shiva in the Hindu trimurti as the principle of rebirth through death and fury – as one commentator noted, Heidegger's interest in religion was especially evocative of his interest in "the East." Perhaps it is an entirely depersonalized echo of Nietzsche's distinction between the Dionysian and the Apollonian, in the mature version of which the destructive dynamic of the Apollonian is needed to reenergize the life of the Dionysian. In any event, in Heidegger's view it is impossible to pass ethical judgements on the destructive dimension of historical change. As the genesis of history, Being must contain both the malice of rage and healing; it must annihilate in order to create.

The *Letter on Humanism* reveals the evolution of Heidegger's critique of the idea of historical progress in light of the way in which he sees the encounter between global technology and man unfolding in the postwar world. It also signals Heidegger's abandonment of any possibility of overt opposition by a people to the unfolding processes of global technology and his apparent deemphasis of the active, aggressive mode of man's relation to Being in favor of the passive, open one. The two developments are plainly linked, since Germany's defeat was the defeat of what Heidegger had taken in 1935 to be the most promising contemporary manifestation of resolve. If there *is* a decisive turn in Heidegger's thought, I believe it is that after 1945, his hopes for the National Socialist revolution having been dashed, Heidegger turns away from any further explicitly political commitment. Already in *An Introduction to Metaphysics* we saw the beginning of the emphasis on "letting-be," inasmuch as the heavens-storming but contentless projection of "resolve" in *Being and Time* had given way to the "unclosedness" of man to Being as revealed in the historical epoch of a people. However, whereas *An Introduction to Metaphysics* had allowed a place along with poetry and thinking for the specifically political role of statesmanship, in the *Letter on Humanism*, only the poet and thinker remain of the original trio of creators. Heidegger now seems to believe that an authentic relation to Being will occur only when man becomes the "Shepherd of Being" – the Shepherd of revelations carefully husbanded by art and thought. We should note the pastoral and millenarian reverberations of this image, whose transformative role in the coming epoch we will continue to explore. The world may yet be transformed, Heidegger intimates, but in an *apparently* more quietistic way (I will explain my implied reservation in due course) than the "creative violence" of the founders of the polis commended in 1935. Poetry and thinking may enable Being to "upsurge" into the beings from which it has drained away, sustaining them once again as a "hale" or "healing" wholeness (*des Heilens*).

Heidegger concludes the *Letter* by pronouncing that the time for philosophy is over, that it must yield to "thinking." As we recall from Chapter 2, Hegel had argued that we can now abandon philosophy in its original Platonic meaning as the "love of wisdom" because wisdom had now been fully actualized through the dialectic of Spirit. For Heidegger, this delusion of Hegel's must be rejected every bit as much as the Platonic original. Hegel's belief that he had found the absolute truth, while purporting to surpass Plato, was in reality grounded in the original Platonic love of wisdom itself: We no longer have to merely long for it, Hegel was saying, because it is here. Just to attempt to return to the Platonic meaning of philosophy as the longing for wisdom would merely be to repeat the whole process over again, until another Hegel came along to announce that he had found the answer to that longing. Instead, Heidegger believes, we have to step outside the entire cycle of the Platonic eros for wisdom, which itself stimulates the claim to have found the absolute metaphysical truth. By "thinking," Heidegger appears to mean a deep meditation on the *Ursprung*, the origins of beings, that resists all systematization; that draws back from all propositional reasoning. As he puts it in another maxim, "thinking is thanking," an act of gratitude to Being for its gifts.

TECHNOLOGY AND THE FUTURE OF BEING

We will complete our discussion of Heidegger's later works by turning to *The Question Concerning Technology*, where Heidegger further develops his view of technology as the "determinate" outcome of the history of man's "fall" from Being (to recall the terms he employed in *An Introduction to Metaphysics*). Technology, he argues, is one of the primordial ways – along with art and thinking – through which Being "presences" or reveals itself. Like the poets, statesmen and thinkers described in 1935, the craftsman does not so much produce things *ex nihilo* as he "lets be." The Greek word for art or craft (*techne*) is a kind of "making" (*poiesis*), and this is also the word for "poetry": Homer was often called "the maker of the Gods." By connecting *techne* with *poeiesis*, Heidegger transforms it from mere technical manufacture into a kind of revelation, in keeping with his earlier revival of the pre-Socratic understanding of *physis* as emergence into the "shining forth" of appearance: Even the objects of the humble crafts are a kind of poetry. The skills by which the craftsman fashions his product are modes by which Being achieves "presencing" through him.

Modern technology, by contrast, although rooted in the original Greek experience of *physis*, has forgotten its openness to Being in pursuit of one (now historically absolute) way of producing. According to Heidegger, modern technology is grounded in instrumentality and the priority of efficient cause. But this modern approach, he goes on, is already latently or incipiently present in Plato and Aristotle. An important subtext here is Book 2 of the *Physics*, where Aristotle likens nature to the productivity of the craftsman in the operation of the four causes, thereby elevating, in Heidegger's view, efficient cause over material, formal and final. "The Greeks," by contrast – meaning the pre-metaphysical horizon of the polis – experienced the causes existentially as four partnering "ways," unranked, for the "occasioning" of Being as the work of craft or art, whether a poem or a chalice: in other words, a revelation. Aristotle's physics of the four causes is, for Heidegger, the metaphysical reification of the Greeks' existential experience of those causes as four coalescing ways for the "occasioning" of Being. Modern technology as it emerges full-blown from its metaphysical antecedent is still a mode of revealing, but in the mode of "challenging" Being. While linked to ancient *techne*, modern technology constitutes a severe modification of it. We "enframe" nature in order to control it, to extract from it "standing reserve," energy for the sake of efficiency. For the very capacity of man to make a stand in the midst of Being in order to let it reveal itself has also enabled him to "block" Being from any *further* revelations, a paradox he first broached in *An Introduction to Metaphysics* as man's "victory" over Being through the elevation of Thinking over Appearance and Becoming.

Hence, in a way that is as yet "unthought," whereas according to conventional chronological history, modern physics gave rise to today's machine technology, ontologically speaking the reverse is true: technology grounds and gave rise to the actual smoke-belching factories all around us. As Heidegger sees it, the conquest of nature by technology summed up in Bacon's formula of "knowledge for the sake of power . . . for the relief of man's estate" *required* the new physics of matter in motion and summoned it into existence, so that the world could now present itself as a field of random, purposeless happenstance fit for man's intervention and reshaping. This is a good example of what Heidegger means by "historicity" as opposed to mere chronology: In ontological history, the new horizon of technology long preceded the industrial and machine technology of the present, which was achieved through technology's summoning forth of the physics of matter in motion.

Where remnants of the old technology still exist today, Heidegger says, they "take care of" nature as they use it. The "old windmill" (a characteristically bucolic example of life "near to Being") illustrates the difference between the older *techne* and modern technology. The windmill's sails turn when the wind unpredictably blows, but the windmill does not attempt to "unlock energy from the air currents in order to store it." Modern technology, by contrast, drains nature of its heterogeneous possibilities and organizes them as a standing reserve of homogeneous undifferentiated energy – not energy for the sake of a local purpose, but for the sake of anything anywhere. Thus, while the old stone bridge connecting the two banks of the Rhine reveals the Rhine as a place and links it to the folk nearby (analogous to the work of art in *The Origin of the Artwork*), the modern power station converts the Rhine into a source of hydroelectricity for distant cities and lands. Its living presence is siphoned off into an ensemble of techniques in no way dependent on the dense textures of local experience. While the hydroelectric plant hums away hidden from view, the river itself now becomes a quaint – meaning dead – object "on call for inspection by a tour group ordered there by the vacation industry." Severed from its local world, it is reduced to a kitschy image on a chocolate box.

In evoking the sway of technology over all aspects of modern life, Heidegger uses terms he employed in *Being and Time* to describe man's ensnarement by inauthentic "everyday" existence: We are "fallen" into and "surrendered" to technology. Our varying attempts to advance, cope with, or evade technology, he claims, only testify to the grip of its power over us. As long as technology is viewed from an "anthropological" perspective – that is, as an objective process standing over against human subjects – we are condemned to veer between the equally fruitless alternatives of trying to restrict technology to serving human purposes or regarding it as simply out of control. To the extent that technology "challenges" man to exploit nature, he himself is organized as a part of the standing reserve. People become "human resources," a "supply of patients," and so forth. But because it is man who, as the conduit for Being's presencing as technology, "orders" the natural environment and "drives" its exploitation, he is never wholly reduced to the standing reserve, but experiences technology "more primordially" than other beings. Man is the locus for Being's revelation as technology, which is nothing less than the entire history of the West. Man belongs to technology. It reveals itself through him, he does not make it. It is the culmination of the reciprocal interaction between Dasein and the larger forces of history that Heidegger began to set forth in *An Introduction to Metaphysics*. The point, therefore, is neither to devise a humanistic code of ethics for the proper use of technology, nor to abandon all hope of resisting it. Rather, we must recognize technology as one pole of a reciprocal relationship between man and the particular "presencing" of Being that has predominated since Plato.

It is "too late" in Western history, Heidegger writes, to choose either to have technology or to abandon it – rather, it "has" us. Our choice is neither to resist nor to submit but to submit freely – to "prepare a free relation" to technology. As in *Being and Time*, therefore, Heidegger is arguing that we can only "choose to make this choice," choose to choose technology, a choice now transposed from *das Volk* to global man. By raising our relationship with technology to full historical consciousness, we become aware retrospectively that it is indeed the "destiny" of the West – just as in *Being and Time* the people's rechoosing of its destiny established retrospectively the full content of its heritage. By submitting freely to technology, we may be able to liberate it from its modern meaning as enframing, returning behind Plato and Aristotle to technology as revealing. Because today's technology is rooted in the original Greek experience of *techne* even while radically distorting it, its green shoots are still there, and can be poetically reevoked. Heidegger's critique of technology is often confused with the standard critiques of its dehumanizing or unethical consequences made on behalf of ordinary liberal politics or Luddism. In reality, it goes much deeper than this. Technology *is* the history of Being, and far from wanting to reverse or curtail it, we need to experience it to the full – the worse, the better. Only today, standing on the verge of technology's complete working out, are we in a position to grasp that technology has been the destiny of Being from the outset.

If the origin of modern technology can be thought through, Heidegger suggests, its capacity to "block" man's relation to Being may be dissolved, opening up the possibility that man "might be admitted more and sooner and ever more primarily to Being." As in the *Letter on Humanism*, the overbearing and oppressive quality of Being's presencing as technology, closing off all other relations to Being, might itself spark the return to Being. In this way, Heidegger fills in with the "determinate" history of the West the a priori relationship expressed in *Being and Time*, whereby the anxiety imposed on man by his everyday existence could provide a liberating insight into its impermanence and, thus, into the possibility of its regeneration. Just as with the *Letter on Humanism*, however, Heidegger no longer places his hopes for the future primarily in "peoples." In widening the crisis of Being to a global scale, Heidegger seems at least here to set aside even the partial palliative of our continuing rootedness in the local "homeland." This may suggest that, just as capitalism had, for Marx, made the unity of mankind a realistic prospect for the first time in history through the scope and intensity of its oppression, global technology has had the same effect in Heidegger's eyes. It is still possible, though, that Heidegger envisions the future more primary relation to Being as one which will be taken up by autonomous peoples once mankind as a whole has been delivered from its global oppressor. In other words, the universal oppressor will not give way (as in Marx) to the universal class, but to an efflorescence of authentic "homelands." (In an interview given in 1966, Heidegger said: "I know that, according to our human experience and history, everything essential and of great magnitude has arisen only out of the fact that man had a home and was rooted in a tradition.") Heidegger's ambiguity on this score resembles the ambiguity we discussed in Nietzsche between his preference for the rootedness of "peoples and fatherlands" and the necessity of their coming assimilation in a new supranational epoch. However this may be, the crisis said to face modern man in Heidegger's postwar works has become ever more international in scope as the role of a specific salvational people has receded.

Heidegger now raises the possibility that the "saving power" of Being may yet be released from within the juggernaut of global technology, ushering in a relation to Being that is freer than ever before. It is nothing less than the hope for a Third Age, overcoming both the ancient and modern epochs. We are currently in grave danger, placed between the possibility that man himself becomes standing reserve or that we use technology as a weapon to become "Lords of the Earth." Transparently a Nazi slogan taken from Nietzsche, Heidegger employs it now to characterize *all* varieties of the nation-state: they are all now "metaphysically the same" as spearheads of technology. The clear implication is that *all* nationalism is tantamount to Nazism. Just as he earlier implied that Hitler was as bad as FDR, now he characterizes today's world as being full of national "Fuhrers," a further controversial aspect of his explanation of National Socialism after the fact, to which we will return. We face the danger, Heidegger continues, of finding our way between the alternatives of the absolute triumph of technology and the annihilation of the human and a future in which man may become "more experienced" with Being; a future in which he will assume, permanently and undistractedly, the guardian's passive role of tending "all that is present on this earth," the "Shepherd of Being." In this either/or dichotomy we can detect a final residue of the choice which Germany was said to face in 1935 – when it was placed between the "pincers" of the two technological superpowers, between the West's resurgence through German resolve and the triumph of "global technology" – but now drained of any recognizably political outcome because it is no longer identified with the destiny of any one people. Commentators including Gadamer have described this either/or choice between a new openness to Being and the "oblivion" of Being as a secularized "eschatological reversal," not in the Hegelian sense of a rational dialectic fulfilling itself in the present, but rather of a millenarian deliverance in which nothing will be as it was before. As with Marx and Nietzsche, one may say that, for Heidegger, a hitherto unprecedented degree of alienation and despair establishes the possibility of a hitherto unprecedented degree of freedom and fulfillment. In this respect, Marx, Nietzsche and Heidegger may all be seen as rebels against Hegelianism. This is why, despite Heidegger's admiration for "the Greeks," a return to them is not enough. Like Nietzsche, his interest in the archaic and tragic horizon of the polis is not nostalgic or antiquarian, but as a foil for our current nihilism and a springboard for its overcoming. Heidegger prefers the pre-Socratics to Plato and Aristotle because their ontology of Being as origination, of *physis* as strife, helps us to revivify the Question of Being, to return to the crossroads and the fork not taken. But the Pre-Socratics themselves, according to Heidegger, may have already harbored the seed of metaphysics even in their evanescent distinctions between Being, becoming and appearance, and in any event, they were not strong enough to resist its suzerainty: Metaphysics has entirely determined our history, including bringing us to the new crossroads of complete devastation or a new millennium far superior even to the heroic age of the Greeks. We cannot *want* technology not to have happened.

As we have observed throughout this book, the Philosophy of Freedom exhibits a millenarian dimension all the way back to Hegel. Politically the most moderate in his attachment to the values of the Enlightenment and the modern nation-state, whose psychological and historical underpinnings he wished to deepen so as to preserve it from its revolutionary and reactionary foes, even Hegel evoked the impending completion of history as "something new that is coming ... a new age," likening it to a newborn baby whose gestation is being spurred by the Labor of the Negative in the form of the French Revolution and Napoleonic wars, a "flash" of Benjamin Franklin's lightning and Napoleon's cannons. Nietzsche also likened the coming "third metamorphosis" after the epochs of the morality of consequences and the morality of intention to a newborn child. Marx located socialism in a realm beyond politics, accompanied by "the withering away of the state." Yet, despite their increasingly counterfactual and utopian visions of the future, Heidegger's historicist predecessors believed the roots of the future must be in the present. Hegel, of course, was still optimistic enough about modern civil society to believe the conditions for its legitimacy could be set forth as a theory of Right, meaning he still had one foot firmly in the camp of Locke and Rousseau. Marx and Nietzsche spurned this enterprise on the grounds that nothing about "the bourgeoisie" or "the Last Man" could be redeemed for the future, the coming era of socialism or the Overman. Yet even their visions retained some roots in the present. For Marx at his most consistent, the transition to the full "human" emancipation of social-ism could not come about without the maturation of the socioeconomic condi-tions brought about by the "political" emancipation of liberalism, an emancipation that was insufficient but still necessary. For Nietzsche, what he terms "our virtues," "peoples and fatherlands," and the watersheds of past great historical creations and refinements of the Will to Power would fuel the leap toward the Overman: the third metamorphosis of the Child is the offspring of the preceding two, the Camel and the Lion. In my view, beginning with *Being and Time* and continuing here, Heidegger goes much further than any of them in his repudiation of the present, is far more radical and uncompromising in his rejection of the "everyday world," including the study of chronological history, substantive human psychology, economics, political science or any notion of public policy. For Heidegger, our alienation is from nothing less than the totality of reality. It cannot be specified as economic, social or psychological – those are mere reformist sops to blunt the experience of our alienation by pretending to care about it and through devising material solutions that remain entirely within the chains of everyday life and the they-self. He abandons the nation-state, its civil society, its class structure, ultimately even *das Volk*, as any kind of benchmark for measuring modern progress.

How is our future deliverance as the "guardians" of Being supposed to emerge from within the maws of technology itself? I am not sure I understand what Heidegger is saying – *The Question Concerning Technology* is one of the most gnomic of his writings – but I think it may be this: Metaphysics launches technology beginning with Plato by erecting the pure rationality of the "the yoke of the Idea" over the rest of existence, and gradually subjugating the rest of existence to conform with it, converting it into sheer material fodder for limitless efficiency in continuing that project of subjugation. Having brought the rest of existence under its yoke, the Idea must turn in on itself to purge itself of any lingering taint from the world of emotional, poetic, customary, trad-itional or religious experience, of any natural empirical impediments to its dynamo of creating standing reserve, and finally, of any limitation imposed by the structure of metaphysical rationality itself, the liquidation of its elevation of thinghood and the thingly account of Being, so that at length technology may dissolve itself and release Being (and all the beings) from its grip. Because technology must dissolve all fixity so that everything is converted into the energy of standing reserve, technology *itself* at length makes us challenge metaphysics. Metaphysics' *own* certainties will have to be dissolved in the pure potent energy of efficiency for the sake of efficiency. Heidegger pronounces the prospect of technology's self-dissolution as "astonishing" or "wondrous" (*Erstaunt*), the historicized and existential equivalent, perhaps, of the "wonder" stirred in Socrates by eros – the release of the beings from their hardened distinctness into pure possibility, inverting the Platonic transcendence of the beings in their hardened distinctness by what is immortally true. Perhaps the self-dissolution of technology is also analogous to Nietzsche's argument that the ascetic ideal, first erected over the rest of existence as Plato's Idea of the Good and as God, must eventually consume any latent traces of personality or emotion in God himself, resulting in God's "death" and the liberation of the will to power. In the case of both Nietzsche and Heidegger, the outcome is an either/or gamble: for Nietzsche, the Overman versus mankind's degeneration into the Last Man; for Heidegger, the fulfillment of man as "the Shepherd of Being" versus his absorption into technology's standing reserve. The pastoral and millenarian resonances of the image of the Shepherd are, we can be certain, intentional.

We recall from Chapter 2 that Hegel believed his *Phenomenology of Spirit* had reconciled Platonism with historicism, assimilating the ascent up the Divided Light to the sunlight of the Good to mankind's progress toward "the spiritual daylight of the present." For this reason, at every turn in the career of his thinking, it seems to me, Heidegger's great antagonist is Hegel. He was the great block in the road, because if he was right, both the ancient and modern assaults on Being – metaphysics followed by modern science – could be redeemed as way stations toward mankind's happiness. One way to bring this into focus is to consider how each thinker related history to some form of transhistorical transcendence, or, put another way, related finitude to infinity. For Hegel, man rises from finitude to infinity through the teleological culmination of history as Absolute Spirit. Both Hegel and Heidegger undercut the subject/object distinction through their understandings of the historicity of existence. But whereas Hegel does this through an ascent to the Absolute, Heidegger achieves that result without ever letting go of the absolute finitude of man and Being. Even philosophical thinking, for Hegel a hallmark of Spirit that can be studied in abstraction from nature and the rest of life and is in some ways the highest human activity, for Heidegger is wholly immanent within the historicity of the existential analytic of Dasein, whose own prompts from "mood" issue in "the Call" from Being to Dasein to question Being. The light of transcendence, once it is glimpsed at the margins of the Call, must be squarely resisted. Conceptual and logical clarity of the kind sought by Hegel in formulating the dialectic of Spirit does not illuminate this Call, but on the contrary takes us further away from it.

Since in Heidegger's view the whole history of metaphysics since Plato is based on the subject/object distinction, the whole history of metaphysics has concealed Being, but it has also revealed Being through the looming power of its increasingly felt absence. So fundamental ontology still needs the history of Being, going back to the false path already taken by the ancient Greeks, as

Heidegger argued in *Being and Time*, when they were early on seduced by logic [26–27]. As we saw in Chapter 2, Hegel's Unity of Subject and Substance may be described as the interactive poles of the modern project for the conquest of nature (Machiavelli, Bacon and Hobbes) and the longing for harmony, community and reconciliation (Rousseau, Spinoza, but also Plato). For Hegel, the conquest of nature works in tandem with the longing for harmony so as to ultimately yield the telos (*das Ende*) of history. Heidegger is arguing that we in the twentieth century now know that the Hegelian progress of history has revealed itself to be driven solely by the subjective side of this polarity, what Hegel termed "the labor of the negative," with no harmonious outcome in prospect. What Hegel regards as the Understanding in its interplay with the longing for wholeness has been revealed to be nothing *but* the domination of nature. The Subject pole of the dialectic of history, what Heidegger terms technology, has been the sole agenda of modernization. The third age, the Shepherd of Being, superseding both the ancients and the moderns, can still come. Alternatively, technology may reduce man to pure energy for the endless transformation of existence. As he awaits the either/or outcome – outside of which no alternative paths are available – Heidegger's final stance toward the twentieth century is, as Fackenheim puts it, one of "absolute composure" which "lets things be." In the meantime, we can cultivate green oases for poetic revelation to re-flourish as sites for the local "happening" of Being.

Throughout my treatment of Heidegger, I have stressed the way in which he radically departs from the Hegelian notion of the progress of history and its dialectical resolution in the present. For Heidegger, Dasein's finitude is the locus or site not only of human history, but of Being altogether. To reiterate an earlier observation: Unlike some who believe that Heidegger with his later works reached a "turn" from the historicity of human existence in *Being and Time* to the historicity of Being as such (including Dasein enfolded in it), I believe that Being and human existence are thoroughly and jointly historical in *Being and Time* itself. The only turn is to an interest in fleshing out the formal structure of fundamental ontology as the conditions for any possible world with a phenomenological depth dimension opened up through the "determinate" history of Being, starting in *An Introduction to Metaphysics* and continuing as we have seen in the *Letter on Humanism* and *The Question Concerning Technology*, including concretized instances of Being's coming-to-presence such as the work of art. It was a shift in emphasis, not a repudiation of the fundamental ontology of *Being and Time*, meant to allay the mistaken perception that, in its abstractness, fundamental ontology was a form of transcendental, even Kantian, apriorism. As I suggested in discussing *An Introduction to Metaphysics*, for Heidegger history is a drama without transcendence, bereft of a rational telos. We cannot transcend finitude because Being itself, including the Question of Being, are finite, whereas Hegel believed that the finitude of history transcends itself progressively through the actualization of wisdom.

As we have observed, Heidegger rejects this proposition by going behind Hegel's dialectic of "determinate negation" in *Being and Time* to uncover the sheer "notness" (*Nichtigkeit*) of open possibility. But while Heidegger eschews a final outcome to history in Hegel's metaphysical sense as a "system," perhaps his own answer, fully reached only in the *Letter on Humanism* and *The Question Concerning Technology*, to the question of how we can transcend finitude if Being itself is altogether finite – how the Question of Being does not inevitably lapse into the relativism of warring worldviews whose only basis is the intensity of their commitment – is that technology is the destiny of Being; that it is bringing us toward a new millennium, a new and complete wholeness, a final resolution of thousands of years of alienation that has accumulated through metaphysical dualism. It will be not so much the reconciliation of history and wisdom, but the liquidation of the very distinction between them under technology's "astounding" self-dispersal, a historicist eschatology hailing the advent of the Shepherd of Being that surpasses in radicalism the millenarianism even of Marx and Nietzsche. The total transformation of everything in the coming third age of the Shepherd of Being will complete the dissolution of all metaphysical distinctions, including that between finitude and transcendence, or wisdom and history, even their latent presence in Heidegger's own thinking. This may explain his peculiar habit, in for instance a letter to Junger regarding nihilism, of inserting marks crossing out any use of the word "being" – as if even his identification of Being with bottomless and contentless possibility remains too limited by the requirements of syntax and the copular verb with which we distinguish between Being and beings, between Being and everything else. For Heidegger, reason's insufficiency for explaining human existence can never be exposed by reason itself, but only by its dismantling and silencing, the "end of philosophy" and its replacement by "thinking" as "thanking," a silent act of piety for the "furrows" of Being that cross into us. In my view, insufficient attention has been paid to how, for Heidegger, his vision in *The Question Concerning Technology* of the either/or choice confronting us between the oblivion of Being and the prospect for its future transition to a new dispensation overcomes a host of earlier problematics in his thinking, including allegations that he himself had not been able to avoid latent metaphysical fixities in his categories of Being, Dasein, fundamental ontology and the ontological question. It is all in the hands of destiny. As he put it in the 1966 interview: "Only a god can now save us."

* * *

A final thought on Heidegger's location of the incipient transition from *techne* as *poisesis* or revelation for "the Greeks" to instrumental reason begun, he claims, by the classical metaphysicians. Heidegger's argument that Hegel's dialectic, along with the metaphysical interpretation of Being altogether, must collapse because it has emerged in the twentieth century that technology has been the sole driver of history from ancient to modern times would be untenable if he is *not* correct in locating its genesis in classical metaphysics. For that would mean that technology was a creature of modernity alone – the Machiavellian conquest of nature and the Baconian use of science "for the relief of man's estate" – leaving the claims of premodern philosophy and political philosophy still open to us. So it is worth noting that Heidegger's tracing of modern instrumentality as already lurking in the classical understanding of nature is highly questionable. To see this, let us return to Aristotle's discussion of nature in Book 2 of the *Physics*, a *locus classicus* for Heidegger's discussion of the origins of technology. At first glance, that discussion might appear to validate Heidegger's characterization of metaphysics as incipient technological domination. For Aristotle argues that the four causes are most clearly delineated in their operation in temporal succession by the productive arts: The craftsman (efficient cause) deploys his knowledge (formal cause) to build a bed out of wood (material cause) guided by the final cause of making equipment for sleeping (the telos). To this extent, Aristotle might appear to confirm Heidegger's notion that classical metaphysics transformed the primary experience of *physis* as the "occasioning" of the causes as pathways to a being such as a chalice into the application of reason on matter to impose its will on nature by commodifying it.

But for Aristotle, the analogy of nature to craft is only a heuristic device to illustrate the four causes because they unfold more distinctly and in temporal succession in the arts than they do, for instance, in a flower blooming, where the four causes are simultaneously at work within one organism. The proper analogy for nature, he concludes, is a doctor who heals himself. Here we see the four causes operate within a single living whole: An ill doctor applies his knowledge of medicine (formal cause) to his own unhealthy body (material cause) to bring about (efficient cause) the telos of his health restored (final cause). Final cause guides the others, but in harmonious cooperation, not through external fabrication. The telos – health – solicits and sets in motion under its rule (*arche*) the application of medicine to the body to achieve its natural fulfillment [199b26–30].

Contrary to Heidegger's interpretation of Aristotle, therefore, efficient cause is the least significant of the causes because it is merely the means by which reason brings about its purpose. The elevation of efficient cause over the other causes takes place only through the assimilation of efficient cause to the creative power of God over nature as chief artificer effected by Christian theology, later transferred (as I have argued elsewhere) by Machiavelli and Hobbes to the secular human agency of the Prince or Sovereign. It is therefore a post-Christian and modern conception. This is a small but telling example of how Heidegger does not let the exegetical evidence get in the way of assimilating ancient metaphysics to incipient technology. Yet, as we have already observed with respect to his interpretation of Plato, Heidegger's likely response would be that he is not interested in what Aristotle actually thought or intended to convey, rather in how Being "speaks" through his language to undermine it. Heidegger's stance for responding to criticisms of his exegeses is an infinite regress further back from "ontic" reasoning into the contentless *Ursprung* of Being, meaning that to criticize him for exegetical inaccuracies is only a sign that one is still trapped within the limitations of metaphysics and propositional reasoning, the creatures of everyday life. An equally acute case is his interpretation of Nietzsche, with which we will conclude our consideration of the eschatological reversal in his later thought.

THE UNACKNOWLEDGED ALLY: HEIDEGGER'S DUBIOUS APPROPRIATION OF NIETZSCHE

Heidegger's magisterial four-volume study of Nietzsche parallels and deepens his ruminations on technology as our global destiny in *The Question Concerning Technology*. For in Heidegger's view, Nietzsche had experienced with agonizing prescience the way in which all of Being was reducing to thinghood, and the realization that "within metaphysics" – that is to say, as the result of all previous history – "there is nothing to Being as such." But when Nietzsche extolls the will to power as the source for creating new, life-enhancing values, Heidegger believes he is committing a fundamental error that ends up exacerbating the very forces of spiritual decomposition he deplores. For, according to Heidegger, Being cannot be instantiated in any hierarchy of values. The very effort to do so drives beings apart from Being. Thinking can only dwell in Being's revelations of itself through beings (such as values), and those beings limit Being in its entirety *by* appearing, and which appear, therefore, by virtue of Being's withdrawal. The proper stance toward Being, then, can never be one of reforming it according to a value system, but of a devotional openness to and gratitude for it, however it may happen to come to presence.

Nietzsche was in error, Heidegger argues, to think that Being could be "mediated" by values or by the genealogy of morals, any more than it could be mediated by Hegel's dialectic of determinate negation. Major transformations in the revelation of Being, the "turning" of its destiny and the "danger" of its magnitude, "can happen only without mediation. For Being has no equal whatever. It is not brought about by anything else nor does it itself bring anything about . . . Sheerly out of its own essence of concealedness, Being brings itself to pass into its epoch." Being reveals itself as a being, and therefore simultaneously withdraws in the entirety of its potential: "That which according to its essence preservingly conceals, and thus remains concealed in its essence and entirely hidden, though nonetheless it somehow appears, is in itself what we call the *mystery*." By presencing as a being while simultaneously withdrawing, that being – say a work of art or a code of morals – is "abandoned by Being itself." The abandonment by Being applies to beings as a whole, not only that being which takes the shape of man. Because man "represents" Being metaphysically as "ontic" beings, "Being itself withdraws from him in its truth, leaving man abandoned" (an echo perhaps of Dasein's "thrownness" in *Being and Time* [135]). Nietzsche's teaching about the Will to Power is the ultimate "representation" of Being as a hierarchy of beings, and therefore its ultimate obfuscation. The Will to Power can only overcome the nihilism consequent upon the withdrawal of Being by attacking Being itself: "To want to overcome nihilism – which is now thought in its essence – and to *overcome* it would mean that man of himself advance against Being ... But who or what would be powerful enough to attack Being itself, no matter from what perspective or with what intent, and to bring it under the sway of man?"

In order to control the world and make it conform to its metaphysical essence, man must uproot all existence, opposing himself to Being as an object which can be isolated and subdued. As the core of life – communal, religious and traditional modes of existence closer to Being – is eaten away, modern man is driven on in a frenzy of appropriation, as if only complete mastery could banish the unease and homelessness caused by the drive for mastery itself. For Heidegger, the essence of twentieth-century life, whether recognized or not, is this "struggle for the mastery of the earth," and Nietzsche was its prophet. The world is drained of meaning; reality becomes empirical; any conviction or faith that cannot be accounted for empirically floats off into a "vapor" of groundless abstraction or arbitrary preferences. The drive to reduce Being to thinghood finally turns on the supersensible itself, which had first enabled Being to be drained from beings – consequently, "God is dead."

But, Heidegger continues, although Nietzsche experienced the incipient planetary alienation from Being that was to become our twentieth-century reality, he thought the solution lay in the conscious creation of values freed from the earlier metaphysical delusion of immortal truth – the willing, not of an eternal truth, but of an eternal return of the chance to create "truth." For Heidegger, this only radicalized the crisis by accepting the very schism between fact and value which is the deeper ground of nihilism. Through Nietzsche, Heidegger argues, Being comes to be viewed as the will to power to create values. What this really means is that the will to power is erected over Being. Although intended to free man from subjectivism – the degraded philistinism and materialism of the Last Man – it in reality completes his subjectivization. For to posit man's will as the creator of all value is, in Heidegger's view, the ultimate reification of Being into subject and object. Nietzsche, then, both foresaw and hastened the battle for planetary mastery, beside which all traditional meanings of justice and community dwindle into pathetic obsolescence: "When God and the gods are dead ... and when the will to power is deliberately willed as the principle of ... value-positing, then dominion over the earth passes to the new willing of man determined by the will to power." And this is why Nietzsche's teaching regarding the will to power is but the final installment in the modern project to erect "values" and "the Ought" over the rest of Being that is outlined in the History of Being in *An Introduction to Metaphysics*, and therefore at bottom the final working out of Platonic metaphysics as technology.

This is a terrible vision. Is it a fair reading of Nietzsche? Some have objected that it exaggerates the importance of the formal and monistic doctrine of the will to power in Nietzsche's thought and underrates the variegated and nuanced psychology and typologies which Nietzsche elaborated to provide content for his doctrine – a phenomenological richness from which, it is arguable, Heidegger's own philosophy would benefit. There are many indications in Nietzsche's philosophy pointing to a dimension of "letting Being be," to use Heidegger's terminology, that mitigate Heidegger's emphasis on the unconditional will to power as its core. A prime example is *The Dancing Song* in *Thus Spake Zarathustra*, one of the most beautiful and elusive sections of the book, which we first discussed in Chapter 3 and which is worth revisiting in the context of Heidegger's critique of Nietzsche. In it, Zarathustra sings a song for Cupid and some girls to dance to it in a meadow. The song tells of Zarathustra's own experience with two women, Wisdom and Life, thereby exploring the relationship of Zarathustra the knower both to what he knows and to the world in which he seeks knowledge. Its details show that Nietzsche did not conceive of willing to be its own ground, but understood it to be grounded in an interplay between man and Being in which Life solicits man to will her interpretation in order that Life can come to presence as the manifold values exhibited throughout history. To put this into a larger frame, we must remember that, as we discussed in Chapter 3, the teaching of the will to power is coupled with that of the eternal recurrence because of Nietzsche's concern that, left to itself, the will to power, animated by the adder's bite of resentment toward the dead hand of past and current history, will be motivated by revenge against it, by a lust to raze it to the ground and raise its own new absolute on its ashes. The eternal return is meant to sublimate the potential bellicosity and narcissism of the will to power with a grateful acceptance of and submission to all that has gone before, of life's "endless play and spectacle." By ignoring the Dionysian and erotic dimensions of the Eternal Recurrence in their interplay with the Will to Power, Heidegger in effect acts as if the Will to Power was fueled by nothing but *ressentiment*.

The circumstantial richness of Nietzsche's genealogy of morals and his treatment of psychology as the superior route to understanding life as opposed to the "prejudices" of philosophy – whose criticisms of which in many ways anticipate Heidegger's critique of metaphysics and constitute Heidegger's summing up of traditional philosophy's chief prejudice – arguably lend Nietzsche's thought a depth of content and sublimity lacking in Heidegger's gnostic evocation of absent Being; an evocation in which the very wish for a phenomenology of Being marks an error and falling away from an encounter which resists any mediation and specification in "ontic" terms. Nietzsche aims to elaborate a typology of values that mediates the will to power without hindering its epochal scope. By contrast, Heidegger rejects the very idea of mediation. According to Heidegger, Nietzsche does not surrender enough of the Will to Power to Being. But Heidegger arguably surrenders too much. That said, however, it cannot be denied that there is an emphasis in Nietzsche's thought on the forward movement of history through multiple levels of mastery ranging from the subtlest inward spiritual self-overcoming to literal outward conquest and subjugation that distinguishes it from that of Heidegger after World War II. For Nietzsche, "thinking" cannot ultimately rest with "thanking," to use a Heideggerian evocation, but must continue to strive for "the enhancement of the type 'man'."

We recall that in *An Introduction to Metaphysics*, Heidegger asked whether Nietzsche was right to conclude that Being was a "fallacy," and then proceeded to reject this alternative which Heidegger attributed to him by attempting to show how the Question of Being might be restored and revived through Heidegger's own non-metaphysical perspective. How accurate was Heidegger's characterization of Nietzsche's thought? It is true in a certain sense, as we observed in Chapter 3, that Nietzsche did indeed regard the traditional conception of Being as a fallacy, as a prejudice which could not account for its own incentive, for its "faith" in the principle of identity and contradiction, a presupposition that made its rationalism possible, but which could not itself be derived *from* reason, but only from an anterior drive – ambition, *ressentiment*, a longing for immortality – to create an interpretation of the world. But it strikes me as puzzling that Heidegger should conclude from this that Nietzsche as it were abandons the Question of Being and turns instead to the Will to Power, which Heidegger conceives of as the radicalization of the modern project for the conquest of nature, a project we can locate in early modern thinkers like Machiavelli, Bacon and Hobbes, that dimension of historical transformation that Hegel identified as the Subjective or Labor of the Negative, and which Heidegger himself locates as already incipient in Platonic metaphysics – in sum, that Nietzsche abandons Being in exchange for the consummation of global technology as the "lords of the earth."

It is certainly true that Nietzsche regards the will to power as an epoch-shaping force that, having reached its current zenith as Platonism/Christianity, can bend its bow and shoot toward an even greater future summed up as the Overman. But, far from amounting, as Heidegger maintains, to the abandonment of Being, it is clear that Nietzsche regards the Will to Power and the teaching about the eternal recurrence of the same with which he pairs it *as* Being. For we saw abundant evidence in Chapter 3 that Nietzsche does not regard the will to power as the projection of power by human subjects, whether individually or collectively. In other words, for Nietzsche, the Will to Power is the furthest thing imaginable from a modern Machiavellian or Hobbesian anthropocentric conception of the human conquest of nature – whether literally and outwardly to create powerful states or internalized as Baconian natural science and Cartesian epistemology – whereby nature is identified from the outset as an external and often hostile force, a force from which man must begin by thoroughly uprooting and alienating himself so as to make it the object of his domination, bending nature to the creation of political power and material wellbeing for mankind. As Nietzsche frequently tells us, *everything* is Will to Power, "and nothing else." Far from being a subjective human projection onto the purposeless chaos of nature, as in early modern liberal thought, the Will to Power is Nietzsche's name for the whole, a field of forces that issues through the human affects, our passions, lusts, love of beauty and glory, and, using us as its conduits, seeks "discharge" through the greatest human creations of philosophy, art and rule, first expressed in *The Birth of Tragedy* as the "world-artist."

It is the bellicose and belligerent dimensions of the will to power that Heidegger criticizes, regarding it as the drive behind the modern project for the technological mastery of the earth, and, as we observed in Chapter 3, it arguably may include such consequences. Nietzsche does endorse the equation of knowledge with power going back to Bacon, and the modern physics of matter in motion does resemble the Will to Power as a field of strife and happenstance, as long as one recognizes that Nietzsche's ontology is meant to thoroughly sublimate and de-subjectivize the physics of matter in motion and link it organically to the historical life-world. (Not accidentally, therefore, Nietzsche recognizes in Spinoza a forebear.) But while Heidegger's identification of the Will to Power as the vehicle for technological mastery is a criticism one could make of Nietzsche within the realm of informed debate about his texts, in my view Heidegger still distorts and covers over the fact that, as an ontological principle, the Will to Power actually bears a great deal of resemblance to Heidegger's own evocation of Being as an "overpowering power," a storm, a force, war and strife, the "malice of rage." Moreover, Heidegger's depiction of man as being in the grip of this power, having to make a stand against it, such that, through that encounter between the strife of Being and "the creators" there issue great philosophy, art and states, resembles Nietzsche's depiction whereby the Will to Power expresses itself through its human avatars, just as for Heidegger, Dasein is the "clearing" for Being's "presencing" as historical greatness.

Furthermore, even though Heidegger eschews Nietzsche's interest in substantive human psychology as it is spiritually deepened by the genealogy of morals on the grounds that the Question of Being is occluded by being tainted by such "ontic" considerations that belong properly to the merely derivative realms of anthropology, narrative history and other "everyday" disciplines that emerge into clarity only in the wake of Being's withdrawal, there is surely a close resemblance between some of the passions that Heidegger grants an "equiprimordial" status as components of the foreground structure of Dasein before it issues in any possible world (resolve and commitment in particular) and Nietzsche's evocation of the Master Morality and the longing for nobility. The difference between them is that, whereas Nietzsche exhibits them as fully rounded, historically richly laden psychological prototypes embedded in the genealogy of morals, Heidegger depicts them as generalized and impersonal forces, bereft of human detail – a difference which, on the level of descriptive phenomenology, may be counted a liability of Heidegger's fundamental ontology in comparison with Nietzsche's genealogy of morals. Similarly, we may detect in Heidegger's use of borrowed religious terminology such as "the Call" and Dasein's silent circumspect attunement to Being his own version of Nietzsche's evocation of authentic faith (as opposed to systematic theology) as centered on sacrifice and reverence, albeit, once again in Heidegger's version, leeched of the circumstantial richness and psychological roundedness of Nietzsche's archetypes such as the Saint. Finally, let us note the parallel between Nietzsche's assimilation of the traditional role of the philosopher to the roles of legislator, prophet and breeder and Heidegger's early identification of philosophy with serving the destiny of the people, the main difference being that for Heidegger this political vocation was limited to his own Volk, whereas for Nietzsche it must aim beyond nationalism to a supranational and ultimately global politics of greatness exercised by a master race.

A final parallel: Like Heidegger, Nietzsche also identified Platonic metaphysics as already incipiently what Heidegger calls global technology, although he did not use that term but wrote instead of the ascetic ideal and its culmination in the secularization of Christianity as modern herd morality. Herd morality is not unlike what is implied by Heidegger's disparagement of "the they-self" as summing up the spiritual debasement of modern liberal individualism with its vulgarity, materialism and eroding of rank, though it is depicted in rather wraith-like terms as opposed to Nietzsche's fiery vigor in his jeremiad about the Last Man. Heidegger depicts Nietzsche's Will to Power culminating in the call for the Overman as the ultimate realization of the agenda of global technology for the total Platonization of existence. But in his later writings, although he has abandoned politics in the ordinary sense of a party or movement, Heidegger also envisions the advent of a savior surpassing what is currently human, "the Shepherd of Being," a figure whose name, like Nietzsche's assimilation of philosophy to rule and prophecy, has millenarian overtones suggesting a new Christ or Pancrator. In the case of both thinkers, the crisis of modernity poses the two forks in the road of continuing degradation or an unprecedentedly shining future. Heidegger interprets Nietzsche's Eternal Recurrence as the Platonization of existence on the grounds that, if reality is governed by the eternal Ideas, then phenomena and events will, as instantiations of them, repeat themselves in the same way forever. But we saw in Chapter 3 that Nietzsche does not equate the Eternal Recurrence with this kind of determinism, arguably an outcome of ancient cosmology (as recognized, for instance, by Cicero) but in precisely the opposite manner: We must say Yes to everything that has happened up until now because we must wish it to always happen in this way so as to deliver us to the crossroads where we might use those accumulated energies, now unraveling into nihilism, as a springboard into a completely new and as yet unanticipated epoch. Heidegger's equation of the Eternal Recurrence with the Platonization of the world is premised upon his mistaken assumption that Nietzsche regarded it as a fixed and already fully known sequence of events, instead of the prelude to an as yet unknown future – not a closed circle, but an open one.

Moreover, Heidegger himself treats technology in a similar way to what I am arguing is the true meaning of Nietzsche's Eternal Recurrence – that it is an open, not a closed circle. For the working out of Platonic metaphysics as technology in every one of its manifestations culminating in the present might, according to Heidegger, bring us to a crossroads where an entirely new relationship to Being can be envisioned – that the working out of Platonic metaphysics will provide just the conditions and energies needed for this millenarian deliverance as it undoes itself. In other words, just as Nietzsche believes we must want Platonism/Christianity to have happened in order to bring us to the either/or of the future (Herd Man or Overman), Heidegger believes we must want technology to run its full course to bring us to the either/or of the oblivion of Being or the Shepherd of Being. Analogously, we might say, Marx believes we must want capitalism to reach its zenith of oppression so as to act as its own gravedigger. Just as Nietzsche envisions the Overman as emerging from an either/or apocalyptic struggle between the Herd Man and the new caste of global rulers, so Heidegger envisions the either/or struggle between the utter annihilation of the human by technology and the prospect of global salvation as a kind of eschatological reversal – although, once again, whereas Nietzsche's drama of reversal is so historically and psychologically circumstantial as to suggest parallels with actual historical events or prognostications for the future at least visibly emerging in the present (such as the Free Spirits), Heidegger's drama is a tension and clash between awesomely impersonal forces depicted only as principles, which does not rob them of their potentially ominous political implications. These were evoked in Heidegger's observation late in life that "only a god can save us," the verb save (*Retten*) having to my mind the political undertone of rescuing or leading us out of captivity, prompting us to wonder: What kind of god does Heidegger envision? A human god? More than human? A prophet? I am not denying that Heidegger presents the Shepherd of Being in a quietistic light, the "saving power" that will heal the earth, while Nietzsche's Overman shares more of the robustly masterful qualities of a Caesar or Napoleon. But as preached by Zarathustra, out of his care for man, the Overman arguably has a similar role to the Shepherd of Being as a kind of balm of love and salvation for a broken mankind. And as regards Heidegger's vision of the future, we must wonder what transitional means this god, the Shepherd of Being, might have to employ in order to bring about the "astounding" transformation of everything.

All of these considerations entitle us to wonder whether there is ultimately not something willful, whether consciously or not, in Heidegger's refusal to recognize the ways in which Nietzsche anticipated many of his fundamental ontological motifs, and in his perverse distortion of what Nietzsche meant by the Will to Power into the ultimate radicalization of Cartesian subjectivity, in order that Heidegger might maintain his stance that he is the *first* and *only* thinker to pose the Question of Being anew, while all of his predecessors succumbed to its previous destiny as "metaphysics ... working itself out as technology." This in spite of Heidegger's otherwise frequently profound insights into Nietzsche's philosophy in his four-volume study, which is scrupulously thought-provoking in its exegeses *short of* what I regard to be this fundamental distortion.

Is it at bottom a case of one great thinker not wishing to acknowledge his debt to a predecessor lest it dim his own claim to uniqueness? Alternatively, it has also been suggested that offloading onto Nietzsche the role of the proto-fascist – through Nietzsche's alleged elevation of the will to power as the "absolute subjectivization of Being" launching the "struggle for the mastery of the earth" – and thereby the spearhead of global technology was rhetorically useful to Heidegger in arguing that he, by contrast, had only supported Nazism's initial "inner greatness" before coming to realize that it had been vitiated by technology like the two superpowers and was therefore "metaphysically the same" as all other nationalisms; that all nationalism is a species of Nazism, of the drive to become "lords of the earth," in contrast with his own emphasis on *die Heimat* as the people's quietistic dwelling near to the source of Being which supposedly eschewed all such aggressiveness. In short, he tries to make Nietzsche the fall guy.

Perhaps it is an overall dynamic of German historicism from Hegel to Heidegger that Hegel's successors had to position themselves as wholly original, while battening off the Hegelian precedent. For it could be said that Nietzsche did not or refused to acknowledge that Hegel had anticipated in his discussion of Greek tragedy much of the substance of Nietzsche's later interpretation of it, and also minimized the sense in which Hegel had already identified the modern project for the mastery of nature in the pursuit of human freedom as the secularization of God's ability to stand outside of nature and reshape it (the ascetic ideal). Only Marx, while recasting Hegel's dialectic, openly acknowledges doing so, and displays a certain fealty to its concepts. This dynamic is arguably connected with the fact that Hegel's successors are also increasingly hostile to his accommodations with liberal modernity and project an increasingly counterfactual vision of the future which bears virtually no resemblance to the bourgeois present. Marx may be more accurate in his depiction of Hegel because the benign version of socialism (not the proto-Leninist one) as an evolutionary and largely nonviolent emergence of socialism from within the bourgeois epoch itself constitutes less of a rupture with Hegel than either Nietzsche's or Heidegger's visions of the third age, although as we noted it was later assimilated by the Bolsheviks to a kind of Nietzschean cult of the Party as Superman. In any case, none of Hegel's three successors saw the point of a Philosophy of Right, because whereas for Hegel the end of history constitutes a kind of cherry on top of what we already are becoming, a festive recollection of freedom, the "foaming forth" of "the chalice of spirits," reconciling past, present and future, for them there is virtually *nothing* in modernity that can be salvaged for the new millennium.

CONCLUSION: THREE PERSPECTIVES ON HEIDEGGER AND AN ATTEMPT AT A GENERAL EVALUATION

Because Heidegger's works signify the end of the Philosophy of Freedom as a grand paradigm, he is the sluicegate through which its many rivulets, along with his own, fertilize the twentieth-century schools of thought into which it disperses. For that reason, I will postpone a detailed consideration of his influence until the Conclusion of this book. But I do want to close our treatment of him with three matters especially close to the themes and texts we have examined in this chapter. The first is a final consideration of his relationship to National Socialism, the second is his contribution to the debate about the relationship between reason and revelation that has been a continuing theme in our discussion of historicism, and the third is a brief suggestion for how Heidegger's ontology of Being might be critiqued from within its own scope and from a Platonic perspective. Finally, I will attempt to sum up Heidegger's contribution to the history of political thought in spite of the moral and theoretical liabilities of his ontology.

* * *

In order to offer a final assessment of Heidegger's retrospective view of National Socialism, his involvement in it, and its consequences, let us return to his silence about the evil of the Holocaust, which we can let stand as a summation of the ethical vacuum of his philosophy as a whole. Was Heidegger's failure to confront the Holocaust inevitable? I would say he confronted it in the only way he could – as a subset of global technology – and therefore did not confront it ethically at all. For Heidegger, an "event" in Being, even Nietzsche's doctrine of the will to power whose impact he viewed as a war against Being, is authentic, and therefore good in the sense of being "hale," a dimension of the dyadic alternation between healing and the malice of rage that is leading us to the either/or choice, and therefore is beyond ethical judgement. If Being is *not* manifested in a magnitude of "danger," then an attempt at an ethical judgement and historical analysis about what happens in human affairs amounts to a banality. Either the Nazis were "a Presence of Being" or they betokened the withdrawal of Being, just one among many forms of technological malaise – which is in fact what Heidegger later judged Nazism to have become after its initial "inner" promise of greatness. Further analysis of its causes, characteristics and events (such as his rectorship) would therefore be, as he wrote, "trivial and irrelevant." Thus, as Emil Fackenheim put it, the "evil uniqueness" of the Third Reich and Holocaust could "never come into view" for Heidegger. In the 1930s, he thought National Socialism was the last hope for the West. When that hope failed, he regarded further dwelling on it as pointless compared to the titanic sway of technology of which it had turned out to be a phase, and technology's assimilation of all merely proximal, now outmoded, moral distinctions and attempts to distinguish between better and worse forms of government. Indignation or repentance were useless in the face of destiny. As a subset of technology, the Holocaust was a revelation of Being, and Being *must* culminate in catastrophe if it is to rank as a true Event – Being is *polemos*, violence, power, "the storm." How could the destruction of metaphysics by its own working-out as global technology, with the Third Reich as its way station, preclude the Holocaust any more than the fire-bombing of Dresden, the Battle of Stalingrad and Hiroshima? And in the face of Being's titanic "destining," what use is moral condemnation, detailed analysis, the assessment of responsibility, or ethical discrimination?

To be sure, nowhere in Heidegger's work do we find an actual endorsement of the Holocaust as the culmination of the National Socialist "revolution," which for Hitler it clearly was. But neither did he condemn it, then or later. The reason he could not atone for or retract his support of National Socialism was that he did not believe a thinker can regret or retract his support for *any* historical event, however terrible. In the "destining" of Being, no event transcends time, and there are no enduring transtemporal standards by which to judge good and bad conduct. Moreover, since, as we have seen, Heidegger rigorously excludes from his exploration of Being the concept of "mediation," of a teleology of historical progress, he cannot even invoke the perhaps limited sense in which Hegel was in a position to deem some historical alternatives in the present as a falling away from the true and correct path of Spirit, as relapses into barbarism that rejected the moderation of our expectations for freedom by precedent and prescription. This criterion for moral evaluation was embedded in his category of determinate negation which, whatever its own vulnerability to relativism may have been, at least provided a moral compass from within the assumptions of historicism. Marcuse thus aptly described Hitler's coming to power as "the day Hegel died." Even Marx's historicism, while utterly opposed to what he viewed as Hegel's deification of history as Spirit and a force transcending human action, could make judgements against political extremism on the basis of his own purportedly rational stage theory of historical development, repeating, for example, Hegel's criticism of the Jacobin Terror.

It may well be that in 1933 Heidegger never foresaw or intended what was to come about through National Socialism – the Nuremberg Laws, World War II and the Holocaust. But, as Fackenheim puts it, neither did his understanding of the people's return to its destiny "expressly exclude" such actions. I would go further and stress that Heidegger's later identification of the Destiny of Being with technology included by implication the Holocaust as a mere subsystem of that global juggernaut along with Fordism, nuclear weaponry and the tourist industry. He made this parallel quite explicit in a 1949 lecture: "farming is now a motorized food industry, in essence the same as the manufacture of corpses in gas chambers and extermination camps, the same as the blockade and starving of the peasantry, the same as the fabrication of the hydrogen bomb." When Heidegger reworked the lecture as *The Question Concerning Technology*, this passage was omitted, presumably because even he realized it would be too much to stomach. For Heidegger, the outcome of the Third Reich may have shattered its original "inner truth and greatness," but that catastrophe – including its effects such as Auschwitz – must now be accepted as necessary phases in technology's global self-dissolution, bringing us to the millennial either/or of mankind's total absorption by it or the birth of a new epoch in which man is the shepherd of Being, closer to Being than ever before, closer even than the pre-Socratics. Technology in all its manifestations has to happen. For Heidegger, the Holocaust would have constituted just another variant of technological mastery, like nationalism, a GM assembly line, or Soviet central planning.

Heidegger's failure to acknowledge the moral evil of the Holocaust along with the Third Reich's devastation of millions of other victims is to my mind consistent with his avoidance of making any such "ontic" ethical judgements about precise historical disasters, crimes or tragedies, or of ethically condemning whatever Being reveals, lest he undermine the openness of fundamental ontology to the "overpowering power" of sheer possibility. Furthermore, for Heidegger, modernity as a whole, including liberal democracy, culminates in the attempt to become, as he puts it in *The Question Concerning Technology*, technological "lords of the earth," a catchphrase, as we observed above, of Nazi rhetoric revived by Heidegger to imply that all modern states are what the Nazis turned out to be. Subsumed under the worldwide destining of technology, Auschwitz was merely one event along a continuum along with mass production, agribusiness and hydroelectric plants replacing windmills. This view is generalized in Heidegger's postwar contention that we now live in a time of "world wars" and "Fuhrers," ignoring the truth that there has only been one Holocaust and one Fuhrer. Nationalism is now stigmatized as a form of technological will to power, in contrast with the rooted "homeland" of a people, where supposedly no aggressiveness obtains, but now in peril of obliteration. Reading between the lines, is he not suggesting that the "inner truth and greatness of National Socialism" rooted in its historical dwelling as a "homeland" was at length the victim of its inauthentic technological version, placing the German people's suffering in the war on a par with that of Hitler's victims?

* * *

Ironically, given his shocking moral indifference to the extermination of the Jews, over time Heidegger's ontology of Being had a considerable impact on religious thinking, including that of Jewish philosophers like Emil Fackenheim, who at the same time, of course, loudly decried his indifference to and lack of remorse over Nazi evil. Throughout this book, we have examined the issue of the debate between reason and revelation in the Philosophy of Freedom, beginning with the observation that there is a kinship – originating with Hegel and largely retained by his successors despite whatever other disagreements they had with him – between the view of existence as "self-origination" and revealed religion. The ground of history, in other words, is analogous to the unfathomable character of divine revelation, of the God who utters the mystery, "I am what/that I am."

Hegel believed that his dialectic of Spirit had reconciled reason and revelation in a new synthesis, and understood the progress of history as the "self-actualization" of God. He depicts Christianity as the "representation" of *Geist*, its symbolization in liturgy and worship. Marx, the only unambiguous atheist and materialist among our quartet, rejected the claims of religion altogether: Faith in God represented the alienation of man's creative powers to a fictitious entity so as to make him accept the capitalist status quo, and that included Hegel's divinization of historical progress as Spirit. Nietzsche, on the other hand, regarded revealed religion as a deeper source of human spirituality than philosophy, one that could explain the motivation to philosophize better than could philosophy itself – that is, as a faith or prejudice. He recoiled from Hegel's synthesis of reason and revelation along with other modern compromises such as Deism as a wan and eviscerated sidekick of democratic leveling, predicting a growing desire in Europe to return to religion's authentic origins. Yet he was deeply conflicted about Christianity's historical influence, viewing it both as a source of tremendous self-overcoming but also as the forebear of today's herd morality.

If Hegel's claim to have ended the debate between reason and revelation by synthesizing both within the dialectic of Spirit had been shattered, along with the entire teleology of progress of which it had been a component, by the subsequent course of historical events and ideas, culminating in the catastrophes of the two world wars, the Great Depression and the rise of Communist and Fascist revolutionary violence and dictatorship along with existentialism, then the tension between them had to reemerge with full vigor, especially since existentialism had forsaken the traditional claims of reason even within philosophy, rendering philosophy doubly unable to be the great synthesizer.

Heidegger's way of posing the Question of Being was an important moment in the breakdown of the synthesis between reason and revelation and the revitalization of faith, now unburdened by the "cosmopolitanism" of the Enlightenment and its claim to have assimilated religion without subverting its independence, disputed by many religious thinkers who believed that the secular side of liberal tolerance and of the separation of church and state always won out over its allegedly equal religious partner, wearing faith down through its relentless materialism and secularization, shrinking it to a tiny preserve of personal avocations. Heidegger shares the view that revelation may, along with poetry, offer a more authentic route into the mystery of Being than metaphysics. But in *Being and Time* he dismisses the systematic theology of Thomas Aquinas, which in his view taints that wordless mystery by interpreting the divine through a metaphysical Aristotelian lens converting God into a "representation," in other words a being [3, 14, 214]. Unsurprisingly, he is favorably inclined by contrast toward St. Augustine, Meister Eckhart and Luther. Nor does he display any interest in Nietzsche's view that human spirituality had been deepened by faith, the source of enduring psychological archetypes like the Saint or the intellectual self-crucifixion of Pascal that could provide a model for the emerging extra-moral perspective. Just as Heidegger's ontology of Being stands radically apart from the everyday world, rejecting the mediation of Being by "ontic" concerns of either a classical or Hegelian variety, opening up Being as a sheer abyss of possibility, so does he favor the view of God as being radically apart, a mystical experience.

This similarity between Heidegger's ontology and an experience of revelation that is anterior to systematic theology is deeply rooted in his way of posing the Question of Being. Heidegger is asking us – not only in his later thought but as early as *Being and Time* – to tarry with the emergence of the phenomenon from Being as possibility, as the hidden roots. This is a pre-discursive experience in which we are attuned to Being through silent wonder, stirred by the moods of care and anxiety by which the finitude of all beings touches Dasein in its uncanny awareness of its own finitude. Not the self-confidence of discursive assertion (what Heidegger, citing St. Augustine, calls "the lust of the eyes" that is the basis of Western reason [215–216]) but a "circumspect" meditation on Being's silent cycles is fostered, the "call of conscience" that summons us away from our obsession with the certainty of metaphysical rationality and our domination by public opinion and dogmatic ideologies back to life's more profound origins in the roots of the whole.

What attracted those looking to revitalize revelation was Heidegger's own stigmatization of systematic theology as hopelessly compromised by classical metaphysics' attempt to think about Being as "representation," as if Being were a being, thereby conceiving of God as an objective entity rather than a mystery. Heidegger's preference for a silent attunement to the mystery of Being over our fascination with "the looks of the world" and the endless prospect they offer of more transparent analysis and classification is, according to Fackenheim, tantamount to a preference for hearing over sight, a kinship with Judaism's preference for the Word of God over man's independent capacity for reason that amounts to nothing less than "the Judaization of the entire history of Western philosophy." Although Heidegger insists in *Being and Time* that his exploration of Being should not be viewed as an interpretation of God [220], we should observe that he does evoke Dasein's alienation from Being in, as is widely noted, distinctly Augustinian metaphors such as "lostness," "fallenness" and the "call of conscience." There are further Augustinian undertones in the derogation of big city life as a realm of "chatter" and the likening of metaphysical "curiosity" to a kind of vanity, "lust" or "fascination" [107].

Heidegger's evocation of Being's all-encompassing power of self-origination points to a singularity reminiscent of the Abrahamic God, and not only the Christian version of the Abrahamic God. It is precisely by insisting that fundamental ontology and religious faith stand apart as authentic alternatives that cannot be synthesized that Heidegger is able to let revelation be independent and autonomous from the spurious claims of the Enlightenment and Hegelianism to have reconciled them, a typical example, for him, of the "dimming down" and "tranquilizing" of our experience of Being by the Dictatorship of the They, and exposes more clearly than before the ways in which these two independent paths might nonetheless resemble each other. In this way, paradoxically, philosophy can be an indirect ally of faith precisely through its distance from it. For instance, while there is no direct evidence of Heidegger's influence on Gershom Scholem's contention that Jewish medieval philosophy including Maimonides sacrifices "the living structure" of Jewish belief by converting it "into a bundle of abstractions," it resonates closely with Heidegger's aversion for metaphysically infused theologies like Thomism in favor of the mystical visions of Augustine or Meister Eckhart.

***

Let us now turn briefly to consider how Heidegger's ontology of Being might be questioned from within its own assumptions. If Heidegger can argue that Hegel's phenomenology of the "shapes of consciousness" occludes Being with a metaphysical overlay, might one not turn this around and ask how an approach to the Question of Being that excludes the possibility of the extraordinary historical and psychological richness of that phenomenology – including principles of moral judgement and political prudence – can possibly be valid as an avenue into Being as a whole? It seems to me there is a very real sense in which the essentials of Heidegger's existential analytic of Dasein are already contained within Hegel's evocation of the Unhappy Consciousness in the *Phenomenology of Spirit*. As we observed in Chapter 2, it has many Augustinian and Lutheran undertones in its evocation of the profound alienation of man from God. But the Unhappy Consciousness is merely one among a whole series of theoretically, psychologically and morally insightful *Gestalten* from which Heidegger seals himself off in the wraithlike abstractions of fundamental ontology.

The reasons for Heidegger's unwillingness to range outside of the Unhappy Consciousness are clear enough from his entire enterprise. Like Kierkegaard, who drew upon this motif in *The Phenomenology of Spirit* for his own evocation of religious despair – a bookend to Marx, who drew upon the Master/Slave encounter, such that the two thinkers opened up a chasm between personal existentialism and revolutionary collectivism – Heidegger does not want to cross over from the landscape of our "lostness" and alienation from God. He does not, that is to say, want to cross over into Hegel's forward-thrusting phenomenology embracing the whole ambit of the individual, communal, aesthetic, religious and political in concrete form, the overlapping spheres of historically actualized reason, faith and freedom, but prefers to tarry with that primordial existential Fall. But neither is Heidegger content with any version of individualism, of a personal withdrawal from life in the manner of Kierkegaard's evocation of "the singular individual." In *Being and Time*, in a brilliant display of originality, he in effect collectivizes Kierkegaard's vision of individual religious *Angst* as the basis for a full-blown ontology of historical existence embracing the personal, the communal and our historical heritage. Whereas the past philosophical tradition had regarded fear of death as individuating, as prompting us through fear of mortality to pursue our own survival and self-interest, Heidegger uniquely turns the individual's experience of dread regarding death into the very basis for Dasein's communality. For Hobbes, anxiety about death was the *summum malum* that dispelled the classical longing for immortality through noble politics and made us focus on our own self-interest. For Heidegger, by contrast, our anxiety over death is the wellspring of our capacity for being in the world and being with others in a community. Still, one must pose the question whether, by so truncating our access to Being and expelling from the outset the merely "ontic" considerations of Hegel's rich phenomenological range, Heidegger does not ultimately reduce the majesty of Being and so narrowly interpret authentic experience as being grounded in anxiety as to jettison virtually all other measures of our dissatisfaction or happiness.

Cognate with the argument that Heidegger's approach to the Question of Being is highly dubious owing to the psychological and historical barrenness it necessitates in order to avoid the taint of "ontic" reasoning and morality is a related question raised by Leo Strauss: Based on our observation of the phenomena of human life prior to philosophical reflection, what justifies Heidegger in the first place in identifying anxiety as the fundamental human relationship to the whole? Why could it not at least as justifiably be love, whether of God or of wisdom? That in turn would argue for philosophy as an eros for wisdom concerning the eternal causes of the whole, in other words Platonic philosophy, rather than Dasein's Question of Being prompted by an awareness of death. Perhaps the most fruitful way into a critique of Heidegger's ontology would be by way of his assessment of Plato – a critique not grounded in the accuracy of Heidegger's exegesis of Plato, which for reasons we have considered is not, quite consistently with Heidegger's own principles, constrained by the obligation to understand the author as he understood himself, but by our own direct reflections on everyday life. In other words, start where Heidegger starts and ask what moves us more profoundly: Anxiety or Love?

There is no way of avoiding the philosophical divide between Plato and Heidegger, regardless of whether Heidegger really grasps Plato's thought or not. All we can do is try to deepen our own grasp of Plato. If Heidegger is correct, Plato's metaphysics are the beginning of a project to impose "the yoke of the Idea" on the rest of existence. If, for Plato, philosophy were only a *techne*, Heidegger might have grounds for finding in it incipient global technology. But if, as I have argued elsewhere, the technical dimension of that philosophizing was at the service of, and entailed by, an erotic longing for knowledge of the eternal order of the whole – a recurrent and never-to-be-completed longing – how could it launch the project for the assimilation of the rest of Being to technology imputed to it by Heidegger?

* * *

I began my examination of Heidegger by promising to aim for a middle course between ignoring the dangerous political implications of his philosophy and reducing it to nothing but a fascist ideology. That entailed alternating between commentary on his texts and a forthright examination of their intrinsic connection with his commitment to National Socialism along with the unsatisfactory character of his attempts to explain it retrospectively. Now, by way of restoring balance, I want to end with an attempt at assessing Heidegger's contribution to the history of ideas.

Heidegger tried to save German historicism – with its aim to provide a comprehensive account of human life on both the individual and the communal level, including social life, emotional depth, poetry and the arts – in the wake of the collapse of the belief in the Hegelian account of the rational progress of history. This he did as a response to how the Hegelian and historicist legacy had been displaced in the academic world by the comeback of modern dualism and its separation of rationality from experience, both in the form of neo-Kantianism, which located reason in a contentless ethical and analytical formalism standing outside of history, and in the form of Weber's fact/value distinction. Both resurgent versions of dualism arguably split the world back into the original Rousseauan chasm between nature and reason, nature and freedom, the Is and the Ought, that Hegel had sought to bridge – Kantianism by dividing reason's account of freedom from psychology and Weber by arguing that reason could only help us implement decisions that were themselves made in a purposeless void, and could provide no guidance itself for what we ought to choose. Both arguably led to a hopeless relativism whereby reason retreated from the rest of life, which in consequence became a battleground of competing and equally arbitrary *Weltanschauungen*. Weber called it "value polytheism," and likened it to an eternal war among gods.

Heidegger aimed to salvage the traditional role of reason in the West as guiding our choices by *completely* historicizing it. (Saving it, a critic might argue, by destroying it altogether.) As I began by observing at the beginning of this chapter, he was the antipodal opposite of Plato. For Heidegger no less than for Hegel, Marx and Nietzsche, there was no way back behind the modern account of nature as matter in motion, nor, for him, was there even any prospect for human wholeness in the chronological unfolding of history to date. By enfolding reason within the analytic of Dasein and its call by the Question of Being, Heidegger maintained that reason need not be viewed as standing apart from existence in the Kantian or Weberian sense, or in the traditional way by which it transcended the here and now in the Platonic sense, but is always already folded *into* human experience as the ontological question, entirely historical, temporal and immanent. Notwithstanding that Heidegger's understanding of commitment was also liable to the charge of being a version of Weberian decisionism arbitrarily projected into an ethical void, hence relativistic, the early Heidegger believed that he had avoided that charge by grounding existential decision in the collective depth dimension of a specific people's heritage and communal roots, which lent fundamental ontology a sociopolitical scope comparable to Hegel and, standing behind him, Plato, while jettisoning their dialectic. Such a decision was not relativistic, in Heidegger's mind, because not *every* historical setting or people was suitable for posing the Question of Being. Moreover, as I have argued, as his new vision of the Third Age bulked ever larger in his later thought, he could maintain in principle that the salvation and wholeness it promised for mankind was unconditional, all-embracing and absolute, the culmination of the destiny of the world, hence not a mere idiosyncratic decision and not a species of relativism.

Whatever may be the validity of the comparison between Heidegger, Hegel and Plato as regards their respective philosophical enterprises, it is certain that Heidegger's ontology of Being was the last of work of the Philosophy of Freedom that aimed for the comprehensiveness of *scope* of those predecessors, notwithstanding the misgivings I expressed above about its *depth*, such that Heidegger can plausibly be mentioned in the same breath with them. Like those predecessors, he tried to make philosophizing once again the key to a vision of the world that integrated human life at every level, from the most deeply inward to the most public and other-related. For reasons we will consider in the general conclusion to this work, none of Heidegger's successors, however much one or another theme from his thought may have influenced their own theories, claimed this ambitious breadth of scope again. On any estimate, therefore, Heidegger's achievement was a tremendous one, which is why it stirred such intense excitement among his students, and why the young Leo Strauss, for example, who had great reservations about it, nevertheless thought that Heidegger blew away Cassirer's defense of humanist individualism in their famous 1929 debate when neo-Kantianism was already waning. Cassirer's uncomfortable mélange of neo-Kantian rationalism, the history of humanist values and the "symbolic forms" of myth and religion that could not be derived from reason was swept aside by Heidegger's self-proclaimed mission as the "lieutenant of the Nothing," meaning to say, the lieutenant of Being in its untapped possibilities, a vortex in which all of Cassirer's careful distinctions collapsed. This achievement was unquestionably compromised by his political commitment in 1933, but the achievement was not simply reducible to it, and many of his philosophy's central premises would not oblige us to follow

Heidegger down this particular political path, as is witnessed by its conditional embrace by Fackenheim and Strauss among others.

I am going to postpone a more detailed discussion of the contemporary significance of Heidegger's works until the Conclusion, where I will present it as part of a larger dynamic in which the Philosophy of Freedom as a whole falls apart and fragments into the various schools of twentieth and twenty-first century political theory, fertilizing those fragments with its now divided rivulets of intellectual inspiration. I will also try to explain why Heidegger's ontology of Being was necessarily the last installment in a pedigree of historicist philosophy stretching back through Nietzsche, Marx and Hegel, and whose roots originated in Rousseau's fateful walk along Lake Bienne.

Conclusion

The Fragmented Legacy of the Philosophy of Freedom

We have examined in this book how Hegel conceived of the teleological progress of history as the way of reconciling the contradictions between nature and freedom, self versus other, and the Is versus the Ought inherited from the thought of Rousseau by way of Kant and Schiller. For Hegel, historical existence as a "self-originating wealth of shapes" provided what he termed the "intersubjectivity" that would ground these contradictions in their underlying temporal sources of collective historical action and possibility, a unifying temporal ground to replace the lost transcendental unity of the classical metaphysics of the eternal whole. This sublimation of the priority of the individual by the currents of collective history – a priority central to the social contract theory of the early moderns, validated by the new physics of matter in motion – would also, Hegel believed, enrich modern life on both an individual and communal level, alleviating the psychological, moral, educational and aesthetic shortcomings of liberalism.

All the thinkers we have considered from Hegel onward sought to uncover this temporal ground. For all of them, history is a movement of self-origination. That was the common ontological premise of the Philosophy of Freedom. Hegel termed it Spirit; for Marx, it was species-being; Nietzsche expressed it as the Will to Power, and Heidegger evoked it as the Question of Being. In the case of every one of these variations of the ontological premise, moreover, it is not viewed as a human creation or projection strictly speaking, and certainly not as individualistic. Instead, life expresses itself *through* the human. As we saw, an early version of Nietzsche's Will to Power was his evocation of "the world-artist" out of which emerged the clashing forces sublimated within Greek tragedy as the civilizational life-force of ancient Greece.

Despite this point of agreement, however, Hegel's successors also launched the great debate regarding whether what I have termed the ontological premise develops and progresses over time; and their disagreements with Hegel in this regard, compounded by their unfolding disagreements with one another, is why they express the ontological premise with very different structures and consequences. Hegel argued that Spirit develops teleologically over time into Reason. But Marx, Nietzsche and Heidegger want to take back the creative drive from what they regard as this objectification of the dynamism of historical action. Hegel had expressed the conceptualization of Spirit as the Unity of Subject and Substance, the key to his system. His successors take that concept and pull its poles apart, or, more precisely, claim that the actual unfolding of history since Hegel has already torn its poles apart. The subjective side of the interaction of the two poles, where Hegel located his concept of modern analytical Understanding, the labor of the negative, and the pursuit of freedom through political, economic and technical mastery, becomes Marx's capitalism, Nietzsche's ascetic ideal and Heidegger's technology. They all agree that there is no synthesis, as Hegel had maintained in the Unity of Subject and Substance, between the pursuit of freedom and the emergence of community; between Kant and Spinoza; between science and Romanticism. That latter side of the dialectic, what Hegel termed Substance, we now know can come about *only* in the future, as an entirely new dispensation, and only through its complete rupture with the irredeemable world of liberal modernity in the present. Gadamer termed it an "eschatological reversal" common to Heidegger and Marx, and I would add, to Nietzsche.

This debate with Hegel over the historical evolution of the ontological premise leads, as we saw, to radically different visions for political life. For Hegel, the fulfillment of history is the modern Westphalian nation-state of the post-Napoleonic era. For Marx, it will be socialism, which is to be both futural and post-national. For Nietzsche, it is the coming epoch of the Overman, also futural and post-national. For Heidegger, after World War II, it is the possibility of a new advent of Being, also to be post-national. We observed a further refinement within the debate. Although Marx and Nietzsche both rejected Hegel's understanding of the teleological progress of history, they did not abandon the idea that history is coherently structured throughout. For Marx, human beings create history through revolutionary struggle, and its successive stages have been necessary in order to bring about socialism in the future. Although it is a purely human, anthropocentric creativity, ungoverned by any objective rationality such as Hegelian Spirit (to say nothing of any notion of natural teleology), Marx's socialism is nevertheless, he maintains, governed by "scientific" principles – arguably a hopeless solipsism that took nothing away from its revolutionary political potency in practice.

For Nietzsche, history does not progress in the Hegelian sense of rationally and cumulatively necessary steps, the principle of "determinate negation" reminiscent in practical terms, as we considered, of Burke. But it is still characterized by important archetypes like Platonism, Christianity, the Saint, the Herd-Man and the emerging dawn of the extra-moral perspective and the Overman. These are benchmarks in the genealogy of morals which allow us to navigate our way through the chaos of the Will to Power and glimpse the promised land that may grow out of its very nihilism. Heidegger, as we have seen, goes furthest in rejecting any notion of historical progress whatever, whether it be Hegelian teleology, Marx's scientific socialism, or Nietzsche's genealogy of morals. In his view, they are all mere way stations in the unstoppable subjectivization of experience set in motion by the juggernaut of global technology already incipient in Platonic metaphysics, the history of our "alienation from Being." In the 1930s, he calls for the people's return to its destiny, to its origins and possibilities in Being as self-origination, a backward and forward-looking leap mediated by none of the shapes of historical experience intervening between "the Greeks" and us, a leap that repudiates liberalism, conservatism and socialism all at once as mere spearheads of that global fate. It culminated in an antipolitical politics bent on destroying both received tradition and modernity. After World War II, Heidegger's faith in a national vehicle for the return to Being is transferred to the emerging global either/or dyad between the "malice of rage" of the technological apocalypse and the "saving power" of the Shepherd of Being.

THE END OF ABSOLUTE KNOWLEDGE

Now that I have provided a broad overview of the unfolding of the Philosophy of Freedom from Hegel to Heidegger, let us consider its legacy for political theory and practice in the twentieth and twenty-first-centuries. Of great importance for understanding its fate is a massive intervening development, the distinction between facts and values crystallized by Max Weber. We touched upon it in Chapter 4, but should delve further to see how it affected the reception of the Philosophy of Freedom in the years to come and to consider how Heidegger may have offered a riposte to it. As we have seen throughout this book, there could be no more dramatic contrast between early modern liberalism and its separation of reason (modeled on the empirical study of nature as matter in motion) from history and received tradition and what unfolded in Europe as the Philosophy of Freedom, beginning with Hegel's magisterial attempt to demonstrate the synthesis of history and received tradition *with* reason, the actualization of wisdom in time at the end of history through the dialectic of Spirit. However, the apparently decisive blow against German historicism and of Hegelianism in particular and the reestablishment of the distinction between nature as matter in motion and the analytical and empirical rationality that studied it was delivered not by the classical liberalism of the early modern social contract theorists, which continued to flourish in the Anglosphere, but by another German, the sociologist Max Weber. The principle that analytical reason operated outside of history and the observation of human existence was crystallized by him as the fact/value distinction.

According to Weber, you cannot derive an Ought from an Is; how man ought to act from how he observably does act. It bears emphasizing that this

Conclusion

had emphatically *not* been true for the early social contract theories of Hobbes and Locke. They claimed to derive from their study of the Is – human nature – a binding rational prescription for just government – the Ought. They undertook this by performing the thought experiment of asking how people would behave by nature were the constraint of political authority to vanish, leading directly to a prescription for how we ought to live based on reason. In other words, Hobbes and Locke maintained that the study of human nature could directly yield a theory of justice and legitimacy, notwithstanding the fact that Rousseau and his historicist successors regarded the early modern account of human nature as narrow, reductionist and psychologically impoverished owing to its focus on appetitive self-interest and their account of reason as limited to empirical observation. Beginning with the Utilitarians, modern English philosophy itself had abandoned the study of nature as the basis for justice (the point at which, Strauss maintained, it ceased to be philosophy). As Bentham famously pronounced, the very concept of natural right – the bedrock of Hobbes' and Locke's prescriptions for just authority – was "nonsense on stilts." Now, further bolstered by the fact/value distinction, liberalism assumed that political authority was legitimized solely and self-evidently by its ability to promote the greatest material good for society. The rationality informing it was no longer guided by the observation of nature, but was purely procedural and analytically self-referential, detailing the mechanisms through which this self-evident utilitarian purpose could best be maximized. In our own era, it culminated in John Rawls' *A Theory of Justice*, which presupposed the validity of the fact/value distinction and maintained that the principle of justice as fairness can be derived without any reference to an understanding of human nature, or the good life and civic virtue, which are matters of personal avocation alone. It was openly based on prevailing American social and political conventions, "our own most cherished notions," hence completely positivistic.

With Weber's crystallization of the fact/value distinction, we come full circle to the seemingly insoluble paradoxes in early modern political theory that were the catalyst for the great protest begun by Rousseau and fully launched by Hegel. For the fact/value distinction was the final installment in the problem we observed going back to Hobbes and covered over by him. Notwithstanding the fact that the original social contract theorists claimed to derive their prescriptions from the rational inquiry into human nature, the Philosophy of Freedom objected: How *could* human reason make judgements based on the observation of nature when human reason had no intrinsic connection to nature understood as matter in motion; when the human mind did not mirror the cosmic intellect as the ancients had averred? If nature is limited to matter in motion, reason is limited to this as well, and spirit, morality and will are outside its purview. Rousseau's response had been to reformulate the question by positing a distinction between human nature and freedom of will. The side of man that was strictly natural, driven by the need for self-preservation, was adequately explained in terms of the new mechanistic science. But the highest part of man was characterized by the pursuit of freedom from nature, including the possibility of resisting the pull of one's own natural inclinations. That faculty could not be explained by modern science because it was beyond the purview of what science could account for in human nature, which was limited to the appetitive and materialistic. But Rousseau's response only unleashed a new flurry of paradoxes. For it appeared that in order to save the noblest side of human existence – that is, freedom – Rousseau had to drive a wedge between freedom and nature and between freedom and rationality, which Rousseau accepted was the rationality of modern natural science. How, then, Hegel and his successors asked, might we heal this rift between nature and freedom, between the Is and the Ought? Weber's answer cut the Gordian's knot: We *can't*. And that answer altered the character of continental political philosophy itself.

Since Hegel, German historicism represented the grand effort to heal this chasm between nature and freedom through the concept of the progress of history. The critiques of Hegel undertaken by his successors Marx, Nietzsche and Heidegger form, as we have seen in this book, a continuous intertextual dialogue from the publication of the *Phenomenology of Spirit* in 1807 until Heidegger's death in 1976. But viewed within its wider historical context, that dialogue unfolded in a manner anything but continuous. As faith in the Hegelian teaching declined after his passing, German historicism as exemplified by the outsiders Marx and Nietzsche left the academy and split off into ever more millenarian and apocalyptic projections of the future. Meanwhile, many academics shared Weber's acceptance of the inescapable truth that we can have objective knowledge about the empirical reality studied by science, but that our ethical choices are made in a void; that we endow a purposeless world with purpose through our choices and commitments. Once we have made that choice, we might *then* employ our capacity for reason and our knowledge of empirical reality to help bring our choices about, while having to admit that our ethical choices had no grounding or justification *in* reason at all. Perhaps there remains a trace of the original European horror at the prospect of this chasm between nature and freedom, between fact and value, in the reports that Weber suffered from crippling depression and insomnia. English utilitarians, by contrast, slept soundly at night.

The growing prevalence of the fact/value distinction was presaged by the return of Kantianism in the late nineteenth century as the dominant paradigm in the German university. Kant's categorical distinction between the theoretical knowledge we might gain of the empirical world through natural science and the realm of freedom which operated beyond its purview harmonized readily enough with the distinction between facts classified according to reason and the rest of life as a matter of decision. Of course, this neo-Kantian revival largely occluded the full Kantian moral and ontological teaching, which, far from believing that autonomous moral acts were projections into a void bereft of reason, believed that they conformed with the rational structure of the whole studied by natural science, such that the exercise of freedom might, on some readings, bring the world into closer conformity to reason itself, an incipient account of historical progress.

In any event, the pervasive influence of neo-Kantianism in the academy throws into sharper relief than we have seen so far just how iconoclastic a figure was Heidegger, even though he enjoyed a conventionally highly success-ful academic career. For he brought the entire grand dialogue about the meaning of history and the whole reaching back to Hegel back into the heart of German academic philosophy, signaled by what almost everyone who observed it agreed was his intellectual rout of the benign neo-Kantian Cassirer in their famous debate. Neo-Kantianism had already begun to wane during the revival of Romanticism in the early 1900s and a growing new appreciation for Hegel and Nietzsche. This was the increasingly anti-Kantian atmosphere in which Heidegger emerged and flourished. Today, we regard it as perfectly ordinary in Great Books or political theory programs to spend an entire semester reading a few books, even just one text. It is hard to recover, therefore, the German philosophic world's astonishment when the word spread that Heidegger was about to devote an entire semester to reading one section of Aristotle's *Metaphysics*. Why, the remaining Kantians asked, would anyone waste their time doing that? Didn't we know that such ancient views had been discarded by the progress of scientific knowledge, by materialism and the fact/ value distinction, and stored in an appropriate cabinet of curios and "myths"?

It is unclear whether or to what extent Heidegger was engaging Weber directly. However, his existential analytic of Dasein certainly can be taken as a riposte to the Weberian argument and the chasm it opened up between facts and values, a dichotomy that, as we observed in *An Introduction to Metaphysics*, certainly preoccupied Heidegger as a sign of cultural crisis in Europe. As he argued there, the meaning of reason had been conceded to empiricism and instrumentality, while everything higher in life including art and philosophy were consigned to the realm of merely arbitrary, idiosyncratic value choices and "holiday ornaments." Art had been shorn of the civilization-shaping prowess of Homer and Sophocles in the emergence of the glorious statesmanship of the Greeks and reduced to a private avocation. Going a step further in the same direction, Fackenheim argued that Weber drove a wedge into Kant's equipoise between the sphere of nature knowable by theoretical (meaning scientific) reason and the sphere of freedom governed by the meta-physics of morals, two spheres thought by Kant to be linked by the formal characteristics of reason as such (universality and necessity). Through Weber's crystallization of the fact/value distinction, the sphere of nature was expanded into the sphere of historical existence generally, while the sphere of freedom became, in anything about human existence that strayed beyond the self-evident canons of utilitarian instrumentality, the sphere of irrational and arbi-trary commitments. This led to an existentialist "war of world-views," as Fackenheim put it, among different cultures, peoples, national loyalties and ideological commitments where reason, having abandoned from the start the possibility of ranking one's choices in the classical mode according to the teleological order of the immutable truth, could offer no rational criteria for choosing one commitment in contrast with another – all that mattered was the intensity of your or your group's preference. Weber recognized the existentialist implications of the fact/value distinction when he coined the term "value polytheism" and likened it to an eternal war among gods.

Heidegger believed that his own conception of Dasein in its pre-reflexive engagement with Being avoided the relativism of another mere worldview or decision made in a void because it did not abandon reason, meaning to say the Question of Being. Instead of abandoning reason's traditional magisterial role in life, in Heidegger's analytic of Dasein, our capacity for reasoning is seamlessly enfolded within Dasein's experience of the world in a community with others – put another way, reason is completely temporalized. Existence itself, touching us inwardly through our awareness of our finitude, prompts us to question the meaning of Being in its rapturous mystery and wondrousness, an experience anterior to any metaphysical settling upon a definition of the essence of Being that nonetheless explains our capacity for such derivative second-order explanations. In this sense, the traditional meaning of philosophy, including the identification of the capacity for reasoning about the whole with man, is rescued by Heidegger from its current Weberian metaphysical dead-end and restored to human existence through the "infinitely finite" (to use Schelling's phrase) possibilities in which we are always already historically engaged.

Whether Heidegger's attempt to avoid the metaphysical dichotomy of the Weberian fact/value distinction and its consequent ethical decisionism through this temporalized evocation of the Question of Being, stirring us to resolve and authenticity as we seek to return to the destiny of our people, does indeed avoid the pitfalls of relativism and of a "war of world-views" is, of course, highly questionable. As I suggested in Chapter 4, one might object that it avoided the fact/value distinction only through the total historicization of reason. But it at least provided a way of encountering the fact/value distinction and the problems it poses in a radically different way from that of neo-Kantianism, by suggesting an underlying pre-rational communality only on the basis of which could one assert such a premise in the first place, which, in its dichotomy between existence and rationality, was metaphysical dualism *par excellence*.

But Heidegger's fundamental ontology is the last gasp of the Philosophy of Freedom in its fully developed form. No one aims for this kind of comprehensiveness again. In the twentieth century, it was no longer considered possible to give an all-embracing historicist account of the whole, not only because of the fact/value distinction but because, in light of the rise of totalitarian political systems, it was believed that attempts to promulgate a theory of everything such as Hegel's "Absolute Knowledge" of history and Marx's "scientific socialism" fed dangerous monistic claims such as the "unity of theory and practice" in Marxism-Leninism, while elements of Nietzsche and Heidegger, as we know, were employed by the Nazis in their deification of the Third Reich. It was increasingly felt that we cannot and should not aim to recover or rearticulate Hegel's "Absolute Science of Spirit," one expression of which was Hegel's claim to have collapsed the distinction between subject and object in the dialectic – now considered tantamount by some to the submersion of individual freedom in the collective. All-encompassing theories such as that of Hegel were no longer considered possible epistemologically owing to Weber, and most certainly not desirable politically because of the totalitarian politics that often aped or invoked their monistic claims. This is where we can see a fundamental break between the Philosophy of Freedom and contemporary continental political thought come plainly into view. Heidegger is the last of the group who, like Hegel, Marx and Nietzsche, offered a complete and absolutely comprehensive teaching providing a unified account of life on every level – individual, communal, political, psychological, moral and aesthetic – within an overarching ontological framework claiming to possess the absolute truth about the whole (Spirit, scientific socialism, the Will to Power, the ontology of Being). After Heidegger, German historicism abandons these sweeping claims to a Platonic kind of breadth, depth and unity – claims for the Philosophy of Freedom that we first saw emerge explicitly with Hegel – maintaining that such an enterprise is neither possible nor desirable. Whereas to my mind it is conceivable to speak of Heidegger in the same breath as Plato or St. Augustine, regardless of whether one would actually place him on Plato's or St. Augustine's level, but simply because of the comprehensiveness of his teaching, twentieth-century political theorists abandon the enterprise altogether. Instead, they break off rich morsels of their predecessors' works and employ them to build their own frequently stimulating but intentionally self-limiting attempts at illuminating the reality of the human condition.

THE BREAKUP: HABERMAS, FOUCAULT AND GADAMER

Among the chief contemporary successors of the Philosophy of Freedom are critical theory, postmodernism and hermeneutics, represented here respectively by Habermas, Foucault and Gadamer. We will undertake a three-sided comparison of their standpoints to illustrate the fragmentation of the Philosophy of Freedom into the contemporary schools of continental political and moral thought. Broadly speaking, what we witness is the fragmentation of Hegel's historical dialectic of the Unity of Subject and Substance into competing dimensions of historical rationality, on the one hand, and existential spontaneity and self-origination, on the other. Habermas attempts to retain something of Hegelian rationality in the service of human emancipation, while Foucault embraces the sheer underlying dynamism and fluidity of historical change, more akin in this respect to Nietzsche. Gadamer attempts to find a kind of middle ground, preserving the richness and complexity of cultural experience while eschewing any Hegelian claim to absolute transcendental knowledge. My comparison of the three thinkers will be made in broad strokes. Readers interested in the nuances are encouraged to consult the Further Reading for the Conclusion.

In order to see how the Philosophy of Freedom began its fragmentation after Heidegger, it is useful to consider Habermas' early schema of the three cognitive interests. Like the thinkers we have considered in this book, Habermas had a profound awareness of the differences between ancient and modern theory and practice, and grounded his evaluation of modernity in the contrasting vision of the Greek polis, a continuing paradigm in European political theory. As he discusses it, the ancients equated knowledge primarily with prudent statecraft and the formation of a virtuous civic character through education and philosophically guided rhetoric. By contrast, the moderns tend overwhelmingly to equate knowledge with the technical, the utilitarian and the economically productive. According to Habermas, we too often try to solve nontechnical problems of alienation and injustice by technical means, which often prompts a flight by the dissatisfied or disenchanted from the norms of civil society.

Marxist socialism is not the answer, according to Habermas, because it, too, succumbed to a scientism and positivism that confused human knowledge with technical rationality and thereby contributed to its own perversion by Leninism. Habermas encourages the rescue of the humanist side of the early Marx, which entertained a much richer understanding of human alienation than his later economistic emphasis. An aid in this process could be Hegel's "shapes of consciousness." Habermas wants to rehabilitate Hegel as a diagnostician of moral experience by freeing these shapes from the overarching teleological monism of Hegel's full-blown theory of historical progress, so that they might emerge on their own as striking examples of individual moral tableaux, like Stoicism or the Unhappy Consciousness, combining elements of psychology, thought and action in a series of discrete historical pictures.

Habermas tries to reconcile these competing humanistic and economic strains in his schema of the three cognitive interests. The technical interest comprehends the realm of modern empirical science and economic productivity. It concedes the necessity that the exercise of our freedom requires a wherewithal of economic security and freedom from want; that it cannot be a purely aspirational ideal like Kantianism which rigorously sets aside the claims of economic self-interest – a view with which Hegel and Marx would both be at home. The second of the trio is the practical interest. This is the realm of the hermeneutical and interpretive, of historical tradition, humanism and liberal education, enabling us to explore our identities either as individuals or as communities. In this way, utilitarian self-interest is balanced by spiritual self-cultivation.

But Habermas is not satisfied with such an equipoise between the necessities of modern economic individualism and the inner richness and shared experience of education and aesthetic pleasure, the balance favored, as we saw earlier, by Schiller. The third interest – the emancipatory – reveals the sense in which

Habermas cleaves to the more aggressive and politically dynamic side of the Philosophy of Freedom, including Hegel and Marx. For its aim is the critique of the status quo led by the social sciences and the acquisition of power through this critique to expose its deficiencies and improve it. The overarching aim of the three interests is to promote "communicative rationality," a situation of free and undistorted public speech, consensual norms, mutual understanding and collective deliberation – all common motifs, in my view, from the Hegelian search for intersubjectivity.

Indeed, the three cognitive interests taken together might well remind us of Hegel's dialectic of Spirit expressed through the concept of the Unity of Subject and Substance: We pursue satisfaction progressively by exercising our freedom of will and thought, transforming nature to create prosperity so that people can flourish both as citizens and as individuals in political societies that promote rational deliberation and cultural self-development. A skeptic might even say that Habermas' three cognitive interests are suspiciously close to a "triad," that preference for trios so widespread, as both Kant and Schiller observed, among philosophers. The "ideal speech situation" also bears a resemblance to Kant's categorical imperative, an aspirational ideal that Habermas contextualizes through a recognition of our material needs and our hermeneutical and psychological complexities, not unlike Hegel's own recognition of the validity of Kantian "morality" and its drive for a disinterested purity of intention while situating it within the mediating context of communal custom and tradition (*Sittlichkeit*) and the modern pursuit of prosperity. There is a sense, then, in which Habermas takes Hegel's dialectic of Spirit and divides it into three distinct but related segments.

How distinct? Habermas is insistent that his three cognitive interests do *not* constitute a unified dialectic like that of Hegel, that they are not a Hegelian triad or "Ladder to the Absolute." He maintains that the three interests do not interact as a dialectical synthesis. Although they do work together, each has its own "quasi-transcendental" status. Not surprisingly, even friendly interpreters wonder whether the term "quasi-transcendental" does not allow Habermas to have his epistemological cake and eat it. But the important thing is that Habermas clearly rejects Hegel's view of a single, unilinear outcome to the progress of history. The ideal speech situation is incomplete and open-ended – "wisdom" and "the truth" are never "actualized" at the end of history, as Hegel claims in the *Phenomenology of Spirit* about the modern present. More akin in this respect to Kant's categorical imperative, Habermas' ideal speech situation is a formal or procedural ethic: It does not endorse or prescribe a specific set of social or institutional political policies, a concrete set of socioeconomic conditions, but limits itself to establishing canons of deliberative rationality by which such outcomes might be legitimately reached. In Habermas' view, such a totalizing philosophical claim as that of the Hegelian progress of history – which, as we saw, according to Hegel literally embodies "the self-actualization of God" – can, intentionally or unintentionally, lead to dangerous political claims, engendering the same tendencies in Marxism and culminating in the divinization of the state dictatorship. This is why Habermas attempted to combine discursive coherence with practical pluralism. The "quasi-transcendental" status of the three cognitive interests enables us to view them as partly embedded in historical existence, partly able to stand outside of it in the pursuit of greater freedom and enlightenment. In practice, it amounted to a politically moderate social-democratic stance.

If we can view Habermas' contribution to critical theory as attempting to salvage what can be usefully taken away from Hegel, Kant and Marx without succumbing to their totalizing claims, postmodernism can be understood as the radicalization of Nietzsche's and Heidegger's protests against the rationality of Hegelianism, embracing the evocation of life as sheer self-origination and the upsurge of power and strife. These contending positions are visible in what we can conjecture would have been the views that Habermas and Foucault entertained about one another's respective theoretical stances. In this encounter, we witness what we can term the uncoupling of the rational and irrational dimensions of the Philosophy of Freedom; the uncoupling of a historical dialectic from the underlying ontological premise of sheer self-origination. Habermas' articulation of the three cognitive interests arose from his concern that the modern tendency to assimilate reason to the technical mode of rationality alone – to utility – can spark a dangerous counterreaction of "irrational decisionism," the revolutionary pursuit of liberation from modern society and its institutions with no rational constraints whatever, a position arguably already lurking in Weber. Habermas identified irrational decisionism with terrorist and authoritarian movements of the far Left and Right. I think we can infer that he would have identified it philosophically with Foucault. Although there was no actual debate between them, one was conducted by their respective followers, and those partial to Foucault tended to assume that Habermas would have made such a critique.

Foucault regards society as a field of power centers. Doctrines of legitimacy like those of the social contact school or the Philosophy of Right are merely a tool by which the dominating power coerces the subordinate power of the others. He urges the growth of dissenting powers to counteract the oppressors' monopoly on power. But in the absence of binding canons of political rationality and ethics to adjudicate the conflict, one might ask, why does that not simply lead to more oppression, this time by the new constellation of dominant powers? (One is put in mind of Hegel's diagnosis of the Jacobin power struggle as constantly attempting to erect a dominant authority over the revolution and then having it overthrown and replaced by another dominant authority.) Based on his own principles of "communicative rationality," I think Habermas would have concluded that Foucault's postmodernism supplies no structure for public debate and the emergence of consensual norms from currently conflicting groups.

Foucault's riposte would likely be that Habermas remains entirely *too much* in the grip of Hegelian and Kantian rationalism; that, despite his claims to have resisted the monism of the Philosophy of Freedom's claims to the absolute truth, he is an authoritarian rationalist and an apologist for the entrenched capitalist, hegemonic and patriarchal status quo. We see vividly here how the rational and irrational polarities of the Philosophy of Freedom split apart into Habermas' attempt to preserve elements of Hegel's dialectic and Kantian ethics, on the one hand, and Foucault's espousal of unmitigated revolutionary spontaneity, on the other. Put another way, our attention is drawn to the neo-Nietzschean emphasis of Foucault in contrast with the neo-Kantian dimension of Habermas.

The other corner of the debate among the remaining fragments of the Philosophy of Freedom is Habermas' engagement with Hans-Georg Gadamer, credited as one of the founders of the hermeneutical school of interpretation. Whereas Habermas' possible critique of Foucault remains a matter of inference or conjecture, Gadamer's and Habermas' disagreements are a matter of record. Gadamer entertains no explicit political project in his writings, not even general principles of legitimacy. Instead, he stresses the need for cultural continuity through education and the transmission of traditions of liberal learning and aesthetic taste to cushion us against the aridity of modern materialism and reductionist utilitarianism, opening up havens of reflection within the prevailing horizon of technology. In a sense, he is the reincarnation of Schiller, relying on a renaissance of liberal education to offset the modern emphasis on economic self-interest while avoiding any revolutionary political crusades (which he had witnessed firsthand under the Third Reich). He wrote brilliant studies of both the classical philosophers and of the Philosophy of Freedom, as well as literary studies.

Gadamer's hermeneutics took from Heidegger the notion that we are always already engaged with the past and with past texts and art, a reciprocal engagement in which both sides of the interaction are transformed. Because, as Heidegger had argued, speech is Being's way of revealing itself, whatever dimension of Being speech reveals, the rest of Being withdraws, meaning that the work of art is both a revealing and a concealing. This is true not only of texts, but of the plastic arts. As we saw in *The Origin of the Artwork* as supplemented by Scully, the semi-concealed presence of the god in the inner sanctuary of the temple visible through the outer columns reveals the simultaneous hiddenness and unhiddenness of Being, the opening up through the temple of the juncture of earth and world. When this insight is transferred to the realm of literature, the hermeneuticist must therefore pay attention not only to what the words make clear, but more importantly to what the words do not make clear, what they leave silent – through that aporia, we experience the silent call of Being.

Gadamer derived from this Heideggerian insight his hermeneutic of the "fusion of horizons," which, simply stated, maintains that the contradictions among the great works of the tradition are precisely what increases our understanding of them, and that as moderns we are in some ways in a better position to understand those works than was possible in their own era through the concerns we bring to them in the present. It follows from this that Gadamer did not believe it was possible to understand the author as he understood himself. For example, as he argues in *Truth and Method*, if we were to find in reading Aristotle that he was "more correct" than "the corresponding modern theories," then would we not have to conclude that "Aristotle could not understand himself in the way that we can understand him" since he was not conscious of "the modern theories"? More generally, according to the hermeneutic of the fusion of horizons, the very conclusion that ancient thought is superior to modern thought transforms the meaning of ancient thought itself.

In addition to Heidegger's influence on Gadamer, I see a direct connection between his notion of the fusion of horizons and Hegel's conception of education as "recollection," which we discussed in Chapter 2. Hegel, too, maintains that our understanding of past culture is transformed by the concerns we bring to it, and we ourselves are transformed by that reciprocal interaction: it is a dialectical and maieutic interaction, the core of *Bildung*. The irreconcilability of these past perspectives need not concern us – on the contrary, they are what infuses liberal education with its liberating indeterminacy, which means it can never be reduced to the ingestion of rote learning. The dialogue among the Great Books is always open, always mutable – there is no settled textbook account of who was right and who was wrong. "Nothing vanishes in Spirit," as Hegel put it; that is, all perspectives are preserved. For instance, when we think through the irreconcilable contradictions between what Sophocles and Kant mean by morality, we will be deepened by both. For we will recognize from our own experience of the world that we have a moral responsibility to choose right actions over wrong actions guided by reason – vindicating Kant – while realizing at the same time that people's capacity for reasonable choice is sometimes overwhelmed by totally undeserved misfortune, ranging from catastrophic weather to terminal disease, or even by an inner psychological turmoil which can rule our actions – vindicating Sophocles. Human existence is intertwined with ethical choice and insurmountable fate.

This stance of reciprocal interaction toward our cultural inheritance, characteristic of Gadamer and Hegel, I hasten to add, does not entitle one to simply make up the meaning of the core texts or works of art by avoiding a close reading. Much less does it elevate the hermeneuticist as the truly creative partner in the interaction, surpassing in his originality as a critic the canonical authors he is interpreting – a baseless pretension. I would liken hermeneutics to taking a light into a vast cave. Wherever you shine that light, you will open up a hitherto invisible pathway, one among a limitless number. But if you attempt to walk into the cave unguided by that light, you will bump into the immovable stone. The work of thought or art can be opened up in limitless ways depending on where we shine the interpretive light, guided by our own concerns. But the work still possesses an objective meaning, one whose full range may never come to light. And not all ontological premises, as we have seen in this book, can be reconciled – there is no way of embracing both the Idea of the Good *and* the Will to Power as one's guide to understanding the whole. Education comes from seeking to understand, and living within, the tension between these fundamental alternatives.

Habermas' response to Gadamer's theory of hermeneutics is to position himself between Gadamer and what I have conjectured would have been his critique of Foucault. In effect, he argues that if Foucault's kind of postmodernism can lead to potentially irrational decisionism and revolutionary terrorism, Gadamer's hermeneutics lead to an altogether *too* complacent, Panglossian and apolitical tolerance for existing injustices, the retreat to an elitist Isles of the Blessed through the study of the Great Books. In other words, Habermas tries to position himself between Foucault and Gadamer by incorporating what for Gadamer was the comparatively unpolitical sphere of hermeneutics – it is contained within one of Habermas' three cognitive interests – while maintaining Hegel's and Marx's interest in political power and justice and Kant's interest in everyone's active pursuit of autonomy, but not at the cost of revolutionary violence. Again, readers interested in further details of this three-cornered debate will find them in Further Reading.

THE LINGERING VISION OF THE ANCIENT GREEKS

The Philosophy of Freedom's persistent motif of looking back to the ancient Greeks as benchmarks for criticizing modernity and envisioning the future continues among the three thinkers just discussed, and like their predecessors they envision that Greek heritage differently depending on their expectations for the present. Habermas leans toward Aristotle and his espousal of prudent statecraft; Foucault embraces the Dionysian and consummately imprudent dimension of ancient Greek hedonism; Gadamer embraces Plato's works as literary masterpieces and Aristotelian theoria as a divine ascent. This continuing invocation of the ancients as a benchmark for understanding the modern age and its deficiencies remained the hallmark of a number of influential scholars of political theory including students of Heidegger such as Arendt and Strauss and those influenced by him including Grant and Voegelin. Strikingly, however, they depart from Heidegger's argument that modernity was a continuous evolution out of ancient metaphysics into global technology and hold instead that there was a fundamental and decisive paradigm shift between ancients and moderns. Strauss locates this shift in the political philosophy of Machiavelli, originator of the project for the conquest of nature and the pursuit of self-interest by both princes and peoples, viewing the low but solid ground of "the natural desire to acquire" as being preferable to the "imagined republics" of the classical and Christian writers. Arendt focuses on Hobbes' inversion of Aristotle's view of the distinction between the public life of the polis and the private realm of the oikos, the household, including economic wellbeing. Whereas Aristotle insisted that the city must circumscribe the household, elevating the good life of civic virtue over the mere life of economic productivity, Hobbes reverses this relationship, in effect assimilating the meaning of statecraft and political reason to the promotion of individual material wellbeing that had been the "economic" realm of the household. (The contrast between Arendt and Heidegger on the origin of modernity is complicated by the fact that she does share Heidegger's view of Plato's metaphysics as productionist, hence an antecedent of modern technology, while endorsing Aristotle as the philosopher of civic life in the agora.) Gadamer, too, viewed the shift from the ancients to the moderns to be a fundamental one. While he encouraged a fusion of horizons through the interpretation of both ancient and modern thought, the energizing nerve of that fusion was precisely the fact that they were fundamentally at odds with each other and could not be homogenized in a tepid syncretism. Moreover, in contrast with Heidegger's unvarnished loathing of modern liberal democracy and belief that it was "metaphysically the same" as Stalinism, among these successors to Heidegger, we encounter varying degrees of enthusiasm for it, ranging from Strauss' view that it was the best available alternative to Voegelin's acknowledgement that it was preferable to totalitarianism but who nevertheless detested its materialistic basis, while we also encounter a partiality to certain aspects of Heidegger's identification of modernity with technology, most notably in George Grant.

These legatees of Heidegger's influence also rejected Heidegger's call in *Being and Time* for the "destruction of metaphysics," meaning to say the uprooting of the entire philosophy and culture of the West stretching back to Plato on the grounds that it was hopelessly vitiated and undermined by the metaphysical agenda now working itself out as technology. Since, according to Heidegger, only the ancient pre-Platonic Greeks and modern man in his encounter with global technology had been offered authentic paths to Being, virtually everything in between the pre-Platonic Greeks and our own age had contributed only to our increasing alienation. For his successors, by contrast, there are redemptive possibilities in the entire history of philosophy, art and literature, including its modern forms, as avenues to different substantive perspectives on the meaning of the good life. Moreover, even if they found the ancients to be on the whole a preferable path to the moderns, they found in certain modern thinkers, artists and statesmen a refuge from modernity's own excesses. But further than these exercises in hermeneutical enrichment so as to offer relief from modern materialistic and technocratic alienation Heidegger's successors cannot venture. Because the modern account of nature as matter in motion continued to hold against the cosmologies of Plato and the ancients, while the possibility of an all-encompassing historicist account of the whole has burned out with Heidegger, they are not able to mount their own attempts to account for human nature within the order of the whole but must remain content with historical studies that further contribute to our understanding of what modernity is and how it attempted to repudiate the ancients.

The dilemma is captured by Strauss in a way that is probably representative of most of the contemporary political theorists we have discussed. In *Natural Right and History*, he distinguishes between the "mechanical" (modern) and "teleological (classical) conception of the universe." Now that the mechanical conception has prevailed, two unsatisfactory alternatives open up. One is that the nonteleological conception of the universe be paralleled by a nonteleological conception of human life. For example, Hobbes argues that human nature is a system of matter in motion within the larger system of matter in motion comprising nature altogether. But this results, according to Strauss, in an "inadequate account of human ends" by reducing them to "desires or impulses." The other path is a characteristically modern dualism between a non-teleological natural science and the attempt to retain a teleological science of man, undertaken, for example, by contemporary Thomism. But this constitutes a break with Aristotle and with Thomas as well, for whom the teleological account of man mirrored the teleological conception of the universe. "Present-day social science," Strauss continues, rejects natural right "in the name of History and in the name of the distinction between Facts and Values."

In this context, by "History" Strauss means the ordinary vulgar and conventional view that regards all ideas and opinions as the products of their time – for example, that modern natural right was the product of social and market forces in seventeenth-century England – and simply leaves it at that. I would add to Strauss' argument the observation that the absence of a fully historicist *and* teleological account of the whole, such as that of Hegel, whatever its drawbacks may have transpired to be, very much intensified the victory of the Fact/Value distinction as the only permissible avenue on human existence. As I have argued here, the Fact/Value distinction brings this about inasmuch as "values" quickly dissolve into sets of historical conventions in which ideas are the products of existential decisionism, battling it out as conflicting worldviews. In other words, the Fact/Value distinction itself militates toward radical historicism. With no solution in sight for restoring a teleological approach to the study of both nature and man, Strauss concludes: "The fundamental dilemma, in whose grip we are, is caused by the victory of modern natural science. An adequate solution to the problem of natural right cannot be found before this basic problem has been solved." Cannot be found, in other words, until someone – not Strauss himself – can refute the modern mechanistic and nonteleological conception of nature. In the meantime, all we can do is examine "the human things" as they emerge within the classical horizon while eschewing any expectation of restoring the larger cosmology in which it they had their place.

A final word about postmodernism. It has many meanings, but for political theory it fundamentally means the abandonment of the Westphalian nation-state as the most reliable and successful vehicle for achieving modern freedom both for individuals and for society as a whole. While Habermas displayed the internationalist and EU leanings of a contemporary European social democrat, he did not abandon this claim, stressing not only the liabilities but the achievements of the nation-state. To me this was symptomatic of how, regardless of his skepticism toward the grand syntheses propounded by his nineteenth-century predecessors, Habermas kept one foot in the rationalist dimension of the Hegelian Philosophy of Freedom and the articulation of principles of political legitimacy, as well in Hegelianism's political moderation and its distrust of revolutionary ardor. By contrast, Jacques Derrida, another leading light of the postmodernist school, called for a new global civil society of the marginalized and dispossessed "beyond the sovereignty of the state," growing up alongside global capitalism and eventually displacing it, a world beyond politics and its hegemonic and patriarchal tools of oppression. This call signals a recrudescence and reconfiguration of Marx's forecast of the growth of the global proletariat and a coming world society accompanied by the withering away of the state, as well as the Leninist dynamic of "the worse, the better," whereby out of the oppressive stranglehold of global capitalism itself at its zenith the new world of complete equality and social justice without private property will emerge.

With this we begin to move beyond the academy into the wider world of political activism. But before discussing it further, I want to round out my assessment of the Philosophy of Freedom's contemporary impact by amplifying my earlier comments on its importance for religious thinking and theology, especially as it relates to Heidegger.

HISTORY AND REVELATION

We can readily establish Heidegger's impact on modern Jewish theology through the thought of Emil Fackenheim, Martin Buber and (at least indirectly) Gershom Scholem. While appalled by Heidegger's Nazism and his refusal to recant or apologize for it, they were intrigued by his critique of modern rationalism both in its early modern and later historicist renditions. Believing that the claims to universal rationality of the philosophies of Kant and Hegel contributed to the assimilation of Judaism by the modern state, they thought that by exploding these claims, the original tension between reason and revelation would reemerge with greater vigor. If modern reason could not satisfy the claims of faith, if indeed, despite its advocacy in principle of universal religious tolerance, modern reason militated in practice toward the demand that it was the Jews who must assimilate their distinctive identity to the Christian or secular majority, then Heideggerian existentialism might be the answer. They saw in Heidegger's call for the repudiation of the arid abstractness and empty universalism of Enlightenment reasoning, its reduction of authentic faith to individual self-interest and economic utility, precisely this battle cry against assimilationism. Moreover, Fackenheim was particularly attracted to Heidegger's notion of the autonomy of distinct, historically rooted peoples, as against the cosmopolitan claims of liberalism, because he thought it might show the path to a distinctly Jewish sense of peoplehood that would resist assimilation and secularization.

Heidegger's argument that our capacity to employ propositional and causal reasoning to make sense of our world was rooted in much deeper, more primordial and prerational existential experiences of mood, anxiety and silent wonder, that poetic revelation was arguably a deeper source of insight into life's mysteries than philosophy, signified to Fackenheim (as we observed in Chapter 4) nothing less than the possibility that it constituted the retroactive "Judaization of the entire history of Western philosophy." With his evocation of the silent call of Being as opposed to the "lust of the eyes" of metaphysical reasoning bewitched by "the looks of the world" (distinctly Augustinian tropes), Heidegger, according to Fackenheim, sides with Moses against Plato: "[W]hereas ever since Plato, philosophers 'see,' ever since Moses, Jews 'hear.'" Although, as I observed earlier, there is no direct evidence for Heidegger's influence on Scholem, one can say that Heidegger's prerational ontology of existence paralleled Scholem's efforts to restore Jewish mysticism and kabbalah in order to combat what he regarded as the arid theological rationalism of Maimonides and Spinoza, whose espousal of secular pluralism arguably contributed to the assimilationist drive. As we observed in Chapter 4, this preference for mystical experience over rational theology dovetailed with Heidegger's own preference for St. Augustine and Luther, who plumbed the existential depths of pristine Christian openness to the awesome mystery of the divine, over the hyper-rationalism and metaphysical systematics of St. Thomas.

Although we have highlighted Heidegger's impact on Jewish theology as an illuminating route into his existentialism and its impact, we should add that his influence on Christian thinking was no less significant, evidenced by Protestant theologian Paul Tillich's call to listen to the "God above God," beyond the routinization of church doctrine and worship, akin to Heidegger's evocation of our openness to the Call of Being beyond the encrustation of metaphysical reasoning (including traditional theology) and the inauthentic everyday world. We should also note Catholic theologian Karl Rahner's deeply challenging attempt to map the inner experience of Christian faith onto Heidegger's existential analytic of Dasein and freedom toward death.

Speaking more broadly, Heidegger's notion of peoplehood is sometimes likened to a variation of Romantic nationalism, which began to take root in Central and Eastern Europe in the second half of the nineteenth century, not coincidentally at the same time as the emergence of Zionism and the longing for a Jewish homeland. Both were symptomatic of the decline of faith in Enlightenment rationalism and the modern nation-state. It is not a coincidence that the melody of the Israeli national anthem the Hatikvah is almost identical to that of the Czech nationalist anthem, the Moldau – both versions originated in a Central European folk song. Fackenheim was very attracted to Strauss' project of restoring classical political thought, but at the end of the day, his attraction to Heidegger's existentialism proved stronger and, he believed, more compatible with his Zionism. Strauss remained more ambivalent than the modern Jewish existentialist-tinged theologians we have discussed regarding the debate between reason and revelation. Although a self-identifying Jew and supporter of the state of Israel, he could never go all the way over to Jerusalem, or even express the wish that he could do so or lament that he could not. He wanted Athens too, or maybe more, which connects us back to his riposte to Heideggerian existentialism discussed earlier: that nothing justified Heidegger in identifying anxiety over the prospect of our mortality as self-evidently the central human experience as opposed to love of the immortal truth.

THE REVOLUTION CONTINUES: THE PHILOSOPHY OF FREEDOM AND THE POLITICAL WORLD

Now let us turn to the more political and real-life side of the contemporary legacy of the Philosophy of Freedom. One arc we observed in its unfolding throughout this book was the decline of the legitimacy of the nation-state (for Hegel the locus for modern freedom) in favor of the proletariat (Marx) or the people (Nietzsche in the qualified sense already discussed in Chapter 3, and Heidegger before the end of World War II). This arc is paralleled by a decline in the Hegelian belief in the benevolent cumulative progress of history and the rise of increasingly millenarian and illiberal expectations for the future (in varying but related ways characteristic of Marx, Nietzsche and Heidegger).

The first practical consequence of this pattern emerges from the Left-Hegelian school of Feurbach and Marx and its development by Lukacs and Kojeve, accompanied by the erstwhile Marxist theorist and real-life putschist Lenin. Partly encouraged, as we saw in Chapter 2, by a reading of Marx's and Engel's own inconsistencies, Lenin changed the meaning of socialism from a largely peaceable evolution out of late capitalism into the seizure of power in a coup d'état in a country that had skipped the bourgeois stage of socioeconomic evolution, and then set about to create the productive capacities of capitalism from above, through rapid industrialization and collectivization, while simultaneously *preventing* the emergence of private property rights, surplus value and bourgeois profit. This was accomplished through forced collectivization and the extermination of the kulaks or "rich peasants," an act of utopian genocide comparable to the Nazi Holocaust. Lenin, fully aware of the fact that the socioeconomic conditions of the bourgeois phase of history regarded by Marx in his lucid intervals as indispensable for the transition to socialism were entirely absent from Russia, believed that the Bolsheviks' seizure of power in the name of socialism would act as a beacon of inspiration for sparking a true proletarian revolution in industrialized Europe, which would then come to the fraternal assistance of Russia in helping it achieve complete economic modernization. This never happened, so Lenin's successor Stalin proclaimed the existence of "socialism in one country," Russia.

Lenin also encouraged the development of national liberation movements in the countries colonialized by the Western powers, something in which Marx, given his preoccupation with a world revolution and the withering away of the state, showed little interest. This helped to inspire the Marxism-Leninism of Mao and Ho Chi Minh, though it should be stressed that Lenin never regarded encouraging nationalist rebellions against colonialism as anything more than a tactic to help bring about a world socialist order led by the Soviet Union. Internally, such "chauvinist" movements within the Soviet Union and Warsaw Pact were ruthlessly suppressed, and relations between Soviet leaders from Stalin onward with their third-world ideological allies like Mao remained turbulent.

The second practical political consequence of the twentieth-century legacy of the Philosophy of Freedom was the cross-fertilization between postwar neo-Marxism and Heideggerian political existentialism. This merger had several features. Under the influence of Heidegger's existential analytic of everyday life, our alienation from modern bourgeois capitalist society is expanded in meaning beyond the socioeconomic dimension stressed by orthodox Marxism to include psychological, spiritual, erotic and aesthetic varieties of alienation, nothing less than what Heidegger termed our "alienation from Being" as such. The expansion of the meaning of alienation coincided with the disappearance of the industrial proletariat in Europe (or, rather, its steady bourgeoisification). It signified the replacement of the Marxist proletariat as the empirically demonstrable vehicle for a socialist revolution with a counterculture of the spiritually disaffected from all strata of society – students, artists, academics, writers, entertainment celebrities, rock stars, mordantly summarized by Kolakowski as "Marxism without a proletariat." This cultural revolution included the rise of Marxist humanism, which stressed (in my view accurately) that the early Marx's understanding of alienation was less about economic determinism and more about the alienation of our full range of creative powers, including the aesthetic. The new Marxist hybrid came to life in the May 1968 "revolution" in Paris of disaffected graduate students and professors and through the New Left in the United States, which was always more of an adversarial counterculture than a political revolution – more Jefferson Airplane than Fidel Castro. Its major academic pied piper was Herbert Marcuse, a once-solid scholar whose vision of the coming cultural revolution culminated in "polymorphous perversity."

A third facet of the Philosophy of Freedom's legacy to real-life political activism was Heidegger's specific influence on Frantz Fanon's theory of third-world socialism, in which the international proletariat is replaced with the destiny of peoples, and the international struggle between proletariat and bourgeoisie is replaced by the struggle of colonialized peoples against the capitalist powers led by the United States. In some versions of third-world socialism, the Soviet model of socialism is also rejected as too materialistic and lacking in revolutionary élan – hence Mao's contemptuous dismissal of

Krushchev's attempts to introduce some meager consumer pleasures into the Soviet economy as "goulash socialism." We can detect another Heideggerian strain in Fanon's theory, namely Heidegger's argument that a people's received opinions about its past traditions may just be an officially promulgated doctrine of conformity meant to condition the people to accept the status quo and to believe that a radical return to the people's authentic underlying destiny was not possible; in other words, that much of what passed for German tradition was a prop for the capitalist status quo or for reactionaries. Similarly, Fanon maintained that what colonialized peoples often mistook for their authentic traditions were "masks" that they had been forced to wear by the colonial power so as to reconcile them to its domination. Finally, Fanon is sometimes taken to be arguing that the violence of revolution is cathartic, that it purges one's latent bourgeois or colonialized instincts, and is not merely a means to an end. Here one can detect echoes of both Marx (when he is in his "seize the day," proto-Leninist mode) and Heidegger, who insists that all great political achievements, like all great events in Being, are violent.

We can throw into the mix of how the Philosophy of Freedom and its culmination or at least its final full-blown installment in Heidegger affected political and social practice by briefly noting Sartre, who, as we discussed in Chapter 4, was heavily reliant on Heidegger's existentialism while very critical of its collectivization of authentic commitment. Lukacs is also of interest: He infused the notion of the Vanguard Party of the Communist state developed by Lenin with the idea that they were world-builders, not mere economic planners; that they embodied Nietzsche's Will to Power and Heidegger's notion of a collective resolve against Being in order to wrest our destiny from that encounter. Interestingly, one of the Bolsheviks' antecedents in Russia had been a Nietzschean sect called the God-builders. Lenin himself was often characterized as attributing this godlike power of the Superman to the Party and especially to his own leadership, a source of criticism from his detractors and of admiration from his comrades such as Pyatakov. Lenin himself, however, in a stupefying illustration of unknowing or willful self-deception, always maintained that he was faithful to Marx's teaching about the laws of "scientific socialism" and the need for mature socioeconomic development before socialism could be successfully implemented, and he criticized Lukacs for what he saw as his deviationism, although I would argue that Lukacs was the true philosophical distillation of Leninism itself and its revolutionary Prometheanism.

I will dwell briefly on Alexandre Kojeve, whose Left-Hegelian reading of Hegel was influential in North America in part because of his debate with Leo Strauss regarding the meaning of modern tyranny, and now that interest in Strauss is growing in Europe, a new generation is thinking about Kojeve. I have argued elsewhere why I believe that Strauss did not agree with Kojeve's interpretation of Hegel apart from assuming it to be true for the sake of argument in a single work, *On Tyranny*, where he referred to it pointedly as "Kojeve's Hegel." I will not repeat that argument here, but I will stress some important differences between Kojeve's transformation of Hegel and Hegel's own teaching that help to illuminate the latter. I could not address Kojeve at length following my discussion of Marx because, although his interpretation of Hegel is massively Marxist-inspired, it contains a dimension of Heidegger's ontology that is less evident, but which enables Kojeve to create a new hybrid version of Hegel's historicism.

The key to understanding how Kojeve's interpretation of Hegel departs from the original is the centrality that he assigns to the Master–Slave dialectic, identifying it as the origin of man's negation and transformation of nature in the pursuit of freedom. In reality, as we observed in Chapter Two, that encounter occupies a brief few pages well along into the *Phenomenology of Spirit*, is not identified by Hegel as being centrally important, and is arguably no more than, if as important as, the Unhappy Consciousness with which this section of the book ends. Indeed, in my view the internalization of the Master–Slave encounter within the Unhappy Consciousness as the inner calling from God (the true Lord) to his servant man is for Hegel a deepening and sublimation of self-consciousness that transcends the merely outward struggle between Master and Slave.

Moreover, as we saw in Chapter 2, this whole sequence of "shapes" – Master, Slave, Stoic, Skeptic, Unhappy Consciousness – is presented by Hegel at this stage in the *Phenomenology of Spirit* as still largely from within the viewpoint of "consciousness," in other words from the perspective of the modern Cartesian self that assumes the priority of the individual. After the full sweep of history has been introduced with the appearance of Spirit roughly halfway through the book, Hegel takes us back through the same sequence of shapes, but now within the broader context of the ancient *polis*, and culminating in the late Roman Empire. As we saw, Hegel is explicit that this second account of the sequence is the fuller one, because the opposed selves of the earlier sequence are now thoroughly contextualized within the realm of the political community and customary ethical being (*Sittlichkeit*): "Earlier we saw the Stoical independence of pure thought pass through Scepticism and find its truth in the Unhappy Consciousness ... If this knowledge appeared then merely as the one-sided view of consciousness as consciousness, here the *actual* truth of that view has become apparent" [483]. In Hegel's cumulative presentation, the "Master" morality, properly considered, was never literally reducible to an individual self, but emerged as a communal historical force from ancient Greek religion and society.

Kojeve argues that, for Hegel, history progresses through the Slave, but this is by no means clear in Hegel's works. In the *Phenomenology of Spirit*, the first historical appearance of "freedom" – as opposed to the mere "independence" of the Master – comes not with the Slave, but with Stoicism, in many ways an aristocratic morality. Finally, for Hegel, modern man is not, as Kojeve argues, simply a synthesis of Master and Slave as the Bourgeois, but of the *entire* "wealth of shapes" including Master, Slave, Stoic, Skeptic and Unhappy

Consciousness, an amalgam that is crystallized in the nineteenth-century cultural battle between Science and Romanticism, or between Kant (the internalization of Jacobinism) and Goethe or Schiller (the Beautiful Soul) – a battle that will, once sublimated within Spirit, usher in the reappearance of God in History in a new era of mutual forgiveness. Of course, in fairness to Kojeve, he never claimed to interpret Hegel as Hegel interpreted himself, but is propounding a new reading for altered historical conditions that might arguably make Hegel's philosophy more consistent with itself, by banishing the mystification of Spirit and replacing it with the historical action of man. That is a plausible rereading, but clearly a Left-Hegelian or Marxist one.

Kojeve writes as if man is the "nihilator" in history, rather than Spirit, Hegel's name for the whole, which contains within itself, as "the labor of the negative," the transformative and destructive energy of historical creation actualized through its human avatars. Kojeve, we might say, combines the reductionist materialism of Marx with the historical and cultural breadth of Hegel. He sees sheer "nothingness" as the continuing historical essence of man, whereas for Hegel, history's accumulated "wealth of shapes" has enriched us teleologically through *Bildung*. Kojeve in effect borrows the "nothingness" of Heidegger's concept of Dasein, the only being, as we saw in Chapter 4, directly touched by the innermost character of all Being: that it is not any fixed thing, it "is" nothing or sheer finitude. But whereas Heidegger, as we observed, employed this concept to argue that, in its bottomless nothingness, Dasein could never be "filled up" by a positive doctrine of the progress of history like that of Hegel, Kojeve maintains that this innermost nothingness is the very engine of historical progress itself.

For Kojeve, the progress of history is purely anthropocentric, borrowing, as I have suggested, the nothingness of Dasein from Heidegger but uprooting it from any larger connection with Being (or with Hegelian Spirit). For Heidegger, the "notness" (*Nichtigkeit*) of Dasein is where Being as such touches human existence and radiates through it into a historical "clearing" through the reciprocal encounter between Dasein and *Sein*. Kojeve, however, turns Dasein into nothing more than a human subject, filling his inner void through the outward and literal conquest of nature. In an analogous manner, Spirit in its indeterminateness was for Hegel the source of our capacity to negate nature in the pursuit of freedom. But as we saw, for Hegel, at bottom, the labor of the negative is not primarily *human* labor, but rather the subjective pole of Spirit (the unity of Subject and Substance), that is, "the Truth" about the whole that operates through its human avatars, progressively transforming the world as Spirit's *own* odyssey of self-actualization.

For Kojeve, in stark contrast, man *alone* negates the sheer inert fodder of nature. Kojeve identifies man with "self-consciousness," an individual human subject. It is man, initially the Slave, who creates history, art and culture, including "ideologies" like Hegelian Spirit itself that legitimize the bourgeois status quo. But for Hegel, Spirit alone is truly self-conscious, progressively so as history unfolds teleologically – at bottom, the self of which I as a human being am aware is the self-consciousness of Spirit operative through me. Whereas for Hegel, Spirit's longing for reconciliation (Substance) and the negation of nature (Subject) operate in tandem through man, bringing about both greater freedom and greater harmony as history evolves, for Kojeve, history is entirely an outward, positivistic, aggressive and uniquely human transformation. In fact, I would argue that Kojeve's closest philosophical cousin is not Hegel at all, but Fichte, the ultimate proponent of man's untrammeled will to conquer and reshape nature, with man having no intrinsic connection to nature itself, which is nothing more than "the material of our moral duty rendered sensuous." Hegel believed that his own ontology of the unity of Subject and Substance in Spirit had anticipated and headed off at the pass this voluntaristic extremism, which also fed the Jacobin tendency in modern politics to impose a rational pattern on human nature by direct action and revolutionary will, regardless of the constraints of precedent and tradition. As Fichte was to Jacobinism, so might we say Kojeve was to Stalinism.

Perhaps the most fundamental divergence between Kojeve's interpretation of Hegel and Hegel's own thought is over the status of revelation. We recall that in Hegel's formulation of the concept of Spirit in the Preface to the *Phenomenology of Spirit*, under the pole of "Subject" is located the modern project for the conquest of nature, modern science and political liberalism, culminating in Kant's ethic of individual moral autonomy. Under the pole of "Substance" is located the contrary longing for reconciliation, love, beauty, community and harmony between man and man and man and the world, characteristic of classical thought, but also including religious revelation, and culminating in Spinoza. The realms of Subject and Substance also crystallize respectively as "morality" (typified by Rousseau's General Will and Kant's Categorical Imperative) and communal or ethical being (*Sittlichkeit*), beginning with the chthonic and Olympian gods of the Greek polis. The conflict in Greek tragedy between the divine law of the gods and the human law of burgeoning philosophic rationality and universality is the first historical actualization of the interplay between Subject and Substance within the whole of Spirit. The divine law of the old hearth religion and "the community of the dead" is the welling up and evolution of "life" out of mere nature into the divine law, buttressing Strauss' criticism of Kojeve for failing to realize that by "life" Hegel meant much more than the modern understanding of nature as matter in motion – it is more akin to the life-world of Spinoza. The welling up of "life" as the oldest chthonic religion of the ancestors displays a continuous evolution from nature into civilization. For Kojeve, by contrast, the realm of the divine law and family life is nothing more than "biological" existence as an alien other pitted against the emergent rationalism of historical progress through the negation of nature. For Hegel, Spirit expresses itself *both* as the Divine Law and the Human Law. For Kojeve, reason, actualized as the negation of nature, is exclusively on the side of the latter.

As I argued in Chapter 2, there is no way of establishing with certainty what kind of believer Hegel was. But there is no evidence at all for Kojeve's characterization of his philosophy as atheistic. While Hegel's Christianity may have been a kind of deism or pantheism that was not in keeping with any traditional understanding of revelation, neither is it the case that, as Kojeve asserts, "according to Hegel – to use the Marxist terminology – Religion is only an ideological superstructure that is born and exists solely in relation to a *real* superstructure," that is, a mere ideological justification for the pursuit of power. Not only, as we earlier observed, is the Unhappy Consciousness arguably more important for human development than the Master/Slave encounter, but the *Phenomenology of Spirit* as a whole culminates in a genealogy of religion from the most distant past down to the present. The way forward, in other words, is the way back – "God manifested" in History. The Marxist reductionism of Kojeve's approach, reducing the realm of "life" to mere biological and physical stuff, is nowhere more evident than here.

One way of grasping the concept of Spirit, as I suggested earlier, is that into the life-world of Spinoza, emerging continuously out of nature toward the aspects of Godhead, and thus repudiating the dualism of Hobbes and Descartes, Hegel introduces the aggressive dimension of progressive historical transformation, the injection of "the labour of the negative" into Schelling's quietistic Spinoza-inspired "Absolute." Finally, whereas for Hegel history fulfills itself as an irreducible plurality of distinct nation-states with their variety of windows on the world through their diverse educational cultures, the "foaming forth" of the Spinozist Kingdom of Spirits in Schiller's *Ode to Joy* with which the *Phenomenology* upliftingly ends, Kojeve forecasts an Orwellian coming world society of pedestrian materialism and uniform psychological emptiness, the Universal Homogeneous State – a variation, we might say, of Heidegger's understanding of the unstoppable spread of global technology, but without regrets.

MORE RECENT HEIDEGGERIAN HYBRIDS

One of Heidegger's students, Hans Jonas, is credited with being among the first to articulate an environmentalist ethic codifying our "responsibility to nature." It was clearly influenced by Heidegger's assessment in *The Question Concerning Technology* of how technology's endless quest for "standing reserve" to be extracted from "challenging" Being threatened the devastation of the earth. Jonas' attempt to set forth a Green ethics, however, clearly departed from Heidegger's own strictures against the whole discourse of modern ethics and humanism as merely more subtle ways by which we arrogate our power over existence as "Lords of the Earth." According to Heidegger, by attempting to codify ethical behavior, we elevate the very metaphysical rationality that is the fuel for technology's subjugation of the planet itself. Jonas' insistence that an environmentalist ethic is possible is another example of a trend I discussed earlier – how those influenced by Heidegger took issue with some of the more draconian implications of his teaching, and stoutly rejected his claim that ethical and humanistic reflection were now hopeless, outmoded and self-vitiating enterprises.

On the other hand, the influence of environmentalist ethics originating with Jonas has certainly unfolded against the backdrop of the apocalyptic motif of the worse, the better – an amalgam, as we have observed, of Heidegger and Marx – because the warning that uncontrolled carbon emissions will rapidly and inevitably bring about the end of the world as we know it is promulgated in the hope that it will spark the needed transformation in human behavior that might avert that catastrophe and bring about a world where nature has been restored. As a final example of this apocalyptic motif, I will mention its popularization a generation ago with regard to the danger of world destruction from nuclear weapons technology: Jonathan Schell argued in *The Fate of the Earth* that precisely the terror of that nuclear annihilation is necessary to shock us into the Augustinian character transformation of peaceful living, humility and love that alone can save us from nuclear Armageddon – another version of the either/or prospect of destruction or salvation shared by Hegel's millenarian successors.

Closer in time to us than the neo-Marxism of Lukacs and Kojeve is the Islamic liberation theology of Ali Shariati, the distinguished Iranian academic who was heavily influenced while a student in Paris by the philosophy of Heidegger and who translated *Being and Time* into Farsi. Considered by many to be the intellectual godfather of the 1979 Iranian Revolution, he had created an amalgam of Shia Islamic religious millenarianism, Marxism and Heidegger's Volkisch revolutionism in which the Iranian people could, by real-world revolutionary action, help advance the millennial era of happiness promised by the return of the Hidden Imam, or indeed speed up his return. Ali Shariati had a huge following among Iranian university students, and while traditional clerics denounced his view, arguing that it was impious to believe that human political action, especially revolution, could advance the aims of God for mankind, one prominent cleric, the Ayatollah Khomeini, endorsed him. Following a pattern we have seen a number of times throughout this book, we can have no certain way of knowing whether and to what degree Ali Shariati's theories were responsible for the enormities carried out by the Khomeinists and whether and to what degree he would have endorsed them, especially since he did not live to see the revolution. It is apposite to observe in this connection that Foucault regarded that upheaval to be the first postmodernist revolution, and he enthused about Khomeini being "a mystic saint."

Finally, a number of motifs from Heidegger's writings from the 1920s and 1930s, which shaped his perception of and commitment to National Socialism, live on today in the writings of Aleskander Dugin and his ideology of National Bolshevist Eurasianism in Russia, a major component of the geopolitical ideology of Vladimir Putin's rule. Dugin basically transferred Heidegger's notion of the German people as the "people of destiny" caught between the pincers of

West and East in the 1930s, capable of making a stand for its destiny that would redeem all mankind, to the position of Russia today, which Dugin envisions as leading a revolution of "archaic values" against the bourgeois world headed by the United States. We observed earlier that both Nietzsche's and Heidegger's existentialist evocations of the rootedness of peoples interwove with the broad rise of Romantic nationalism in Europe from the late nineteenth century, including arguable parallels between Nietzsche and Dostoyevsky. In Russia itself, there had always been a tension, sometimes an outright cultural war, between its westward-looking attachment to Europe and its Slavophilic, eastern roots. This tension was embodied in the novels of Turgenev on the Western-looking side, and Dostoyevsky on the other. In the novels of Tolstoy, a great devotee of Rousseau – in whom, as we have seen, Enlightenment rationalism and Romanticism converge without reconciling – we encounter a balanced tension between these Western and Eastern forces embodied by the cultures of St. Petersburg and Moscow. The tension continued into the twentieth century, reflected in the different varieties of dissidence against the Soviet regime – Sakharov speaking for Russia's foothold in the Enlightenment, Solzhenitsyn evoking its Slavophilic roots and Orthodoxy.

Without making any judgements about their respective merits, Dugin fits squarely into the latter stream, as does Putin himself, an admirer of Berdyev. Dugin's campaign against "bourgeois" America in favor of "archaic" Russian conservative values clearly implies that the struggle extends to whatever remains of a "bourgeois" Enlightenment liberal culture in Russia itself. In drawing upon Heidegger to ground his Eurasianist perspective, Dugin has written extensively about his works, and has been a highly valued advisor of Vladimir Putin, who gave him a mandate to expunge from the Russian education system all mention of the Gorbachev reformist (and Westernizing) interval of *glasnost* and *perestroika*. He has influenced elements of the Alt-Right in Europe, including Putin admirers such as Victor Orbán and Marine Le Pen, who appear to see in Putin a possible Fuhrer to stave in the rotten liberalism of the European Union, the Alt-Right's Weimar.

As we leave the fragments of the Philosophy of Freedom currently strewn across the landscape, it is time for a final reflection on its original animating impulse – the pursuit of political wholeness and the end of human alienation – and to think about whether it retains any plausibility as the twenty-first century unfolds in its increasingly mysterious way. What have been its gains and losses? What if anything does it have left to contribute? Or is it best to bid it farewell as a path that should never have been taken in the first place, especially in light of its arguably extremist political implications? To begin this reflection, let us turn to one of German historicism's earliest and most prescient diagnosticians.

APOCALYPSE NOW?

We have traced the legacy of the Philosophy of Freedom largely through its impact on the academic world and on some contemporary political movements.

But not all the thinkers we have considered in this book as representatives of the Philosophy of Freedom were academics, much less all their followers, who spread their influence around the world both in culture and in politics. For much of the twentieth century, huge regimes bore the names of Marx and Lenin or sported slogans drawn from Nietzsche and Heidegger, and that has not entirely vanished even after the collapse of the Soviet Empire. The millenarian potential of the earlier Jacobin, Marxist, Nazi and Maoist revolutions, fueled by the same passions for honor, combat, righteous wrath and collectivist justice, is alive and well today in the international jihad and in the emerging global movement for white supremacism.

That is why it is appropriate to conclude these reflections with an assessment of the Philosophy of Freedom offered by one of the nineteenth century's greatest poets, Heinrich Heine, who foresaw the millenarian danger inherent in its way of thinking as early as 1837, seven years before the birth of Nietzsche and while Marxism was as yet a fledgling movement. Heine saw with eerie foresight the coming "politics of greatness" for the "mastery of the earth" (to use Nietzschean language) already implicit in the most Promethean dimensions of German historicism.

In a stunning and famous passage from *Religion and Philosophy in Germany*, Heine predicts a coming revolution in which the forces of Kantianism and historicism will ally. He identifies the Kantians with the Fichtean call for man to assert his will to shape nature without limit, treating it, as Fichte said, as inert fodder for the application of our moral duty. Because they believe in the godlike omnipotence of the will to transform the future, the Kantians, Heine says, are not in awe of the restraints of tradition and have no fear of danger, which "has no existence" for them because nothing can withstand the power of the human will.

But the coming upheaval will be even more terrible and sinister because of the alliance of the Kantians with "the philosophy of nature." This is Heine's term for historicism, and it requires a word of explanation in light of our earlier observation that, strictly speaking, historicism has no conception of human nature as a permanent substratum of behavior because human beings are purely historical self-makers. Heine is using the term "nature" here in a different sense, meaning that German historicism liberates the passions and a love of action, thereby appealing to the emotions and instincts instead of the intellect, illustrated in Hegel's maxim that history is a "slaughter bench" and that the ambition and bloodlust of great conquerors like Caesar and Napoleon is what drives the progress of history, including the achievement of moral ideals.

In this way, Heine warns, historicism is conjuring up from the primordial past the "demoniacal forces of old German pantheism," a Viking spirit celebrated by "the Northern poets" that loves combat above all else – almost a prediction of Wagner's restoration in his operas of the Nordic heroism of old as a flashpoint for Germany's revulsion for bourgeois modernity, inspiring would-be Nietzscheans of the future like Hitler to burn down the Enlightenment world, with film footage of the Wehrmacht crashing into Poland accompanied by a sound track taken from *The Ride of the Valkyries.*

For a time, Heine observes, Christianity had tamed the "brutal warrior ardor" of primordial Nordic Germany. But now, under the impact of both secular liberalism and revolutionary radicalism, the Cross "has fallen to pieces," releasing the "frantic Berserker rage" to come roaring back as the hammer of Thor shatters the Gothic cathedrals. Heine warns the French in his pseudo-biblical language – "Ye French, be on your guard" – about the coming apocalypse, compared with which their own Terror of 1793 will seem like chickenfeed. The French should retreat when they hear "the trampling of feet and the clashing of arms" from across the Rhine: resistance will be futile. The "outburst of revolution" that German philosophy had created in "the region of intellect" is now coming about in reality: "The thought precedes the deed as the lightning precedes the thunder": Heine continues:

German thunder is of true German character: it is not very nimble, but rumbles along somewhat slowly. But come it will, and when ye hear a crashing such as never before has been heard in the world's history, then know that at last the German thunderbolt has fallen. At this commotion, the eagles will drop dead from the skies and the lions in the farthest wastes of Africa will bite their tails and creep into their royal lairs. There will be played in Germany a drama compared to which the French Revolution will seem but an innocent idyl.

I began this book by asking what is the purpose of political life? Should it be a politics that promotes individual self-interest and economic well-being, securing the rights of the individual, and enabling them to enjoy their personal leisure time as they wish? If so, then liberalism is the answer – a social contract that protects us from tyrannical treatment and creates a maximum net gain in prosperity for its individual participants, who accept its legitimacy for those reasons. But what if we believe that political life should provide something greater, nobler than the facilitation of self-interest? What if we long for a full sense of community in which citizens participate in a deliberation about public affairs; a community that promotes civic virtue along with compassion for the worst off; a community that, in its harmony and the nobility of its aspirations, takes on a quality of beauty akin to that of an aesthetic experience. That is what the Philosophy of Freedom aimed to create, inspired by the ancient polis.

Given the illiberal consequences, intended or unintended, that Heine identified so early on, and the utopian longings and millenarian extremism that intensified as the debate within the Philosophy of Freedom about the meaning of history and the future ran its course from Hegel to Heidegger, perhaps one ought to conclude that the alternative to liberalism toward which it summoned us ought to be avoided at all costs, both philosophically and in practice. The issue of political violence is a fulcrum for this possibility. The ancients could give the passions of honor-seeking, combat and glory their proper place within the political community because they were subordinated to a higher realm, the hierarchy of reason over political ambition embodied in Diotima's Ladder, the tripartite city of Plato's *Republic* and Cicero's *Dream of Scipio*. A passion for honor (Plato's Diotima proclaimed this to be the distinctive trait of humans) could, if left undirected, serve the unjust ends of tyranny and exploitation – or it could be sublimated and redirected through a proper education in character (*paideia*) to provide energy for serving the common good and receiving the honor of one's fellow citizens. In the case of extraordinarily virtuous rulers, their entirely legitimate longing for honor might lead to their immortalization in the poetry and art of future generations.

In stark contrast to this classical attempt to redirect potentially tyrannical passions toward honorable public service, early liberal thinkers such as Hobbes discouraged these passions as politically subversive under any pattern of authority. The new natural science of matter in motion identified the satisfaction of human nature with material self-interest, thereby attempting to deflate the pretensions to immortality through civic virtue and statesmanship encouraged by classical political thought. Classical political philosophy believed that potentially tyrannical passions could be redirected toward the pursuit of civic virtue because civic virtue was a proper end for human beings given in the order of nature itself, and closer to the harmony and repose of the immortal cosmos than the chaos and disarray of tyrannical ambition, which lived in the lower realm of accident and impulse. Civically motivated honor-seeking, in other words, had a place in the best regime prescribed by nature and reason. But according to the new natural science, that eternal cosmic pattern of which the best regime was a reflection had been completely disproven. The early liberal thinkers intended the new physics of matter in motion and the new psychology of appetitive self-interest derivable from it to shatter once and for all the alliance proposed in the *Republic* between philosophy and *thumos*, whereby honor-seeking, governed by reason, could seek its outlet within the well-ordered polis. Instead, they envisioned a future in which *thumos* itself would dwindle into a desire for self-preservation and pedestrian pleasures.

That of course did not prevent the honor-seeking passions from emerging. But the crucial transition is that when they did so, they were now envisioned – due to liberalism itself – as independent of reason altogether. Rousseau initiated the great countermovement against bourgeois materialism and the smallness and venality of modern political life, but because he did not reject the modern account of nature and reason, these aggressive passions could only be defended *because* they were irrational. They were irrational because they belonged to the realm of republican collectivism, patriotism and manliness; they occupied the higher sphere of freedom as opposed to the "mechanistic" account of human nature concerned only with self-preservation. In principle, these aggressive passions could not be governed by reason inasmuch as reason – identified in the modern age with utility – could not give an account of their psychological characteristics or their potential for rehabilitation as civic virtue, since it was no longer believed that there was an eternal order of the whole which prescribed civic virtue as one of man's ends.

After Rousseau's bifurcation between freedom and reason, the only hope for moderating these aggressive passions lay in a belief in the rationality of the progress of history; a hope that the new Hegelian historicist vision of an ordered whole (Spirit) would take the place of the classical hierarchy of the soul *sub specie aeternitatis* according to which wisdom would govern thumos so as to ensure its moderation. Moderation would now be replaced by mediation, by Hegel's axiom of "determinate negation" meant to retard fanaticism and revolutionary violence through cumulative and limited reform. That worked to a degree and for a time. But the underlying historicist ontology of existence as spontaneous "self-origination," of (to cite Heidegger) existence as Heraclitean strife or war, upon which the Hegelian dialectic itself had been erected, eventually blew up and swept away the simulacrum of moderation that Hegel believed was provided by the teleological progress of history, a belief systematically dismantled by the critiques of Marx, Nietzsche and Heidegger that culminated in philosophy standing aside and letting youthful passion roar out of its box. To sum up: The central liability of historicism as regards the danger of political violence is that, especially as it lost its faith in the teleological progress of history, in order to rescue honor-seeking from the psychological reductionism of liberal materialism, it could not avoid defending it *as irrational*. It could only be moderated by a belief in the rational progress of history, and when that belief failed, so did the effort at moderation.

That all said, attempting to suppress or ban the Philosophy of Freedom from our educational horizon on the grounds of its flirtation with political extremism or inability to retard it would, in addition to constituting an incalculable sacrifice of intellectual brilliance, be pointless, because the passions it both released and tried to control will never go away. The essentials of liberal political philosophy were in place by the time of Locke and Hume, and have not changed in important ways since then. In order to embrace liberalism to the total exclusion of the Philosophy of Freedom, therefore, one would have to be entirely satisfied with its account of human nature, psychology and reason: In other words, Hume is as good as it gets. Some may well believe this. But others will always want more, both from philosophy and from life – an exploration of the passions for honor, glory and civic-spiritedness; in short, of the longing for nobility in political life. The distinctive improvement over liberalism contributed by the Philosophy of Freedom is that it did explore these passions, notwithstanding the fact that it often did so in a way that flirted with encouraging them. In this way, historicism offered a breadth of insight into human nature that at least aspired to the breadth of the ancients, and was nowhere to be found in early modern thought. Hegel extolled the role of supreme political ambition in advancing the transformation of the world. Nietzsche provided a breathtaking landscape of human creativity and ambition as expressions of the Will to Power. Heidegger extolled the glory of the statesmanship of the polis.

Without that expansion of the meaning of human existence, whatever its liabilities, political philosophy would have been the poorer.

This is not the only argument to be made in favor of the Philosophy of Freedom. As we saw in Chapter 2, beginning with Hegel's identification of liberal education with "recollection," including its Platonic echo, the Philosophy of Freedom tried to recapture the depth and richness of the classical account of the soul. Habermas' attempt to rehabilitate Hegel as a diagnostician of moral experience bereft of the overarching claims of the dialectic of Spirit was plausible. But it sacrificed the longing for a unified life, both inwardly and outwardly, promised by the Platonic ascent of the soul and by Hegel's attempt to reenact that ascent through the teleological progress of history. Whatever we may ultimately think of Hegel's attempt to reconcile the holistic account of the soul and the political community provided by Plato with the freedom of the individual established by liberalism, that attempt provides one of the only portals in modern philosophy through which we can encounter that Platonic original. By contrast, liberalism in its essential principles does not need Plato at all.

For Hegel and his successors, the enrichment of modern life beyond the narrowness of liberalism's utilitarian account of human satisfaction included not only the ontological speculations of philosophy regarding the character of all reality, but recollecting the grandeur of ancient art and poetry. I do not share the reductive view of liberalism as being utterly pedestrian with respect to high culture that runs throughout the thinkers we have considered – Rousseau on the venal hypocrisy of the bourgeois; Schiller on the modern reign of Utility and Necessity in the "noisy mart" of economics; Kant's disdain for material self-interest; Hegel's contempt for bourgeois moralizing about the evils of great political ambition; Marx's view of liberalism as "the animal kingdom of man"; Nietzsche's imprecations against "herd morality"; and Heidegger's horror over a boxing match being placed on the same level as a symphony concert. Liberalism is not exclusively defined by the right to private property, which is but one of a constellation of liberties including freedom of thought and worship, and many liberal thinkers and statesmen placed a high value on liberal education, including the classics, and sometimes even on the love of beauty – think of Locke, Hume or Jefferson. But I do not think it is unfair to ask whether these avocations were absolutely *central* to the formation of liberal individualism, as they *were* absolutely central to the pursuit of wholeness and communality explored by the thinkers we have considered in this book. Liberalism supports higher education as one of the finest pastimes with which the social contract equips the individual with the economic leisure and freedom of choice to pursue. But at the end of the day, it is chiefly that: a personal pastime. As we observed earlier, Rawls' theory of justice does not in his view require supplementation by, let alone integration with, an account of the good life. Within the horizon of liberalism, studying the birth of tragedy, for example, can be interesting and rewarding. But it is not literally essential to unfolding the human soul, as it was for Hegel and Nietzsche.

A prime example of how the Philosophy of Freedom might enrich the modern soul beyond what is available from within the confines of liberalism is, in addition to its veneration for ancient culture, its relationship to the art, literature and music of its own era. Throughout this book we have stressed the intimate connection between German philosophy as far back as Schiller and the German high culture of that period. Nietzsche captured it beautifully in the aphorism from Part Eight of *Beyond Good and Evil* where he writes that Beethoven's music was the voice through which Schiller, Shelley and Byron sang as they "dreamed with Rousseau and danced around the freedom tree." The thinkers knew about the artists and the artists knew about the thinkers. Schiller read Kant; he was Germany's greatest playwright (who influenced English Romantic poetry through Coleridge) and close friend of Goethe, whose verse Schubert set to music. Beethoven read Rousseau and set Schiller to music. Moreover, the creativity of the thinkers and the artists was not merely parallel or complementary to one another, but fully interacted with each other in a process of cross-fertilization.

Consider, for instance, this passage from Goethe's *Faust*, which could be read as echoing Schiller's and Hegel's view of modern rationality as a kind of dissection when Mephisto says: "Who would study and describe the living starts / By driving the spirit out of its parts: / In the palm of his hands he holds all the sections / Lacks nothing except the spirit's connections" [1935–1940]. Mephisto could also be read as embodying Hegel's labor of the negative when he says: "I am the spirit that negates / And rightly so, for all that comes to be / Deserves to perish wretchedly." But out of negation comes a restored unity: "I am part of the part that once was everything" [1345–1350].

Viewed from various angles, these verses could be taken as a poetic evocation of what Hegel conceptualized as the Unity of Subject and Substance, and how its two reconciliatory and aggressive dimensions grew out of an original passive organic unity of life – Spirit "in itself" – and, having evolved into Spirit "for itself," now seek a new and higher unity. They might also put one in mind of what Nietzsche will later characterize, in reference to Pascal, as the will to superficiality and the will to profundity, the two poles of Hegel's dialectical synthesis exploded into an irreconcilable tension so as to revivify it. Was there an echo of *Faust*, knowingly or unwittingly, in Nietzsche's later deconstruction of Hegel? Lines 1070–1100 of *Faust* seem to presage the language of Nietzsche's *The Dancing Song*, where Zarathustra sings a song for Cupid and some girls to dance to in a meadow, while lines 1100–1104 ("I shall never envy birds their wings / Far greater are the joys that spirit brings") makes one think ahead to the poem ending *Beyond Good and Evil*, where Nietzsche compares his thoughts to "birds" who can be caught only when they are weary of flying. And what could better sum up the whole theme of this book, the theme of dualism and the divided self of modern man going back to Rousseau, than when Faust says: "You are aware of only one unrest / Oh never learn to know the other! / Two souls, alas, are dwelling in my breast / And one is striving to forsake its brother" [1110–1115].

I earlier suggested a kind of affinity between Hegel's *Phenomenology of Spirit* and Beethoven's Ninth, both of which chronicle man's emergence from the primordial swamp into the daylight of Schiller's *Ode to Joy*, while of course Nietzsche's early enthusiasm for Wagner's creation of a new epic Arthurian myth cycle as "the music of the future" is well-known. Finally, I personally detect in Richard Strauss' 1948 composition *Four Last Songs*, and the last song in particular ("In the Twilight"), a musical rendering of the *Weltschmerz* and longing for a lost closeness to Being that saturated the writings of Heidegger and Holderlin, particularly in its backward glance at the dark valley of the struggle we have come through and the possibility of a coming dawn, as if surveying in retrospect the catastrophe unleashed by the National Socialist revolution to which Heidegger had dedicated himself, but looking ahead to the unfolding destiny of the postwar world:

> Through adversity and joy
> We've gone hand in hand;
> We rest now from our wanderings
> Upon this quiet land.

The seemingly infinite E flat major chord with which the song wordlessly ends sets the tone for Heidegger's stance of "absolute composure" (to use Fackenheim's characterization) as our destiny unfolds. That destiny may be Death, but the larks evoked by flute trills at the beginning of the song reappear reassuringly in its long, dark final chord, like lights on the horizon of a new day.

I am not saying that these were conscious influences on Richard Strauss, only that they are of a temperamental quality akin to themes in Heidegger's thought. The main point I want to make through these examples is that, in addition to its frequent philosophical profundity and psychological depth, the Philosophy of Freedom has always been a gateway into these cultural treasures, with which it possesses a symbiotic relationship that, as far as I know, is not true of the connection between philosophy and art in the Anglosphere, and whose only precedent is perhaps the Classical Age of ancient Greece. (The reverse is true, by the way – not only does the philosophy help open up the art, but the art also opens up the philosophy.) In my view, this body of thought, while often giving rise to disturbing political implications, also remains essential to anyone who regards themselves as liberally educated both philosophically and culturally.

If we ignore the attempt made by the Philosophy of Freedom to give a coherent account of history such as Hegel and, in their ways, Marx, Nietzsche and Heidegger undertook, then we will possess no intellectual equipment for identifying the possibly constructive side of passions that are not satisfied by the psychology of liberalism; for distinguishing between, on the one hand, the meritorious side of honor, manliness, the struggle against injustice, a reverence for tradition and the sublimation of the passions by the aesthetic experience, and on the other, sheer anarchistic and revolutionary violence, the spirit of nihilistic destruction and an uncompromising hatred of modernity which has continually re-erupted since the Jacobins. Until we can acknowledge and try to account for modern man's continuing eros for nobility, despite the dangerous forms it may have taken in some reaches of the Philosophy of Freedom, we will never be able to distinguish that noble longing from the temptations of barbarism.

Throughout this book, we have seen how Hegel's successors discovered or envisioned – it is not always possible to say which – a draconian division in the world portending a terrible struggle and a new dawn, whether it be Marx's polarity between bourgeois and proletarian, Nietzsche's polarity between Herd-Man and the Overman, or Heidegger's either/or scenario for our annihilation by global technology or its ushering in of the Shepherd of Being. They were already glimpsed in outline by Heine's dichotomy between the political Romantics and the armed Kantians. A similar draconian polarity is emerging again today. Its two divisions have not yet assumed the clarity of their predecessors. But when we think of the words "populism" and "global elite," everyone senses what those forces are and how the hostility between them is building toward who knows what outcome in the century ahead.

Further Reading

Introduction

As regards German Idealism and the Philosophy of Freedom, intellectual historians are not at one as to whom they would include in these categories, which can be extended to other rubrics such as the historical school and continental thought. Most would agree, however, that Hegelianism was central to all of them. Consider Henrich (2008), Steiner (2011) and Zizek (2013). I will be using these terms pretty much interchangeably in what follows, giving special prominence to the Philosophy of Freedom. For reasons I explore at length in Chapter 1, I believe that Rousseau should be included in this pedigree, because he identifies our freedom of will to oppose nature as the faculty that distinguishes human "spirituality" in contrast with other living beings, and also because he proposes a historical account of the evolution of mankind from its primitive origins to the present. Both these themes are taken up and developed by his successors including Kant, Schiller, Hegel and Marx.

With regard to other synoptic approaches to the pedigree of the Philosophy of Freedom, I am greatly indebted to Fackenheim (1967), whose model of the Hegelian "middle" of the teleological progress of history that subsequently underwent a series of challenges from Left and Right is basically the one I have adopted as my own, although my cast of philosophical characters is somewhat different. Lowith (1967) is still the best general introduction to the Philosophy of Freedom, although it omits Heidegger. I am also a longtime admirer of Yack's book on historical longing (1986), still one of the best such works out there. I am particularly indebted to his view of how Schiller's cultural aestheticism was perversely assimilated to the aestheticization of political life (including revolution) that began with Marx. Zuckert (1996) provided an exceptionally useful analysis of postmodernist thinkers including Nietzsche, Heidegger, Gadamer, Derrida and Strauss through the focused lens of how they read Plato, an arc of influence not unlike the one I trace in this book, although I deal more extensively with the rough and tumble of actual political life, extend the classical heritage beyond Plato alone, and am also more inclined to highlight the irreconcilable contradictions between Platonic philosophy and its postmodernist devotees. Abram's study of the influence of German

Romanticism on English poetry (1973) remains a masterpiece, not least because, in the course of explaining his main theme, he branches into brilliant overviews of the German philosophical works that engaged artists like Schiller, including those of Hegel and Schelling, who often employed literary symbolism themselves. Megill (1987) was an early and very helpful attempt to think through the roots of postmodernists such as Foucault and Derrida in the historicism of Nietzsche and Heidegger, although I am more struck by their truncation and obfuscation of the work of those predecessors. As regards relatively more pragmatic as opposed to relatively more ontological interpretations of the historicist thinkers I consider, I will cite these in the respective chapters devoted to them. But provisionally one can point to a number of such ontological-leaning versus pragmatic-leaning pairings: for Hegel, Rosen (1974) versus Avineri (1972); for Nietzsche, Danto (2005) versus Drochon (2016); for Heidegger, Marx (1971) versus Wolin (1993). For an earlier treatment of the vision of the Greek polis as a foil for the historicist critiques of modernity undertaken by Schiller, Hegel and Marx, see Kain (1982).

As regards my argument about how a veneration for the Greek polis is a common motif among the thinkers considered, Marx is obviously something of the odd man out. Marx held no veneration for the polis because he regarded it as based on the exploitation of the slaves by the masters. Nevertheless, Marx is not entirely bereft of a debt to the ancients because of his interest in the materialism and philosophical hedonism of Epicurus and Lucretius which, as I argue in Chapter 2, contributed significantly to his understanding of the socialist future. Moreover, we cannot exclude a consideration of Marx's subversive adaptation of Hegelianism if we wish to understand the full legacy of the Philosophy of Freedom for contemporary political theory.

This book grew out of my previously published work on Rousseau, Kant, Schiller, Hegel, Marx, Nietzsche, Heidegger, Lukas and Kojeve, some traces of which survive here, included in the Bibliography for interested readers. *Tyrants: A History of Power, Injustice, and Terror* (2017) provides further materials for considering the arguably dangerous political implications of the Philosophy of Freedom in their real-world impact on revolutionary violence. Finally, beginning in the Introduction and continuing throughout this book, I often use images from Plato's dialogues of the ascent of the soul – the Image of the Cave and Diotima's Ladder especially – as a foil for German historicism. These draw upon my earlier books about Plato (2000) and ancient versus modern tyranny (2013).

Chapter 1

Cranston's three-volume biography of Rousseau (1991) remains the go-to guide for his colorful life. Goethe's estimation of Rousseau's influence is in his autobiography *Poetry and Truth* (1913).

Cassirer (1989) remains one of the most impressive synoptic interpretations of Rousseau's works, attributing to him the view that "society" now takes the place of the biblical Fall as being responsible for human evil and injustice, and sees him as riven by his vision of a society in which the individual sacrifices everything to the collective and his personal belief that he needed to live entirely outside the realm of convention. Arendt (1963) in a sense completes the thought that society is responsible for injustice with the conclusion, which she attributes to Rousseau, that society must therefore relieve injustice through a politics of compassion promoted by the General Will. That lends extra force to Rousseau's argument in the *Second Discourse* that a capacity for pity is innate to natural man and can be built upon within the social contract. Melzer (2016) has stood the test of time in his systematic and insightful interpretation of the whole range of Rousseau's seemingly disparate works as being unified by his central concern with the natural goodness of the original human condition, whereas in my view that unifying thread was provided by his own intermittent experience of that condition in the present. Maclean (2003) by contrast stresses Rousseau's understanding of freedom of will as the concept around which he built his teachings on the evolution of human society and the social contract. Also standing the test of time, Miller (1984) provides a robust reading of Rousseau, whom he credits with our high expectations from democracy as a society that will unite a just political community with individual personal fulfillment, and judiciously distinguishes Rousseau's actual views of the social contract from the perversion of them by totalitarian politics. It reminds us of a period when Rousseau in general inspired more enthusiasm than is presently the case. Velkley's very fine study (2002) emphasizes the path from Rousseau to thinkers such as Kant, Schelling and Heidegger who sought to find a cultural resolution to the contradiction between nature and society that Rousseau first explored, although he is not centrally concerned with the explicitly political dimension of attempts by Rousseau's successors to bridge that same chasm. Horowitz (1987) offers an energetic "Marcusean" reading of Rousseau which focuses on the pathologies introduced into the human character by the imposition of an abstract utilitarian individualism at the expense of passion and happiness, and maintains that the *Second Discourse* contains the germ of a historicist conception of human labor that points toward Marx. Lund (2016) reads Rousseau for illumination over many pressing contemporary political issues, including the rights of women and the role of family life in society. Neuhouser (2013) argues for the hypothetical character of Rousseau's history in the *Second Discourse*, but in my view takes it too far by overlooking what I regard as the minimal sense in which Rousseau had to posit his understanding of human nature as historically real. The general study of Rousseau's moral theory by Dent (1989) stirred new interest in Rousseau in the Anglosphere by emphasizing the positive dimension of *amour-propre* in seeking recognition and respect from others.

For the impact of Lucretius on the *Second Discourse*, see Wilson in Norbrook (2015) and Plattner (1979). Menon (2015) and Colman (2012) question the apoliticality usually attributed to Lucretius, suggesting that he wished to introduce the Roman ruling class to the Epicurean philosophy, but I do not believe their approach calls into question Lucretius' fundamental aversion for participating directly in civic life. Griswold (2017) constructs an imaginary dialogue between Rousseau and Adam Smith over their contrasting understandings of human nature, sociability and selfhood. Strauss' chapter on Rousseau in *Natural Right and History* (1974) is perhaps the best single summing up of the deeply paradoxical character of his thought, flowing from his insistence that man's natural capacity for happiness is pre-political, which arguably created insurmountable difficulties for any conception of a just political order. Shklar (1985) also asks how Rousseau can conceive of a legitimate civil society when the state of nature is irrecoverable and modern civilization is irredeemably corrupt. She emphasizes (as in my discussion of the David painting) Rousseau's starkly opposed conceptions of the virtuous collectivist republic and the sweet bonds of family life, and concludes that, in Rousseau's pessimistic outlook, these two alternatives are unlikely ever to be reconciled.

Berlin (1958) cited Rousseau's political theory as an illustration of a dangerous potentiality in positive freedom – that it could legitimize a state that violated our negative freedom in the pursuit of "collectivist holism." Pateman's reading of the _Social Contract_ (1975) provides, in my view, a convincing refutation of its association with totalitarianism, locating it squarely in the social democratic camp, and arguing, as against Berlin, that Rousseau's theory of the social contract entailed negative liberty while aspiring to a higher conception of civic freedom, my own position as well. However, the fact that Pateman's reading is arguably the correct one does not resolve the difficulty regarding the extent to which Rousseau's inflammatory rhetoric inspired Robespierre and his totalitarian successors. As for the totalitarian reading, the most powerful exponent remains Talmon (1952). Schama (1990), who provided the Roussseauan interpretation of the David painting that I draw upon here, in my view offers the best history of the French Revolution in the English language. He also restores the place of Rousseau as the dominating intellectual antecedent of that upheaval. Belloc's biography of Robespierre (1927), including Rousseau's influence on him and his contemporaries, in my view remains unsurpassed. For further reading on the French Revolution and how Robespierre saw himself as carrying out the political intent of "Jean-Jacques," see Newell (2017).

In a deep reading of Rousseau's interpretation of the Book of Judges, Kochin (2007) argues that for Rousseau the Bible is a source for shaping our characters to resist self-interest, not a guide for action, which may shed some light on Rousseau's view of the value of religion for sustaining the General Will. Cassirer (1970) astutely observes that, although Rousseau believes that nature displays a harmonious arrangement, his religious philosophy contains little enthusiasm or transports like other varieties of pantheism such as that of Shaftesbury. Instead, the "miracle of human freedom and conscience" is at its core. In this way, Rousseau's religious philosophy is consistent with his conceptions of citizenship and the rule of law, and at their service. It is primarily an "ethical" and not an "aesthetic" religion, a part of his proto-Kantian dimension.

In this connection, a further word about the civil religion of the _Social Contract_ is in order. According to Rousseau, the religions of the ancient world were seamlessly at the service of the state – their gods were national gods. The spread of the universal message of the Christian Gospel made this impossible, introducing an irresolvable conflict between the authority of the state and of the priesthood. Among modern thinkers, only Hobbes tried to resolve this conflict by making the sovereign responsible for prescribing religious belief. Rousseau proposes something different, a "purely civil profession of faith." Its aim is not to breed any particular religious creed in the citizenry, but "sentiments of sociality." Citizens need only believe in a Deistic Supreme Being and must practice complete tolerance toward all other faiths. Anyone rejecting this minimalistic belief in the Supreme Being can be expelled for being "unsociable" and "incapable of loving the laws."

In the introduction to his translation of the _Emile_, Bloom (1979) provides strong reasons for regarding that work as Rousseau's overall preferred solution for resolving the contradictions between nature and freedom or nature and society, an aesthetic synthesis (cultivated through education) entailing family and political life, a synthesis that arguably addressed the conflicts in Rousseau's own personality as revealed by his autobiographical writings. Starobinski (1998) remains the most sustained and interesting attempt to root Rousseau's reflections on human nature in the trauma of his early life and how his wanderings as a "tramp" instilled in him a compassion for the oppressed.

Meier (2016) provides a rich exegesis of the *Reveries*, but in my view conflates Rousseau's poetic stance toward nature with the traditional meaning of the philosophic life, thereby occluding its originality. No classical philosopher could have described happiness, as Rousseau does, as being attainable "without taking the trouble to think." Davis (2000) reads works of Heidegger, Nietzsche and Plato as philosophical autobiographies, culminating in an insightful discussion of Rousseau's *Reveries* which, in my view, like that of Meier, does not adequately question whether and to what degree Rousseau can be conceived of as a philosopher. Shklar (1985) by contrast makes a strong and, to me, convincing case that Rousseau did not consider himself to be a philosopher, that he did not particularly value logical consistency, and that he saw himself instead as the first "painter of nature and the historian of the human heart" – that is to say, an unprecedented type. Consider also Reisert (2003). Kelly (2019) provides the most detailed commentary available on Rousseau's *Confessions*, and argues persuasively for its organic connectedness to the corpus of Rousseau's other writings.

Chapter 2

Bracketed references to the *Phenomenology of Spirit* are by section number. The scholarship on Hegel is extraordinarily diverse, and some of it is of philosophic value in its own right. I will begin with some general works. The authors I mentioned in the Introduction as providing synoptic treatments of the Philosophy of Freedom as a whole also contain valuable specific discussions of Hegel. I have already indicated my indebtedness to Fackenheim (1967) for his approach to that tradition in general, and I should also stress his impact on my understanding of Hegel in particular, especially his insistence that Hegel's philosophy cannot be grasped in isolation from its religious dimension. Gadamer has also contributed some fine essays on Hegel's dialectic (1982). Solomon (1993) provides a robust reading of the *Phenomenology of Spirit*, showing the political and intellectual climate from which it emerged, and conveying its boldness and idiosyncrasies. Shklar (1976) stresses that Hegel's aim is to harmonize the development of individual citizens with the ends of the community through their mutual creativity, drawing attention to Hegel's multileveled critique of the modern concept of individualism. Kelly (1978, 2010) offers an overarching view of the sweeping ambition of Hegel's aims, culminating in his claim to have reconciled classical thought with Christianity and showing how they were still wellsprings for modern historical consciousness, including morality and political life. Franco (2002) offers a solidly satisfying reading of Hegel in the tradition of the Hegelian Middle, arguing that Hegel attempts to reground liberalism and its defense of freedom in a way that remedies its narrowness and capacity for dogmatism without succumbing to a romantic communitarianism. Especially helpful is his commentary on Hegel's *Philosophy of Right*.

Among general works on Hegel, two in particular have stood the test of time. Rosen (1974) provides a magisterial study of Hegel's effort to synthesize a historicist approach to human existence that will enable us to achieve a degree of reconciliation with the classical approach while acknowledging the limited possibilities of that reconciliation and indeed claiming to arrive at a "science of wisdom" transcending both the ancients and the moderns, an approach very congenial with my own. That said, I am not sure I would go as far as to say, as does Rosen, that "Hegel is first and foremost a logician, not a philosopher of history, a political thinker or a *Lebensphilosophe*." In my understanding, Hegel's logic emerges as the result of his phenomenology, and is the discursive crystallization of the Ladder to the Absolute. The study by Taylor (1975) to me remains perhaps the single most impressive, combining rigorous textual exegesis of all of Hegel's major concepts – phenomenological, logical, aesthetic and political – with an encyclopedic knowledge of the historical and biographical contexts informing Hegel's thought. I also believe that, among the major interpreters, Taylor comes closest to an accurate interpretation of what Hegel means by the modern state as a synthesis of the individual and the community, one that I share here, and an implicit repudiation of Kojeve's understanding of the Hegelian end of history. Taylor also suggests that Hegel's phenomenology is divided between an "ontological" and an "historical" dialectic, which, while admitting that they are distinctively derived – the first being conceptual and the second being based on empirical evidence and hypothesis – Hegel claims to reconcile in the overall science of Spirit. Taylor employs this distinction as a useful fulcrum for assessing the meaning of Hegel's thought as a whole, and I have posed a similar question as to whether Hegel's pragmatic political prescription (based on historical observation and a moderate progressivism) can be disentangled and treated separately from its ontological and metaphysical grounding in the Concept of Spirit, the Unity of Subject and Substance as the conceptual pie-crust for the empirical pie-filling of historical phenomenology.

Finally, in considering general approaches, although I defer until the Conclusion a discussion of Hegel's legacy, many North American students of Hegel, especially members of the Straussian school, received their introduction to his thought through the massively influential study by Kojeve (1969). While I have laid out my reservations about it as an attempt to understand Hegel as he understood himself – see Newell (2016) – there is no denying its brilliance, and it deserves particular credit for drawing attention to the historical importance for Hegel of the transition from the Greek polis to the world empires of Alexander the Great and Rome. Kojevian-inspired works on Hegel and the end of history include Darby (1990). Last but not least, Hypollite's line by line commentary on the *Phenomenology of Spirit* (1979) remains unsurpassed for its comprehensiveness and rigor of insight. While echoing some Kojevian themes, it has no interpretive axe to grind.

Coming to more recent work, in the world of academic philosophy, Pippin's non-metaphysical reading of Hegel (1989) remains perhaps the single most influential one. Pippin also stresses the continuity between Kant's ethical philosophy and that of Hegel. While this reading is plausible, to me it overlooks the extent to which Hegel's historicism radically undermines the analytically static framework of Kantianism, synthesizing the Is and the Ought in historical action, and also overlooks Hegel's strong criticisms of the implications of Kantianism for political and ethical practice, which I discuss in this chapter. Wood (1990) departs from Pippin in regarding Hegel as more of an Aristotelian than a Kantian, but shares Pippin's leaning toward a non-metaphysical reading. Other examples of this approach are Longuenesse (2007), Neuhouser (2003), who presents a non-metaphysical reading of the *Philosophy of Right*, and Pinkard (1996), whose theme of the "sociality of reason" stresses the pragmatic dimension of Hegel's *Phenomenology*. Redding (1996) claims that Hegel built upon Kant's critique of ancient reasoning so as to demolish it altogether, while supplementing the psychological thinness of Kantianism with a historicist "hermeneutics" that remains non-metaphysical – an approach which, to me, shares Pippin's tendency to see too close an affinity between Kantianism and Hegelianism, and overlooks Hegel's related claim to have assimilated the wisdom of Platonic thought to the dialectic of Spirit. The edited volume by Hartman (1988) presents a variety of perspectives on the non-metaphysical reading.

Within the world of academic political theory, examples of a comparatively pragmatist approach would include Smith (1989), though he does not altogether omit the broader ontological considerations. Smith sees Hegel as wanting a psychologically richer basis for rights-based liberalism than it had been able to provide for itself, a view I share. This could be done by supplanting its individualistic psychology with sources of cultural and historical intersubjectivity, including adapting from the ancients a concern with teleological character development. Other more straightforwardly pragmatic readings of Hegel include Avineri (1972). This interpretive approach to Hegel generally coincides with the defense of his credentials as a friend of liberalism or social democracy, viewing his pragmatic political teaching as not differing essentially from the moderate progressivism of Burke, Mill or Tocqueville. Beiser (1999) usefully distinguishes between those who think that Hegel's entire body of thought should be rejected because of the "mysticism" or logical fallacies of his metaphysics and those who, while agreeing with that critique, believe that much of pragmatic interest can be extracted from it, including Hegel's defense of liberalism and rights. Going back to the realm of philosophy, more recently there has been a renewed interest, initiated by Rosen (2013), in Hegel's metaphysics as being essential to a full consideration of his system. Examples include Stern (2012), Bowman(2015), Kreines (2015) and Zambrana (2015).

Having looked at these general perspectives on Hegel, I now turn to the argument I make in this chapter about Hegel's historicism as a response to the contradiction between nature and freedom inherited from Rousseau and the responses to it by Kant and Schiller. Korner's introduction to Kant's system (1974) is still the place to begin for understanding the relationship among his mature works, written for nonspecialists in jargon-free prose. With regard specifically to political theory, the study by Shell (1980) was a pathbreaking attempt to ground Kant's theory of right in the dual character of human beings as both natural and capable of freedom of will, a concept inherited from Rousseau. Velkley (1989) carefully unearths the influence of Rousseau on Kant's philosophy and, like me, argues that there is an intrinsic connection between Kant's understanding of theoretical reason and the metaphysics of morals, which I locate in the concept of freedom as a "fact of reason." For those hardy enough to climb the Mount Everest of the central premise of Kantian rationality, "the transcendental unity of apperception," Dryer is your best guide (2017). Basically, it is about how Kant believes unified judgements are possible about purely empirical matters and purely conceptual matters, or, to put it another way, his famous question: How are synthetic judgements a priori possible? Or: How are judgements based on empirical observation combinable with contentless causal concepts? This only bears on our theme in the form of Kant's paradox, once again, that freedom is a "fact of reason" – that it combines the universal structure of causality as such with an observable phenomenon, namely freedom, and that it is the only observable fact to do so. The best discussions of freedom as a fact of reason, in my view, are to be found in Fackenheim (1996) and Grant (1985). Fackenheim engaged in an ongoing reflection on the dualism of Kantianism, an anticipation of Weber's fact/value distinction, and how it provoked in response existentialism and the war of competing "worldviews," until historicism was revived by Heidegger as a unified account of existential commitment and reason (interpreted as fundamental ontology). This discussion is therefore properly reserved for Chapter 4. As I argue in the current chapter, the status of freedom as a "fact of reason" arguably acts as a bridge between the natural world studied by "pure reason" and "the metaphysics of morals," such that the second formulation of the Categorical Imperative elevates it from being a mere human maxim into a summons to transform all of reality in the pursuit of freedom, the bridge to Fichte and Kojeve. On the basis of the view that lurking inside of Kant's alleged balance between nature and freedom lies the summons to an open-ended dynamic of transformation, Rosen (2003) lays at Kant's feet the most devastating consequences of this project for the conquest of nature culminating in all the depredations of modern technology. It is a bracing gallop, but at the end of the day I remain unconvinced that it is fair to Kant. Henrich's 1973 lectures (2008) remain valuable for suggesting how the philosophies of Fichte and Hegel emerge as plausible answers to questions that Kant inevitably prompts about the possibility of a unified ontology of historical existence that might overcome the dualism of his own system.

Yack's analysis of Schiller's place in the pedigree of the Philosophy of Freedom remains one of the best (1986). Baumann (1998) offers a very illuminating study of Schiller as a healthy alternative to the attempt to achieve human fraternity through direct political means. Examining the New Left of the 1960s and the Terror of the French Revolution, culminating in what he sees as Sartre's attempted philosophical justification of terror as being necessary to achieve fraternity, Baumann concludes that no effort to achieve harmonious community on a political level can fail to contradict itself by necessitating the use of terror, which is the antithesis of community. He then encourages us to turn to Schiller for an example of how a peaceable sense of human community might be fostered through aesthetic education. Although Schiller largely employs the Kant of the *Groundwork* as the foil for his argument about aesthetic education, in the *Critique of Judgement*, as we observed, Kant attempts to provide his own account of aesthetic experience and how it harmonizes with pure and practical reason. Zuckert (2020) helpfully argues that the Third Critique grounds both our appreciation of beauty and our understanding of organic life in its empirical character in an underlying ability to anticipate the whole. On the way in which the German thinkers often viewed art as a revelation of life on a par with anything that philosophy could furnish, see Gadamer's excellent study of Goethe – who, Gadamer claims, went so far as to argue "that a separate discipline of philosophy was not at all necessary because it is already part and parcel of religion and poetry" – and Goethe's intellectual relationship with Schelling, Hegel and Schiller (1994).

I should dwell a bit further on Kant's complex view of the relationship between happiness and virtue. In the "Antinomy of Practical Reason" in the *Critique of Practical Reason*, Kant argues that happiness cannot be an inducement to virtue because the desire for happiness cannot be moral. Since man is both determined by nature and capable of freedom, "it is not impossible" that virtue may cause happiness in the sense that if we live morally, our empirical lives are likely to arrange themselves in such a way – orderly, productive, sensible – as to make us happy as well. But the relationship between morality and happiness is, strictly speaking, "indirect," because morality exists outside the bounds of the "theoretical," whose understanding is confined to nature. The link between virtue and happiness is unintelligible within the bounds of either pure or practical reason, and our experience of it cannot be clarified further than to assume that "an intelligible Author of nature" has provided for their connection to be observable in human life.

There are several studies of the Concept of Spirit and of the Unity of Subject and Substance which I have found to be exceptionally insightful. Rosen (1982) engages what critics view as the hopeless circularity of Spirit: any criticism of the system can be relegated by Hegel as "one-sided," and folded back into the system itself as a dimension of its evolution. This renders it immune to the charge of formal self-contradiction, or, put another way, it can be viewed as a classic Popperian circular argument in which it is impossible to state the conditions under which it could be falsified. Rosen's response is that, for Hegel, Spirit is not primarily a conception of pure rationality, but a "mystical" experience that itself makes speculative rationality possible. In other words, as I would put it, for Hegel, *Geist* is inexplicable apart from the Absolute Religion, Christianity. Lauer (1982) maintains (as I do) that, for Hegel, *Geist* is indistinguishable from God, meaning that if the Hegelian system is intelligible, then Hegel's concept of God must be intelligible. Harris (1972) draws attention to Hegel's early theological and philosophical writings and how, following Schiller, they argue that philosophy must fall silent in face of the claims of love and of religion, a standpoint Hegel transcends in the *Phenomenology*. Kojeve's interpretation, of course, remains the most striking rejection of Hegel's religiosity, maintaining that his philosophy is explicitly atheistic. As Fackenheim used to remark in his classes, *if* Hegel was an atheist – which he wasn't – then Kojeve's interpretation would unquestionably be the best. Otherwise, Fackeneheim's was. For my first attempt to view Hegel's concept of Spirit as the historicist reenactment of the Platonic ascent of the soul toward wisdom, see Newell (2009).

Similar to the approach I take, Marx (1975) regards the Preface and Introduction to the *Phenomenology* as providing the foundation for the rest of the system. By focusing on this ontological grounding, Marx is able to identify and reject the speculative liberties taken with the rest of Hegel's texts by Marxism, Existentialism and other movements, which have mined it selectively for their own purposes. Particularly useful is his discussion of the paradox surrounding the principle of determinate negation, and how it constitutes the "retroactive logicizing" of past history from the privileged access to the truth of "we phenomenologists" in the present. Heidegger's essay on Hegel's concept of experience (1989) can be described in the same way as many of his exegeses of other thinkers: Brilliant, but proceed with caution. Characteristically, he assimilates Hegel as one of his predecessors stretching back to Plato, all of whom embraced a "metaphysical" interpretation of Being against which he alone, for the first time in history, has taken a stand. Because it is relevant to my discussion of Heidegger in Chapter 4, I will postpone further comments until then.

As regards the roles played by Spinoza, Schelling and Fichte in Hegel's concept of Spirit, I understand Schelling and Fichte to be furnishing an account of the whole from opposite starting points. For Schelling (echoing Spinoza), the world evolves out of nature into the completed harmonious *Lebenswelt*, where all things are interchangeable as I = I. For Fichte, by contrast, the will imposes its freedom on nature, transforming it through action into a whole, and the free self, by distinguishing itself from itself as nature and then negating that other, can also be expressed as I = I. In other words, for Schelling, the world grows organically into I = I. For Fichte, by contrast, man constructs the world in pursuit of the ideal of I = I. These two approaches correspond respectively to the Substance side of Hegel's Unity of Subject and Substance (where Spinoza is alluded to for "submerging" existence within the whole) and the Subjective side (including analytical understanding and "the labour of the Negative"). Hegel's legacy among his followers split into Spinozist and Fichtean axes, which, according to Bauer, Hegel had never been able to successfully reconcile. See the discussion of Bauer by Moggach in Quante (2015).

I have touched upon Hegel's philosophical relationship to Spinoza, Schelling and Fichte only tangentially, but readers may want to explore this rich subtheme further. Machery (2007) presents Hegel and Spinoza as sharply opposed, favoring Spinoza as an early non-foundationalist who has no place for a teleological structure such as that of Hegel, which is arguably overstated. By contrast, Moder (2017) regards Hegel and Spinoza as being in constant dialogue. Zizek (2007) offers an interesting but to my mind unconvincing reading of Schelling as a materialist, and even less convincingly argues that he anticipates Marx's critique of idealism, although Marx's concept of species-being admittedly does have a Spinozist and Schellingian tinge. Ostaric (2014) offers an excellent array of interpretive issues in Schelling. Neuhouser's study of Fichte's concept of subjectivity is comprehensive and solidly done (1990). The edited volume by Forster (2015) provides a useful overview of the somewhat neglected theme of Spinoza's influence on German Idealism. Scruton's short introduction to the philosophy of Spinoza (1998) is lucid and comprehensive. Smith (1998) stresses Spinoza's attempt at a synthesis between Judaism and liberalism. The penetrating study of Schelling by Heidegger (1985) is subject to the same caveat as I stated above with respect to Hegel, but not to the same degree. Heidegger responds positively to Schelling's understanding of existence as "the infinitely finite" (1984) because it really does bear a kinship to Heidegger's own attempt at a non-metaphysical account of historicism, which we will take up in Chapter 4.

In regard to specific themes in the *Phenomenology* that I take up after the Introduction and the Preface, including education and *Bildung*, I would begin by drawing attention to the edited volume by Moggach (2011), who locates Hegel in the wider context of the intense philosophical creativity that blossomed in his era, involving Kant, Schiller and Fichte, and touching on multiple spheres of human experience including culture, politics, society and our relation to the ancients. Surprisingly little attention has been paid to my suggestion that the *Phenomenology of Spirit* be regarded primarily as a pedagogical classic of teleological character development, an issue I first broached in Newell (2015). The edited volume by Ricci (2013) discusses "recollection" as a general property of Hegel's dialectic, but not specifically as it relates to education. However, Buchwalter (1992) comes at the issue in another way, arguing that Hegel attempted to revive certain aspects of ancient Greek virtue ethics under the changed conditions of modern social life. Rutter (2010) reminds us that, despite what I have identified as Hegel's critique of Schiller and Romanticism in general for fleeing from the unedifying side of historical experience, aesthetic education remained indispensable to Hegel's conception of a fulfilling modern life, and to this extent his early debt to Schiller was preserved. Rosen (1974) touches on Hegel's educational enterprise and how it forestalls political revolution in favor of teleological character development: "According to Hegel, man can never return to the Garden of Eden ... Wisdom is acquired by a turn inward, a process of education which is also a 'recollection,' not of separate Platonic Ideas, but of the concrete historical experience of the human race ... Hegel is a conservative rather than a revolutionary."

Wood in Beiser (1999) argues that Hegel is attempting to revive the virtue ethics of Plato and Aristotle on the basis of Kantian moral autonomy despite Kant's objection to the eudaemonism of the classics. In his view, the result cannot be "comfortably classified" as either teleological like the theory of Aristotle or "de-ontical" like Kant's. which is based on a rule. For reasons I discuss in this chapter, the status of freedom as a "fact of reason" means that the Categorical Imperative is not merely a rule for human conduct but has an implicitly ontological status. Wood concludes that Hegel's theory is an "agent-oriented" theory of "self-actualization," which is useful, but arguably overlooks the sense in which Hegel's principle of determinate negation endows the historical process itself with a substantive teleology. Wood also observes the ambivalence in Hegel's employment of the term *Sittlichkeit*, which on one level possesses its previous meaning of "customary morality," that is, a defense of tradition, while on another level being compatible with "rational harmony." There is no denying this, and the success of Hegel's enterprise stands or falls by his success or failure at reconciling these two meanings. Regarding my discussion of Legal Right superseding the polis, see the useful essay by Baumgardner (2016). On how the Enlightenment tried to transform Socrates into a modern rationalist, as opposed to a precursor of Christ, see Leonard (2010).

The first rendition of the shapes of consciousness – Master and Slave, Stoicism, Skepticism and the Unhappy Consciousness – has sparked a long debate with important consequences for later philosophical schools. As I discuss in this chapter, Marx adapts Hegel's Master/Slave dialectic to his own theory of the role of the proletariat versus the bourgeoisie. This privileging of the Master/Slave motif in the *Phenomenology* is the lynch-pin for Kojeve's entire reconstruction of Hegel. On the other hand, the Unhappy Consciousness motif informed Kierkegaard's religiously based existentialism, and the superior significance of the Unhappy Consciousness within the whole sequence of shapes was defended by Wahl (1951) in his famous riposte to Kojeve. Thus, Mastery/Slavery and Unhappy Consciousness stand as the two perhaps irreconcilable bookends of the sequence, pointing to the way in which Hegel's purported synthesis of the Unity of Subject and Substance may have flown off into those two conflicting directions of radical political action and spiritual inwardness. As regards Hegel's understanding of the French Revolution as the destructive exaggeration of the Subject dimension of the Unity of Subject and Substance – the aim to achieve "absolute freedom" through the total negation of nature – Ritter (1982) remains a useful guide to how it shaped Hegel's larger political and social theory and understanding of the dynamics of modernity.

Turning to Marx: Up until the 1940s, Marx was best known for his later works culminating in *Capital*. Drawing upon the British classical economists including Smith and Ricardo, Marx and Engels claimed that their version of socialism was "scientific" because it was guided by the "laws" of economic development and was entirely materialistic and empirically verifiable. Subsequently, renewed attention was paid to Marx's earlier writings, including some that had only been recently discovered (such as the *1844 Manuscripts* and the *German Ideology*) which led to a "humanist" interpretation of Marx. Its central theme was man's alienation from the modern world – not merely economic, but, as I have stressed, on all levels including psychological and aesthetic.

According to the humanist reading, the true context for Marx's thinking lay in the Philosophy of Freedom, including Kant, Hegel and Feuerbach. Tucker (1965) and others of this leaning including Marcuse (1969) argued that the later, allegedly "scientific" Marx grew organically out of his earliest concern with our alienation from species-being. Avineri (1975) stresses the centrality of Marx's notion of labor as humane creative potential throughout all the periods of his thought. Althusser (1988) offered a strong rebuttal, arguing that the mature Marx of "scientific socialism" constituted a complete break with the earlier humanist Marx, meaning that the humanist reading was a distortion. In its place, Althusser offered an interpretation of Marxism as "theoretical anti-humanism." Hyppolite (1973) took more of a middle ground, arguing that Marx's theory reveals an organic relationship with that of Hegel, but also a sharp materialistic critique and inversion of the dialectic of Spirit, which is fair enough.

I remain persuaded that the humanist reading is preferable, because it grounds mature "scientific" Marxism in its broader presuppositions from within the Philosophy of Freedom without denying the increasingly sharp departure from those presuppositions in later years, culminating in *Capital*, an approach I take in my own commentary. As I argue, when the "laws" of economic development advanced by Marx appear to be completely contradicted by the actual unfolding of the capitalist economy, Marxists can always retreat to Marx's earlier and all-encompassing humanistic judgement that improved conditions for the workers are, as he put it in the *1844 Manuscripts*, "nothing but better payment for the slave." As I suggest in this chapter, the core assumption from his earliest writings that no amount of mere economic reform can ameliorate the psychic agony of our alienation under capitalism goes a long way to explaining why Marx could never wholeheartedly approve of social democracy or trade unionism.

Hence, as Lukes (1987) puts it, Marxist reasoning is primarily perfectionist and only secondarily utilitarian. I especially like Lukes' approach, which is, given the fragmentary quality of Marx's writings, to identify major themes and then systematically review Marx's writings and extract a coherent account of each theme, or suggest evidence of their incoherence. This is the most profitable approach – one cannot engage the jumble of journalism, notebooks, manuscripts and pamphlets making up the Marxist *oeuvre* as a pure exegete.

Marxist humanism generated a dizzying array of offshoots and influences, from Lukacs to Lacan to the Frankfurt School, and I am going to postpone a further discussion of them to the Conclusion, when I examine the legacy of German Idealism for the twentieth and twenty-first centuries. For now, let me recommend Kolakowski (1981) for his exhaustive three-volume study of Marxism and its manifold variations and successors.

Chapter 3

I began this chapter by arguing that Nietzsche is a systematic thinker in a way that belies the aphoristic and seemingly disjointed style of his writing. In looking at some of the rich literature surrounding his works, I will begin with some general studies that attempt to render the overall structure of his thinking, then proceed to a consideration of specific themes like the Will to Power, the Eternal Recurrence and the meaning of history, ending with the debate over Nietzsche and politics.

As regards general studies, Fink (1960) was an early distinguished attempt to treat Nietzsche as coherent philosopher. He uncovers the development in Nietzsche's thought from the aestheticism of *The Birth of Tragedy* to his mature works and their twinned doctrines, the Will to Power and Eternal Recurrence, a path I also follow. He is a subtle exegete of Nietzsche's texts. The only drawback, in my view, is his tendency to view Nietzsche as searching for the expression of his own personal ontological experience, whereas to me, the greatest expressions of the Will to Power are never strictly personal, but occur on the level of whole civilizations and peoples. Moreover, Nietzsche is not so much concerned about his own personal experience in the present as with the prospect for the redemption of mankind in the future.

Danto's interpretation of Nietzsche (2005) was another pioneering effort to prove that Nietzsche had a coherent and systematic philosophy whose work anticipated and contributed to the philosophy of science, language and logic. His argument, however, was muddied by his concession that Nietzsche was not necessarily aware of himself as this systematic thinker, and that his purported influence on later philosophy was a kind of accident. In a later edition, he tried to combat the appropriation of Nietzsche by extremists by constructing a response from within Nietzsche's philosophy itself to this "rabid" version of him. To me, it could not overcome the intrinsic evidence from within Nietzsche's thought that it was more than open to employment by political extremism, and contained no absolute and binding ethical prohibition against such movements.

The study by Schacht (1983), beginning with what Nietzsche meant by philosophy, mapped it onto a series of themes including epistemology, metaphysics, ontology, anthropology, morality and art. He also stressed the unity of Nietzsche's thought across a whole range of his works. This effort contributed to Nietzsche's rehabilitation in the Anglosphere as a thinker, and not – as Rudolf Carnap had put it – a "poet." For a discussion of Carnap's and Nietzsche's differing angles of attack on metaphysics, see Moreira (2020).

Stern (1985) is sometimes criticized for leeching Nietzsche of what excites about his work by scrupulously sorting out its main themes and evaluating them as neutrally as possible. But Nietzsche will always excite us; there is no danger of Stern ending that, and Stern's sobriety reminds us that there is more to Nietzsche as a thinker than excitement.

Deleuze's reading of Nietzsche (1962) captures the sharp break between Nietzsche and his systematic predecessors such as Kant and Hegel. Nietzsche's stress on what Deleuze terms "difference" (the Will to Power) as opposed to "identity" took direct aim at Hegel's dialectic of history and its claim to have synthesized all social and political contradictions. Nevertheless, I think that Deleuze overlooks the historical depth dimension that was all-important to Nietzsche's enterprise – how to find a way of deepening ourselves from an exposure to past history without it paralyzing us or making us want to destroy the past completely. He also pays little heed to the archetypes of the Will to Power to which Nietzsche points as inspiration for the future – the Saint, the Free Spirits, the Roman Caesar and the soul of Christ. Above all, he does not pay enough attention to Nietzsche's own resolution of history's contradictions, the coming epoch of the Overman, which, Nietzsche argues, will provide mankind at last with the goal he has pursued but never been able to hold on to. Hence Deleuze's Nietzsche is ultimately too much of an anarchist and decisionist.

Richardson (1993) makes a valuable contribution by stressing that Nietzsche, beneath his beguiling prose, advances a complete philosophical worldview centered on the ontological principle of the will to power, and constituting a direct reversal of Platonic metaphysics by replacing the classical account of Being with his own belief that "becoming" is at the heart of all existence. I am arguing that the ontological premises of Nietzsche's thought, as well as his account of the whole as will to power, stands out in even greater relief when we contrast it with Hegel's philosophy of history.

Pippin (2011) undertakes what is supposed to be a fresh approach to Nietzsche, interpreting him as above all else a psychologist in the mold of La Rouchefoucauld and Stendahl, eschewing grand metaphysical theories in favor of life experiences. This to my mind is a reductive approach. While it is true that Nietzsche called for a return to psychology to take the place of the "prejudices" of philosophers, he meant a new kind of psychology that was inseparable from the doctrine of the will to power and the eternal recurrence. Nietzsche certainly did admire the figures named above as signs of contemporary creative health, but they were no more than way stations to the only hope for mankind, the Overman, and the psychological finesse of the Free Spirits was to be at the service of this new epoch. In predictable postmodernist fashion, Pippin by contrast pushes these central ontological concerns of Nietzsche to one side and converts his work into nothing more than a series of images and metaphors.

Turning to Nietzsche's specific themes, very early in the first of his four-volume study of Nietzsche (1981), Heidegger establishes the connection between the Will to Power and the Eternal Recurrence, though he goes on to suggest that, as Nietzsche's understanding of the whole, the Eternal Recurrence may be the primary premise of his thought. This is close to my own approach in this chapter. Gillespie (2019) argues for the unqualified priority of the Eternal Recurrence as the key to Nietzsche's final teaching. He strikes the right balance in arguing that Nietzsche regarded this doctrine as the key to mankind's future redemption, a redemption that would, however, involve unprecedented struggle and violence – while at the same time insisting that Nietzsche cannot be seen as a forerunner of fascism. I am more ambivalent about that latter point.

While I also entertain the possibility that, of his two fundamental premises, the Eternal Recurrence may take precedence over the Will to Power – because in my view it contains the remedy for the resentment and desire for revenge against the past that tends to envelop the Will to Power left entirely to its own devices by asking us to affirm everything that has taken place in life to bring us to the current crossroads of past and future – Lowith (1997) argues that the eternal recurrence is actually incompatible with the will to power because the infinite repetition of a finite number of events would render freedom impossible, since all such actions would be predestined. I argue in this chapter that this is precisely why Nietzsche could *not* have understood the eternal recurrence in this way. Instead, we will not know until after the advent of the Overman what the full sequence of events is that has eternally recurred, nor does anything exclude the creation of new values after the advent of the Overman that will in turn retroactively open up our knowledge of the full sequence of events that have eternally recurred. For other interesting discussions of the eternal recurrence, see Klossowski (1969) and Schrag (1970).

Reginster (2009) makes a valuable contribution by stressing the centrality of nihilism to Nietzsche's enterprise, why it is generated by Christianity, and how the Will to Power is meant as an antidote to nihilistic despair through a reaffirmation of life. More stress, I think, could be laid on the profoundly ambivalent character of Nietzsche's assessment of Christianity, including its positive role as the greatest "will to untruth" to date, and therefore the source of tremendous spiritual deepening, while it is at the same time the drive for herd-morality and democratic leveling.

In his reflections on how ethics should avoid formalism in favor of experience and temperament without thereby also abandoning truthfulness, Williams (1985) was taken with Nietzsche's argument that morality cannot go on as it has before in the absence of religious belief. Moral categories like Ought, Right and Good lose their authority without "the prerogatives of a Pelagian God."

Shaw (2010) offers an interesting variation on the observation made in this chapter that Nietzsche's project is "beyond politics" in a way not dissimilar to Marx, and therefore can provide no specific details about its norms or institutions. According to Shaw, Nietzsche's resistance to any form of state ideology, coupled with the modern decline of religious belief, leaves him unable to suggest how his own prescription could provide a basis for political authority.

Church (2014) argues that Hegel and Nietzsche share in common the wish to harmonize the modern defense of individual liberty with the classical conception of the community as having a higher claim than individuality, resulting in the "historical individual," incorporating the distinctive contributions of both ancients and moderns. As a general thesis this is unexceptionable, but I think it leads Church to soften or underplay the intransigent differences between what Hegel and Nietzsche mean by these terms, summed up in the complete incompatibility of their visions for the future – the "end of history" versus the Overman.

Hill (2005) makes an interesting and erudite argument that, in spite of what appears to be Nietzsche's deprecatory view of Kant throughout his works, his philosophy can only be understood in relation to Kant, and that Nietzsche had a much deeper grasp of Kant's three critiques than is commonly supposed. For instance, according to Hill, Nietzsche's *The Birth of Tragedy* emerged from his close reading of Kant's *Critique of Judgement*. I recognize a kind of pedigree connecting the two works inasmuch as in the Third Critique Kant, not unlike Schiller, denies that art can be comprehended by pure reason or by the metaphysics of morals, and claims instead that the sentiments of the artist emerge out of nature and are sublimated by their interaction with artistic form, thus yielding the work of art as a synthesis of nature and thought. In some ways, this is not far from Nietzsche's evocation of "the world-artist" in *The Birth of Tragedy*. Nevertheless, we have Nietzsche's own word for it that he regarded Schiller's conception of the artwork, as exemplified by Homeric poetry, as too smooth a synthesis of nature and beauty, at bottom a species of Rousseau's Romanticism, whereas for Nietzsche, Homeric poetry erupted from a titanic clash of warring forces. In my view, this critique of Schiller's aesthetics would extend *mutatis mutandis* to Kant's understanding of the artwork.

The deeper problem with Hill's argument that Nietzsche is philosophically indebted to Kant, however, is over Nietzsche's conception of the self. Nothing could be further than Kant's assumption of a fixed individual subject – in this respect at one with the early liberal theories of the Age of Reason and the Enlightenment – from Nietzsche's insistence that the self originates in the pre-self; that what we identify as a self is only the final expression of a field of forces that radiate through the human affects, and that to understand selfhood, we must regress behind it into the affects that link us to life as Will to Power. As Nietzsche puts it in *The Genealogy of Morals*, there is no such thing as human nature or an independent self: "There is no such substratum, there is no 'being' behind doing, affecting, becoming; 'the doer' is merely a fiction added to the deed – the deed is everything." In other words, the will to power is utterly de-subjectivized. For this reason, there is no parallel in Nietzsche's thought to the rights-bearing individual capable of moral autonomy in Kant's ethical system; indeed, for Nietzsche, it is altogether impossible to conceive of a binding formal ethic such as Kant's Categorical Imperative because life is historical and timebound through and through. I think the most appreciative remark Nietzsche makes about Kant is when he calls him "the great delayer." I take him to mean that, by attempting to erect the rational framework of the Categorical Imperative over the maelstrom of nature as matter in motion so as to tame its chaos, Kant was the last attempt at building a bulwark of modern rationality to hold back the Will to Power – a "scarecrow" of morality, as Nietzsche put it in *The Will to Power*.

Nietzsche's fullest discussion of the Ascetic Ideal and how it is not refuted by modern science but is its culmination is in the *Genealogy of Morals*: "[The Ascetic Ideal] believes that no power exists on earth that does not first have to receive a meaning, a right to exist, a value, as a good of the ascetic ideal, as a way and means to *its* goal, to *one* goal. But it has not yet 'found its match,' the new 'one goal,' the Overman." Science does not refute the ascetic ideal, but is "rather the latest and noblest form of it." But left to itself, it has "absolutely no belief in itself." It has bled itself of "passions, love, ardor and suffering," another permutation of the sacrifice of God to the Idea of God. Incidentally, while Marx's name does not appear in Nietzsche's writings, he does remark that after the destruction of "the great chain of being" modern man "has become an animal," perhaps alluding to Marx's "animal kingdom of man."

Rosen (2004) is the originator of the view I discuss in this chapter that Nietzsche has an esoteric and an exoteric teaching. The esoteric teaching is that reality is sheer unintelligible chaos. The exoteric teaching includes the doctrines of the Will to Power, the Eternal Recurrence, and the endurance of nobility, which Rosen interprets as Nietzsche's wish to give us something to cling to rather than be swept away by the purposeless maelstrom of becoming. I am *partly* convinced by this interpretation, but find that I cannot follow it as far as Rosen does, for whom it leads to an irreconcilable contradiction between the prospect of a revolutionary transformation in the future that is promised by the exoteric teaching and the utter meaninglessness and hopelessness of life in the esoteric teaching. In my view, the principles of the will to power and the eternal recurrence are meant quite literally by Nietzsche as ontological premises that explain the whole, out of which history has generated archetypes of greatness that endow the past with meaning and point the way to our ultimate salvation, the Overman. This does not preclude the possibility that Nietzsche may rhetorically *overstate* the certainty of these archetypes – the Free Spirits, the Saint, the Noble, the Roman Caesar with the soul of Christ – in order to give us ladder rungs, so to speak, to avoid being sucked into the vortex of the abyss. And, as I repeatedly stress, Nietzsche cannot speculate on what precise form the advent of the Overman will assume or evince any certainty that it will happen at all. But I am not convinced of the need to drive a wedge into such possibly rhetorical overstatements that lops the two teachings into an irreconcilable contradiction. An indisputable merit of Rosen's book is that he believes that, in what Rosen views as his exoteric teaching, Nietzsche envisioned a world-scale revolution, not only philosophically but politically. Rosen also believes the exoteric teaching is philosophically coherent. So he rejects both the contemporary wish to defang Nietzsche and make him into a liberal lifestyle coach and the postmodernist attempt to deconstruct his thought into a series of stylistic tropes.

Lampert's books on Nietzsche (1989, 2004, 2013, 2018) have deservedly gained him an admiring following for their exegetical rigor. He undertakes his reflections on Nietzsche partly mediated by his reflections on Leo Strauss, and he employs Nietzsche in turn to open up what he sees as some core themes of Strauss' own teaching. Like myself and others mentioned above, he regards the will to power and the eternal return as the essential and interrelated themes in Nietzsche's thought. He interprets Strauss as thinking that the eternal return and the future to which it pointed represented Nietzsche's return to the concept of nature, which had been wounded or fragmented by the modern Machiavellian and Baconian project for its conquest: Having once been integrated within nature, modern man had been torn from it. Through the eternal return and the new era to come, the possibility of man's natural wholeness will be reinstated.

Regarding the accuracy of Lampert's interpretation of how Strauss interprets Nietzsche, I will leave it at questioning whether an understanding of "nature" so entirely assimilated to historicism, even if that historicism is not mere random flux but points toward a future fulfillment, does not stretch the meaning of the concept of nature past the breaking point: in other words, *any* concept of the whole is tantamount to a concept of nature. The difficulty to which this assumption is exposed, I think, is clear from this chapter and Nietzsche's lifelong defense of the thoroughgoing historicity of human experience, indeed of all existence, culminating in the identification of the whole as "will to power, and nothing else," to say nothing of his strictures against Platonism's assumption of an eternal transhistorical truth and against the metaphysical subversion of historicity that he believes was undertaken by Hegelianism. I will also leave it at observing that I am not convinced Strauss believed that Plato and Nietzsche shared the same belief about the whole, differing only in that Plato disguised it exoterically while Nietzsche did not. It is clear that Strauss identified Nietzsche with "the historical school," and as a follower of Callicles rather than Socrates. I have written about this elsewhere (2010) and plan to do so again.

For the purposes of my discussion of Nietzsche here, Lampert's main argument is that Strauss and Nietzsche agree that eros is the fundamental principle of existence, the "being of beings," and since Lampert identifies eros with will to power, he concludes that Strauss implicitly agrees with Nietzsche that the character of all reality is will to power. However, as Zuckert (2014) usefully observes, Strauss *distinguishes* between eros and will to power: "Nietzsche [Strauss wrote] replaces eros by the will to power – a striving which has a goal by a striving which has no goal." This comports with my consistent use of Plato's eros for knowledge of the eternal truth as a foil for Nietzsche's ontology of the will to power in particular and for historicism in general. Nietzsche's replacement of eros with will to power, according to Strauss, demonstrates "the serious *opposition* of Nietzsche to Socrates." Platonic eros cannot be will to power because eros is the longing for the good, that is, a "love of the truth that is independent of will or decision" (Strauss in Zuckert, 2014). I tried to highlight the differences between Platonic eros and Nietzsche's evocation of erotic longing and the relationship between life and wisdom in my discussion of *The Night Song* in *Zarathustra*, which Nietzsche expands upon in the final aphorism of *Beyond Good and Evil*, writing of his "painted thoughts," his "loved ones," likening them to birds he can only catch and "immortalize" when they are tired and "can no longer live or fly, only weary and mellow things." For my full interpretation of *The Dancing Song*, see Newell (Spring 1990).

I follow Strauss' suggestion that *Beyond Good and Evil* is divided into two parts, separated by the *Epigrams and Interludes*. The first "is devoted chiefly to philosophy and religion and the second chiefly to morals and politics" (Strauss, 1983). Pangle's brief discussion of the three songs from *Zarathustra* discussed in this chapter is very helpful (1986). The work of Heber-Suffrin (2015) drew my attention to the theme of Zarathustra's second coming; that in Nietzsche's resuscitation of the Iranian sage, he came "to contradict his first message." As regards Jung's reception of Nietzsche focusing on "the Dionysian self," consider Bishop (1995). I should add in this connection that Eliade (1981) furnishes evidence of the broader mythological context for Nietzsche's evocation of the Apollonian and the Dionysian in *The Birth of Tragedy* and their reconciliation at Delphi. A variation on Nietzsche's critique of Socrates in *Beyond Good and Evil* can be found in *The Twilight of the Idols* (1978), where he faults Socrates' use of dialectic for inviting others from the "lower orders" to dispute their betters, for whom argumentation was considered to be in bad taste. Nietzsche sums up Socrates' creed of utility as the equation of reason, virtue and happiness. For Nietzsche's early enthusiasm for Spinoza, see his postcard to Overbeck: "[I]n five main points of his doctrine I recognize myself; he denies the freedom of the will, teleology, the moral world order, the unegoistic, and evil. Even though the divergences are admittedly tremendous, they are due more to the difference in time, culture, and science" (in Turner, 2014). For an example of how historicism lost its politically conservative character after Hegel, see Marx's critique of Gustav Hugo, who identified the validity of the law with tradition even when it legitimized oppression, discussed in Levine (1987).

Now to Nietzsche and politics. As regards the Old Nietzsche versus the New Nietzsche, let's start with the Old. The best-known war horse for the indictment of Nietzsche as a forerunner of fascism remains McGovern (1941), whose title says it all: *From Luther to Hitler: The History of Fascist-Nazi Political Philosophy*, published at the height of the Western allies' life and death struggle with the Third Reich. Unfortunately, McGovern believed that the entire previous 400 years of German history had been a single, relentless movement forward to the Fuhrer, involving virtually every philosopher and religious and cultural figure of note. He did this by defining fascism as authoritarianism and *etatisme*, that is to say, as essentially indistinguishable from the Great Power imperialism of Napoleon III, Bismarck or the Kaiser, and regarded any conservative critique of the Enlightenment and modern democratic society going back to the French Revolution as synonymous with what became National Socialism. In other words, anything that was not unreservedly liberal must have been fascist. This was an understandable if utterly provincial perspective given the danger of the era and the fact that so little was clearly understood about Nazi ideology even as the West struggled against it. Genuine proto-fascist Volkisch ideologues like Moeller van den Brucke go unmentioned, while Hegel is unreservedly and absurdly claimed for the fascist camp. Heidegger's name never appears because he was virtually unknown outside of Germany at this time. Still, I prefer McGovern's morally decent provincialism to the absurdities of Nietzsche's rehabilitation as a liberal.

The New Nietzsche begins in a moderate enough way with the study by Kauffman (1975), first published shortly after World War II. Kauffman attempts to separate what he regards as Nietzsche's authentic ideas from the way they had been distorted and exploited by the Nazis and other extremists. While conceding the inflammatory quality of his writing, Kauffman insists that the doctrine of the will to power should not be identified with literal and ruthless domination, but contextualized by connecting it to Nietzsche's ideas about sublimation and psychological self-development. One can never be grateful enough to Kauffman for his fine translations of Nietzsche. His interpretation of Nietzsche can be appreciated for its attempt at fair-mindedness, but in my view it played a large role in defanging the dangerous political implications of Nietzsche's thought by reducing the will to power to a purely personal, inward creed of askesis and, with no justification at all, excluding the possibility that Nietzsche was entirely serious about his call for a coming global struggle for the mastery of the earth by a new master race.

Hunt (1993) argues that Nietzsche's philosophy does contain a coherent ethical theory and that one can extract from it a "Nietzschean liberalism," although he admits that it is at odds with much of the content of Nietzsche's own writings. As regards the first claim, I have tried to show that since Nietzsche rejects the Platonic account of the whole, embraces a radical historicism that makes it impossible to find a Kantian purchase for an ethics that stands outside of historical events, while at the same time eschewing a Hegelian account of the teleological progress of history, it is impossible to find a binding ethical principle in his writings (unless it is synonymous with a certain kind of teaching about character formation). As regards the second claim, Nietzsche's writings are so brimming with a coruscating and cheerful illiberalism and hatred of democracy that in order to extract from them any variety of liberalism would be, as I suggested, like converting his works into those redacted FOIA documents where nine out of every ten words are blacked out. Hunt's Nietzschean liberalism reduces to the unexceptionable claim that Nietzsche encourages us to think critically.

In their edited volume, Golomb and Wistrich (2003) try to strike a balance between conceding that "there is much that is disturbingly anti-egalitarian and anti-democratic in Nietzsche" while maintaining that his "emphasis on individualism and contempt for German nationalism put him at stark odds with Nazi ideology." If I am right, however, Nietzsche is anything but a defender of individualism in the strict sense, and his contempt for German nationalism did not preclude – indeed it stimulated – his vision of the twentieth century as a global battle for the mastery of the earth.

The New Nietzsche gathers force with the edited volume of the same name from Allison (1985). It contains essays of varying insightfulness by Derrida, Heidegger, Deleuze, Klossowski and others. But its central claim is, as Allison puts it, that "it seems practically impossible for a contemporary reader of Nietzsche not to encounter Nietzsche's texts except by way of Heidegger or Derrida," thereby claiming Nietzsche for contemporary postmodernism. This new deconstructionist approach to Nietzsche aims to dismantle all earlier attempts to systematize his philosophy and turn it into a series of "non-theses." Critics rightly observed that the assertion that one can only encounter Nietzsche through Heidegger or Derrida was baseless, given the existence of numerous other interpretative studies including the ones we discussed earlier. As I will argue in the next chapter, we must be particularly wary of using Heidegger as a guide to Nietzsche because of his gross distortion of some of Nietzsche's ideas. As for Derrida, to view Nietzsche through the lens of his writings reduces Nietzsche to nothing more than a stylist. As I will argue in the Conclusion, one cannot understand either Nietzsche or Heidegger adequately through relying on their epigones like Derrida, who mined their works for a few useful hooks and ignored the rest. In contrast with this deconstructionist approach to Nietzsche, I have tried to make the case that he was both a profound and a systematic thinker in the great tradition of philosophy.

Many contemporary social movements have also invoked Nietzsche's ideas. Call (2001), who mistakenly views Nietzsche as an anarchist, also purports to find in his writings a postmodernist feminism based on the idea that, since truth is nothing but metaphors, we can make truth into anything we want. Hallman (1991) argues there is a "latent" ethic in Nietzsche's writings that is "compatible with an ecologically oriented, environmentally concerned philosophizing." It must be very latent indeed. Hutter (2005) may be taken as an extreme case of the wishful thinking rejigging and bowdlerization of Nietzsche into a lifestyle coach of personal askesis, a Socratic despite all appearances to the contrary whose chief concern is the modern soul. My response to these variations on the New Nietzsche is the same as my responses to Hunt, Deleuze and Kauffman.

Drochon (2016) has speculated in an article that Nietzsche would have opposed Brexit and supported staying in the European Union on the grounds of his opposition to the nationalism of his own era, an untenable assumption that I addressed in this chapter by suggesting that, although Nietzsche did believe mankind must advance beyond the "petty politics" of nationalism, guided by the dream of a united Europe, its ultimate aim – the advent of the Overman – resembled in no way, shape or form the capitalist and bureaucratic European Union of today, which Nietzsche would have seen as the ultimate realization of the modern bourgeois nation-state as "the beast with a thousand eyes." Drochon's book (2016) is based on the interesting contention that we should not attempt to view Nietzsche in terms either of his appropriation by the Nazis or by postmodern democratic theory, but should view him strictly in the terms of his own era and his adaptation of Bismarck's notion of a unified Europe as his own. It is a well-argued book, but to my mind cannot be reconciled with Nietzsche's low opinion of Bismarckian Great Power nationalism or with his belief that mankind's redemption can come only through a future in which the human condition is entirely transformed in an apocalyptic and revolutionary reversal.

Chapter 4

Bracketed references to *Being and Time* and *An Introduction to Metaphysics* are to the pagination in the original German editions. I am going to begin with some general works about Heidegger's philosophy before proceeding to the impact of his writings on political and social thought and the controversy surrounding his involvement with National Socialism. However, it is sometimes hard to disentangle the general works from a discussion of Heidegger's political significance. That is because, whereas Nietzsche's political impact took place largely after his writings were complete, in Heidegger's case, the philosophical and political significance of his writings were intertwined from the beginning.

Steiner (1978) still provides the best introduction to Heidegger for a first-time reader. He performs the great service of taking Heidegger's notoriously abstruse terminological lexicon and illustrating, in straightforward colloquial language, how its terms emerge from real-life experiences that all of us are likely to have had – loneliness, anxiety and doubt about the possibility of happiness or purpose. Barrett (1976) offers a similar evocation of why we should care about Heidegger's account of everyday life, stripped of its peculiar jargon, centering on man's feeling of homelessness in the modern world.

To me, the best general discussion of Heidegger's philosophy for specialists remains that of Marx (1971), particularly because of its use of Aristotle and Hegel as two alternatives against which Heidegger orients his own call for a renewed Question of Being. Whereas I have stressed the seamless intertwining of Heidegger's philosophical speculations and his engagement in the politics of his day, Marx's treatment is scrupulously empty of all political implications and associations, which can be justified on the grounds that, before one can assess the political implications of Heidegger's ontology, one must make the most painstaking and technically rigorous efforts to comprehend it. But there is a surprise ending – see below.

Poggeler (1974) provides a still-durable overview of the grand themes of Heidegger's philosophical enterprise, from his encounter with the ancient Greeks, his understanding of historicity, his engagement with Nietzsche and Holderlin to his postwar vision of a new beginning for mankind – always stressing the provisional character of his "paths." The volume by Velkley on Heidegger and Strauss (2011) together with his study already cited of Rousseau and his legacy to the Philosophy of Freedom (2002) provide a deeply insightful study of Heidegger's thought. It is a merit of Velkley's examination of Heidegger and Strauss that he stresses that Strauss never simply turned his back on Heidegger's work after an early attraction to it, but continued to engage Heidegger on the origins of philosophy and its continuing possibility.

Dahlstrom (2000) offers a fresh take on what Heidegger meant by existential truth in his early work through exploring the interconnectedness of truth, being and time, and in particular Heidegger's confrontation with his early mentor Husserl. Polt (1997) offers a widely admired introduction to Heidegger's philosophy, written in a clear and accessible manner, linking the emergence of his thought to his personality and background. Focusing on Heidegger's central concern, the Question of Being, Polt anchors his analysis in *Being and Time* and ties it to the major features of his later thought. He enters into the controversy over Heidegger's involvement with National Socialism and parses reactions to it that run the gamut from exculpation to unmitigated condemnation. Copobianco (2011) focuses attention on the way in which, for Heidegger, Being comes to presence as *lichtung* and locates it within his engagement with ancient Greek and Eastern thinking. Kisiel (1995) provides a genetic account of the emergence of *Being and Time* from a combination of Heidegger's personal and intellectual biography. In this connection, for an account of how neo-Kantianism was displaced in the German university beginning in the early 1900s, leading to a Hegel revival and Heidegger's emergence, see Gadamer (1983).

As I discuss in this chapter, some interpreters detect a "turn" in Heidegger's thought away from *Being and Time*, whereas others see a continuity between it and the later works. Heidegger himself discouraged the notion of a turn in his works. See the discussion in Krell (1977). Richardson (1993) provides perhaps the most influential defense of the notion of a "turn" from the existential analytic of Dasein to the "thinking" of Being, although he stresses that the latter stage does not constitute a contradiction of the former. I have argued in this chapter that, while a shift of emphasis from the reciprocal engagement of Dasein and *Sein* in *Being and Time* to the "determinate" history of Being beginning in *An Introduction to Metaphysics* certainly takes place, the history of Being is already implicit in the opening pages of *Being and Time* itself, such that the turn is no more than a shift in perspective – which I am not sure is appreciably different from Richardson's position. Harries (1976) aptly describes *An Introduction to Metaphysics* as "developing new themes" whose "roots" are in *Being and Time*.

The reading of *Being and Time* by Dreyfus (1990) drew attention by attempting to assimilate Heidegger's existential analytic of Dasein to mainstream Anglo-American analytic philosophy, including the philosophy of mind and cognitive science. While this attempt at a marriage between the two schools was admirable, unless I am wrong in my reading of Heidegger and his critique of "productionist" reasoning, including positivism, it must come perilously close to being shotgun. As Heidegger put it in *The Anaximander Fragment* (1984): "As it reveals itself in beings, Being withdraws," which would appear to scotch the case for analytical philosophy – an impression heightened when we remember Heidegger's strictures against the very notion that Being can be understood as "mediated" by reason.

Having considered some general interpretations that at least, relatively speaking, try to keep Heidegger's politicality on the margins of considering the intrinsic content of his thought, let us now proceed to the direct impact of his writings on political thought and practice. Scholarship assessing Heidegger's significance for political theory has tended to fall into three categories – his impact on other thinkers; his own reflections on the political; his specific involvement with National Socialism. For an overview of Heidegger's impact on other political theories, see Steiner (1978) and Jay (1973). I will offer an analysis of these linkages in the Conclusion. For an assessment of Heidegger's works for their own direct significance as political theory, see Poggeler (1974), Schwan (1965) and Palmier (1968). There is no general study of Heidegger's political thought in English comparable to, for example, Avineri's volumes on Hegel and Marx because, for the reasons explored in this chapter, he did not regard the enterprise of establishing the legitimacy of the modern state to be a viable one. However, as we also observed, his works after World War II continue to exhibit traces of a certain understanding of politics. The study of Heidegger by Blitz (1981) performed the very useful service of reflecting on whether Heidegger's fundamental ontology in *Being and Time* could give rise to any positive account of political philosophy, including the theme of the best regime or legitimate political order, a question I have pursued in my own way in this chapter.

As for Heidegger's indubitable commitment to the Third Reich, opinion has been divided between those who regarded it as a personal aberration with no intrinsic connection to Heidegger's philosophy (Arendt, 1978; Krell, 1977; Waehlens, 1946; Weil, 1946) and those – including this author – who have seen a connection, more or less direct, between Heidegger's political commitment and his philosophy of the period (Adorno, 1973; Grant, 1978; Harries, 1976; Lowith, 1946; Rosen, 1969; Steiner, 1978). Schmitt (1969) and Nicholson (1971) argued that the political teaching of *Being and Time* is anarchistic. While there is a degree of truth to this (in, for example, Heidegger's insistence in the Rectoral Address on a dimension of "resistance" between the movement and its leader), as Harries (1976) points out, it involves a selective reading which downplays Heidegger's overall massive insistence that "man exists essentially with others" and shares "the destiny of a people." Hoy (1978) writes similarly of Heidegger's insistence that "Dasein (man) is not an isolated, private ego but most primordially a social, communal and historical being." None of those just cited who see an intrinsic connection between Heidegger's philosophy of the 1920s and 1930s and National Socialism, however, would have argued that his philosophy was entirely reducible to a fascist ideology – as Nicholson put it (1971), a third way must be found of addressing the political implications of Heidegger's thought besides the two extremes of characterizing it as "fascist" or "unpolitical." That is the approach I follow in this chapter.

Some interpreters who do not identify Heidegger's significance as being exhausted by his Nazi commitment nevertheless speculate about the ways in which fundamental ontology was open to such a temptation. As Hoy (1978) remarks, "an important feature of Heidegger's ontological analysis of historicity is that nothing follows from the analysis about what the *content* of history must be. Hegel's concept of history, in contrast, is far more prescriptive." In other words, because Heidegger's understanding of historicity is incapable of providing criteria for choosing between morally good and bad courses of action, it leaves a vacuum bereft of ethics into which a movement like Nazism could flow. Adorno (1973) makes the interesting argument that precisely because fundamental ontology is so abstract, it "succumbs to cultural mediations all the more; they recur as social aspects of that ontology's own purity." Hence, fundamental ontology becomes the hostage and legitimizer of the "here and now." Again, because it contains no ethical prescription or positive historical teleology, Heidegger's ontology of Being can be swamped by whatever political and social forces happen to prevail (for example, National Socialism), which would not be the case with the far more prescriptive historical dialectics of Hegel or Marx. Although Adorno is correct to point out the unmediated quality of fundamental ontology, I think he overestimates its merely passive receptivity to whatever political forces overwhelm it and underestimates the "revolutionary radicalism," to use Lowith's phrase (1946) of Heideggerian "resolve" to recover the people's destiny. In other words, as Fackenheim formulates it (1982), did fundamental ontology merely "permit" Heidegger to embrace National Socialism, or did it demand that commitment? I have argued for the latter. Lowith (1946) saw in Heideggerian "resolve" the decisionist philosophy of Carl Schmitt placed at the service of a unified and historically unique German community. It should be added that, while setting no moral limits on resolve itself, Heidegger directs this resolve toward a definite *kind* of political alternative, if only by the exclusion of other alternatives (such as, in the 1920s and 1930s, liberalism and communism). Thus, as Blitz remarks (1981), "authentic political resolve ... would not be true of every political alternative."

A further word about Blitz: I have argued in this chapter that Heidegger's relegation of the realm of opinion (with which the Platonic Socrates argued in the *Phaedo* the dialectic of the Ideas must begin) to everyday "chatter" reflecting conformism to the status quo made the activity of political philosophy in the traditional sense impossible, including the character of the best regime. The study by Blitz was an early and distinguished engagement with this issue in the field of political theory. Blitz's work also stood out in the ranks of political theorists of the Straussian school because of his competence to address the technical philosophical issues surrounding Heidegger's ontology. This was not widespread. Another early and worthy work was that of Gillespie (1984), who carefully contrasts the approaches to historical existence of Hegel and Heidegger, although I think at times that he does not distinguish with sufficient clarity between what Plato means by Being and what Heidegger means by Being, seeming to take it for granted that they shared the same view, but that Heidegger claimed to have identified its terrible contemporary outcome. This is defensible exegetically, insofar as one wants to get it right about what Heidegger thought Plato meant by Being, or about how the history of Being had worked out. But if, as I have tried to do here, one keeps in mind the enormous contrast between their respective approaches – such that their views of the whole are antipodal opposites – not only does one bring into sharper relief Heidegger's originality as a thinker, but one is in a position to attempt a Platonic critique of his ontology.

Further to the frequently remarked-upon abstractness of fundamental ontology, Megill (1987) astutely observes that the Rectoral Address conflates the need for the reform of the German university, of higher learning, and the "coordination" of the German people without distinguishing among these "equally abstract" aims. German students are "on the march," but is it "toward a true understanding of the essence of science or toward the complete overthrow of the Treaty of Versailles?" To me, this conflation of purposes is symptomatic of how all such concrete and proximal distinctions are lost in Heidegger's originary account of Being as a vortex of sheer possibility. The important studies by Lacoue-Labarthe (2007) suggest that Heidegger's stance toward politics can best be understood through his interpretation of Holderlin's poetry, including his original commitment to National Socialism and his qualified and implicit repudiation of it in favor of the quietistic *Heimat* or "dwelling place" after World War II. In this chapter, I too have discussed the connection between Holderlin and Heidegger's understanding of the political, but I would not attach as much weight to it as does Lacoue-Labarthe, because I believe that Heidegger's political leanings emerged directly from his meditations on the Question of Being, of which the Holderlin strain would be but one manifestation, and I would also limit Holderlin's impact on Heidegger's understanding of the political mainly to his post-Nazi period. I have argued in this chapter that Heidegger's post-Nazi millenarian vision of the coming self-unwinding of technology and advent of the Shepherd of Being resolves many of the paradoxes in his thought regarding the relationship between reason and existence, and contains an implicitly political undertone. My use of the phrase "eschatological reversal" comes from Gadamer's characterization of Heidegger's later thought: "Philosophy would recognize itself as a kind of secularized eschatology, establishing a kind of expectation of a possible historical reversal" (1982). See also Mehta (1976), who writes that "Heidegger's philosophy represents the historic moment of self-abrogation, the 'reversal' of the metaphysical tradition and is itself conditioned by this tradition."

I have mentioned my admiration for the rigor of Marx's book and its scrupulous adherence to a purely theoretical perspective. However, in the last few pages Marx departs from that approach and concludes with a brief but remarkably insightful attempt to characterize Heidegger's approach to the political, referring directly to National Socialism and its aftermath. As he argues, the fact that, for Heidegger, "the National Socialist revolution" could only take place violently, permeated with "evil as well as error and sham," was entirely to be expected from its status as "an occurrence of truth." For Heidegger, a violent political founding was "only a consequence of the coordination of evil and good in the clearing of Being," meaning that such founders could not be held guilty on the basis of "moral considerations." Far from having "erred" about the violence and evil of National Socialism out of naivete, therefore, "on the contrary, he must have *a priori* assessed it correctly, since he viewed it as an 'occurrence of truth.'" In other words, Heidegger foresaw the potential of National Socialism for tyranny from the outset, and knowingly embraced it. And for these reasons, to emphasize the arguments made in this chapter, it never occurred to him after World War II to repudiate or condemn it in retrospect, including the Holocaust.

I argue in this chapter that the timeline in the response to Heidegger's National Socialism followed a different trajectory from the response to Nietzsche's alleged political extremism. Whereas the assessment of Nietzsche in the Anglosphere went from condemnatory to exculpatory (hardening again just recently in some quarters into the condemnatory), with Heidegger it was more nearly the reverse. At first neither Heidegger nor his commitment to National Socialism were widely known outside of Germany and France. When he did begin to gain attention in the Anglosphere, at first his commitment in 1933 was treated with reticence if not ignored, either out of a wish to preserve his reputation or perhaps because it was not widely known about. Mosse's study of the intellectual origins of the Third Reich, first published in 1964, makes no mention of Heidegger, whereas Schmitt and Nietzsche are discussed – a sign of the extent to which Heidegger was still very little known in the United States. The volume by Runes (1965) was published a year later. Though it had little impact (and was misleadingly entitled *German Existentialism* with Heidegger identified as the author), it was for its time a very informative compendium of public statements by Heidegger supporting the Nazi regime (including a shortened version of the Rectoral Address) as well as newspaper items about Heidegger's daily activities on behalf of the movement as rector. Despite the reams of new material that have been published since then on Heidegger's commitment to the Party, everything essential one needs to know about it is in fact here – one could have easily inferred in 1965 what was later established with complete documentary certainty about what attracted him to National Socialism and how he served it. And it was inconceivable even then, to anyone with a knowledge of the history of that era, that Heidegger could have accepted such a prestigious university appointment and the public endorsement of the Third Reich that it entailed while remaining oblivious to the violent anti-Semitism that was at the movement's core.

After that, as critical theory and postmodernism gained increasing influence in the academy, Heidegger, too, became more widely known, and, as we have observed, the debate about the meaning and extent of his National Socialism followed his influence across the Atlantic. Beginning in the 1990s, the evolution from reticence to discuss the controversy to the search for a middle ground that would combine an acknowledgement of its connection to his ontology of Being but not reduce Heidegger's significance to his Nazi period alone (my approach in this book) increasingly gave way to an extreme of unqualified condemnation.

Faye (2011) kicked off this new phase, drawing upon previously unpublished material by Heidegger to argue that his commitment to National Socialism was much deeper than previously supposed, to the point that its philosophical value was entirely vitiated by that commitment, with the consequence, in Faye's view, that Heidegger's works should be removed from the Philosophy section of the library and placed in the History of Fascism shelves. Farias (1991) makes a similar argument to the effect that Heidegger never recanted his commitment to National Socialism, remained personally faithful to its core principles even after World War II, offered no criticism of the Holocaust, and was a lifelong anti-Semite. The publication of Heidegger's so-called Black Notebooks in 2014 claimed to have confirmed at last that Heidegger had been an anti-Semite and remained one even after giving up on National Socialism. See Mitchell and Tawney (2017).

Although these works offer some important insights into Heidegger's commitment to the Third Reich based on newly available documentary evidence, they are characterized, in my view, by the typical academic publishing ploy of erecting a straw man – that is to say, a position which almost no informed person holds – and then knocking it down to prove that one is offering an original new interpretation. They depict interpretations of Heidegger's Nazism before their own works as uniformly naive and exculpatory, when in fact, as we have outlined, the full-throated criticism of Heidegger's Nazi commitment and its undeniably intrinsic connection to his ontology of Being had emerged as early as 1946 and battled with Heidegger's apologists throughout the ensuing decades. The same is true of Wollin (1993), who believes that, after the appearance of his own books, "we cannot help but read [Heidegger] differently ... insofar as we know that his enthusiasm for National Socialism, far from being a fortuitous political flirtation, was philosophically overdetermined," despite the previous appearance of the article by Harries on Heidegger as a political thinker (1976), my own article on the political implications of Heidegger's early thought (1984), and the critiques already cited by Rosen, Steiner, Lowith and Adorno among others. In other words, it had been established well before 1991 that Heidegger's Nazism was not a fortuitous flirtation. Again, the existing evidence about Heidegger's Nazi commitment going back decades, while not exhaustive, had been more than ample to establish that fact.

As for Heidegger's anti-Semitism, there is no denying this ugly fact. But the evidence offered by the Black Books in 2014 did nothing to alter the fact that, as I have argued in this chapter, Heidegger – quite consistently with his ontological principles – did not embrace the biological racism and pseudoscience that was at the core of Nazi anti-Semitism. This, as I suggested, differentiates his anti-Semitism during the Nazi period from that of Carl Schmitt, who did embrace the Nazis' biological racism much more directly in his campaign to remove "Jewish influence" from German law and in his support of the Nuremberg Laws, the subject of a very good book by Gross (2007). The prejudices about Jews that Heidegger entertained in his diary are of a piece with the standard cultural anti-Semitism of his era – that "world Jewry" stands for capitalistic greed and a rejection of tradition and honor, just like the Americans and the British. As for the fact that Heidegger never recanted his National Socialism, never apologized for it or expressed his regret about the Holocaust, I have tried to show in this chapter how those actions followed necessarily from his understanding of the History of Being working itself out as global technology – in other words, that his refusal to repudiate his earlier National Socialist commitment was intrinsically connected to his ontology of Being, just as had been his earlier commitment to it.

Now let us turn, in conclusion, to some interpretations of specific texts and themes of Heidegger that we examine in this chapter and to some of Heidegger's interpretations of other major thinkers. My opening discussion of the Tree of Being as an overview of Heideggerian ontology is a variation on Heidegger's use of this comparison (1972), where he evokes the tree as rooted "on that soil upon which we live and die, if we are honest with ourselves." In contrast with our meditation upon the temporal Being of the tree, according to Heidegger, metaphysics presents a "glittering deception" limited to "the objective and static surfaces and foreground facets of all things as alone valid and valuable – a setup with whose help man carries on and degrades everything."

As I observed in this chapter, Heidegger's approach to fundamental ontology in *Being and Time* was sometimes mistaken for a kind of neo-Kantian subjective individualism, even though, as I argue, there is abundant evidence to the contrary in *Being and Time* itself and throughout his subsequent works. Reflecting this perspective, Korner (1974) wrote that Heidegger's analytic of Dasein employs "provocatively Kantian terminology." In my view, by contrast, Heidegger commends Kant for emptying his concept of selfhood of all "soul substance" – that is to say, of all traditional accounts of character formation and psychological motivation, making it the very opposite of Korner's assertion that for Heidegger selfhood "is no more than a variation of the old theme of rational psychology." Heidegger then takes Kant to task for, in effect, a failure of nerve: having reached the point of intersection between Dasein and *Sein* in the vortex of temporality, he hesitated on the brink and ended up reaffirming the modern Cartesian individual self.

Since the debate about whether and to what extent Heidegger clung to a subjectivist Kantian account of Dasein in *Being and Time* is important for establishing whether or not his later works represented a "turn" from the history of Dasein to the history of *Sein* – I have maintained they do not, in any fundamental sense, because the history of *Sein* is already implicit in *Being and Time* – it is worth supplementing my account of Heidegger's critique of Kant in *Being and Time* with his more extensive discussion in his book on Kant and the problem of metaphysics (1975). There, Heidegger writes, Kant establishes "the intrinsic possibility of ontology as the disclosure of transcendence, i.e. the subjectivity of the subject." But Kant falls short of establishing this "pure anthropology" because his anthropology remains "empirical," a criticism that is consistent with what Heidegger wrote in *Being and Time*. Although Kant marched up to the edge of "the revelation of the subjectivity of the subject, Kant recoiled from the ground which he himself had established." In other words, according to Heidegger, Kant could not abandon the reified individual self and follow subjectivity back behind this fixed entity into its temporal origins in the encounter between Dasein and *Sein*. He confused the temporality of subjectivity with the ontic classification of the subject. Kant thereby got distracted from asking how the "foundation of metaphysics" is disclosed through human subjectivity by asking "the question of the essence of man." That is to say, he gave a metaphysical answer to the question of how metaphysics is possible. For Kant, metaphysics is possible because man has the capacity for metaphysics, rather than, as Heidegger would put it, because metaphysics emerges into "presence" out of the temporal horizon of the summons to Dasein by the Call of Being.

Deng Xiamang (2009) provides a succinct critique of what is arguably Heidegger's distortion of Hegel in *Hegel's Concept of Experience* (1989). The central distortion is that Heidegger reduces Hegel's understanding of Being (*Sein*) to a being (*Seiende*), assimilating Hegel to the Western tradition originating with Plato that sought to understand Being through a metaphysical lens as, to quote Heidegger, "another and higher kind of thing." Heidegger thereby occludes what I argue is the intrinsic ontological similarity between his view of Being as possibility and what Hegel termed "a self-originating wealth of shapes." The ontological debate between Hegel and Heidegger is not over this fundamental premise, but over its historical working-out. As Deng Xiamang observes, Heidegger also reduces Hegel's dialectic of Spirit to the "will," thereby identifying it with the metaphysics of Presence and incipient global technology, or, as I have put it, recasts the Unity of Subject and Substance as the subjective drive alone for the mastery of existence. Kolb (1991) offers an analogous critique of Heidegger for reducing Spirit to the Cartesian and Fichtean metaphysics of pure subjectivity, and attempts to rescue Hegel from this charge by stressing his concept of intersubjectivity and the grounding of the "empty" individualism of modernity in its surrounding historical contexts, thereby enlisting Hegel in the ranks of the postmodernists – to my mind not convincingly, given Hegel's fidelity to the modern nation-state.

Further to this issue, see also Heidegger's discussion of Hegel's *Phenomenology of Spirit*, where, similar to his argument in *An Introduction to Metaphysics*, he locates in Platonism the beginning of "Idealism" in the history of Being, meaning the imposition of metaphysical rationality on the rest of existence, and then asserts that Hegel's work "is the deliberate, explicit and absolute justification of idealism," that is to say, the completion of the Platonic project (1994). As noted, this conclusion can only be reached by attributing to Hegel the understanding of Being as a being, and is arguably contradicted at every point by Hegel's stress on the plasticity, indeterminacy, contingency and dialectical exchange of opposites that are constitutive of Spirit, not least, for instance, in his concept of "Force" discussed in this chapter.

One could only arrive at the conclusion that Hegel identified Being with a being by isolating the Subjective pole of the Unity of Subject and Substance, which contains analytical and empirical Understanding (*Verstand*), and act as if the Substance pole, where all distinctions among beings are collapsed and reunited within the indeterminacy Spirit, did not exist. While that is not to deny that Hegel accords more independent status to the realm of concrete beings than does Heidegger, since their negation mediates historical progress, we still must ask: Is Heidegger unwilling to recognize the extent to which his ontology of possibility is compatible with Hegel's view of historical existence as self-origination?

For his part, Sartre does not object to Heidegger's critique of his version of existentialism in the *Letter on Humanism* for its emphasis on individual autonomy – he regards this as evidence of its superiority to what he sees as Heidegger's collectivization of experience. As he comments (1966): "The empirical image which may best symbolize Heidegger's intuition is not that of a conflict but rather a *crew*. The original relation of the Other to my consciousness is not the *you* and *me*; it is the *we*."

As regards what I argue is Heidegger's distortion of Nietzsche's doctrines of the Will to Power and the Eternal Recurrence into the absolute subjectivization of experience in the service of global technology, see Fink (1960), who criticizes Heidegger for ignoring the Dionysian dimension of Nietzsche's thought – a playful, passionate openness to the mutability of existence which mitigates any monistic potential those doctrines may contain. Klossowski (1969) argues that the eternal recurrence should not be seen, as Heidegger sees it, as an inversion of Platonism which preserves the metaphysical dichotomy between Being and becoming, but as an *ekstasis* comparable to Heidegger's own evocation of our "unclosedness" to Being. This is the dimension of Nietzsche's thought to which I drew attention through the example of *The Dancing Song* from *Thus Spake Zarathustra*.

Not unlike Nietzsche, Heidegger's regard for poetry and art as revelatory experiences equal if not superior to philosophy connects his thought to the profundity of both beauty and faith and what they may share in common. The study by Yates (2013) on the poetic imagination in Heidegger and Schelling points to an underlying link between Heidegger's understanding of the work of art as the revelation of Being and Schelling's ontology of "the infinitely finite" (1984) that expresses itself in music and poetry. My evocation of the example of the unnamed Greek temple in *The Origin of the Artwork* is amplified by drawing on Scully's interpretation of the temple of Apollo at Delphi in his book on Greek sacred architecture (1979), an approach that shows a clear indebtedness to Heidegger's essay. Heidegger likely had in mind a temple at Paestum that he had visited. He did eventually make it to Delphi, but not until after the essay had been completed.

Again not unlike Nietzsche, Heidegger's radical rejection of both modern Western subjectivism and classical metaphysics in favor of a "non-thingly" account of Being as possibility and revelation led to a natural association between his thought and mysticism, sometimes acknowledged by Heidegger himself. McGrath (2013) explores Heidegger's relationship to Christian theology, and is especially illuminating about his assessment of Luther, who, as I have suggested in this chapter, Heidegger greatly preferred to the metaphysically vitiated theology of Thomas. According to McGrath, distantly inspired by Luther, Heidegger attempted to overturn the medieval Aristotelian-Scholastic tradition, consonant with my argument in this chapter. In *Being and Time* Heidegger credits Luther with the insight that a theological "foundation" for faith is not an inquiry in which faith itself is primary: on the contrary, faith is concealed and distorted by such doctrines. The implicit comparison is with Thomas, who in Heidegger's view posits a "representation" of God derived from Aristotelianism which reduces God to a being [214]. For a consideration of Meister Eckhart's place in the mystical dimension in Heidegger's thought, see Caputo (1986). May (1996) persuasively uncovers common ground between Heidegger's account of Being and elements of Daoism and Buddhism, an interpretation extended by Zhihua Yao (2010). In his essay on Heidegger, Strauss (1989) traces Heidegger's interest in revelation to his interest in "the East": as he characterizes Heidegger's view, "the Bible is the east within us, Western men. Not the Bible as Bible, but the Bible as Eastern, can help us in overcoming Greek rationalism."

Heidegger's announcement of man's future role as "the Shepherd of Being" who will transcend the annihilation of the earth by technology not surprisingly has led to a "Green" reading of his works, sometimes conjoined with the theme of Eastern mysticism. See the essay by Zimmerman in the edited volume by Guignon (1993). As mentioned, I am going to postpone a more detailed assessment of Heidegger's impact on contemporary thought until the Conclusion. For the present, I recommend the highly stimulating book by Duff (2018), who, based upon a rigorous explication of Heidegger's writings, traces their many rivulets of influence on the political and social analysis and activism of the twentieth and twenty-first centuries, ranging beyond the now well-worn theme of his National Socialism.

As I touched upon in this chapter, there is also a specifically Jewish dimension to Heidegger's impact on contemporary religious thought. Fackenheim's years-long engagement with Heidegger, the subject of an ongoing study by this author, is strung intermittently throughout a number of works (1961, 1973, 1982, 1996). In them, he wrestles with the prospects opened up by Heidegger's fundamental ontology for a uniquely Jewish peoplehood juxtaposed against Heidegger's monstrous indifference to the radical evil of the Holocaust as an outcome of the German people's destiny. For Scholem's slighting reference in this chapter to Maimonides for turning "the living structure" of Judaism into a "bundle of abstractions" in contrast with studying the Kabbala, which I have suggested is analogous to Heidegger's preference for Augustine, Meister Eckhart and Luther over Thomism, see Scholem (1946). For a more recent engagement between Judaism and Heidegger's thought, see Chighel (2020), who argues that Heidegger's prejudices against Judaism as revealed by the Black Books are actually a facet of his relationship with Judaism as brought out in his philosophy. For the arbitrariness of Heidegger in stressing anxiety over love – whether of wisdom or of God – as the fundamental human experience, see Strauss' essay on Heideggerian existentialism (1989a).

As regards my attempt in this chapter to mount a Platonic critique of Heidegger, it is part of an extended argument I made in my first Plato book (2000). In the Platonic account of the soul, the two primordial passions are eros and thumos. Eros is the longing for completion through gaining knowledge of the eternal order of the whole. Thumos, by contrast, is the seat of warlike and aggressive desires, and is the psychological drive for the Socratic elenchus or refutation, a form of dialectical warfare Socrates wages against his interlocutors. Thumos is therefore the closest parallel in Platonic psychology to what Heidegger identifies as the project originating with Platonic metaphysics for the conquest of existence in accordance with the Ideas, culminating in technology. For that to be the case, however, thumos would have to take priority over eros in the Platonic account of the soul and guide its passionate energies in the imposition of reason on the rest of existence. However, as I argue, for Plato the opposite is the case: eros, the never-to-be-completed longing for knowledge of the whole, entails thumos as its ancillary ally in the aggressive dimension of technical philosophical refutation and guides it in the erotic pursuit of wholeness. Thus, as I argue in this chapter: "if [for Plato] the technical dimension of that philosophizing was at the service of, and entailed by, an erotic longing for a knowledge of the eternal order of the whole – a recurrent and never to be completed longing – how could it launch the project for the assimilation of the rest of Being to technology imputed to it by Heidegger?" Of course, as noted, Heidegger can always elude these exegetical arguments through his conviction that Being speaks *through* Plato regardless of Plato's own self-understanding.

This is the place to record my debt to Stanley Rosen for stimulating my thinking in this direction as regards Plato, and to acknowledge his own challenging attempt to "reverse" Heidegger on Platonic grounds (1993). According to Rosen, Heidegger's interpretation of the Idea of the Good and its analogy to the sun mistakenly attributes to Plato a conception of the "utility" of Being and beings. By contrast, Rosen stresses that what Plato means by utility is the pursuit of goodness, a pursuit which is not itself metaphysical, but through which the doctrine of the Ideas "emerges from a commonsensical reflection on the nature of ordinary experience" (as in, for example, the *Phaedo*). I would identify the goal of this pursuit as an erotic one in the sense just sketched – a longing for happiness through knowledge of the whole. Rosen also argues that

Heidegger takes an analogy drawn by Socrates between nature and the productive arts – for example, in Book Ten of the *Republic* – and, ignoring the fact that it is merely an analogy, identifies the productive arts with a direct account of nature, thereby attributing a "productionist" account of Being to Plato. This in spite of the fact that Socrates "sharply distinguishes between *physis* on the one hand and both *techne* and *mimesis* on the other." There is an even more fundamental reason why Plato's metaphysics could never culminate in Heidegger's account of technology. According to Rosen, for Plato, metaphysics is possible, but never actual. It can never provide a blueprint for action. We possess a noetic intuition of the unity of the Ideas which enables us to clarify the distinctions among them through dialectic. But there can be no dialectic regarding the Idea of the Good – the Idea of Ideas – as such, because our intuition of the unity of the Ideas that participate in the Idea of the Good is prior to all discursive clarity about Being as such. Therefore, in contrast with Aristotle, for Plato there cannot be a "science" of Being.

Conclusion

In the suggested *Further Reading* for the previous chapters, I have already cited a number of general works about the Philosophy of Freedom and its ramifications for more recent political theory, and they are helpful for the themes considered in the Conclusion as well. I remind the reader as well of my own articles on Hegel, Marx, Nietzsche, Heidegger, Lukacs and Kojeve cited in the Bibliography. As for general works about the roots of Critical Theory and Postmodernism in German Historicism and its problematics, I recommend Bernstein (1978), Jay (1973) and the more recent work by Young (2018). For the origins of Critical Theory in particular as "Marxism without the proletariat," Kolakowski (1981) remains unsurpassed in breadth and theoretical acumen. For the way in which Marxism was repurposed by modern revolutionary movements and Communist regimes, I recommend Leonhardt (1974). For more detailed discussions of Marxism-Leninism and the varieties of neo-Marxism and their impact on real-world revolutionary politics, including profiles of their leaders (who often claimed to be theoreticians), I would direct the reader to my book *Tyrants: A History of Power, Injustice, and Terror* (2017), which also features an extensive bibliography of history, biography and political analysis.

The conjectural debate between Habermas and Foucault centered on whether Foucault's discussion of "power analytics" provided a better basis for assessing modern social and political life than Habermas' emphasis on "communicative rationality." There was no actual debate between the two – it was carried out by their respective followers (see King, 2009). Martire (2012) believes that there is an implicit attack on Foucault by Habermas on the grounds that Foucault's emphasis on society as a field of powers embracing different groups departs from Habermas' own subjectivistic perspective, which I discussed in connection with the Kantian dimension of the ideal speech condition, and which Martire goes so far as to equate with the notion of the "unencumbered self" of classical liberalism. That strikes me as a distortion of Habermas' position, which attempts to account for our intersubjective experiences through the second and third cognitive interests. King convincingly characterizes Foucault's likely assessment of Kant's aspirational ethics and expectations for world peace as one of "scorn."

Kogler (1999) attempts to find a middle way between the subjectivism of Habermas' model of communicative rationality and dialogue and Foucault's understanding of the collective forces of power and how social power "constructs" interpretation in a way that outstrips "individual subjectivity." But Kogler does acknowledge that Foucault has been faulted for his ignoring of individual freedom in social interaction. And I think we can infer that this absence of an emphasis on the individual would be the core of an explicit critique of Foucault by Habermas, whose stance I believe would constitute for Habermas an instance of what he terms "irrational decisionism" with its implications for political extremism, including terrorism.

Tarintseva (2014) offers a stimulating argument to the effect that Gadamer's interpretation of tradition can be "supplemented" by Foucault's emphasis on the dynamics of power. The "common ground" between them, according to the author, is that they both reject Habermas' claim that undistorted communication be guided by "universal criteria of rationality" because both believe that individuals are "inextricably embedded within a particular tradition." Self-understanding can only emerge from the dynamic within this tradition, and not according to an "Archimedean point of view outside of any tradition," probably an allusion to Habermas' Kantian dimension. But I am skeptical that Gadamer's understanding of how we are embedded in tradition would leave room for a Foucauldian critique of "ideological distortions." In short, Foucault's understanding of power dynamics is politically too revolutionary for Gadamer, who places far more emphasis on our reconciliation with tradition, more in the spirit of Hegel's understanding of education as "recollection."

In contrast with the attempt to construct a debate between Habermas and Foucault based on the views of their exegetes, Habermas' and Gadamer's criticisms of each other are open and explicit. Gadamer addresses Habermas' dubious notion of the "quasi-transcendental" status of the cognitive interests by arguing that if, as Habermas otherwise maintains, human existence is finite and temporal, "he cannot escape the question of how his own thinking as transcendental is empirically possible" (1987). Gadamer maintains that this is not a problem for his own hermeneutic of the "fusion of horizons," in which the interpreter is always already involved with the tradition under interpretation back to its earliest beginnings, constituting a kind of historical infinity. Gadamer's hermeneutic of the fusion of horizons is, he believes, a holistic interaction between self and world that overcomes dualism but stops short of claiming to be "fulfilled in an absolute consciousness," as Hegel had claimed. In other words, it is Hegelian "recollection" immanentized and severed from the transcendental claims of Hegel's Absolute Science of Spirit.

At the same time, from another angle, Gadamer disputes the rationality of Habermas' model for undistorted communication. By driving a wedge between tradition and communicative discourse as two categorically distinct cognitive interests, Gadamer claims, Habermas consigns tradition to "pure romanticism" bereft of rationality, and therefore unable to assist us in clarifying our present discourse, which is reduced to an empty husk of positivism. One can detect an echo here of Hegel's critique of the dichotomy between modern reason and Romanticism in the *Phenomenology of Spirit* – it impoverishes the former psychologically and reduces the latter to sheer capricious impulse.

In Gadamer's view, by presupposing a distinction between the methodology of the social sciences and hermeneutics, placing the latter at the service of the former so as to bring about the "emancipation" of that methodology from tradition – that is, drawing upon tradition to destroy its influence over us – Habermas renders himself unable to embrace hermeneutics "with all its bridge building and recovery of the best in the past."

In other words, for all his claims to have opened up modern technical rationality to the riches of tradition, Habermas remains an ultra-rationalist. Gadamer claims that Habermas regards Gadamer's own immersion in the prejudgments of inherited tradition as "treason" against the Enlightenment because it might "lead to an acknowledgement of authority." In Gadamer's view, hermeneutics is not incompatible with an "emancipating criticism of authority." But as against Habermas, he adds: "Authority is not *always* wrong." Habermas' riposte is that Gadamer's uncritical immersion in tradition exhausts itself in mere cultural ornamentation, and thus displays a "sorry powerlessness" in the face of "modern alienation and injustice" (quoted in Gadamer, 1987).

Kolakowski (1981) dismisses critical theory in general as "an inconsistent attempt to preserve Marxism" without a proletariat, and "offering no replacement for what it leaves out." Habermas, Kolakowski observes, criticizes Marxism for reducing human self-reflection to "patterns of material production." But Habermas does not clearly define what he means by "emancipation." In the spirit of German Idealism, Kolakowski writes, Habermas is seeking a point at which theory and practice, cognition and will, knowledge and change "all become identical." But he has not found this point or shown us how to get to it. Bernstein (1978) also examines Habermas' ambivalence toward Hegel and German Idealism. Habermas sharply criticizes Hegel for collapsing the distinction between subject and object in the synthesis of Spirit. "But," Bernstein observes, "his own cognitive interests are analogous to Hegel's forms of consciousness ... It is this movement [of self-reflection in Hegel] that Habermas wants to recover." But his own key concepts make it impossible for him to recover this unity of self-reflection. There is a "deep unresolved conflict in Habermas" between the a priori and transcendental status of his categories and his "pragmatic" recognition of the huge heterogeneity of "all forms of rational inquiry" as they are embedded in real-world circumstances. To maintain nevertheless that there are "categorically different" types of inquiry, some transcendental while others are not, "is a fiction." In reality, the competition among the realms of technical, practical and emancipatory cognitive interests "continues to rage."

Arendt's disagreement with Heidegger that modern technology originated in classical thought is less clear-cut than in the case of Strauss or Grant. Regarding Aristotle, she is unequivocal that in his view the technical realm of the household must be subordinated to the public realm of the city: "Aristotle's definition of man as zoon politikon" was "unrelated and even opposed to the natural association experienced as household life" (1982). The household was the realm of bodily necessity; the city "on the contrary, was the sphere of freedom." But she argues the opposite as regards Plato, who, she claims, proposed that the polis be administered exactly as a "well-ordered household." The *Statesman* in her reading contended that no difference existed between the constitution of the oikos and of the state. Therefore the modern world did not reject Platonic thinking but on the contrary "liberated it" from the prejudices of ancient society against the craftsmen.

Her considered view seems to be that Plato's thought was an agenda for pure managerial technocracy, echoing Heidegger's interpretation. Aristotle's elevation of the polis over the household was, by contrast, for Arendt a reflection of "Greek" thought and culture. In sum, then, Arendt shared Heidegger's interpretation of Platonism as incipient modern technology. She also shares Heidegger's distinction between classical metaphysics and the authentic "Greek" life of the historical polis. But whereas Heidegger lumped Aristotle in with Plato as the originators of the technological project,

Arendt approves of him for embodying "Greek" authenticity in contrast with Plato's productivist account of Being.

For an analysis of Weber's significance for later German philosophy up to Heidegger, see Young (2018). As to whether Heidegger explicitly addresses Weber and his work, I argue that his arguments in *Being and Time* and *An Introduction to Metaphysics* could readily be interpreted as addressing a Weberian position about the Fact/Value distinction. Thompson (2003) argues that both Spengler and Weber are among Heidegger's unnamed interlocutors, especially when writing about the reform of the university. Perhaps the clearest indication of this is the recollection by Gadamer, who was Heidegger's student, of how his contemporaries viewed Weber's thought in the 1920s and 1930s: "This inner-worldly asceticism of a value-free science which is then perfected by a certain kind of decisionism, we found it majestic but impossible. Heidegger felt that too ... One saw [Weber] as a symbol of a kind of scientific life with which we could not identify" (quoted in Thompson, 2003). Weber is mentioned parenthetically in Heidegger's early lecture course on the phenomenology of religious life compiled from Heidegger's notes and notes by a student (2010). See also Barash (1992).

For those interested in the displacement of neo-Kantianism in German philosophy beginning in the early 1900s, the return of Hegel, and the growing posthumous influence of Nietzsche, see Gadamer (1983). Hegel's grounding of his dialectic in the notion of the life-world, derived from Schelling, along with the emphasis in his early writings on love, liberated his philosophy from any claims that it was pan-logistic or hyper-rational. Heidegger's student Marcuse found a linkage between Heidegger – by way of Dilthey – to Hegel's concept of Objective Spirit as the interaction of life, consciousness and mind. See also Jay (1973). Gadamer also makes the shrewd observation that it was precisely *because* Heidegger from early on was attracted to Hegel's philosophy in furthering his own critique of the "idealized subject" of Kant's thought and its reification of freedom as a "fact of reason" that led Heidegger to rigorously distinguish Hegel's thought from his own, at the cost, as we have observed, of arguably distorting it. In other words, as Gadamer puts it, Hegel was "close enough" to Heidegger for Heidegger to feel called upon to "challenge him all the more." For the hermeneutic of the "fusion of horizons," see Gadamer (1975).

For a critique of Kojeve's interpretation of Hegel and proof that Strauss entertained it solely for the purpose of their debate about tyranny, see Newell (2016). For Grant's partiality toward Heidegger's identification of modernity with technology, see Newell (2021). The book by Pelluchon (2014) is illustrative of the recent interest being taken in Strauss in Europe. For the characterization of Marx and Heidegger envisioning the future as an "eschatological reversal," see Gadamer (1982). For the three cognitive interests see Habermas (1971) and for his critique of Marxism and contrast between classical and modern political theory see Habermas (1973). For the argument that Heidegger's ontology amounted to the Judaization of Western philosophy, see Fackenheim (1973). Voegelin's scorn for modern liberalism in contrast with Strauss' qualified endorsement of it is nicely conveyed by their exchange regarding Locke (Emberley, 2014). When Voegelin branded Locke a "nihilistic destroyer," Strauss gently reproved him for overlooking the fact that Locke's study of human nature was genuinely philosophic and that the first wave of modernity was politically preferable to the "fanatical obscurantism" of the third.

Heidegger is sometimes taxed for retaining the concept of Being in any form, even the concept of sheer possibility, tying it to his attachment to Nazism, as if that lamentable and imprudent choice had stemmed from Heidegger's failure to be relativistic enough.

Merely to conceive of Being in any way led straight to the Third Reich. Admittedly, Heidegger might have invited this repudiation of *any* coherent way of addressing his own Question of Being when he began to cross out the word for Being in his works, in horror at the prospect that it might contain even the slightest trace of metaphysics owing to the constraints of predicative syntax. We need not wander too far down this self-vitiating rabbit hole, a contest over who can get the furthest in jettisoning any slight tincture of discursive rationality or "logocentrism" on the grounds that it immediately justifies Hitler. For the argument that Heidegger's ontology of Being remains metaphysical, see Bronner (1977), who argues that Heidegger "reifies" Being into the distinction between ontic and authentic, which somehow (Presto!) leads to Nazism. According to Derrida (1987), Heidegger avowed a metaphysical concept of Spirit that implicated his philosophy in Nazism, a "spiritual racism" that paralleled the Nazis' biological racism, to my mind a highly questionable interpretation of Heidegger's arguments. For Derrida's call for a new International see Parry (2004).

Bibliography

Abrams, M. H. *Natural Supernaturalism*. New York: Norton, 1973.

Adorno, T. *The Jargon of Authenticity*. Kurt Tarnowski and Frederic Will trans. Evanston, IL: Northwestern University Press, 1973.

Allison, D. ed. *The New Nietzsche: Contemporary Styles of Interpretation*. Cambridge, MA: MIT Press, 1985.

Althusser, Louis. *For Marx*. Ben Brewster trans. New York: Verso, 1988.

Arendt, Hannah. *The Human Condition*. Chicago, IL: University of Chicago Press, 1982.

"Martin Heidegger at Eighty." In *Heidegger and Modern Philosophy*. M. Murray ed. New Haven, CT: Yale University Press, 1978.

On Revolution. New York: Viking, 1963.

Avineri, Shlomo. *Hegel's Theory of the Modern State*. Cambridge: Cambridge University Press, 1972.

The Social and Political Thought of Karl Marx. Cambridge: Cambridge University Press, 1975.

Barash, J. "Martin Heidegger in the Perspective of the Twentieth Century." *Journal of Modern History* 64:3 (1992).

Barrett, William. "Homeless in the World." *Commentary* (March 1976).

Irrational Man. Garden City, NY: Doubleday, 1985.

Baumann, Fred. *Fraternity and Politics: Choosing One's Brothers*. Santa Barbara, CA: Praeger, 1998.

Baumgardner, Paul. "Legal Right and Personhood in Hegel's Phenomenology of Spirit. *Birkbeck Law Review* 4:1 (2016).

Beiser, Frederik C. *The Cambridge Companion to Hegel*. Cambridge: Cambridge University Press, 1999.

"Introduction: Hegel and the Problem of Metaphysics." In *The Cambridge Companion to Hegel*. Frederik C. Beiser ed. Cambridge: Cambridge University Press, 1999.

Belloc, Hilaire. *Robespierre: A Study*. London: Nisbet, 1927.

Berlin, Isaiah. *The Roots of Romanticism*. Princeton, NJ: Princeton University Press, 1982.

Two Concepts of Liberty. Oxford: Clarendon Press, 1958.

Bernstein, Richard. *The Restructuring of Social and Political Theory*. Philadelphia: University of Pennsylvania Press, 1978.

Bishop, Paul. *The Dionysian Self: C. G. Jung's Reception of Friedrich Nietzsche*. Berlin: de Gruyter, 1995.

Blitz, M. *Heidegger's "Being and Time" and the Possibility of Political Philosophy*. Ithaca, NY: Cornell University Press, 1981.

Bloom, Allan. Introduction. *Emile or On Education*. New York: Basic Books, 1979.

Bowman, Brady. *Hegel and the Metaphysics of Absolute Negativity*. Cambridge: Cambridge University Press, 2015.

Bronner, S. E. "The Consequences of Political Mystification." *Salmagundi* (1977): 38–39.

Buchwalter, Andrew. "Hegel's Concept of Virtue." *Political Theory* 20 (1992).

Call, Lewis. "Toward an Anarchy of Becoming: Postmodern Anarchism in Nietzschean Philosophy." *Journal of Nietzsche Studies* 21 (2001).

Caputo, John D. "Meister Eckhart and the Later Heidegger: The Mystical Element in Heidegger's Thought." *Journal of the History of Philosophy* (1975).

The Mystical Element in Heidegger's Thought. New York: Fordham University Press, 1986.

Cassirer, Ernst. *The Question of Jean-Jacques Rousseau*. New Haven, CT: Yale University Press, 1989.

Rousseau, Kant, Goethe. James Gutmann trans. Princeton, NJ: Princeton University Press, 1970.

Chighel, Michael. *Kabale: Das Geheimnis des Hebraischen Humanismus im Lichte von Heideggers Denken*. Berlin: Klostermann, 2020.

Church, Jeffrey. *Infinite Autonomy: The Divided Individual in the Political Thought of G. W. F. Hegel and Friedrich Nietzsche*. University Park, PA: Penn State University Press, 2014.

Colman. J. *Lucretius as Theorist of Political Life*. New York: Palgrave, 2012.

Copobianco, Richard. *Engaging Heidegger*. Toronto: University of Toronto Press, 2011.

Cranston, Maurice. *Jean-Jacques: The Early Life and Work of Jean-Jacques Rousseau*. Chicago, IL: University of Chicago Press, 1991.

Dahlstrom, Daniel. *Heidegger's Concept of Truth*. Cambridge: Cambridge University Press, 2000.

Danto, Arthur C. *Nietzsche as Philosopher*. New York: Columbia University Press, 2005.

Darby, Tom. *The Feast*. Toronto: University of Toronto Press, 1990.

Davis, Michael. *The Autobiography of Philosophy*. Lanham, MD: Rowman and Littlefield, 2000.

Deleuze, Gilles. *Nietzsche et la Philosophie*. Paris: Presses Universitaires de France, 1962.

Deng Xiaomang. "Heidegger's Distortion of Dialectics in 'Hegel's Concept of Experience.'" *Frontiers of Philosophy in China* 4:2 (2009).

Dent, N. J. *Rousseau: An Introduction to His Psychological, Social and Political Theory*. London: Blackwell, 1989.

Derrida, Jacques. *Of Spirit: Heidegger and the Question.* Chicago, IL: University of Chicago Press, 1987.

Dreyfus, Hubert. *Being-in-the-World: A Commentary on Heidegger's Being in Time.* Cambridge, MA: MIT Press, 1990.

Drochon, Hugo. "Nietzsche and Brexit." *Medium* (July 9, 1916).

Nietzsche's Great Politics. Princeton, NJ: Princeton University Press, 2016.

Dryer, D. P. *Kant's Solution for the Verification of Metaphysics.* London: Routledge, 2017.

Duff, Alexander. *Heidegger and Politics: The Ontology of Radical Discontent.* Cambridge: Cambridge University Press, 2018.

Eliade, Mircea. *A History of Religious Ideas, Volume 1: From the Stone Age to the Eleusinian Mysteries.* Willard R. Trask trans. Chicago, IL: University of Chicago Press, 1981.

Emberley, Peter ed. *Faith and Political Philosophy.* Columbia: University of Missouri Press, 2014.

Engels, Friedrich. "On Social Relations in Russia." In *The Marx–Engels Reader.* Robert Tucker ed. New York: W. W. Norton, 1972.

Fackeneheim, Emil L. *Encounters between Judaism and Modern Philosophy.* New York: Basic Books, 1973.

"Historicity and Transcendence of Philosophic Truth. In *The God Within: Kant, Schelling and Historicity.* John Burbidge ed. Toronto: University of Toronto Press, 1996.

To Mend the World. New York: Schocken Books, 1982.

Metaphysics and Historicity. Milwaukee, WI: Milwaukee University Press, 1961.

The Religious Dimension in Hegel's Thought. Boston, MA: Beacon, 1967.

Fanon, F. *The Wretched of the Earth.* New York: Grove, 2005.

Farias, Victor. *Heidegger and Nazism.* Philadelphia, PA: Temple University Press, 1991.

Faye, Emmanuel. *Heidegger: The Introduction of Nazism into Philosophy in Light of the Unpublished Seminars of 1933–1935.* Michael Smith trans. New Haven, CT: Yale University Press, 2011.

Fichte, J. G. *The Science of Knowledge.* A. E. Kroeger trans. Ann Arbor: University of Michigan reproduction. 2006.

Fink, Eugen. *Nietzsches Philosophie.* Stuttgart: W. Kohlhammer, 1960.

Forster, Eckhart. *Spinoza and German Idealism.* Cambridge: Cambridge University Press, 2015.

Foucault, M. *Discipline and Punish.* New York: Vintage, 1995.

A History of Sexuality. New York: Vintage, 1990.

Franco, Paul. *Hegel's Philosophy of Freedom.* New Haven, CT: Yale University Press, 2002.

Gadamer, Hans-Georg. *Hegel's Dialectic.* P Christopher Smith trans. Albany, NY: SUNY Press, 1982.

Literature and Philosophy in Dialogue. Robert Paslick trans. Albany, NY: SUNY Press, 1994.

On Education, Poetry and History. Albany, NY: SUNY Press, 1992.

Philosophical Hermeneutics. D. E. Linge trans. Berkeley: University of California Press, 1987.

Reason in the Age of Science. Frederick G. Lawrence trans. Cambridge, MA: MIT Press, 1983.

Truth and Method. New York: Continuum, 1975.

Gillespie, Michael. *Hegel, Heidegger and the Ground of History.* Chicago, IL: University of Chicago Press, 1984.

Nietzsche's Final Teaching. Chicago, IL: University of Chicago Press, 2019.

Goethe, Johann Wolfgang von. *Goethe's Faust.* Waller Kauffman trans. New York: Doubleday, 1963.

Poetry and Truth. Minna Smith trans. London: G. Bell, 1913.

Golomb, J. and Wistrich, R. eds. *Nietzsche Godfather of Fascism?* Princeton, NJ: Princeton University Press, 2003.

Grant, George P. *English-Speaking Justice.* Notre Dame, IN: University of Notre Dame Press, 1985.

George Grant in Process. Toronto: Anansi, 1978.

Griswold, Charles. *Jean-Jacques Rousseau and Adam Smith: A Philosophical Encounter.* London: Routledge, 2017.

Gross, Raphael. *Carl Schmitt and the Jews: The "Jewish Question," the Holocaust, and German Legal Theory.* Joel Golb trans. Madison: University of Wisconsin Press, 2007.

Guignon, Charles ed. *The Cambridge Companion to Heidegger.* Cambridge: Cambridge University Press, 1993.

Habermas, Jurgen. *Knowledge and Human Interests.* Jeremy Shapiro trans. Boston, MA: Beacon Press, 1971.

Theory and Practice. Boston, MA: Beacon Press, 1973.

Hallman, Max. "Nietzsche's Environmental Ethics." *Environmental Ethics.* 13 (1991).

Harries, Karsten. "Heidegger as Political Thinker." In *Heidegger and Modern Philosophy.* Michael Murray ed. New Haven, CT: Yale University Press, 1976.

Harris, H. S. *Hegel's Development: Toward the Sunlight.* Oxford: Oxford University Press, 1972.

Hartmann, K. "Hegel: A Non-Metaphysical View." *Studies in Foundational Philosophy.* Amsterdam: Editions Rodopi, 1988.

Heber-Suffrin, Heber. *Introduction au Zarathoustra de Nietzsche.* Paris: Kime, 2015.

Hegel, G. W. F. *Early Theological Writings.* T. M. Knox trans. Philadelphia, PA: University of Philadelphia, 1948.

Elements of the Philosophy of Right. H. B. Nisbett trans. Cambridge: Cambridge University Press, 1991.

Hegel on Tragedy. Henry Paolucci ed. New York: Doubleday, 1962.

Introduction to Hegel's Philosophy of Fine Art. Bernard Bosanquet trans. BiblioBazaar, 2009.

Introductory Lectures on Aesthetics. Bernard Bosanquet trans. London: Penguin, 2004.

Lectures on the History of Philosophy. E. S. Haldane trans. 3 vols. New York: Humanities Press, 1963.

Lectures on the Philosophy of Religion. E. B. Speirs trans. London: Kagan, Paul, Trench, Turner, 1895.

Phanomenologie des Geistes. Johannes Hoffmeister ed. Hamburg: Meiner, 1975.

The Phenomenology of Mind. J. S. Baillie trans. New York: Harper and Row, 1967.

Phenomenology of Spirit. A. V. Miller trans. Oxford: Oxford University Press, 1979.

The Philosophy of History. J. Sibree trans. Mineola, NY: Dover, 1956.

The Science of Logic. George DiGiovanni trans. Cambridge: Cambridge University Press, 2010.

Heidegger, Martin. *Being and Time.* Martin Macquarrie and Edward Robinson trans. New York: Harper and Row, 1962.

Early Greek Thinking. David Krell and Frank Capuzzi trans. New York: Harper and Row, 1984.

Einfuhrung in die Metaphysic. Tübingen: Max Niemeyer Verlag, 1953.

Hegel's Concept of Experience. Kenley Dove trans. New York: Harper Collins, 1989.

Hegel's Phenomenology of Spirit. Parvis Emad and K. May trans. Bloomington.: Indiana University Press, 1994.

An Introduction to Metaphysics. Ralph Mannheim trans. New Haven, CT: Yale University Press, 1975.

Kant and the Problem of Metaphysics. James Churchill trans. Bloomington: Indiana University Press, 1975.

"Letter on Humanism" and "The Question Concerning Technology." In *Basic Writings.* D. F. Krell ed. San Francisco, CA: Harper Collins, 1993.

Nietzsche. D. F. Krell trans. Vols. 1, 2, 4. New York: Harper and Row, 1981, 1984, 1982.

The Phenomenology of Religious Life. Matthias Fritsch trans. Bloomington: Indiana University Press, 2010.

"Plato's Doctrine of Truth." In *Pathmarks.* W. McNeill ed. Cambridge: Cambridge University Press, 1998.

Schelling's Treatise on the Essence of Human Freedom. Joan Stambaugh trans. Athens: Ohio University Press, 1985.

Sein und Zeit. Tubingen: Max Niemeyer Verlag, 1957.

"The Self-Assertion of the German University (Rectoral Address)"; "The Rectorate 1933/34: Facts and Thoughts." Karsten Harries trans. *Review of Metaphysics* 38 (1985).

"Uberwindung der Metaphysik." In *Vortage und Aufsätze.* Pfullingen: Gunter Neske, 1954.

What Is Called Thinking? J. Glenn Gray and F. Wieck trans; J. Glenn Gray intro. New York: Harper and Row, 1972.

Heidegger, Martin and Jung, E. *Correspondence 1949–1975.* Lanham, MD: Rowman and Littlefield, 2016.

Heine, H. *Religion and Philosophy in Germany.* J. Snodgrass trans. Albany, NY: SUNY Press, 1986.

Henrich, Dieter. *Between Kant and Hegel: Lectures on German Idealism.* Cambridge, MA: Harvard University Press, 2008.

Herf, Geoffrey. *Reactionary Modernism.* Cambridge: Cambridge University Press, 1986.

Hill, Kevin. *Nietzsche's Critiques: The Kantian Foundations of His Thought.* Oxford: Clarendon Press, 2005.

Horowitz, Asher. *Rousseau, Nature, and History.* Toronto: University of Toronto Press, 1987,

Hoy. David C. "History, Historicity and Historiography in Being and Time." In *Heidegger and Modern Philosophy.* Michael Murray ed. New Haven, CT: Yale University Press, 1978.

Hunt, Lester. *Nietzsche and the Origin of Virtue.* London: Routledge, 1993.

Hutter, Horst. *Shaping the Future: Nietzsche's New Regime of the Soul and Its Ascetic Practice.* Lanham, MD: Lexington, 2005.

Hyppolite, Jean. *Genesis and Structure of Hegel's Phenomenology of Spirit.* S. Cherniak trans. Evanston, IL: Northwestern University Press, 1979.

Studies on Marx and Hegel. New York: Harper, 1973.

Inwood, Michael, ed. *A Hegel Dictionary.* Cambridge, MA: Blackwell, 1992.

Jay, Martin. *The Dialectical Imagination.* Boston, MA: Little, Brown, 1973.

Kain, Philip. *Schiller, Hegel and Marx: State, Society and the Aesthetic Ideal of Ancient Greece.* Montreal: McGill-Queen's University Press, 1982.

Kant, Immanuel. *Groundwork of the Metaphysics of Morals.* M. Korsgaard trans. Cambridge: Cambridge University Press, 2012.

Prolegomena to Any Future Metaphysics. London: Hackett, 2002.

Three Critiques. W. S. Pluhar trans. London: Hackett, 2002.

Kauffman, Walter. *Hegel: Texts and Commentary.* New York: Doubleday, 1966.

Nietzsche: Philosopher, Psychologist, Anti-Christ. Princeton, NJ: Princeton University Press, 1975.

Kelly, Christopher. *Rousseau's Exemplary Life: The Confessions as Political Philosophy.* Ithaca, NY: Cornell University Press, 2019.

Kelly, George Armstrong. *Hegel's Retreat from Eleusis.* Princeton, NJ: Princeton University Press, 1978.

Idealism, Politics and History. Cambridge: Cambridge University Press, 2010.

King, M. "Clarifying the Foucault–Habermas Debate." *Philosophy and Social Criticism* (March 2009).

Kisiel, Theodore. *The Genesis of Heidegger's Being and Time.* Berkeley: University of California Press, 1995.

Klossowski, Pierre. *Nietzsche et le cercle vicieux.* Paris: Mercure de France, 1969.

Kochin, Michael. "Living with the Bible: Jean-Jacques Rousseau Reads Judges 19–21." www.tau.ac, 2007.

Kogler, Hans-Herbert. *The Power of Dialogue.* Boston, MA: MIT Press, 1999.

Kojeve, Alexandre. *Introduction to the Reading of Hegel.* James H. Nichols trans. New York: Basic, 1969.

Kolakowski, Leszek. *Main Currents of Marxism.* P. S. Falla trans. Oxford: Oxford University Press, 1981.

Kolb, David. *The Critique of Pure Modernity: Hegel, Heidegger and After.* Chicago, IL: University of Chicago Press, 1991.

Korner, S. *Kant.* Baltimore, MD: Penguin, 1974.

Kreines, James. *Reason in the World: Hegel's Metaphysics and Its Philosophical Appeal.* Oxford: Oxford University Press, 2015.

Krell, D. F. "Analysis." In *Nietzsche.* Martin Heidegger. Vol. 2. New York: Harper and Row, 1984.

"General Introduction." *Martin Heidegger: Basic Writings.* New York: Harper and Row, 1977.

Lacoue-Labarthe, Phillipe. *Heidegger and the Politics of Poetry.* Jeff Fort trans. Champagne, IL: University of Illinois Press, 2007.

Lampert, Lawrence. *The Enduring Importance of Leo Strauss.* Chicago, IL: University of Chicago Press, 2013.

Nietzsche's Task: An Interpretation of Beyond Good and Evil. New Haven, CT: Yale University Press, 2004.

Nietzsche's Teaching: An Interpretation of "Thus Spoke Zarathustra." New Haven, CT: Yale University Press, 1989.

What a Philosopher Is: Becoming Nietzsche. Chicago, IL: University of Chicago Press, 2018.

Lauer, Q. *Hegel's Concept of God.* Albany, NY: SUNY Press, 1982.

Leonard, Miriam. "Greeks, Jews, and the Enlightenment: Moses Mendelssohn's Socrates." *Cultural Critique* 74 (Winter 2010).

Leonhardt, Wolfgang. *Three Faces of Marxism.* London: Holt, 1974.

Levine, N. "The German Historical School of Law and the Origins of Historical Materialism." *Journal of the History of Ideas* 48:3 (1987).

Longuenesse, Beatrice. *Hegel's Critique of Metaphysics.* Nicole Simek trans. Cambridge: Cambridge University Press, 2007.

Lowith, Karl. *From Hegel to Nietzsche.* David Green trans. New York: Anchor, 1967.

"Les implications politiques de la philosophie de l'existence." *Les Temps Modernes* (1946): 2.

Nietzsche's Philosophy of the Eternal Recurrence of the Same. Harvey Lomax trans. Berkeley: University of California Press, 1997.

Lukes, Steven. *Marxism and Morality.* Oxford: Oxford University Press, 1987.

Lund, Nelson. *Rousseau's Rejuvenation of Political Philosophy.* London: Palgrave Macmillan, 2016.

Macherey, Pierre. *Hegel ou Spinoza.* Paris: Decouverte, 2007.

Maclean, Lee. *The Free Animal: Rousseau on Free Will and Human Nature.* Toronto: University of Toronto Press, 2003.

Marcuse, Herbert. *Hegels Ontologie und die Theorie der Gestchitlichkeit.* Frankfurt am Main: Klostermann, 1968.

Reason and Revolution. Boston, IL: Beacon, 1969.

Martire, Jacopo. "Habermas contra Foucault." *Law and Critique* 23 (2012).

Marx, Karl. "On the Jewish Question"; "Economic and Philosophic Manuscripts of 1844"; "For a Ruthless Criticism of Everything Existing"; "Contribution to the Critique of Hegel's *Philosophy* of Right"; "The German Ideology"; "The Communist Manifesto"; "The Eighteenth Brumaire of Louis Bonaparte." In *The Marx–Engels Reader.* Robert C. Tucker ed. New York: W. W. Norton, 1972.

Marx, Werner. *Hegel's Phenomenology of Spirit.* New York: Harper and Row, 1975.

Heidegger and the Tradition. T. Kisiel and M. Greene trans. Evanston, IL: Northwestern University Press, 1971.

May, Richard. *Heidegger's Hidden Sources: East-Asian Influences on His Work.* London: Routledge, 1996.

McGovern, William M. *From Luther to Hitler: The History of Fascist-Nazi Political Philosophy.* Boston, IL: Houghton Mifflin, 1941.

McGrath, Daniel. *The Early Heidegger and Medieval Philosophy.* Washington, DC: Catholic University of America Press, 2013.

Megill, Alan. *Prophets of Extremity.* Berkeley: University of California Press, 1987.

Mehta, J. L. *Heidegger: The Way and the Vision.* Honolulu: University of Hawaii Press, 1976.

Meier, Heinrich. *On the Happiness of the Philosophic Life*. Chicago, IL: University of Chicago Press, 2016.

Melzer, Arthur. *The Natural Goodness of Man*. Chicago, IL: University of Chicago Press, 2016.

Menon, M. "An Unpolitical Political Philosophy?" *Dradek* 1:2 (2015).

Miller, James. *Rousseau: Dreamer of Democracy*. New Haven, CT: Yale University Press, 1984.

Mitchell, Andrew and Tawney, Peter eds. *Heidegger's Black Notebooks: Responses to Anti-Semitism*. New York: Columbia University Press, 2017.

Moder, G. *Hegel and Spinoza*. Evanston, IL: Northwestern University Press, 2017.

Moggach, Douglas ed. *Politics, Religion, and Art: Hegelian Debates*. Evanston, IL: Northwestern University Press, 2011.

Moreira, F. "Overcoming Metaphysics: Nietzsche and Carnap." *Nietzsche Studien* 47:1 (2020).

Mosse, George. *The Crisis of German Ideology: Intellectual Origins of the Third Reich*. New York: Grosset and Dunlop, 1964.

Murray, M. ed. *Heidegger and Modern Philosophy*. New Haven, CT: Yale University Press, 1978.

Neuhouser, Frederick. *Fichte's Theory of Subjectivity*. Cambridge: Cambridge University Press, 1990.

Foundations of Hegel's Social Theory: Actualizing Freedom. Cambridge, MA: Harvard University Press, 2003.

Rousseau's Critique of Inequality. Cambridge: Cambridge University Press, 2013.

Newell, Waller R. "Did Plato Believe in His Own Metaphysics?" In *Recovering Reason: Essays in Honor of Thomas L. Pangle*. Timothy Burns ed. Lanham, MD: Lexington Books, 2010.

"The Distant Command of the Greeks: Thoughts on Heidegger's Rectoral Address." Proceedings. Annual Meeting of the American Political Science Association 1988.

"A Fruitful Disagreement: The Philosophical Encounter Between George P. Grand Leo Strauss." In *Leo Strauss and Contemporary Thought*. Jeffrey Bernstein and Jade Schiff eds. Albany, NY: SUNY Press, 2021.

"Heidegger on Freedom and Community: Some Political Implications of His Early Thought." *American Political Science Review* (September 1984).

"Heidegger's Ontological Politics." *Kritika and Kontext* 1 (1997).

"Kojeve's Hegel, Hegel's Hegel, Strauss's Hegel: A Middle Range Approach to the Debate about Tyranny and Totalitarianism." In *Philosophy, History, and Tyranny: Reexamining the Debate between Leo Strauss and Alexandre Kojeve*. Timothy Burns ed. Albany, NY: SUNY Press, 2016.

"Origins of Enchantment: Conceptual Continuities in the Ontology of Political Wholeness." In *Logos and Eros: Essays Honoring Stanley Rosen*. Nalin Ranasinghe ed. South Bend, IN: St. Augustine Press, 2006.

"Philosophy and the Perils of Commitment: A Comparison of Lukacs and Heidegger." *History of European Ideas* 9 (1988).

"Politics and Progress in Heidegger's Philosophy of History." In *Democratic Theory and Technological Society*. Richard Day and Ronald Beiner eds. London: M. E. Sharpe, 1988.

"The Recollection of Freedom: Hegel as Educator." In *Search of Humanity: Essays in Honor of Clifford Orwin*. Andrea Radasanu ed. Lanham, MD: Lexington Books, March 2015.

"Redeeming Modernity: The Ascent of Eros and Wisdom in Hegel's Phenomenology." *Intepretation* (Fall 2009).

"Reflections on Marxism and America." In *Confronting the Constitution*. Allan Bloom ed. Washington, DC: American Enterprise Institute Press, 1990.

Ruling Passion: The Erotics of Statecraft in Platonic Political Philosophy. Lanham, MD: Rowman and Littlefield, 2000.

Tyranny: A New Interpretation. Cambridge: Cambridge University Press, 2013.

Tyrants: A History of Power, Injustice and Terror. Cambridge: Cambridge University Press, 2017.

"Zarathustra's Dancing Dialectic." *Interpretation* (Spring 1990).

Nicholson, G. "The Commune of Being and Time." *Dialogue* (1971): 10.

Nietzsche, Friedrich. *Also Sprach Zarathustra*. Munich: Wilhelm Goldmann, 1985.

Beyond Good and Evil. Walter Kauffman trans. New York: Vintage, 1966.

The Birth of Tragedy. Walter Kauffman trans. New York: Vintage, 1967.

Ecce Homo. Walter Kauffman trans. New York: Vintage, 1969.

Die Geburt der Tragödie aus dem Geiste der Musik. Munich: Wilhelm Goldmann Verlag, 1895.

On the Advantages and Disadvantages of History for Life. Peter Preuss trans. London: Hackett, 1980.

On the Genealogy of Morals. Walter Kauffman trans. New York: Vintage, 1969.

Philosophy in the Tragic Age of the Greeks. Thomas Cowan trans. Chicago, IL: Regnery, 1962.

"Thus Spake Zarathustra." In *The Portable Nietzsche*. Walter Kauffman ed. and trans. New York: Viking, 1978.

"The Twilight of the Idols." In *The Portable Nietzsche*. Walter Kauffman ed. and trans. New York: Viking, 1978.

Norbrook, David. *Lucretius and the Early Modern*. Oxford: Oxford University Press, 2015.

Ostaric, Lara. *Interpreting Schelling*. Cambridge: Cambridge University Press, 2014.

Palmier, J. M. *Les Ecrits Politique de Heidegger*. Paris: l'Herme, 1968.

Pangle, Thomas L. "The Warrior Spirit as an Inlet to the Political Philosophy of Nietzsche's Zarathustra." *Nietzsche-Studien* 15 (1986).

Parry, B. *Postcolonial Studies*. New York: Routledge, 2004.

Pateman, Carol. *Participation and Democratic Theory*. Cambridge: Cambridge University Press, 1975.

Pelluchon, Corinne. *Leo Strauss and the Crisis of Rationalism*. Robert Howse trans. Albany, NY: SUNY Press, 2014.

Pinkard, Terry. *Hegel's Phenomenology: The Sociality of Reason*. Cambridge: Cambridge University Press, 1996.

Pippin, Robert. *Hegel's Idealism: The Satisfactions of Self-Consciousness*. Cambridge: Cambridge University Press, 1989.

Nietzsche, Psychology and First Philosophy. Chicago, IL: University of Chicago Press, 2011.

Plattner, Marc. *Rousseau's State of Nature: An Interpretation of the Discourse on Inequality*. De Kalb, IL: Northern Illinois University Press, 1979.

Poggeler, Otto. *Philosophie und Politik bei Heidegger*. Freiburg: Karl Alber, 1974.

Polt, Richard. *Heidegger: An Introduction*. Ithaca, NY: Cornell University Press, 1997.

Quante, Michael. *Die linken Hegelianer: Studien zum Verhältnis von Religion und Politik im Vormärz*. Paderborn: Wilhelm Fink, 2015.

Rawls, John. *A Theory of Justice*. Cambridge, MA: Harvard University Press, 1971.

Redding, Paul. *Hegel's Hermeneutics*. Ithaca, NY: Cornell University Press, 1996.

Reginster. B. *The Affirmation of Life: Nietzsche on Overcoming Nihilism*. Cambridge, MA: Harvard University Press, 2009.

Reisert, Joseph. *Jean-Jacques Rousseau: A Friend of Virtue*. Ithaca, NY: Cornell University Press, 2003.

Renault, Emmanuel. *Hegel: La Naturalisation de la Dialectique*. Paris: Bibliotheque D'Histoire de la Philosophie, 2001.

Ricci, Valentina ed. *Hegel on Recollection*. Cambridge: Cambridge Scholars Publishing, 2013.

Richard, John. *Nietzsche's System*. Oxford: Oxford University Press, 2002.

Richardson, William. *Heidegger: Through Phenomenology to Thought*. New York: Fordham University Press, 1993.

Ritter, Joachim. *Hegel and The French Revolution*. Cambridge, MA: MIT Press, 1982.

Rosen, Michael. *Hegel's Dialectic and Its Criticism*. Cambridge: Cambridge University Press, 1982.

Rosen, Stanley. *G. W. F. Hegel*. New Haven, CT: Yale University Press, 1974.
    Hermeneutics as Politics. New Haven, CT: Yale University Press, 2003.
    The Idea of Hegel's "Science of Logic." Chicago, IL: University of Chicago Press, 2013.
    The Mask of Enlightenment: Nietzsche's Zarathustra. New Haven, CT: Yale University Press, 2004.
    Nihilism. New Haven, CT: Yale University Press, 1969.
    The Question of Being. New Haven, CT: Yale University Press, 1993.

Rousseau, Jean-Jacques. *The Confessions*. J. M. Cohen trans. London: Penguin, 1953.
    Emile or On Education. Allan Bloom trans and intro. New York: Basic Books, 1979.
    The First and Second Discourses. Roger Masters trans. New York: St. Martin's Press, 1969.
    On the Social Contract. Roger Masters trans. New York: St. Martin's Press, 1976.
    Les Reveries du Promeneur Solitaire. Jacques Voisine ed. Paris: Garnier-Flammarion, 1964.

Runes, Dagobert. *German Existentialism*. New York: Wisdom Library, 1965.

Rutter, Benjamin. *Hegel on the Modern Arts*. Cambridge: Cambridge University Press, 2010.

Sartre, J.-P. *Being and Nothingness*. Hazel Barnes trans. New York: Washington Square Press, 1966.

Schacht, Richard. *Nietzsche*. London: Routledge & Kegan Paul, 1983.

Schama, Simon. *Citizens*. New York: Vintage, 1990.

Schelling, F. W. J. *The Ages of the World*. Wolfe Bolman trans. New York: Ungar, 1942.
    Bruno, or On the Natural and Divine Principle of Things. Micheal Vater trans. Albany, NY: SUNY Press, 1988.

Schiller, Friedrich. *Letters on the Aesthetic Education of Man*. Reginald Snell trans. New York: Ungar, 1965.
   On Naive and Sentimental Poetry. New York: Ungar, 1980.
Schmitt, Richard. *Martin Heidegger on Being Human*. New York: Random House, 1969.
Scholem, Gershom. *Major Trends in Jewish Mysticism*. New York: Shocken Books, 1946.
Schrag, Calvin. "Heidegger on Repetition and Historical Understanding." *Philosophy East and West* (July 1970).
Schwan, A. *Politische Philosophie in Denken Heideggers*. Cologne: Westdeutschere Verlag, 1965.
Scruton, Roger. *Spinoza*. London: Phoenix, 1998.
Scully, Vincent. *The Earth, the Temple, and the Gods: Greek Sacred Architecture*. Rev. ed. New Haven, CT: Yale University Press, 1979.
Shaw, Tamsin. *Nietzsche's Political Skepticism*. Princeton, NJ: Princeton University Press, 2010.
Shell, Susan Meld. *The Rights of Reason*. Toronto: University of Toronto Press, 1980.
Shklar, Judith. *Freedom and Independence*. Cambridge: Cambridge University Press, 1976.
   Men and Citizens: A Study of Rousseau's Social Theory. Cambridge: Cambridge University Press, 1985.
Smith, Steven B. *Hegel's Critique of Liberalism: Rights in Context*. Chicago, IL: University of Chicago Press, 1989.
   Spinoza, Liberalism, and the Question of Jewish Identity. New Haven, CT: Yale University Press, 1998.
Solomon, Robert. *In the Spirit of Hegel*. Oxford: Oxford University Press, 1993.
Starobinski, Jean. *Jean-Jacques Rousseau: Transparency and Obstruction*. Chicago, IL: University of Chicago Press, 1998.
Steiner, George. *Heidegger*. Glasgow: Fontana/Collins, 1978.
Steiner, Rudolf. The Philosophy of Freedom. lulu.com, 2011.
Stern, J. P. *Nietzsche*. New York: Harper Collins, 1985.
Stern, Robert. *Hegel's Metaphysics*. Oxford: Oxford University Press, 2012.
Strauss, Leo. "An Introduction to Heideggerian Existentialism." In *The Rebirth of Classical Political Rationalism*. Thomas Pangle ed. Chicago, IL: University of Chicago Press, 1989.
   Natural Right and History. Chicago, IL: University of Chicago Press, 1974.
   "Note on the Plan of Nietzsche's *Beyond Good and Evil*." *Studies in Platonic Political Philosophy*. In Thomas Pangle ed. Chicago, IL: University of Chicago Press, 1983.
   "The Problem of Socrates." *Interpretation* 22:3 (2014): 324.
   "Progress or Return?" In *The Rebirth of Classical Political Rationalism*. Thomas Pangle ed. Chicago, IL: University of Chicago Press, 1989.
Talmon, J. L. *The Origins of Totalitarian Democracy*. London: Penguin, 1952.
Tarintseva, Tatiana. "In Defense of Gadamer's Notion of Understanding." *Horizons* 3:1 (2014).
Taylor, Charles. *Hegel*. Cambridge: Cambridge University Press, 1975.
Thompson, Iain. "Heidegger and the Politics of the University." *Journal of the History of Philosophy* 41:4 (2003).
Tucker, Robert. *Philosophy and Myth in Karl Marx*. Cambridge: Cambridge University Press, 1965.

Turner, Zeynep Taray. "Nietzsche and Spinoza: Thinking Freedom." *Uludag University Journal of Philosophy* 26 (2014): 2–16.

Velkley, Richard. *Being after Rousseau: Philosophy and Culture in Question.* Chicago, IL: University of Chicago Press, 2002.

Freedom and the Ends of Reason. Chicago, IL: University of Chicago Press, 1989.

Heidegger, Strauss, and the Premises of Philosophy: On Original Forgetting. Chicago, IL: University of Chicago Press, 2011.

Voegelin, E. *The New Science of Politics.* Chicago, IL: University of Chicago Press, 1987.

Waehlens, A. "De la Philosophie de Heidegger et le Nazism." *Les Tempes Modernes* (1946): 2.

Wahl, Jean. *Le Malheur de la Conscience.* Paris: Presses Universitaires de France, 1951.

Weber, Max. "Science as a Vocation." In *From Max Weber: Essays in Sociology.* H. Gerth and C. Mills trans. New York: Oxford University Press, 1945.

Weil, E. "Le Cas Heidegger." *Les Tempes Modernes* (1946): 2.

Williams, B. *Ethics and the Limits of Philosophy.* Cambridge, MA: Harvard University Press, 1985.

Wolin, Richard. *The Heidegger Controversy.* Cambridge, MA: MIT Press, 1993.

Wood, Allen. *Hegel's Ethical Thought.* Cambridge: Cambridge University Press, 1990.

"Hegel's Ethics." In *The Cambridge Companion to Hegel.* Frederik C. Beiser ed. Cambridge: Cambridge University Press.

Yack, Bernard. *The Longing for Total Revolution.* Princeton, NJ: Princeton University Press, 1986.

Yates, Christopher. *The Poetic Imagination in Heidegger and Schelling.* London: Bloomsbury, 2013.

Young, Julian. *Germany Philosophy in the Twentieth Century.* London: Routledge, 2018.

Zambrana, R. *Hegel's Theory of Intelligibility.* Chicago, IL: University of Chicago Press, 2015.

Zhihua Yao. "Typology of Nothing: Heidegger, Daoism and Buddhism." *Comparative Philosophy* 1 (2010).

Zizek, Slavoj. *The Indivisible Remainder: On Schelling and Related Matters.* New York: Verso, 2007.

Less Than Nothing: Hegel and the Shadow of Dialectical Materialism. New York: Verso, 2013.

Zuckert, Catherine. *Postmodern Platos.* Chicago, IL: University of Chicago Press, 1996.

Zuckert, Michael. "Review of Lampert, The Enduring Importance of Leo Strauss." *Notre Dame Philosophical Reviews* (February 19, 2014).

Zuckert, Rachel. *On Beauty and Biology: An Interpretation of The Critique of Judgement.* Cambridge: Cambridge University Press, 2020.

Index